HOUGHTON MIFFLIN

Spelling and Vocabulary

Senior Author
Shane Templeton

Consultant
Rosa Maria Peña

HOUGHTON MIFFLIN

Boston • Atlanta • Dallas • Denver • Geneva, Illinois • Palo Alto • Princeton

Acknowledgments

For each of the selections listed below, grateful acknowledgment is made for permission to excerpt and/or reprint original or copyrighted material as follows:

Select definitions in the Spelling Dictionary are adapted and reprinted by permission from the following Houghton Mifflin Company publications: Copyright © 1998, 1994 *The American Heritage Student Dictionary*. Copyright © 1989 *The Houghton Mifflin Student Dictionary*. Copyright © 1991 *The American Heritage Dictionary, Second College Edition*. Copyright © 1997 *The American Heritage High School Dictionary, Third Edition*.

Selection from "A Crown of Wild Olive," by Rosemary Sutcliff, in *Heather, Oak, and Olive: Three Stories*. Copyright © 1971 by Rosemary Sutcliff. Originally published by E. P. Dutton. Reprinted by permission of Murray Pollinger and Hamish Hamilton.

Selection from *The Gulls of Smuttynose Island*, by Jack Denton Scott. Copyright © 1977 by Jack Denton Scott. Reprinted by permission of G. P. Putnam's Sons, a division of Penguin Putnam Inc.

Selection from "The Slim Butte Ghost," by Virginia Driving Hawk Sneve, in *Houghton Mifflin Reading*. Copyright © 1986 by Houghton Mifflin Company. Reprinted by permission of the publisher.

Selection from *The Upstairs Room*, by Johanna Reiss (Thomas Y. Crowell). Copyright © 1972 by Johanna Reiss. Abridged and reprinted by permission of HarperCollins Publishers and Oxford University Press.

Selection from "Urban Archaeology," in *Houghton Mifflin Reading*. Copyright © 1989 by Houghton Mifflin Company. Reprinted by permission of the publisher.

ISBN: 0-395-97045-8

23456789-DW-05 04 03 02 01 00 99

Contents

Contents

Contents

Contents

Contents

Contents

Student's Handbook

How to Study a Word

1 ▶ Look at the word.

- How is the word spelled?
- Do you see any familiar word parts?

2 ▶ Say the word.

- How are the consonant sounds pronounced?
- How are the vowel sounds pronounced?

3 ▶ Think about the word.

- What does it mean?
- What do you know about the word's origin?
- Would thinking of a related word help you remember the spelling?

inspire
inspiration

4 ▶ Write the word.

- Think about the sounds and the letters.
- Form the letters correctly.

succeed
succession
submit
submissio

5 ▶ Check the spelling.

- Did you spell the word the same way it is spelled on your word list?
- Do you need to write the word again?

Using Spelling Strategies

Sometimes you want to write a word that you are not certain how to spell. For example, one student writer wanted to spell the word that named the document at the right. She followed these steps to figure out the spelling.

1 Say the word softly. Listen to all the sounds. Then think about the letters and patterns that usually spell each sound. Listen for familiar word parts, such as roots, prefixes, suffixes, and endings.

> The word root *script* at the end of the word is clear.

mannuscript
manyuscript

2 Write the word a few different ways to see which way looks right.

> I didn't find it spelled m-a-n-n-u.

3 Do you recognize one spelling as the correct one? If you're not sure, look up your first try in a dictionary.

4 It's not there? Look up your second try.

> Oh, here it is. It's spelled m-a-n-u-s-c-r-i-p-t.

5 Write the word correctly to help you remember its spelling.

Spelling Strategies

1. Listen for familiar sounds and patterns.
2. Listen for familiar word parts—roots, prefixes, suffixes, and endings.
3. Use the Spelling-Meaning Strategy. Is there a word related in meaning that can help you spell your word?
4. Write the word a few different ways.
5. Use a student dictionary.

The American Heritage
Student Dictionary

11

Consonant Changes

Read and Say

Basic	READ the sentences. SAY each bold word.
1. commit	Did she really **commit** that crime?
2. commission	The city planning **commission** meets at noon.
3. emit	Will the new factory **emit** smoke into the air?
4. emission	Smoke **emission** pollutes the air.
5. intercede	Please **intercede** with the principal for me.
6. intercession	My **intercession** ended their argument.
7. succeed	The prince will **succeed** the king someday.
8. succession	It rained for three days in **succession**.
9. submit	Will you **submit** an application for the job?
10. submission	Your **submission** for the contest is too late.
11. remit	Please **remit** the payment for your bill.
12. remission	She is so glad her illness is in **remission**.
13. transmit	Some insects **transmit** disease to people.
14. transmission	The storm interrupted radio **transmission**.
15. concede	Will she **concede** defeat after the election?
16. concession	Her **concession** helped them to compromise.
17. omit	Don't **omit** your name from your homework.
18. omission	An **omission** of one word changed the meaning.
19. recede	We will return when the flood waters **recede**.
20. recession	Fewer jobs are available in a **recession**.

Spelling Strategy   Knowing how consonants change in one pair of words can help you predict changes in words with similar spelling patterns.

Think and Write   Write each pair of Basic Words under the heading that tells how the final consonant changes when the suffix *-ion* is added.

Final *t* Changes to *ss*   **Final *d* changes to *ss***

Review	23. detect
21. violate	24. detection
22. violation	

Challenge	27. provoke
25. revoke	28. provocation
26. revocation	

Independent Practice

Vocabulary: Using Context Write the Basic Word that completes each sentence. Use your Spelling Dictionary.

1. Many factory smokestacks _____ harmful fumes into the air.
2. The Wildlife Society will _____ on behalf of animals whose habitat is threatened by the proposed industrial park.
3. For five days in _____, we spotted Canada geese flying north.
4. Some shorelines _____ a little each year as the sand on the beach washes into the ocean.
5. A special _____ was formed to study the problem of acid rain.
6. Erin's brothers must usually _____ defeat when they argue with her about air pollution.
7. Ticks can _____ Rocky Mountain Spotted Fever to people.
8. Ned's only _____ to the stormy weather was to take a rain poncho on his nature hike.
9. The _____ of automobile fumes contributes to air pollution.
10. Thanks to the mayor's _____, the dispute between the factory officials and the protestors was resolved.

Vocabulary: Definitions Write the Basic Word that matches each definition. Use your Spelling Dictionary.

11. a temporary lessening
12. something that has been left out
13. to offer for consideration
14. to send money
15. the act or process of sending
16. obedience
17. to do or pledge
18. to follow or replace
19. the act of going back
20. to leave out

Challenge Words Write the Challenge Word that fits each clue. Use your Spelling Dictionary.

21. You might do this to make something happen.
22. This reverses permission.
23. This is a reason to speak or act.
24. An official might do this to a license.

Review: Spelling Spree

Rhyme Time Read each clue. Then write a Basic or Review Word to complete each rhyme.

Example: cancel an angry mood

_____ a snit   *remit*

1. pledge a glove
   _____ a mitt
2. save the dandelion
   _____ for a weed
3. cancel the cardigan
   _____ the knit
4. yield to the front-runner
   _____ to greater speed
5. obey one who's funny
   _____ to a wit
6. discovery in a mirror
   _____ reflection
7. leave out a little
   _____ a bit

8. ask to move back
   plead to _____
9. history of a fume
   tradition of an _____
10. illness that is lessening
    condition in _____
11. admission of guilt in sequence
    confession in _____
12. follow a feat
    _____ a deed
13. crime at a train stop
    station _____
14. find admiration
    _____ respect

Syllable Scramble Rearrange the syllables to form a Basic or Review Word. Write the words correctly.

15. mit   e
16. mis   sion   sub
17. mit   trans
18. sion   o   mis
19. com   sion   mis
20. sion   ces   con
21. trans   sion   mis

22. late   vi   o
23. ces   re   sion
24. ces   ter   sion   in

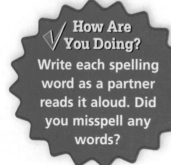

How Are You Doing?
Write each spelling word as a partner reads it aloud. Did you misspell any words?

Proofreading and Writing

Proofread: Spelling, Commas in Compound and Complex Sentences Use a comma before the conjunction in a **compound sentence**.

The rain fell, and the smog cleared.

Use a comma after a **subordinate clause** that begins a **complex sentence** but not before one that ends a sentence.

After the rain fell, the smog cleared.
The smog cleared after the rain fell.

Find five misspelled Basic or Review Words and two missing commas in this excerpt from a letter to the editor. Write the letter correctly.

To the Editor:

The new dam is a violasion of nature. It prevents salmon from swimming up the river to lay their eggs. The dam needs fish lifts, pools arranged in steps. The salmon leap from pool to pool in sucession to reach the top of the dam. As the ommission of the lifts is a threat to the salmon we must interceed. Fish lifts are necessary and we can convince the planning commision of this fact. Together we will succeed in achieving this goal.

Michellene DeGeorge, Salmon Falls

Write a Letter Think of your favorite park, beach, forest, or street. How would you feel if someone dumped trash there? Write a firm but polite letter to that person. Try to use five spelling words and at least one compound or complex sentence.

Basic

1. commit
2. commission
3. emit
4. emission
5. intercede
6. intercession
7. succeed
8. succession
9. submit
10. submission
11. remit
12. remission
13. transmit
14. transmission
15. concede
16. concession
17. omit
18. omission
19. recede
20. recession

Review

21. violate
22. violation
23. detect
24. detection

Challenge

25. revoke
26. revocation
27. provoke
28. provocation

Proofreading Marks
¶ Indent
∧ Add
⅄ Add a comma
ᵛᵞ ᵛᵞ Add quotation marks
⊙ Add a period
⌐ Delete
≡ Capital letter
/ Small letter
∪ Reverse order

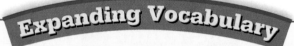

Expanding Vocabulary

Spelling Word Link

transmit
emission

The Latin Root *mit* *Transmit* and *emission* both grew from the Latin root *mit*, meaning "to send, let go, or throw." Other words from this root also have to do with sending or releasing.

promise   mission   dismiss   permit

Write a word from the list above to complete each sentence. Use your Spelling Dictionary.

1. Columbus's _____ was to find a new route to the East.
2. Do beach rules _____ picnicking on the sand?
3. Mr. Thomas decided to _____ the class early.
4. Carla made Angie _____ to wait for her after school.

TEST-TAKING TACTICS

Vocabulary-in-Context The critical reading section of a verbal test may include vocabulary-in-context questions. These questions often present a reading passage with margin line references. Your task is to use the context of the passage to choose the correct meaning of a given word.

Sample passage excerpt and question:

> Some species of algae are minute, one-celled organisms. Much larger species, such as seaweeds and kelps, contain many cells. Depending upon their variety, algae can multiply rapidly in polluted
> (35) rivers and lakes. This, in turn, may disturb the natural balance of life in the water.

The word "minute" in line 32 most nearly means

(A) blue-green   (B) microscopic   (C) sixty seconds
(D) active   (E) slimy

To answer this question, search the sentence that contains the tested word, *as well as surrounding sentences,* for clues about the tested word's meaning.

Review the sample, and then write the answers to these questions.

5. Which answer choice correctly completes the sample question? Write its letter.
6. What context clues helped you determine the correct meaning?

Real-World Connection

Science: Ecology All the words in the box relate to ecology. Look up these words in your Spelling Dictionary. Then write the words to complete this paragraph.

Spelling Word Link

emission

conservation
endangered
contaminate
toxins
by-product
hazardous
biodegradable
aquifer

A factory creates waste as a __(1)__ of its manufacturing process. Many wastes contain poisons, called __(2)__. Improper disposal of __(3)__ waste continues to __(4)__ our water supply. The waste can seep into an __(5)__, an underground layer where water collects. When it reaches a lake or river, the animals that depend on that water are __(6)__. Some factories help by creating __(7)__ wastes, which decompose without harming soil or water. Others recycle waste materials by turning them into useful products. Water __(8)__ relies on methods such as these.

TRY THIS!

Yes or No? Write *yes* if the underlined word is used correctly. Write *no* if it is not.

9. The park ranger had a <u>conservation</u> with three hikers.
10. Cutting down the forest has <u>endangered</u> the wildlife.
11. We should help factories <u>contaminate</u> our waterways.
12. <u>Biodegradable</u> waste is our most serious problem.

Fact File

In 1962, Rachel Carson, a writer and biologist, issued a warning in her famous book *Silent Spring*. Carson said that chemicals used to kill insects could also harm birds and other animals, even humans. The book made many people aware of the need to protect wildlife.

Greek Word Parts I

Read and Say

Basic

READ the sentences. **SAY** each bold word.

1. pathology — Our class in **pathology** was on blood diseases.
2. symptom — Sneezing is a **symptom** of many colds.
3. syndrome — Most doctors know the signs of this **syndrome**.
4. synthetic — Nylon is a **synthetic** fabric made here.
5. protein — Eggs and fish are sources of **protein**.
6. oxygen — Tanks of **oxygen** allow divers to breathe.
7. hydrogen — Did you know that water contains **hydrogen**?
8. homogenized — Fat is spread evenly in **homogenized** milk.
9. synonym — I need a **synonym** for this overused word.
10. sympathy — Cards of **sympathy** helped to ease her grief.
11. pathetic — A starving dog is a **pathetic** sight.
12. apathy — His lack of concern borders on **apathy**.
13. photogenic — Fashion models must be **photogenic**.
14. synagogue — We worship at a beautiful **synagogue**.
15. genealogy — How did you trace your family **genealogy**?
16. empathy — Her tears showed her **empathy** for the victim.
17. pathological — This disease can cause a **pathological** rash.
18. symmetrical — It is easy to divide a **symmetrical** pattern.
19. protoplasm — Plant and animal cells contain **protoplasm**.
20. syndicate — Farmers formed a **syndicate** to sell the crops.

Spelling Strategy   Knowing the Greek word parts *path* ("disease; feeling"), *syn/sym* ("together; same"), *gen* ("born; produced"), and *prot* ("first") can help you spell and understand words with these parts.

Think and Write   Write the Basic Words. Underline the Greek word part *path*, *syn*, *sym*, *gen*, or *prot* in each word.

Review	
21. gene	23. generalize
22. genetic	24. symphony
	25. bacteria

Challenge	
26. synthesis	28. synchronize
27. protocol	29. pathos
	30. protagonist

Independent Practice

Vocabulary: Definitions Write the Basic Word that matches each definition.
Use your Spelling Dictionary.

1. an outward sign of a disease or other condition
2. the study of diseases
3. a set of signs that together indicate a disease
4. the gas that fish, birds, animals, and humans need to live
5. a lack of interest or feeling
6. the study of ancestors and family histories
7. the ability to identify with someone else's feelings
8. likely to look attractive in a photograph
9. affection or understanding between persons
10. the jellylike material that forms all living cells
11. a class of food essential to the body
12. a word with a meaning similar to that of another word
13. the lightest gas; the most abundant element in the universe

Vocabulary: Analogies An **analogy** shows a relationship between two pairs
of words. The first two words are related to each other in the same way as the
last two. Write an analogy as a sentence or with colons.

> Doctor is to hospital as teacher is to school.
> doctor : hospital :: teacher : school

Write the Basic Word that completes each analogy. Use your Spelling Dictionary.

14. flour : sifted :: milk : _____
15. real : fake :: natural : _____
16. pretty : lovely :: balanced : _____
17. unhappy : miserable :: pitiful : _____
18. athletes : team :: executives : _____
19. funny : amusing :: sick : _____
20. study : library :: worship : _____

Challenge Words Write the Challenge
Word that answers each question. Use your
Spelling Dictionary.

21. Whom does the action revolve around in a novel?
22. What could two people do with their watches or clocks?
23. What might be expressed with tears, sighs, or mournful words?
24. What determines how a diplomat should behave?
25. What process combines substances to form a new material?

Dictionary

Alphabetical Order/Guide Words At the top of each dictionary page are two **guide words** that indicate the first and last entries on the page. All of the other words on the page come between the guide words alphabetically.

Practice Write each list of words in alphabetical order.

1. protrude, prospect, protoplasm, protozoan, proton
2. genetic, generalize, genealogy, generous, generation

1. _____ ? _____

_____ ? _____

2. _____ ? _____

_____ ? _____

Look up the words below in your Spelling Dictionary. Write the guide words that appear at the top of the page that contains each word.

3. symphony   4. oxygen   5. photogenic   6. bacteria

3. _____ ? _____   5. _____ ? _____

4. _____ ? _____   6. _____ ? _____

Review: Spelling Spree

Word Part Completion Add a Greek word part to complete each Basic or Review Word. Write the word correctly.

7. a _ _ _ _ y
8. _ _ _ metrical
9. _ _ _ ealogy
10. photo _ _ _ ic
11. _ _ _ thetic
12. _ _ _ agogue
13. homo _ _ _ ized
14. _ _ _ onym
15. _ _ _ dicate
16. _ _ _ _ ology

17. _ _ _ phony
18. hydro _ _ _
19. em _ _ _ _ _ y
20. oxy _ _ _
21. _ _ _ _ _ etic
22. _ _ _ pathy
23. _ _ _ _ _ ein
24. _ _ _ _ e
25. _ _ _ _ _ oplasm

Proofreading and Writing

Proofread for Spelling Find six misspelled Basic or Review Words in this paragraph. Write each word correctly.

Diseases have a variety of causes. Some diseases are genedic, or passed from parent to child through a gene. Others are transmitted from person to person by bacterea or viruses. Each disease has a characteristic pattern called a sindrome. Doctors must be careful not to genaralize from part of this pattern. Instead, they must consider each pathalogical symtom that a patient displays before determining a course of treatment.

FHR MHR 67867
FHR —240
FHR —240
MHR
—210
MHR
HRZ BM WAM SCALE
—210
—180
150
—120 165
—165
—120
—90 120
—120 75
—90 90
—75 60
—60 30 30

Write a Description If you could make one major contribution to medicine, what would it be? Would you discover the cure for a disease or invent a piece of equipment? Write a paragraph describing your contribution. Try to use five spelling words.

Basic

1. pathology
2. symptom
3. syndrome
4. synthetic
5. protein
6. oxygen
7. hydrogen
8. homogenized
9. synonym
10. sympathy
11. pathetic
12. apathy
13. photogenic
14. synagogue
15. genealogy
16. empathy
17. pathological
18. symmetrical
19. protoplasm
20. syndicate

Review

21. gene
22. genetic
23. generalize
24. symphony
25. bacteria

Challenge

26. synthesis
27. protocol
28. synchronize
29. pathos
30. protagonist

Proofreading Marks

¶ Indent
∧ Add
⅄ Add a comma
⋎⋏ Add quotation marks
⊙ Add a period
⌿ Delete
≡ Capital letter
/ Small letter
∽ Reverse order

Expanding Vocabulary

Spelling
Word Link

empathy

Context Clues When you see an unfamiliar word, you can often gather its meaning by using **context clues,** or hints from other words around it. Suppose you did not know the word *empathy*. The context clues in the sentence below would help you determine its meaning.

The **sensitive, caring** nurses felt empathy for the patients.

Write the meaning of each underlined word. Then write the other words in the sentence that provide clues to the meaning of the underlined word.

1. Dr. Lu stared at the x-ray, hoping that his <u>scrutiny</u> would uncover a clue to the patient's illness.
2. Ali received <u>accolades</u> from her admiring coworkers for her remarkable research findings.
3. Sal regretted his hasty, <u>imprudent</u> advice to the patient.
4. The fake diploma confirmed our suspicions that the woman known as Dr. Walker was a <u>charlatan</u>.

TEST-TAKING TACTICS

Analogies Analogy questions on standardized tests often begin with a pair of capitalized words, known as **stem words,** that form the basis of the analogy. Test-takers decide how the stem words are related, and then choose an answer pair that is related in the same way. Look at this analogy stem:

BRIGHT : INTELLIGENT ::

To decide how the stem words are related, first try stating their relationship in a sentence. A sentence that states the relationship between the stem words above might read as follows:

BRIGHT is a synonym of INTELLIGENT.

Once you are satisfied that your test sentence works, replace the stem words with the words in each answer choice. One answer choice pair will clearly have the same relationship as the stem words.

Now study this analogy test question and answer the questions that follow.

SEDAN : AUTOMOBILE ::   (A) chair : desk   (B) atlas : map
(C) cumulus : cloud   (D) rain : snow   (E) weather : geography

5. What sentence might you use to define the relationship between SEDAN and AUTOMOBILE?
6. Which answer correctly completes the analogy? Write its letter.

Real-World Connection

Health: Medicine All the words in the box relate to medicine. Look up these words in your Spelling Dictionary. Then write the words to complete this paragraph.

Spelling Word Link

pathology

diagnostic
prognosis
stethoscope
biopsy
radiology
infectious
microbe
inflammation

Dr. Ramos uses a variety of __(1)__ procedures to identify his patients' illnesses. Lee, one of his patients, complained of a cough. Dr. Ramos listened to Lee's lungs with a __(2)__. He then took a sample from Lee's throat to test for the presence of a __(3)__, an organism that causes an __(4)__, or contagious, disease. He also sent Lee to the __(5)__ department for an x-ray. Because the x-ray was clear, Dr. Ramos did not need to take a __(6)__ of Lee's lung tissue. After checking all the test results, Dr. Ramos decided that Lee had a respiratory __(7)__. His final __(8)__ was that with medication, Lee would recover within a week.

TRY THIS!

True or False? Write *T* if the sentence is true and *F* if it is false.

9. X-rays are used in radiology.
10. A microbe is a type of medical test.
11. To see inside the body, doctors use a stethoscope.
12. An infectious disease is one that is likely to spread.

Fact File

To view the brain or any organ deep inside the body, doctors use computerized axial tomography (CAT). A CAT scan is a series of x-rays taken from many angles. A computer combines the x-rays into a clear, detailed image.

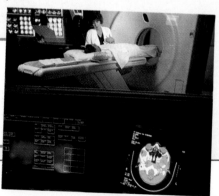

Latin Prefixes I

Read and Say

Basic

	Word	Sentence
1.	transportation	The bus is one form of **transportation**.
2.	subway	A **subway** ran beneath the city.
3.	transit	She is in **transit** between airports.
4.	submerge	Do not **submerge** an electric pot in water.
5.	suburban	Our **suburban** home is near the city.
6.	substance	What is the major **substance** in moon rocks?
7.	translate	Can you **translate** it into another language?
8.	transplant	Please dig up and **transplant** those bushes.
9.	submarine	The captain ordered the **submarine** to dive.
10.	transform	Can we **transform** the gym into a theater?
11.	transfusion	This patient needs a blood **transfusion** now!
12.	subdivide	They will **subdivide** the land into three lots.
13.	sublet	Will the lease allow me to **sublet** the house?
14.	subscription	Shall I renew this magazine **subscription**?
15.	transparent	Cover the pan with **transparent** plastic wrap.
16.	subtotal	What was the **subtotal** before tax was added?
17.	transaction	Which teller handled your bank **transaction**?
18.	subtitle	Each **subtitle** was on the screen briefly.
19.	subside	The pain will **subside** as your leg heals.
20.	transition	Our **transition** to a new school was easy.

Spelling Strategy   Remember the meanings of the Latin prefixes *trans-* ("across; over; through") and *sub-* ("under; near; beneath").

Think and Write   Write each Basic Word under its prefix.

trans-   sub-

Review
21. subscribe
22. transcribe
23. arrival
24. depot
25. vehicle

Challenge
26. subterranean
27. transient
28. subsequent
29. subculture
30. subconscious

Independent Practice

Vocabulary: Using Context Write the Basic Word that completes each sentence. Use your Spelling Dictionary.

1. Some people commute every day from their _____ homes to their jobs in the city.
2. After rush hour, the loud noises from the trains _____.
3. On the train to New York, the executives completed an important business _____.
4. The plane is in _____ between the runway and the terminal.
5. While riding in the ambulance, the medical technician prepared the accident victim for a blood _____.
6. The maps _____ large sections of town into smaller bus zones.
7. After the rain, the once grimy bus windows were again _____.
8. We request your patience during this _____ from the old subway system to the new one.
9. This coupon offers a weekly _____ to *Riders Read Magazine*.
10. The _____ of the mayor's plan is an overhaul of city buses.
11. Colorful murals can _____ the dismal station into a bright area.
12. The apartment that Anne _____ is on the bus route.
13. Add the cost of each taxi fare; then add a trip to the _____.

Vocabulary: Analogies Write the Basic Word that completes each analogy. Use your Spelling Dictionary.

Example: club : membership :: magazine : _____   *subscription*
14. photograph : caption :: movie : _____
15. sky : airplane :: sea : _____
16. highway : automobile :: tunnel : _____
17. climber : rise :: diver : _____
18. telephones : communication :: trains : _____
19. employee : transfer :: shrub : _____
20. currency : convert :: language : _____

Challenge Words Write the Challenge Word that matches each definition. Use your Spelling Dictionary.

21. coming next or after; following
22. a group of people in a society who share beliefs or lifestyles
23. passing away with time; temporary
24. underground; beneath the surface of the earth
25. not completely aware

Review: Spelling Spree

Using Clues Write the Basic Word that fits each clue.

1. This sub is an underwater vehicle.
2. This sub brings you a monthly magazine.
3. This sub is the material something is made from.
4. This sub lies between the country and the city.
5. This sub helps you understand a foreign movie.
6. This sub is a way to rent an apartment.
7. This sub cuts something into smaller pieces.
8. This sub comes before the final sum.
9. This sub takes you underground.
10. This sub is what storms do eventually.

Word Subway 11–25. Find the Basic and Review Words hidden in this subway map. Write the words in the order in which you find them. Begin at Myles Station and end at Union Station.

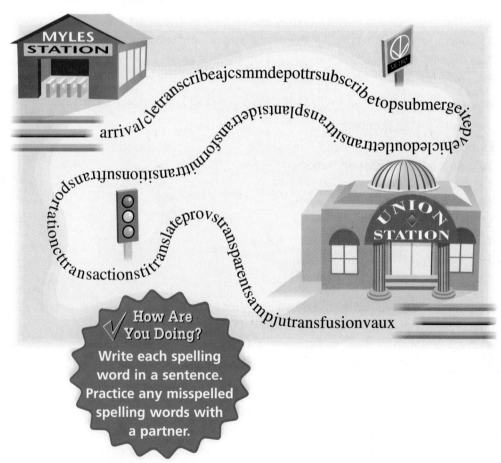

How Are You Doing?

Write each spelling word in a sentence. Practice any misspelled spelling words with a partner.

Proofreading and Writing

Proofread: Spelling and Fragments or Run-ons Correct a **sentence fragment** by adding a subject or a predicate. Correct a **run-on sentence** by creating two separate sentences or one compound or complex sentence.

FRAGMENT:	Ran to the station
CORRECTION:	**I** ran to the station.
RUN-ON:	I ran to the station the train was gone.
CORRECTION:	I ran to the station. The train was gone.
CORRECTION:	I ran to the station, **but** the train was gone.
CORRECTION:	**Though** I ran to the station, the train was gone.

Find five misspelled Basic or Review Words, one fragment, and one run-on in this notice. Write the notice correctly.

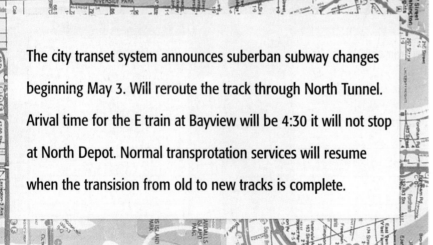

The city transet system announces suberban subway changes beginning May 3. Will reroute the track through North Tunnel. Arival time for the E train at Bayview will be 4:30 it will not stop at North Depot. Normal transprotation services will resume when the transision from old to new tracks is complete.

Basic

1. transportation
2. subway
3. transit
4. submerge
5. suburban
6. substance
7. translate
8. transplant
9. submarine
10. transform
11. transfusion
12. subdivide
13. sublet
14. subscription
15. transparent
16. subtotal
17. transaction
18. subtitle
19. subside
20. transition

Review

21. subscribe
22. transcribe
23. arrival
24. depot
25. vehicle

Challenge

26. subterranean
27. transient
28. subsequent
29. subculture
30. subconscious

Write a Persuasive Essay How would an increased use of public transportation affect air quality, traffic flow, and highway safety in your area? Write an essay to convince readers to use public transportation. Try to use five spelling words, and be sure to avoid sentence fragments and run-ons.

Proofreading Marks

¶	Indent
∧	Add
⌄	Add a comma
⌄⌄	Add quotation marks
⊙	Add a period
℘	Delete
≡	Capital letter
/	Small letter
∿	Reverse order

Expanding Vocabulary

Spelling Word Link

transaction

Using a Thesaurus Have you ever been stuck trying to think of the perfect word to express an idea? Use a **thesaurus** to find exact or precise words and to add variety to your writing. Look at the thesaurus entry below.

main entry word   part of speech   definition   sample sentence

transaction *n.* a business deal or operation. *I made a transaction with Barbara to buy her bicycle.*

subentries

▶ *exchange* trade. *The scarf for the hat is an even exchange.*
▶ *negotiation* discussion to reach an agreement. *The negotiation for the sale for the company lasted months.*

Find each word in your Thesaurus. Then write the subentries.

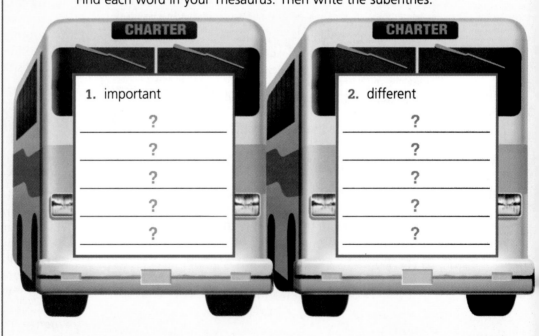

CHARTER

1. important

?
?
?
?
?

CHARTER

2. different

?
?
?
?
?

Now write two sentences, using a different subentry from above in each one.

3. _____?_____

_____?_____

4. _____?_____

_____?_____

Vocabulary Enrichment

Real-World Connection

Social Studies: Public Transportation All the words in the box relate to public transportation. Look up these words in your Spelling Dictionary. Then write the words to complete this paragraph.

Spelling Word Link

transportation

commuter
intercity
elevated
trolley
toll
token
turnstile

Ellen Stein is a __(1)__ who travels each day from the city where she lives to another __(2)__ area where she works. She and other riders share a van that travels the __(3)__ turnpike. The driver pays the __(4)__ with money that the riders contribute. When Ellen arrives at the train station in the city, she puts a small, round __(5)__ in a slot and walks through the __(6)__. Upstairs on the platform, she boards an __(7)__ train, riding on tracks high above the ground. Downtown, she transfers to a __(8)__, an electric bus that runs on tracks on the city streets. At night, she does it all again in the opposite direction.

TRY THIS!

Clue Match Write a word from the box to match each clue.

9. This metal disk shows that you have paid your way.
10. This lets people in, one at a time.
11. This kind of person goes back and forth.
12. You often must pay this to cross a bridge.

Fact File

The magnetic levitation vehicle (MLV) is a recent form of land transportation. Magnets hold this train above its tracks, so friction does not slow it. Gone are the noises and fumes as the MLV whooshes to its destination.

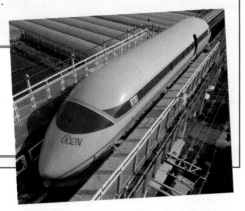

Words from Names

Read and Say

READ the sentences. **SAY** each bold word.

1. atlas	Which world **atlas** has the most recent maps?
2. mercury	Thermometers are filled with **mercury**.
3. narcissus	The **narcissus** blooms early in the spring.
4. psyche	Your **psyche** and body work together.
5. odyssey	Her **odyssey** took her around the world.
6. museum	When will the **museum** exhibit his art?
7. hypnosis	Her doctor uses **hypnosis** to treat pain.
8. Fahrenheit	This thermometer uses the **Fahrenheit** scale.
9. czar	The **czar** ruled over a vast empire.
10. pasteurize	Dairies **pasteurize** milk to kill germs.
11. fate	The **fate** of a candidate rests with the voters.
12. jovial	I am always cheered up by **jovial** people.
13. tantalize	Their music will **tantalize** you to dance.
14. hygiene	Brushing your teeth daily is good **hygiene**.
15. mentor	My **mentor** taught me how to study.
16. psychiatrist	A **psychiatrist** treats emotional problems.
17. mosaic	Thousands of tiny tiles formed the **mosaic**.
18. Celsius	What is the temperature in degrees **Celsius**?
19. fury	His rudeness filled me with **fury**.
20. galvanized	Rust will not harm **galvanized** steel.

Spelling Strategy   Knowing the origin of words that come from names can help you spell and understand the meanings of the words.

Think and Write   Write the Basic Words.

Review	23. Braille
21. boycott	24. leotard
22. silhouette	25. saxophone

Challenge	28. thespian
26. iridescent	29. epicure
27. nemesis	30. gargantuan

Independent Practice

Vocabulary: Definitions Write the Basic Word that matches each definition.
Use your Spelling Dictionary.

1. a doctor who specializes in mental illness
2. the temperature scale on which water freezes
    at 32 degrees and boils at 212 degrees
3. the mind or soul
4. rage or violent anger
5. a silvery-white liquid metal used in measuring
    temperature
6. a former emperor of Russia
7. a guide or teacher
8. a final result or outcome; destiny
9. a picture made with small pieces of glass or
    stone
10. a building in which artistic, scientific, or
    historical works are exhibited
11. a plant with a white or yellow trumpet-shaped flower
12. coated with zinc as protection against rust
13. a sleeplike condition

Vocabulary: Question Clues Write the Basic Word that answers each
question. Use your Spelling Dictionary.

14. What would you be on if you took a trip around the world?
15. What does the smell of food do to you when you are hungry?
16. What might you learn about in health class?
17. What can be done to purify milk?
18. How do you feel when you are very happy?
19. What could you look in to find a map of your state?
20. If you were heating water, and it began to boil at 100 degrees, what
    temperature scale would you be using?

Challenge Words Write the Challenge Word that completes each sentence.
Use your Spelling Dictionary.

21. An _____ eats only food fit for the gods.
22. Because of its _____ size, the Greeks believed that Mount Olympus was the
    home of the gods.
23. Iris, goddess of the rainbow, wore an _____ robe of many colors.
24. The Greek hero waged war against his long-time _____.
25. The _____ was famous for his role as Zeus, ruler of the gods.

Dictionary

Parts of a Dictionary Entry You can learn a lot about a word from its dictionary entry. Look at the sample below.

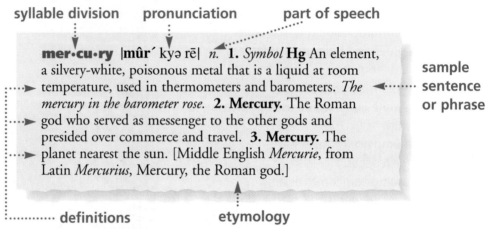

syllable division   pronunciation   part of speech

mer·cu·ry |mûr´ kyə rē| *n.* **1.** *Symbol* **Hg** An element, a silvery-white, poisonous metal that is a liquid at room temperature, used in thermometers and barometers. *The mercury in the barometer rose.* **2. Mercury.** The Roman god who served as messenger to the other gods and presided over commerce and travel. **3. Mercury.** The planet nearest the sun. [Middle English *Mercurie*, from Latin *Mercurius*, Mercury, the Roman god.]

sample
sentence
or phrase

definitions   etymology

Practice Use the sample entry to answer each question below.

1. What part of speech is *mercury*?
2. What Latin word does *mercury* come from?
3. How many definitions are given for *mercury*?
4. Which definition of *mercury* is used in this sentence? *When the temperature falls, so does the mercury.*

Review: Spelling Spree

Code Breaker The Basic and Review words below are written in code. Use the following code key to figure out each word. Write the decoded words correctly. Capitalize when necessary.

CODE:	z	y	x	w	v	u	t	s	r	q	p	o	n	m	l	k	j	i	h	g	f	e	d	c	b	a
LETTER:	a	b	c	d	e	f	g	h	i	j	k	l	m	n	o	p	q	r	s	t	u	v	w	x	y	z

Example: nfhvfn   *museum*

5. zgozh
6. uzsivmsvrg
7. tzoezmravw
8. kzhgvfirav
9. nvmgli
10. sbkmlhrh
11. nvixfib

12. ylbxlgg
13. qlerzo
14. ufib
15. hzclkslmv
16. xazi
17. uzgv
18. mzixrhhfh

19. khbxrszgirhg
20. xvohrfh
21. sbtrvmv
22. khbxsv
23. ovlgziw
24. lwbhhvb

Proofreading and Writing

Proofread for Spelling Find five misspelled Basic or Review Words in this announcement. Write each word correctly.

This month, the City Gallery has an exhibit devoted to Greek mythology. A silouette hangs above the entrance showing Ares, the god of war, in all his fury. In the far corner of the gallery, a huge mosiac of a scene on Mount Olympus is sure to tantilize even a casual observer. Collections of myths are on sale in the muzeum shop. Most are also available in Braile.

Write a Cause and Effect Paragraph Where does lightning come from? How is a rainbow formed? Ancient myths held the gods responsible for such things. Today, we rely on scientific explanations. Write a cause and effect paragraph explaining a natural event. If you do not know the real cause or effect of the event, make one up. Try to use five spelling words.

Proofreading Marks
¶ Indent
∧ Add
⩑ Add a comma
⌄⌄ ⌄⌄ Add quotation marks
⊙ Add a period
∽ Delete
≡ Capital letter
/ Small letter
∾ Reverse order

Expanding Vocabulary

**Spelling
Word Link**

psychiatrist

Slang If you heard a friend say "My mother is a shrink," your friend would be using a **slang** word to mean that his or her mother is a psychiatrist. Slang is our most informal type of speech. Slang words are often peculiar to specific groups within a culture.

Write a standard word or phrase that means the same thing as the underlined slang expression in each sentence below. Use your Spelling Dictionary.

1. I prefer to hang out with forest nymphs and hunting dogs.

2. Can you please give me directions to the main drag?

3. My sister Muses can be real pills.

4. If those giants razz me, I'll just strike them with a thunderbolt.

Now write a sentence for each slang word from above.

5. _____ ? _____
   _____ ? _____

6. _____ ? _____
   _____ ? _____

7. _____ ? _____
   _____ ? _____

8. _____ ? _____
   _____ ? _____

**Unit 4
BONUS**

Real-World Connection

Language Arts: Mythology All the words in the box relate to mythology. Look up these words in your Spelling Dictionary. Then write the words to complete this paragraph.

Spelling Word Link

atlas

epic
immortal
phenomena
Muse
nectar
ambrosia
chariot
labyrinth

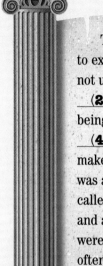

The ancient Greeks created gods and goddesses to explain natural events, or ___(1)___, that they did not understand. According to the stories, art, and ___(2)___ poems of Greek mythology, these ___(3)___ beings surrounded themselves with pleasure. They ate ___(4)___ and drank ___(5)___. Vulcan, the ___(6)___ maker, provided them with transportation. Knowledge was also important to the gods. A special goddess, called a ___(7)___, presided over each type of science and art. Despite their luxurious existence, the gods were easily angered. Those who displeased them were often imprisoned. One prison, called a ___(8)___, was a maze from which only magic could provide escape.

TRY THIS!

Possible or Impossible? Write *possible* if the activity described could be done or *impossible* if it could not.

9. building a Muse
10. seeing a chariot
11. riding an epic
12. walking in a labyrinth

Fact File

The most powerful of all the gods in Greek mythology was Zeus. He ruled the universe from the top of Mount Olympus. Zeus is represented in many works of art, sometimes as a bearded man and sometimes in the form of an animal.

Homophones

Read and Say

| Basic | READ the sentences. SAY each bold word. |

1. chord — Play the **chord** noted on your sheet music.
2. cord — Should I tie a **cord** around the package?
3. choral — Which singers performed the **choral** concert?
4. coral — The divers gazed at the lovely **coral** reef.
5. cymbal — He tapped a brass **cymbal** with his drumstick.
6. symbol — The flag is a **symbol** of our country.
7. aisle — Our theater seats are on the center **aisle**.
8. isle — We sailed around an **isle** in the lake.
9. ascent — The balloon began its **ascent** into the sky.
10. assent — Did your mom give her **assent** to a party?
11. stationary — A **stationary** dock is in the lake all winter.
12. stationery — He wrote his note on beautiful **stationery**.
13. site — The new school will be built on this **site**.
14. cite — Please **cite** the books used in your report.
15. canvas — I need a large **canvas** for my new painting.
16. canvass — Can you help us **canvass** the town for votes?
17. phase — The baby is entering the crawling **phase**.
18. faze — Loud music did not **faze** the sleeping child.
19. descent — The jet began its **descent** to the runway.
20. dissent — Those who did not agree voiced their **dissent**.

Spelling Strategy   Remember to think about meaning when using a **homophone**, a word that sounds like another but has a different spelling and meaning.

Think and Write   Write the pairs of Basic Words.

Review	23. capital
21. compliment	24. capitol
22. complement	

Challenge	27. caret
25. callous	28. carat
26. callus	

Independent Practice

Vocabulary: Using Context Write the Basic Word that completes each sentence. Use your Spelling Dictionary.

1. In a concert, the singers usually remain _____, but in a musical they may dance and move around while singing.
2. Many singers perform at Tanglewood in Massachusetts, the _____ of summer concerts by the Boston Symphony.
3. The barbershop quartet sang the first _____ of "Anabel."
4. Some singing groups perform "doo-wop," a type of _____ music that features syllables like *shoo-be-doo* as well as lyrics.
5. Maria's opera company began its last _____ of rehearsal.
6. The soprano's voice made an _____ to a thrilling high note.
7. Music historians _____ traditional hymns and spirituals of the American South as the inspiration for many modern songs.
8. The noise of a passing siren did not _____ the calm singer.
9. The actress playing Peter Pan sings the opening song while riding a steel cable in a dizzying _____ to the stage.
10. The glee club will _____ the school to sell concert tickets.
11. A quarter note is a common musical _____.

Vocabulary: Classifying Write the Basic Word that fits each group. Use your Spelling Dictionary.

12. agreement, approval, consent, _____
13. lobby, stage, row, _____
14. disagreement, disapproval, difference, _____
15. drum, gong, tambourine, _____
16. rope, string, ribbon, _____
17. fish, seaweed, sand, _____
18. pen, stamp, envelope, _____
19. peninsula, mountain, plateau, _____
20. burlap, muslin, linen, _____

Challenge Words Write the Challenge Word that fits each clue. Use your Spelling Dictionary.

21. You may have one on your toe or heel.
22. Proofreaders use this often.
23. This describes a diamond's weight.
24. This kind of person needs to be softened up.

Review: Spelling Spree

Letter Math Add and subtract letters from the words below to make Basic or Review Words. Write the new words.

Example: was + century – w – ury = *ascent*

1. can + vast – t + s =
2. ph + base – b =
3. cap + item – em + ol =
4. city – y + rare – rar =
5. co + implement – i =
6. co + floral – flo =
7. anchor + al – an =
8. sta + dictionary – dic =
9. astray + sen – tray + t =
10. lunch – lun + order – er =
11. complain – ain + im + ent =
12. c + ant – t + vase – e =
13. car – r + hospital – hos =
14. ai + bobsled – bob – d =
15. stationed – ed + very – v =
16. cy + imbalance – i – ance =
17. cope – pe + word – wo =

Verse Venture Write a Basic Word to complete each rhyme in this ballad.

We sail in fine style
round the tropical __(18)__,
on a sightseeing trip
in our seaworthy ship.
The flying fish amaze us
but soon barely __(19)__ us,
as they sparkle and flash,
leap, soar, and splash!
Next we alight
at a dry landing __(20)__,
then make our __(21)__
to the top of Mount Kent.

Next day we agree
that we long for the sea,
and soon are intent
on a rapid __(22)__.
Again under sail,
feeling hearty and hale,
we look back and say,
"The mountain's so far away!"
Yes, it looks like a thimble,
but to us it's a __(23)__
of something we like
quite enough for a hike.
Now over the deep,
the waves suggest sleep.
No sound of __(24)__;
all on board are content.

How Are You Doing?
List the spelling words that are difficult for you. Practice them with a partner.

Proofreading and Writing

Proofread: Spelling and Commas with Appositives If an **appositive**, a noun or phrase that identifies or renames another noun, is not necessary to the meaning of a sentence, set it off with commas. Do not use commas with an appositive that is necessary to the meaning.

Enrico Caruso, an Italian, was a great tenor.
The pop star Luis Miguel is known mainly in Latin America and Spain.

Find five misspelled Basic or Review Words and two appositives with missing commas in these notes from a CD cover. Write the notes correctly.

Basic

1. chord
2. cord
3. choral
4. coral
5. cymbal
6. symbol
7. aisle
8. isle
9. ascent
10. assent
11. stationary
12. stationery
13. site
14. cite
15. canvas
16. canvass
17. phase
18. faze
19. descent
20. dissent

Review

21. compliment
22. complement
23. capital
24. capitol

Challenge

25. callous
26. callus
27. caret
28. carat

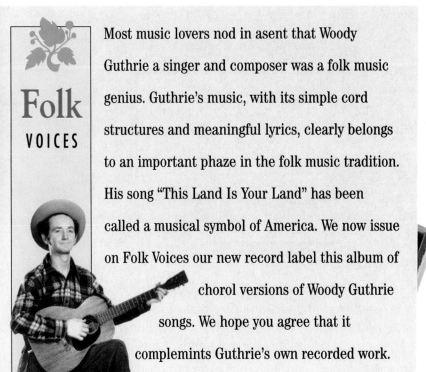

Folk

VOICES

Most music lovers nod in asent that Woody Guthrie a singer and composer was a folk music genius. Guthrie's music, with its simple cord structures and meaningful lyrics, clearly belongs to an important phaze in the folk music tradition. His song "This Land Is Your Land" has been called a musical symbol of America. We now issue on Folk Voices our new record label this album of chorol versions of Woody Guthrie songs. We hope you agree that it complemints Guthrie's own recorded work.

Proofreading Marks

¶ Indent
∧ Add
⩟ Add a comma
∀ ∀ Add quotation marks
⊙ Add a period
⌐ Delete
≡ Capital letter
/ Small letter
∿ Reverse order

Write a Review of a Musical You have just seen a musical based on a story you know. Was the show good or bad? How well did the actors perform their roles? Write a review of the musical. Try to use five spelling words and at least one appositive.

Expanding Vocabulary

**Spelling
Word Link**

symbol

Synonyms **Synonyms** are words that have the same or nearly the same meaning.

symbol = sign   rhythm = beat

Write the word in parentheses that is a synonym for each numbered word. Use your Thesaurus.

1. stationary (fixed, lifeless)
2. site (region, place)
3. assent (eagerness, agreement)
4. phase (season, mood)

1.   ?
2.   ?
3.   ?
4.   ?

Now read the following sentences. Review the Thesaurus entry for each underlined word. From the subentries for that word, choose the synonym that best fits in the sentence. Do not reuse any of your answers from items 1–4. Write the subentries that replace the underlined words.

5. Last year, our City Council gave its <u>assent</u> to building a new Symphony Hall.
6. Construction of the building at its beautiful, hilltop <u>site</u> is well underway.
7. Even at this <u>phase</u> of the building's development, hints of its grand design are visible.
8. Also, if you stand quite <u>stationary</u>, you can almost hear the strains of a lovely concerto coming from the hall.

Real-World Connection

Performing Arts: Music All the words in the box relate to music. Look up these words in your Spelling Dictionary. Then write the words to complete this paragraph.

Location	Section	Row	Seat	NO REFUNDS
Rear Orch Ctr	E	N	2	

2:00 PM

Location	Section	Row	Seat	
Rear Orch Ctr	E	N	1	NO REFUNDS

A serious vocal student might study at a special music school, or __(1)__ . Singers in the school __(2)__ are grouped by vocal range. The highest female part is the soprano, while the highest male part is the __(3)__ . These parts are often sung in a different __(4)__ than the alto or __(5)__ voice parts. A girl who wants to be a __(6)__ must practice solos, perhaps learning an __(7)__ from an opera each week. To relax, many students sing folk or rock songs, either __(8)__ or to guitar or piano accompaniment.

Spelling Word Link

choral

chorus
tenor
baritone
a cappella
octave
diva
aria
conservatory

TRY THIS!

Yes or No? Write *yes* or *no* to tell whether a person or thing is needed for the activity.

9. a piano to perform a cappella
10. notes to form an octave
11. a singer to perform an aria
12. a group to form a chorus

Fact File

Marian Anderson began her singing career in the church choir and went on to become one of the greatest concert artists of our time. She first became well known in Europe. Then, in 1955, she became the first African American ever to perform with the Metropolitan Opera.

6 Review: Units 1–5

Unit 1 Consonant Changes   pages 12–17

commit	intercede	succeed	remit	recede
commission	intercession	succession	remission	recession

 Spelling Strategy Knowing how consonants change in one pair of words can help you predict changes in words with similar spelling patterns.

Write the word that completes each sentence.
1. During a period of _____, symptoms of an illness may disappear.
2. The _____ of a neutral person can help end an argument.
3. A balding man may notice that his hairline has begun to _____.
4. All evidence indicated that she did not _____ the crime.

Write the word that matches each definition.
5. persons or things following in order
6. a group with specific duties
7. to plead on another's behalf
8. to send money
9. to replace in an office or position
10. the act of withdrawing

Unit 2 Greek Word Parts I   pages 18–23

syndrome	sympathy	hydrogen	synonym	protein
genealogy	pathological	symmetrical	protoplasm	synagogue

 Spelling Strategy Knowing the Greek word parts *path* ("disease; feeling"), *syn/sym* ("together; same"), *gen* ("born; produced"), and *prot* ("first") can help you spell and understand words with these parts.

Write the word that fits each clue.
11. *Bright* is this for *brilliant*.
12. This involves one's ancestors.
13. This is a jellylike part of cells.
14. This gives comfort.
15. Food labels list this.
16. This is a gas.

Write the word that belongs in each group.
17. signs, symptoms, _____
18. unhealthy, diseased, _____
19. church, temple, _____
20. equal, balanced, _____

Unit 3 Latin Prefixes I   pages 24–29

| translate | transit | submerge | suburban | substance |
| subscription | sublet | transaction | transition | transfusion |

 Spelling Strategy Remember the meanings of the Latin prefixes *trans-* ("across; over; through") and *sub-* ("under; near; beneath").

Write the word that completes each analogy.
21. city : outskirts :: urban : _____
22. owner : sell :: tenant : _____
23. swap : trade :: deal : _____

Write the word that matches each definition.
24. an injection into the bloodstream
25. a purchase made by a signed order
26. to express in another language
27. passage from one place to another
28. matter
29. to plunge under water
30. the process of change

Unit 4 Words from Names   pages 30–35

| narcissus | psyche | odyssey | Fahrenheit | czar |
| hygiene | mentor | Celsius | psychiatrist | mosaic |

 Spelling Strategy Knowing the origin of words that come from names can help you spell and understand the meanings of the words.

Write the words that complete the paragraph.
   Dr. Byrd, a young __(31)__ , works at a mental health clinic. He has learned a great deal from his __(32)__ , Dr. Clay. Together, they have studied human behavior and the human __(33)__ . For Dr. Byrd, this exploration has been like an __(34)__ through a fascinating land.

Write the word that fits each clue.
35. yellow flower
36. design of stones
37. Russian ruler
38. science of health
39. scale on which freezing is 0 degrees
40. scale on which freezing is 32 degrees

Unit 5 Homophones

pages 36–41

cymbal	aisle	ascent	stationary	descent
symbol	isle	assent	stationery	dissent

Spelling Strategy   Remember to think about meaning when using a **homophone**, a word that sounds like another but has a different spelling and meaning.

Write the word that is an antonym for each word below.

41. disagreement
42. moving
43. agreement
44. climb

Write the word that completes each sentence.

45. An usher looked at our tickets and led us down the _____.
46. I selected some paper and envelopes from the _____ department.
47. The view from the mountaintop made the long _____ worthwhile.
48. Bonnie kept rhythm by beating the drum and tapping the _____.
49. A tropical _____ is no place to be during a hurricane.
50. The eagle on a dollar bill is a _____ of strength and freedom.

Challenge Words   Units 1–5

pages 12–41

revoke	callous	subterranean	protagonist	transient
revocation	callus	synchronize	gargantuan	iridescent

Write the word that means the same thing as the underlined word or words in each sentence.

51. Water flowed into the lake from underground streams.
52. The waves tossed rainbow-colored seashells onto the shore.
53. Unsafe driving can lead to the cancellation of a license.
54. Tight shoes can make a hardened area of skin form on your foot.
55. Chorus line dancers make their steps occur at the same time.

Write the word that belongs in each group.

56. unfeeling, heartless, _____
57. brief, temporary, _____
58. main character, hero, _____
59. huge, gigantic, _____
60. cancel, withdraw, _____

Spelling-Meaning Strategy

The Latin Root *cess*

Did you know that the words *succession* and *necessary* are related in spelling and meaning? Both words contain the Latin root *cess*, meaning "to go" or "to yield." The meaning of the root contributes to the meaning of each word. A succession is a group of people or things that follow, or go, in order, one after another. Something that is necessary is needed; therefore, it must not go. Another form of the root *cess* is *cede* or *ceed*.

Below are more words that contain a form of *cess*.

pro**ceed**	an**ces**tor	suc**cess**or
re**cess**	ante**ced**ent	prede**cess**or

succession

necessary

Think

- How is the root spelled in each word?
- How does it contribute to the meaning of each word? Look up the words in your Spelling Dictionary.
- In Unit 1, you learned that when you add *-ion* to a word ending in *cede* or *ceed*, the *d* often changes to *ss*. What word do you get when you add *-ion* to *proceed*?

Apply and Extend

Complete these activities on a separate piece of paper.

1. Write six sentences. Use one word from the box above in each sentence.
2. What other words belong to the same family as *succession* and *necessary*? With a partner, make a list of related words. Then look up the Latin root *cess* in your Spelling-Meaning Index. Add to your list any other related words that you find there.

Summing Up

The Latin root *cede* or *cess* means "to go" or "to yield." Words that contain the same root are often related in spelling and meaning. Knowing some of the words in a family can help you to use and spell the others correctly.

During World War II, a Dutch family hid two Jewish sisters, Annie and Sini, behind the false wall of a closet. Here Annie tells of a terrifying search by Nazi soldiers. How do you know Annie was frightened?

from

The Upstairs Room
by Johanna Reiss

Loud voices. Ugly ones. Furniture being moved. And Opoe's protesting voice. The closet door was thrown open. Hands fumbled on the shelves. Sini was trembling. She tightened her arms around me. I no longer breathed through my nose. Breathing through my mouth made less noise.

A man was speaking German. Then another was saying, "We want to know where all those pieces of cloth came from."

"What's he doing? He can't just take all of that. It's mine," Opoe said, "Tell'm that."

A stick pounded once on the floor and then again. The closet door was slammed. My heart was beating too loudly. What if they could hear us? Would they stick a bayonet through the closet wall? They could. All over the wall, to be sure to hit whoever was behind the wall.

My mouth was dry, yet I didn't dare breathe through my nose. They might still be there. But you clearly heard them storm down the stairs, didn't you? I know, but what if they had left a soldier behind? Sini must think so, too, or she wouldn't be holding me so tightly.

There were noises on the stairs again. They're coming back? No, only wooden shoes this time.

"They're gone, girls."

Think and Discuss

1. What **details** does Annie use to show that she was frightened? What details show that Sini was frightened?

2. What information does Annie give you through **dialogue**? What makes the dialogue sound real?

The Writing Process
Personal Narrative

What thrilling, terrifying, funny, or tragic events have occurred in your life? Write a personal narrative about something that happened to you. Use the guidelines, and follow the Writing Process.

1 ▶ Prewriting
- Use these starters for ideas: *Some days are unforgettable. I had dreamed of this for years. I heard the warning shout, "Look out!"*
- Choose a topic, and then tell a friend what happens in your story. Try to make your listener see the event. List some of the details you will include.

2 ▶ Draft
- Start to write. Do not worry about mistakes now.
- Write an interesting beginning.
- Use details and dialogue to make your story seem real.

3 ▶ Revise
- Revise your beginning to assure that it will encourage readers to read on.
- Add vivid details where you can. Use your Thesaurus to find exact words.
- Add realistic dialogue where possible.
- Have a writing conference.

4 ▶ Proofread
- Did you spell each word correctly?
- Did you use commas correctly in compound and complex sentences and with appositives?
- Do you need to correct any fragments or run-ons?

5 ▶ Publish
- Copy your narrative neatly and give it an interesting title.
- Share your story. Make a poster to advertise it.

Guidelines for Writing a Personal Narrative

✓ Write a beginning that captures your readers' interest.
✓ Use natural dialogue and vivid details to help your readers see, hear, and feel your experience.
✓ Present the events in sequential order.
✓ Write an ending that *shows* rather than *tells* the outcome.

Composition Words

succeed
sympathy
transform
submerge
odyssey
fate
ascent
faze

Absorbed Prefixes

Read and Say

Basic

READ the sentences. SAY each bold word.

1. communication — Phones have made **communication** easier.
2. announcer — Which radio **announcer** is reading the news?
3. commentary — Her **commentary** helps to explain the issues.
4. accent — He speaks with a strong **accent**.
5. colleague — My **colleague** and I met at the conference.
6. apparent — Her tears made her sadness **apparent**.
7. allude — Did he **allude** to me in his speech?
8. aggressive — Your **aggressive** playing won the game.
9. immerse — Just **immerse** the sponge in water.
10. illusion — Was the trick with the mirror an **illusion**?
11. collaborate — Two writers will **collaborate** on the book.
12. appliance — Does the **appliance** store carry gas stoves?
13. collision — We must change course to avoid a **collision**.
14. accessory — A pin was the only **accessory** on her dress.
15. immaculate — There is no dust in this **immaculate** room.
16. accumulate — Pennies tend to **accumulate** on my dresser.
17. allegiance — The coach demands **allegiance** to the team.
18. aggravate — Will running **aggravate** the pain in your leg?
19. collapse — A light wind will **collapse** a house of cards.
20. illuminate — Oil lamps **illuminate** the log cabin.

Spelling Strategy   Remember that *ad-* ("to; toward"), *in-* ("in; not"), and *con-* ("with; together") can be **absorbed prefixes** when their last letter changes to match the beginning consonant of the base word to which they are added.

Think and Write   Write each Basic Word under the heading that shows how its original prefix can be spelled when the prefix is absorbed.

con- (com-, col-)   ad- (an-, ac-, ap-, al-, ag-)   in- (im-, il-)

Review   23. alliance
21. commercial 24. appropriate
22. acceptable 25. illegal

Challenge   28. commemorate
26. irrelevant   29. alliteration
27. corroborate 30. commiserate

Independent Practice

Vocabulary: Using Context Write the Basic Word that completes each
sentence. Use your Spelling Dictionary.

1. To be a radio _____, you must have a strong, pleasant voice.
2. After being on the air for twenty-four hours without a break, the newscaster
   was ready to _____.
3. Radio and television are two forms of _____.
4. Today, headphones are as common an _____ as a hat or scarf.
5. Sarah Greenberg interpreted the senator's vague statement in the political
   _____ segment of her news program.
6. Most newscasters speak without a regional _____.
7. Because of his _____ to WJAX, Jack never listens to any other radio station.
8. Sound effects in a radio drama create the _____ of a storm.
9. The winner of the radio quiz show gets a kitchen _____.
10. Maria and Julio plan to _____ on a series of radio jingles.

Vocabulary: Synonyms Write the Basic Word that has the same meaning as
each word below. Use your Spelling Dictionary.

11. refer
12. submerge
13. clarify
14. bold
15. crash
16. spotless
17. obvious
18. collect
19. coworker
20. worsen

Challenge Words Write the Challenge Word that matches each definition. Use
your Spelling Dictionary.

21. to honor the memory of a person or event
22. the repetition of beginning consonants for poetic effect
23. having no relation to a subject or situation
24. to sympathize
25. to support or confirm by new evidence

Review: Spelling Spree

Invisible Letters Decide which letters should be added to complete each Basic or Review Word. Write the words correctly.

1. c o l _ i s i _ _
2. _ c _ e _ _ _ b _ e
3. _ _ p _ i _ n _ e
4. _ l _ u _ i _ a _ e
5. c o m _ _ n _ a _ y
6. a _ _ o u _ c _ r
7. i _ l _ g _ _
8. _ g _ r _ s _ i _ _
9. c _ m _ u _ i _ a _ i _ n
10. a p p _ _ p _ i _ _ e

Word Combination In each item, add the beginning letters of the first word to the last letters of the second word to form a Basic or Review Word. Write the words.

Example: common + momentary   *commentary*

11. immense + verse
12. college + vague
13. accessible + story
14. alley + reliance
15. immature + articulate
16. collage + elaborate
17. altitude + conclude
18. collect + relapse
19. accurate + formulate

20. apartment + transparent
21. illustrate + junction
22. commerce + facial
23. accident + rent
24. aggregate + excavate
25. allege + variance

> **✓ How Are You Doing?**
> Write each spelling word in a sentence. Practice any misspelled spelling words with a partner.

Proofreading and Writing

Proofread: Spelling and Subject-Verb Agreement The subject and the verb of a sentence must **agree** in number. Use a singular verb with a singular subject. Use a plural verb with a plural subject and with compound subjects joined by *and*. With subjects joined by *or* or *nor*, use a verb that agrees with the nearest subject.

Mr. Marquez announces the names of the guests.
The two **guests work** for the National Safety Council.
Safety <u>and</u> **seat belts are** the topics of the program.
Mr. Marquez <u>or</u> the **guests answer** listeners' calls.

Find five misspelled Basic or Review Words and two verbs that do not agree with their subjects in this excerpt from a radio script. Write the excerpt correctly.

ANNOUNCER: Many people find seat belts a bother.

The apparant inconvenience of wearing a seat belt

seems to aggrevate these riders. Yet the

evidence in favor of seat belts continues

to acumulate. In a colision, neither the

driver nor the passengers is safe without

seat belts. The National Safety Council and

this station urges you to use a seat belt. It

is one accessery that could save your life.

Write a News Bulletin   Write a brief news bulletin about an event related to the weather, politics, a famous person, or any other topic you choose. Try to use five spelling words, and check that the subject and verb of each sentence agree in number.

Basic

1. communication
2. announcer
3. commentary
4. accent
5. colleague
6. apparent
7. allude
8. aggressive
9. immerse
10. illusion
11. collaborate
12. appliance
13. collision
14. accessory
15. immaculate
16. accumulate
17. allegiance
18. aggravate
19. collapse
20. illuminate

Review

21. commercial
22. acceptable
23. alliance
24. appropriate
25. illegal

Challenge

26. irrelevant
27. corroborate
28. commemorate
29. alliteration
30. commiserate

Proofreading Marks

¶   Indent
∧   Add
⋏   Add a comma
⌄⌄   Add quotation marks
⊙   Add a period
ℐ   Delete
≡   Capital letter
/   Small letter
∿   Reverse order

Expanding Vocabulary

Spelling Word Link

communication

Exact Words What do you picture as you read this sentence?

I received a <u>communication</u> from the radio station.

Do you picture a letter? a broadcast? a telegram? Use exact, or precise, words when you write to give your readers a clear picture. A thesaurus can help you find exact words.

Write the exact word from the list below that best replaces *communication* in each sentence. Use your Thesaurus.

leaflet   report   telegram   message

1. The announcer read the news <u>communication</u> on the air.
2. A glossy <u>communication</u> from a new store was in the mail.
3. The urgent <u>communication</u> read, "Return home. Jane ill."
4. The bottle bobbing in the sea held an odd <u>communication</u>.

TEST-TAKING TACTICS

Vocabulary-in-Context One strategy for answering vocabulary-in-context test questions is to ignore the answer choices until you have figured out your own meaning for the tested word. Then compare your meaning with those given in the answer choices. The answer choice that most nearly matches your meaning is likely to be correct.

Try using this technique. Read the sample passage excerpt below, and then read only the part of the question that locates and names the tested word. Ignore the answer choices for now.

Sample passage excerpt and question:

(40) In broadcasting's golden age, radio dramas were extremely popular. Families gathered around the radio night after night to hear the daring adventures of their intrepid heroes. These courageous characters were never afraid to do what was necessary to save the day.

In line 42, the word "intrepid" most nearly means   (A) attractive
(B) brilliant   (C) dramatic   (D) clumsy   (E) fearless

Now write the answers to these questions.

5. Using only context clues, what do you *think* "intrepid" means?
6. After reviewing the answer choices, which one most nearly matches your meaning of "intrepid"? Write its letter.

Real-World Connection

Performing Arts: Radio Broadcasting All the words in the box relate to radio broadcasting. Look up these words in your Spelling Dictionary. Then write the words to complete this paragraph.

ON AIR

> Though there are many types of radio shows, most center around music. Each show has a __(1)__ , who chooses and announces the musical selections. Some announcers read from scripts, but most __(2)__ instead. With the help of a __(3)__ , the announcer operates CD players, microphones, and other types of equipment. If parts of a program are __(4)__ , the announcer must know when to insert the proper __(5)__ into the tape player. The announcer must also remember to give a station __(6)__ at least once per hour. All of this is transmitted to your radio __(7)__ , sometimes mingled with unwelcome __(8)__ , or electrical interference.

Spelling Word Link

announcer

disc jockey
ad-lib
identification
prerecorded
cartridge
antenna
static
technician

TRY THIS!

True or False? Write *T* if a sentence is true and *F* if it is false.

9. Another name for a radio advertisement is an ad-lib.
10. When you turn a radio dial, you often hear static.
11. A prerecorded show is taped before it is broadcast.
12. A disc jockey is the host of a radio talk show.

Fact File

Orson Welles's 1938 radio show *The War of the Worlds* alarmed much of the United States. The show's news flashes reporting a fictional Martian invasion sounded so real that many listeners hid or fled, panicked by the prank.

Greek Word Parts II

Read and Say

Basic

READ the sentences. **SAY** each bold word.

1. chronology — A time line shows the **chronology** of events.
2. terminology — This document is full of legal **terminology**.
3. catalog — Can I order from that **catalog** by phone?
4. technology — New **technology** makes many tasks easier.
5. geology — Bring some rock samples to **geology** class.
6. zoology — This **zoology** book does not cover apes.
7. logic — Use **logic** to solve this math problem.
8. biology — Our next **biology** lesson is on human growth.
9. apology — I offered my **apology** for breaking the cup.
10. psychology — Students of **psychology** learn how minds work.
11. dialogue — I overheard the **dialogue** between them.
12. sociology — Human groups are the focus of **sociology**.
13. ecology — Oil spills harm the **ecology** of oceans.
14. meteorology — Do weather reporters study **meteorology**?
15. theology — Our minister has a degree in **theology**.
16. anthology — Is my poem in the new **anthology** of poetry?
17. astrology — Fans of **astrology** study stars and planets.
18. analogy — An **analogy** shows how things are related.
19. mythology — The gods of ancient **mythology** interest me.
20. trilogy — I read all three books of the **trilogy**.

Spelling Strategy Knowing the Greek word parts *log* and *logy* ("an oral or written expression; the science, theory, or study of") can help you spell and understand words with these parts.

Think and Write   Write the Basic Words.

Review
21. fragment
22. professor
23. assistant
24. corrode
25. analyze

Challenge
26. archaeology
27. logistics
28. etymology
29. prologue
30. epilogue

Independent Practice

Vocabulary: Definitions Write the Basic Word that matches each definition.
Use your Spelling Dictionary.

1. the expression of a similarity between two things
2. an arrangement of events in time
3. the vocabulary of technical terms specific to a trade, science, or art
4. a collection of writings by various authors
5. a statement that expresses regret or asks pardon for a mistake or offense
6. conversation between two people
7. the scientific study of animals
8. clear reasoning
9. a group of three related dramatic or literary works
10. the study of religion
11. a list of items, usually alphabetical and containing descriptions
12. the application of scientific knowledge, especially to business and industry

Vocabulary: Categorizing Write the Basic Word that names the field in
which each pair of items is studied. Use your Spelling Dictionary.

13. clouds, wind
14. legends, heroes
15. people, animals
16. pollution, conservation
17. volcanoes, rocks
18. fears, mental illness
19. cultures, institutions
20. planets, stars

Challenge Words Write the
Challenge Word that fits each clue.
Use your Spelling Dictionary.

21. This comes at the beginning of a book or play.
22. This comes at the end of a book or play.
23. People who plan events must think about this.
24. This digs up the past.
25. This traces the origin of a word.

Dictionary

Spelling Table Suppose you did not know how to spell the beginning of the word *chronology*. How would you look it up in the dictionary? Many dictionaries provide a **spelling table** that shows the different ways in which each sound can be spelled. To spell *chronology*, you would look under |k| in the spelling table.

SOUND	SPELLINGS	SAMPLE WORDS
|k|	c, cc, ch	pi**c**nic, a**cc**ount, s**ch**ool
	ck, k, que	sti**ck**, **k**eep, anti**que**

Practice Write the actual spelling for each phonetic spelling below. Refer to the Spelling Table and your Spelling Dictionary.

1. |fär´ mə sĭst|
2. |kən fûr´|
3. |rĕch´ ĭd|
4. |sĭm bol´ ĭk|
5. |shō´ fər|
6. |no͞o mōn´ yə|
7. |rīn´ stōn´|
8. |păj´ ənt|

Review: Spelling Spree

Code Breaker The Basic and Review Words below are written in code. Use the following code key to figure out each word. Write the decoded words correctly.

CODE:	m	n	o	p	q	r	s	t	u	v	w	x	y	z	a	b	c	d	e	f	g	h	i	j	k	l
LETTER:	a	b	c	d	e	f	g	h	i	j	k	l	m	n	o	p	q	r	s	t	u	v	w	x	y	z

Example: rdmsyqzf   *fragment*

9. yqfqadaxask
10. mbaxask
11. eaouaxask
12. qoaxask
13. sqaxask
14. bekotaxask

15. laaxask
16. ftqaxask
17. mzmxask
18. pumxasgq
19. oaddapq
20. fduxask

21. xasuo
22. mefdaxask
23. mzmxklq
24. mzftaxask
25. nuaxask

Proofreading and Writing

Proofread for Spelling Find seven misspelled Basic or Review Words in this journal entry. Write each word correctly.

Today, I will cataloge the finds from the San Rego dig. Every fraggment of pottery must be numbered and recorded. I will have to analyze all of the test results myself. My asistant, Gina, is inexperienced and has little knowledge of either the tecknology or the terminalogy. There is good news, however—I have discovered tablets that record the mithology of the San Rego people. The writings will help establish a cronology of their culture.

Basic

1. chronology
2. terminology
3. catalog
4. technology
5. geology
6. zoology
7. logic
8. biology
9. apology
10. psychology
11. dialogue
12. sociology
13. ecology
14. meteorology
15. theology
16. anthology
17. astrology
18. analogy
19. mythology
20. trilogy

Review

21. fragment
22. professor
23. assistant
24. corrode
25. analyze

Challenge

26. archaeology
27. logistics
28. etymology
29. prologue
30. epilogue

Proofreading Marks

¶ Indent
∧ Add
⁏ Add a comma
⌄⌄ Add quotation marks
⊙ Add a period
⟋ Delete
≡ Capital letter
/ Small letter
∩ Reverse order

Write a Summary You are applying for a summer job as a helper on an archaeological dig. Why do you think you would qualify for the job? Write a summary of your qualifications. Try to use five spelling words.

Expanding Vocabulary

Spelling Word Link

astrology

The Greek Word Part *ast* The word *astrology* contains the Greek word part *ast*, meaning "star." Several other English words also contain this word part.

astronaut	asteroid	astronomy
astronomical	disaster	

Write the word from the list above that completes each sentence. Use your Spelling Dictionary.

1. Telescopes are used in _____, the study of the universe.
2. Computers can perform an _____ number of calculations in minutes.
3. Did a _____, such as a flood, kill off the dinosaurs?
4. Aboard the lunar orbiter, the _____ checked the controls.
5. Scientists spotted a rocky _____ orbiting near Mars.

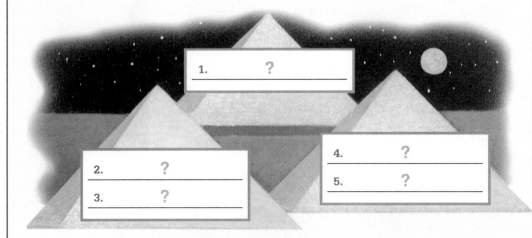

1. _____ ?

2. _____ ?

3. _____ ?

4. _____ ?

5. _____ ?

Now write three sentences. In each one, use *two* words from above that contain the Greek word part *ast*.

6. _____ ?
_____ ?

7. _____ ?
_____ ?

8. _____ ?
_____ ?

Real-World Connection

Science: Archaeology All the words in the box relate to archaeology. Look up these words in your Spelling Dictionary. Then write the words to complete this paragraph.

Spelling Word Link

chronology

expedition
excavate
civilization
strata
relic
implement
shard
classification

In 1870, archaeologist Heinrich Schliemann led a digging __(1)__ in Turkey. He and his helpers hoped to __(2)__ the lost city of Troy. In the attempt, Schliemann's crew dug through several __(3)__ of earth and rock. Each layer revealed the remains of a different city, dating as far back as 2500 B.C. Every tool, or __(4)__, found on the site gave clues about the ancient __(5)__ that existed there, as did every tiny __(6)__ of pottery. Toward the end of the dig, Schliemann found five royal graves full of jewels, weapons, and other treasures. One especially lovely __(7)__ was a crown containing 16,000 gold bits. The identification and __(8)__ of these finds took many years.

► TRY THIS!

Yes or No? Write *yes* if the underlined word is used correctly. Write *no* if it is not.

9. Dr. Wang kept all of his <u>strata</u> on the computer.
10. Ancient Greeks used this <u>implement</u> to grind grain.
11. The worker used a <u>shard</u> to sift the dirt.
12. To <u>excavate</u> a site, workers must dig carefully.

Fact File

The eruption of Mount Vesuvius in A.D. 79 covered the Roman city of Pompeii in twenty-one feet of ash. Excavations at the site have uncovered temples, bathhouses, mansions, and miles of perfectly preserved streets.

Latin Prefixes II

Read and Say

Basic

	Basic Words	READ the sentences. SAY each bold word.
1.	*intramural*	I am on the **intramural** hockey team.
2.	*interstate*	An **interstate** highway connects both capitals.
3.	*supervise*	A teacher must **supervise** your project.
4.	*interference*	We are picking up **interference** on the radio.
5.	*intercept*	Try to **intercept** the ball before she gets it.
6.	*counteract*	Will sugar **counteract** a strong salty taste?
7.	*intermediate*	The **intermediate** class is not for beginners.
8.	*superlative*	A top award is for **superlative** performance.
9.	*counterfeit*	Making **counterfeit** money is illegal.
10.	*superficial*	His cuts are just **superficial** wounds.
11.	*counterpart*	A paw is the **counterpart** of a foot.
12.	*intervention*	Her **intervention** ended the conflict.
13.	*intersection*	Two major streets meet at the **intersection**.
14.	*intrastate*	The law regulates **intrastate** trucking only.
15.	*supermarket*	Buy some milk and soap at the **supermarket**.
16.	*interchangeable*	These parts are **interchangeable** with those.
17.	*superintendent*	A **superintendent** oversees all the schools.
18.	*counterclockwise*	A **counterclockwise** turn is to the left.
19.	*interpret*	Could you **interpret** the meaning of his poem?
20.	*intravenous*	Tiny babies may need **intravenous** feeding.

Spelling Strategy   Remember the meanings of the Latin prefixes *inter-* ("between"), *intra-* ("within"), *super-* ("over; greater"), and *counter-* ("opposing").

Think and Write   Write each Basic Word under its prefix.

inter-	*intra-*	*super-*	*counter-*

Review
21. superstition   24. athletic
22. interjection   25. spectator
23. interruption

Challenge
26. interscholastic   29. interrogate
27. superfluous   30. intersperse
28. counterproductive

Independent Practice

Vocabulary: Replacing Words Write the Basic Word that means the same thing as the underlined word or words in each sentence. Use your Spelling Dictionary.

1. The Ramsay twins are <u>able to be switched</u> as shortstops.
2. Lin belongs in the <u>middle</u> gymnastics group.
3. Harvey was taken out of the basketball game for <u>the illegal blocking of another player</u>.
4. We want to form a tennis team that is <u>within one school</u>.
5. Our field hockey team played a <u>first-rate</u> game.
6. Pam has only a <u>slight</u> knowledge of the rules of lacrosse.
7. The basketball championship will be <u>within one state</u>.
8. The Blues tried in vain to <u>oppose the effect of</u> the Cubs' strong defense by throwing more long passes.
9. Kim couldn't <u>understand</u> the referee's expression.
10. Thanks to Ben's <u>coming between the two</u>, Julio and Matt avoided an argument over the broken bat.
11. Jack's throw looked like a sure touchdown, but one of the opponents managed to <u>seize</u> the ball.

Vocabulary: Word Clues Write the Basic Word that fits each clue. Use your Spelling Dictionary.

12. A shot in the arm can be this.
13. This is someone doing what you do, only somewhere else.
14. This kind of bill isn't worth the paper it is printed on.
15. This place sells breakfast, lunch, and dinner food all day.
16. Parallel roads never form this.
17. If you went back in time, your watch would move this way.
18. The person in charge of a school system has this title.
19. Bosses get paid to do this.
20. A highway that runs through Ohio and Pennsylvania is this.

Challenge Words Write the Challenge Word that matches each definition. Use your Spelling Dictionary.

21. to question closely
22. extra
23. to scatter here and there among other things
24. not helpful; harmful
25. conducted between or among schools

Review: Spelling Spree

Meaning Match Add the prefix to a word that fits the definition to create a Basic Word. Write the Basic Words.

Example: inter + "scene" =   *interview*

1. counter + "segment of a whole" =
2. super + "store" =
3. inter + "subdivision of a country" =
4. counter + "the direction a clock's hands move" =
5. intra + "wall painting" =
6. inter + "able to be altered" =
7. counter + "perform" =
8. inter + "part" =
9. intra + "declare" =
10. inter + "act as agent between two parties in conflict" =

Word Track 11–25. Find the Basic and Review Words that are hidden in this cross-country race course. Write the words correctly in the order in which you find them. Begin at the starting line.

✓ How Are You Doing?
Write each spelling word as a partner reads it aloud. Did you misspell any words?

Proofreading and Writing

Proofread: Spelling, Agreement in Inverted and Interrupted Order A sentence is in **inverted order** when all or part of the verb comes before the subject. A sentence is in **interrupted order** when a word or phrase interrupts the subject and the verb. In either case, be sure that the subject and the verb agree.

INVERTED: On the team **are** two **players** from California.
INTERRUPTED: **Ray**, one of the Tigers, **is** a great player.

Find five misspelled Basic or Review Words and two errors in subject-verb agreement in this interview excerpt. Write the excerpt correctly.

QUESTION: You are a superletive softball player. You hold every intermural batting record. Is there any secrets behind your success?

ANSWER: Well, atheletic skills help, but the real trick is concentration. Any interuption can ruin a game. Also, I twirl the bat conterclockwise before I swing.

QUESTION: Wouldn't you call that a superstition?

ANSWER: Maybe. People on the team calls it crazy!

Proofreading Marks
¶ Indent
∧ Add
⩗ Add a comma
∀ ∀ Add quotation marks
⊙ Add a period
⌐ Delete
≡ Capital letter
/ Small letter
∩ Reverse order

Write a Personal Narrative Have you ever been the team hero in an important competition? Have you ever helped your team lose? How did you feel? Write a paragraph about your most memorable sports or other competitive experience. Try to use five spelling words and at least one sentence in inverted or interrupted order.

Expanding Vocabulary

Spelling Word Link

interference

Jargon As you know, *interference* means "the act of intruding or getting in the way." In sports, *interference* has a more specialized meaning: "the illegal obstruction of a player." Language that is used by a particular group of people in this specialized way is called **jargon**.

Write a word from the list to replace each underlined example of jargon. Use your Spelling Dictionary.

bounced   basket   shot   removed

With seconds to go in the game, Coach West (**1**) <u>benched</u> Tia Luca and put in Peg Gibb. Gibb caught the ball, (**2**) <u>dribbled</u> it down the court, and with a sweeping (**3**) <u>hook</u> sent the ball through the (**4**) <u>hoop</u> to win.

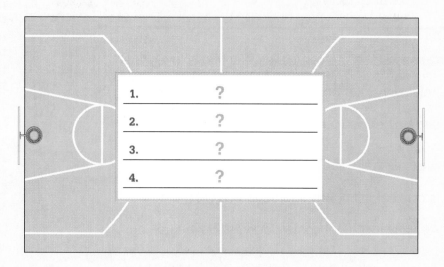

1. _____ ?
2. _____ ?
3. _____ ?
4. _____ ?

Now, using the jargon of the sport, write your own short description of an exciting basketball game. If you like, you may pick another sport and describe a game using that sport's jargon.

_____ ?

_____ ?

_____ ?

_____ ?

_____ ?

_____ ?

Real-World Connection

Physical Education: Intramural Sports All the words in the box relate to intramural sports. Look up these words in your Spelling Dictionary. Then write the words to complete this paragraph.

| TEAM | | RUNNING SCORE | | 1 | 2 | 3 | 4 | 5 | 6 | 7 | 8 | 9 | 10 | 11 | 12 | 13 | 14 | 15 | 16 | 17 | 18 | 19 | 20 | 21 | 22 | 23 | 24 | 25 | 26 | 27 | 28 |
| COACH | T1 | T2 | 29 | 30 | 31 | 32 | 33 | 34 | 35 | 36 | 37 | 38 | 39 | 40 | 41 | 42 | 43 | 44 | 45 | 46 | 47 | 48 | 49 | 50 | 51 | 52 | 53 | 54 | 55 | 56 | 57 | 58 | 59 | 60 |

Yesterday Legrath School held a ___(1)___, or practice game, between the Tigers, the school's ___(2)___ basketball team, and the Stringbeans, a team from the local ___(3)___ league. Although this was supposed to be a relaxed game, the players took it seriously. Their keen sense of rivalry and ___(4)___ made the game lively. At first, the Tigers' greater skill kept the less-practiced team on the ___(5)___. Once the Stringbeans hit their stride, however, their ___(6)___ was unstoppable, and they won the game 86–72. Addressing both teams after the game, Coach Orsini congratulated every ___(7)___ for playing his or her best . "My only problem," he said, "is deciding which team to train for the city ___(8)___ title!"

Spelling Word Link

intramural

recreational
participant
competition
championship
varsity
scrimmage
defensive
offense

TRY THIS!

Yes or No? Write *yes* or *no* to answer each question.

9. Do teams score points for defensive plays?
10. Would a team play a scrimmage to win a state title?
11. Would a school's top athletes be on varsity teams?
12. Would a volleyball game at the beach be recreational?

Fact File

A lacrosse player uses a stick with a net pocket at one end to move the ball toward the other team's goal. First played by Canadian Iroquois, the game of lacrosse is now popular in many parts of the world.

Words from Spanish

Read and Say

Basic

1. coyote	Is the **coyote** related to the wolf?
2. mesa	We camped on the **mesa** high above the desert.
3. savanna	Lions roamed free on the grassy **savanna**.
4. adobe	Bricks made of **adobe** are baked in the sun.
5. pueblo	One man lived on the top floor of the **pueblo**.
6. stampede	The **stampede** of elephants shook the ground.
7. lariat	She tied a loop in the rope to form a **lariat**.
8. bronco	Can you catch and ride that **bronco**?
9. barbecue	Clean the grill before lighting the **barbecue**.
10. tornado	The winds of the **tornado** caused much damage.
11. indigo	The night sky was a deep **indigo** blue.
12. jaguar	Is a **jaguar** as fast as a tiger?
13. mosquito	The **mosquito** is my least favorite insect.
14. sierra	Snow covered the sharp peaks of the **sierra**.
15. avocado	Chop up an **avocado** for the salad.
16. alfalfa	Our cattle are fed hay and **alfalfa**.
17. cafeteria	Does the school **cafeteria** serve good food?
18. mascara	Use **mascara** to make your eyelashes look long.
19. pimento	He likes the red **pimento** in green olives.
20. armada	Each ship in the **armada** was ready for war.

Spelling Strategy   Knowing how to pronounce a word from Spanish will often help you spell it.

Think and Write   Write the Basic Words.

Review		**Challenge**	
21. cargo	23. chocolate	26. bravado	28. incommunicado
22. hammock	24. vanilla	27. renegade	29. flotilla
	25. cocoa		30. aficionado

Independent Practice

Vocabulary: Using Context Write the Basic Word that completes each sentence. Use your Spelling Dictionary.

1. Riding a bucking _____ is nearly as dangerous as riding a bull.
2. The explosive noise caused the cattle to _____.
3. The outlaws fled, heading for the jagged peaks of the _____.
4. Center Falls is holding its annual chicken _____ Sunday.
5. Hank roped the calf with a quick throw of his _____.
6. A herd of buffalo grazed on the flat, grassy _____.
7. Maria peeled the _____ and cut up its soft pulp.
8. The only cosmetic sold at Jeb's General Store is _____.
9. An _____ sailed into the harbor soon after talk of war began.
10. The _____ rose out of the desert like an enormous table of rock.
11. The _____ whirled through the hills, uprooting many trees in its path.
12. Zeke's Grill is famous throughout the Southwest for its hamburgers cooked with onion and bits of red _____.
13. Some Hopi families still lived in the _____.

Vocabulary: Classifying Write the Basic Word that fits each group. Use your Spelling Dictionary.

14. lion, leopard, cheetah, _____
15. horsefly, wasp, gnat, _____
16. scarlet, violet, aqua, _____
17. cement, wood, stone, _____
18. wolf, fox, jackal, _____
19. restaurant, diner, snack bar, _____
20. hay, grass, wheat, _____

Challenge Words Write the Challenge Word that completes each sentence. Use your Spelling Dictionary.

21. Someone forced to be out of touch with others is _____.
22. Someone who is a deserter or an outlaw is a _____.
23. Someone who enthusiastically admires rodeos is an _____ of the western competitions.
24. Someone sailing in a fleet of ships is traveling with a _____.
25. Someone who struts and bluffs is full of _____.

Dictionary

Variations in Spelling and Pronunciation Sometimes there is more than one acceptable way to spell a word. If so, the dictionary entry will show the variations.

> **sa·van·na** or **sa·van·nah** |sə văn´ ə| *n.* A flat, treeless grassland of warm regions. [Earlier *zavana*, from Spanish.]

Dictionary entries also indicate variations in the pronunciation of a word. Although each pronunciation shown is acceptable, the one listed first is usually the preferred or most common one.

> **coy·o·te** |kī ō´ tē| or |kī´ ōt´| *n.* A wolflike animal common in western North America. [Mexican Spanish from Nahuatl *cóyotl.*]

Practice Write the other acceptable spelling for each word below. Underline the letter or letters that are spelled differently. Use your Spelling Dictionary.

1. catalog   2. omelet   3. dialogue   4. encyclopedia

Write the number of acceptable pronunciations for each word below. Use your Spelling Dictionary.

5. adverse   6. dossier   7. versatile   8. diversion

Review: Spelling Spree

Letter Math Add and subtract letters from the words below to make Basic or Review Words. Write the new words.

Example: ham + mockery – ery =   *hammock*

9. pi + mental – al + o =   18. large + giant – geg – n =
10. ad + obey – y =   19. bin – b + dig + o =
11. stamp + edit – it + e =   20. v + anthill – th + a =
12. ja + guard – d =   21. torn + adore – re =
13. car + goat – at =   22. choke – ke + co + late =
14. barbed – d + cute – t =   23. ma + scary – y + a =
15. cafe + term – m + ia =   24. avoid – id + cad + o =
16. all – l + fall – l + fa =   25. mo + squirt – r + o =
17. float – a + ill + a =

Proofreading and Writing

Proofread for Spelling Find seven misspelled Basic or Review Words in this excerpt from a travel brochure. Write each word correctly.

Come to the Southwest for a wild western experience. Climb the rugged seirra or roam with buffalo across the open savvanna. Enjoy the sun-baked beauty of adobe dwellings in an ancient peublo. Picnic atop a meysa and listen to the distant call of a coyotee. Straddle a fence and watch as a cowhand twirls a lariat or tames a bronko. If you prefer to rest, you can grab a bunkhouse hamock and wait for the barbecue to begin. Come to the Southwest—you'll never want to leave.

Basic

1. coyote
2. mesa
3. savanna
4. adobe
5. pueblo
6. stampede
7. lariat
8. bronco
9. barbecue
10. tornado
11. indigo
12. jaguar
13. mosquito
14. sierra
15. avocado
16. alfalfa
17. cafeteria
18. mascara
19. pimento
20. armada

Review
21. cargo
22. hammock
23. chocolate
24. vanilla
25. cocoa

Challenge
26. bravado
27. renegade
28. incommunicado
29. flotilla
30. aficionado

Proofreading Marks

¶ Indent
∧ Add
⩘ Add a comma
⋎⋎ Add quotation marks
⊙ Add a period
⌇ Delete
≡ Capital letter
/ Small letter
∪ Reverse order

Write a Descriptive Paragraph Think of what you know about the Southwest, through personal experience, films, or books and articles you have read. Write a paragraph describing the sights, sounds, and smells someone might experience in the Southwest. Try to use five spelling words.

Unit 10 BONUS

Expanding Vocabulary

Spelling Word Link

adobe

Context Clues Because an appositive identifies another noun, it is often an excellent context clue. Suppose you did not know the word *adobe*. The appositive in this sentence might help.

The house was made of adobe, **brick made of clay and straw.**

Write the meaning of each underlined word.

1. The sirocco, a hot southerly wind, blew along the plain.
2. Horses roam on the pampa, a South American grassland.
3. The woman photographed a paloverde, a small thorny shrub.
4. The skink, a desert lizard, sat by the rock.
5. The naturalist spotted two rheas, ostrichlike birds.

1. _____ ? _____
2. _____ ? _____
3. _____ ? _____
4. _____ ? _____
5. _____ ? _____

TEST-TAKING TACTICS ✔

Sentence Completion Sentence completion test questions consist of a sentence with one or two blanks and four or five choices of answers to fit in the blanks. You are to read the sentence and choose the word or set of words that *best* fits the sentence's meaning. Look at this sample question.

Although the surface land in much of the Southwest is _____, these deserts are rich in concealed mineral deposits.

(A) scenic   (B) scarce   (C) barren   (D) valuable   (E) dry

Many sentence completion questions, including the one above, contain words such as *but, however, nonetheless,* or *although.* These words signal a contrast between two ideas. When you see one of these words, scan the answer choices for a word that means the opposite of another word in the sentence. Use this tactic to answer the following questions.

6. Which word in the sample sentence serves as the contrast signal?
7. For which word in the sentence should you find an antonym?
8. Which answer choice correctly completes the sentence? Write its letter.

Real-World Connection

Social Studies: The American Southwest All the words in the box relate to the American Southwest. Look up these words in your Spelling Dictionary. Then write the words to complete this paragraph.

The American Southwest boasts a landscape rich in wonders. From the towering flat top of a __(1)__ to the shallow, winding bottom of a __(2)__, this dry land is full of life. The prickly __(3)__ cactus, its branches like upraised arms, stands guard over the desert. The thorny __(4)__ tree graces the land with small shade pools. Scuttling among the cacti and rocks are such creatures as the plate-covered __(5)__ and the __(6)__ with its poisonous tail. On mountain slopes, the stately __(7)__ bears pine cones containing nutlike seeds. The clustered white flowers of the __(8)__ plant add beauty to the barren landscape.

Spelling Word Link

mesa

mesquite
butte
scorpion
saguaro
gulch
armadillo
yucca
piñon

TRY THIS!

True or False? Write *T* if a sentence is true and *F* if it is false.

9. A scorpion makes a good house pet.
10. The armadillo burrows for shelter.
11. A butte wanders aimlessly along the desert floor.
12. The mesquite protects itself with a stinging tail.

Fact File

Death Valley got its name in 1849 from some prospectors who lost their way in this California desert. The prospectors managed to cross the mountains that ring the desolate expanse, but their fearful name for the region stuck.

Words Often Confused

Read and Say

READ the sentences. SAY each bold word.

1. immigrate	When did you **immigrate** to our country?
2. emigrate	From which country did they **emigrate**?
3. adverse	An **adverse** reaction to medicine is serious.
4. averse	I am **averse** to the idea of higher taxes.
5. persecute	We do not **persecute** people for their beliefs.
6. prosecute	Which lawyer will **prosecute** the suspect?
7. accede	I hope my parents **accede** to my request.
8. exceed	It is unsafe to **exceed** the speed limit.
9. liable	You are **liable** to fail if you don't study.
10. libel	Lies stated in print are grounds for **libel**.
11. rational	His careful thought led to a **rational** plan.
12. rationale	Explain the **rationale** for your choice.
13. prospective	I met my **prospective** boss at the interview.
14. perspective	The van looks huge from this **perspective**.
15. vocation	My chosen lifetime **vocation** is acting.
16. avocation	A hobby is a kind of **avocation**.
17. vial	The sour milk had a **vile** taste.
18. vile	Pour each blood sample into a small **vial**.
19. regimen	Does your exercise **regimen** include running?
20. regiment	The **regiment** of soldiers marched all night.

Spelling Strategy   To avoid confusing words with similar spellings and pronunciations, think of the meanings of the words.

Think and Write   Write the pairs of Basic Words.

Review	23. bizarre
21. conscious	24. bazaar
22. conscience	

Challenge	27. eminent
25. antidote	28. imminent
26. anecdote	

Independent Practice

Vocabulary: Word Clues Write the Basic Word that fits each clue. Use your
Spelling Dictionary.

1. A family that is planning to move away from its native country is going to do this.
2. A scientist might store a chemical solution in this.
3. A person who is legally responsible for an accident is this.
4. This is the reasoning behind a decision.
5. This is an activity that someone does in his or her spare time.
6. This is a large group of soldiers.
7. You are following this when you stay in bed and drink liquids to fight a cold.
8. A journalist who prints lies about a person may be accused of this.
9. The legal system will do this to someone who is accused of breaking a law.
10. A Greek family that has left Greece and will soon settle in the United States is about to do this.

Vocabulary: Synonyms Write the Basic Word that has the same meaning as each word below. Use your Spelling Dictionary.

11. unfavorable
12. agree
13. profession
14. disgusting
15. future
16. opposed
17. logical
18. view
19. overstep
20. torment

Challenge Words Write the Challenge Word that fits each clue. Use your Spelling Dictionary.

21. judge
22. poison
23. danger
24. humorous

Review: Spelling Spree

Word Change Change a letter in each word to write a Basic Word.

1. dial
2. label
3. viable

4. tile
5. vacation
6. national

Puzzle Play Write the Basic or Review Word that fits each clue. Circle the letter that would appear in the box.

Example: a profession _ _ _ ☐ _ _ _ _   voc(a)tion

7. feeling opposed ☐ _ _ _ _ _
8. a method of treatment _ _ _ _ ☐ _ _
9. to take legal action against _ _ _ _ ☐ _ _ _ _
10. to leave a native country _ _ _ _ ☐ _ _ _
11. a sense of right and wrong _ _ _ _ _ _ ☐ _ _ _ _
12. to consent or yield _ ☐ _ _ _ _
13. an outdoor market _ ☐ _ _ _ _
14. expected to happen _ _ _ ☐ _ _ _ _ _ _ _
15. to cause to suffer _ _ _ _ _ _ ☐ _ _
16. a unit of army troops ☐ _ _ _ _ _ _ _
17. very odd ☐ _ _ _ _ _ _
18. negative or hostile ☐ _ _ _ _ _ _
19. reasons for something _ _ _ _ _ ☐ _ _ _
20. to settle in a new country _ _ _ _ _ _ ☐ _ _
21. a way of viewing something _ _ ☐ _ _ _ _ _ _ _
22. to go beyond the limits of ☐ _ _ _ _ _
23. a hobby ☐ _ _ _ _ _ _ _ _
24. aware _ _ _ ☐ _ _ _ _ _

Now write the circled letters in order. They will spell mystery words that tell where many immigrants live.

Mystery Words:

_ _ _ _ _? _ _ _

_ _ _? _ _

_ _ _? _ _

PASSPOR

United States
of America

Proofreading and Writing

Proofread: Spelling, Comparing with Adjectives and Adverbs To compare two things or actions, use the **comparative degree** of an adjective or adverb. Use the **superlative degree** to compare three or more things or actions. In most cases, form the comparative degree with -*er* or *more* and the superlative degree with -*est* or *most*. Some adjectives and adverbs have irregular forms.

	POSITIVE	COMPARATIVE	SUPERLATIVE
ADJECTIVE	good	better	best
	bad	worse	worst
ADVERB	much	more	most
	far	farther	farthest

Find five misspelled Basic or Review Words and two incorrect adjectives or adverbs of comparison in this journal entry. Write the journal entry correctly.

Today has been the better day of my life. The years of waiting to imigrate to America are over. Mama and I left our village yesterday, consious of many fears. Would my hopes for happiness excede reality? I tried to be rationale, but my heart spoke most forcefully than my head. When I saw my prospective home, however, my fearful pirspective changed. I have arrived not only in a new country but also in a completely new world.

Write a Poem Every day, many immigrants enter the United States. Write a short poem to welcome them to our country. Try to use five spelling words and at least one comparative or superlative adjective or adverb form.

Expanding Vocabulary

Spelling
Word Link

prosecute

Antonyms *Prosecute* means "to conduct a legal action against a person accused of a crime." *Defend* has the opposite meaning, "to represent, or argue for, a person accused of a crime." Words with opposite meanings are called **antonyms**.

Write the Basic or Review Word that is an antonym for each word below.

1. pleasant
2. favorable

3. agreeable
4. ordinary

5. irrational
6. immigrate

1. ___?___
2. ___?___

3. ___?___
4. ___?___

5. ___?___
6. ___?___

TEST-TAKING TACTICS

Analogies Being familiar with the common types of analogy relationships can help you recognize these relationships when you see them on analogy tests. Here are some of the kinds of relationships you will encounter: *object* and its *characteristic*, *object* and its *category*, and *cause* and its *effect*.

Study the following analogy question.

MICROWAVE : APPLIANCE ::

(A) cutlery : sharpness
(B) fire : warmth
(C) wire : flexibility
(D) bottle : container
(E) joke : laughter

Now write the answers to these questions about the sample analogy.

7. What type of relationship exists between the stem words?
8. What type of relationship exists in answer choices A and C?
9. What type of relationship exists in answer choices B and E?
10. Which answer choice correctly completes the analogy? Write its letter.

7. ___?___

8. ___?___

9. ___?___

10. ___?___

Real-World Connection

Social Studies: Immigration All the words in the box relate to immigration. Look up these words in your Spelling Dictionary. Then write the words to complete this paragraph.

Spelling Word Link

immigrate

asylum
aliens
quota
exile
refugee
assimilation
naturalized
citizenship

Beginning in the 1870s, thousands of Ukrainians immigrated to the United States. These newcomers bravely chose voluntary __(1)__ over the harsh lives they had been leading. America offered them __(2)__ from hardship and unfair laws. Many Ukrainians settled in Pennsylvania, where their __(3)__ into the culture was slow but steady. Although the life of a __(4)__ was often difficult, most eagerly awaited the day when they could be __(5)__ and gain their American __(6)__. By the 1920s, however, few Ukrainians were coming to America. The United States government had established a __(7)__ system restricting the number of __(8)__ allowed to enter the country each year.

TRY THIS!

True or False? Write *T* if the sentence is true and *F* if it is false.

9. Exile is always voluntary.
10. Asylum offers a person safety.
11. A quota is a tax put on goods that enter a country.
12. Assimilation is the process of leaving a country.

Fact File

Ellis Island, located in New York Harbor, was the chief United States immigration center from 1892 to 1943. Known as the Gateway to the New World, it was the first American stop for millions of immigrants.

12 Review: Units 7–11

Unit 7   Absorbed Prefixes

pages 48–53

communication	colleague	apparent	immerse	aggressive
allegiance	accessory	appliance	immaculate	illuminate

 Spelling Strategy   Remember that *ad-* ("to; toward"), *in-* ("in; not"), and *con-* ("with; together") can be **absorbed prefixes** when their last letter changes to match the beginning consonant of the base word to which they are added.

Write the word that is a synonym for each word below.
1. loyalty
2. addition
3. message
4. device
5. forceful
6. dip

Write the words that complete the paragraph.
   The supervisor received a memo from a __(7)__ regarding the dim lighting in their department. He said it was __(8)__ that if she would __(9)__ the dark work space, the employees might be more likely to keep the area __(10)__.

Unit 8   Greek Word Parts II

pages 54–59

catalog	chronology	technology	psychology	logic
dialogue	meteorology	sociology	astrology	trilogy

 Spelling Strategy   Knowing the Greek word parts *log* and *logy* ("an oral or written expression; the science, theory, or study of") can help you spell and understand words with these parts.

Write the word that completes each sentence.
11. I finished the second book of the _____ and began the last one.
12. Students of _____ believe that the stars affect human events.
13. Advancements in _____ have made many jobs easier.
14. A time line showed the _____ of the major events in her life.

Write the word that fits each definition.
15. the study of human society
16. the study of mental processes
17. a book that lists items
18. the study of weather
19. the study of reason
20. speech between two people

Unit 9   Latin Prefixes II   pages 60–65

intramural	supervise	counterfeit	superficial	intercept
intrastate	interpret	counterpart	superintendent	interchangeable

💡 **Spelling Strategy**   Remember the meanings of the Latin prefixes *inter-* ("between"), *intra-* ("within"), *super-* ("over; greater"), and *counter-* ("opposing").

Write a word by replacing the underlined prefix in each word below with a prefix from the list above.
21. official   22. exchangeable   23. depart   24. forfeit   25. advise

Write the word that fits each clue.
26. This kind of game is between two teams from the same school.
27. This person is in charge of maintaining an apartment building.
28. This kind of highway connects two cities in Kansas.
29. A football player might do this to a forward pass.
30. You may have to do this to a signal to understand its meaning.

Unit 10   Words from Spanish   pages 66–71

coyote	mesa	adobe	indigo	barbecue
mascara	pimento	avocado	cafeteria	mosquito

💡 **Spelling Strategy**   Knowing how to pronounce a word from Spanish will often help you spell it.

Write the word that fits each definition.
31. a green fruit
32. brick made of clay and straw
33. a type of restaurant where food is served from a counter
34. a red pepper
35. a wild desert animal
36. a dark blue color

Write the word that completes each analogy.
37. cheeks : rouge :: eyelashes : _____
38. rounded : hill :: flat-topped : ____
39. oven : bake :: grill :
40. bird : sparrow :: insect : _____

Unit 11   Words Often Confused   pages 72–77

immigrate	adverse	liable	rational	prospective
emigrate	averse	libel	rationale	perspective

 Spelling Strategy   To avoid confusing words with similar spellings and pronunciations, think of the meanings of the words.

Write the word that is an antonym for each word below.

41. beneficial   **43.** unlikely

42. unreasonable   **44.** willing

Write the word that matches each definition.

45. a point of view

46. a written statement that unjustly damages a person's reputation

47. expected to be or to occur

48. to leave a native country to settle in another

49. the basic reason for something

50. to settle in a country in which one is not a native

Challenge Words   Units 7–11   pages 48–77

interrogate	commiserate	superfluous	epilogue	antidote
alliteration	archaeology	aficionado	flotilla	anecdote

Write the word that is either a synonym or an antonym for each word below.

51. poison

52. sympathize

53. admirer

54. question

55. necessary

Write the word that completes each sentence.

56. The poet who wrote *wild, whistling wind* was using _____.

57. Ancient ruins are fascinating to anyone who likes _____.

58. The comedian told an _____ about his first time on a horse.

59. A _____ of colorful sailboats approached the harbor.

60. The _____ of the book told what happened after the story ended.

Spelling-Meaning Strategy

The Latin Root *reg*

You have learned that the words *regimen* and *regiment* are often confused because they have similar spellings, pronunciations, and meanings. One of the reasons for this is that both words contain the Latin root *reg*, meaning "guide, rule, or law." A regimen is a set of rules you follow. *Regiment* was originally used to describe a government but now describes a military unit. Both a government and a military unit follow strict sets of rules.

Below are more words that contain the root *reg*.

regimen

regiment

region	irregular	regalia
regal	regime	regulation

Think

* How does the root *reg* contribute to the meaning of each word? Look up the words in your Spelling Dictionary.

* In Unit 7, you learned that an absorbed prefix is one in which the final consonant of the prefix changes to match the beginning consonant of the root to which it is added. Which word in the box above contains an absorbed prefix?

Apply and Extend

Complete these activities on a separate piece of paper.

1. Write six sentences. Use one word from the word box above in each sentence.

2. Can you think of other words that belong to the same family as *regimen* and *regiment*? Work with a partner to make a list of related words. Then look up the Latin root *reg* in your Spelling-Meaning Index. Add to your list any other related words that you find.

Summing Up

The Latin root *reg* means "guide, rule, or law." Words that contain the same root are often related in spelling and meaning. Knowing some of the words in a family can help you to use and spell the others correctly.

Two types of sea
gulls inhabit
the island of
Smuttynose.
How do the two
types differ from
one another?

from The Gulls of
Smuttynose Island

by Jack Denton Scott

The two species of gulls that dominate Smuttynose,
although closely related, have one dissimilarity. The
herring gull (so called because it gathers in flocks to dive and
feed upon schools of tiny herring, often driven to the surface
by savage bluefish), with its mantle of pearl-gray, is often seen
near populated areas. The black-back (the great black-backed
gull), with the ebony saddle that gave it the name, prefers
solitude.

Both come to Smuttynose in the early spring for the same
purpose: to mate in a natural, protected breeding ground used
by themselves and their gull ancestors for many years.

Territorial imperative—claiming a certain area of space and
defending it against others—is the law at Smuttynose. The
black-backs are larger (28 to 31 inches in length, with a 5 ½-foot
wingspread, compared with the herring gull's 22 ½- to 26-inch
length and 4 ½-foot wingspread) and therefore select the higher
reaches of the island, the pinnacles of rock and the knolls. This
forces the herring gulls to keep to the lower areas closer to the
water. Black-back guards patrol their territories, both land and
air, and fiercely drive off the herring gulls that try to trespass.

Think and Discuss

1. What is the main idea of the first paragraph?
2. How are the herring gulls and the black-back gulls alike?
3. What is the major difference between the two types of
   gulls? What are some other differences?

The Writing Process
Comparison and Contrast

You can gain a better understanding of a given pair of items by comparing and contrasting them. Compare and contrast a pair of similar subjects. Use the guidelines, and follow the Writing Process.

1 Prewriting
- What topic ideas do you get from these pairs: rock music and jazz, baseball and softball, TV and movies, frogs and toads?
- Choose a topic and explore it. List the features of each item you are comparing and contrasting. Draw lines to connect similar features.

2 Draft
- Write, making each major similarity or difference a separate point. Correct errors later.
- State the main idea of each paragraph in a topic sentence. Include supporting details that give examples of the similarities and/or differences.

3 Revise
- Check each paragraph to be sure that all sentences support the main idea.
- Add specific details to make your points of comparison and contrast clear. Replace weak words with exact words.
- Have a writing conference.

4 Proofread
- Did you spell each word correctly?
- Do your subjects and verbs agree in number?
- Did you use adjectives and adverbs of comparison correctly?

5 Publish
- Copy your work neatly. Add an interesting title.
- Turn your paper into a pamphlet with headings and artwork.

Guidelines for Comparing and Contrasting

✓ For each paragraph, write a topic sentence that states the main idea.
✓ Include supporting details and examples.
✓ Use terms such as *similarly*, *like*, *unlike*, and *in contrast* to help make your points clear.

Composition Words

rational
immaculate
counterfeit
ecology
superficial
exceed
vile
adverse

Vowel Changes I

Read and Say

Basic

READ the sentences. SAY each bold word.

1. vegetable — Spinach is my favorite **vegetable**.
2. vegetation — Rain forest **vegetation** is thick and lush.
3. strategy — My **strategy** is to study first and play later.
4. strategic — Forts are built in **strategic** locations.
5. stability — Will another pole add **stability** to the tent?
6. stable — Is this ladder **stable** enough not to tip?
7. alternative — An **alternative** to running is fast walking.
8. alternate — My parents **alternate** driving on long trips.
9. definition — Check the exact **definition** in a dictionary.
10. define — Please **define** what you really mean.
11. remedy — The **remedy** for a cold is rest and juice.
12. remedial — My **remedial** class has improved my reading.
13. immunize — Will this shot **immunize** me against the flu?
14. immune — Her pride keeps her **immune** from insults.
15. deprivation — Calcium **deprivation** makes bones weak.
16. deprive — Avoid diets that **deprive** you of iron.
17. indicative — His tears were **indicative** of his pain.
18. indicate — Are there trail markers to **indicate** the path?
19. infinite — The universe seems **infinite**.
20. finite — We have a **finite** amount of time and money.

Spelling Strategy   To remember the spelling of |ə| in some words, think of a related word in which the pronunciation and spelling of the vowel are more obvious.

Think and Write   Write the pairs of Basic Words. In each pair, underline the letter that has the schwa sound in one word and the long vowel sound in the other.

Review
21. narrative
22. narrate
23. harmony
24. harmonious

Challenge
25. mandatory
26. mandate
27. initiative
28. initiate

Independent Practice

Vocabulary: Definitions Write the Basic Word that matches each definition.
Use your Spelling Dictionary.

1. a choice or option
2. to take something away from or prevent from having
3. intended to correct something
4. safe from or protected from
5. having limits
6. pertaining to a plan
7. resistance to sudden change or movement
8. to state the precise meaning
9. to show or express
10. without limit
11. the statement of the meaning of a word or phrase
12. plants or plant life

Vocabulary: Using Context Write the Basic Word that completes each sentence. Use your Spelling Dictionary.

13. Doug raises an herb commonly used as a cold _____.
14. Blue Hill Farm runs a _____ stand, where they sell their produce.
15. When drought destroyed their crops, farm families suffered great _____.
16. The veterinarian arrived to _____ the newborn calves against disease.
17. Keesha liked to _____ the animals she showed at the summer fair; one year she would take a calf, the next, a pig.
18. Weight loss and fever in cattle are usually _____ of disease.
19. Mike's late arrival at the county fair was actually a clever _____ meant to draw attention to his sheep.
20. The frame must be completely _____, or the entire barn could collapse.

Challenge Words Write the Challenge Word that fits each clue. Use your Spelling Dictionary.

21. A club might do this to a new member.
22. A boss might give this.
23. For many jobs, a college degree might be described as this.
24. This helps a person succeed at school or at work.

Dictionary

Homographs **Homographs** are words that have the same spelling but different meanings. Because they also have different origins, homographs are listed as separate dictionary entries.

> **sta·ble¹** |stā´ bəl| *adj.* **sta·bler, sta·blest.** **1. a.** Not likely to change position; firm: *a stable foundation of a house.* **b.** Not likely to change, as in condition: *a stable economy.* **2.** Not likely to be affected or overthrown: *a stable government.*
>
> **sta·ble²** |stā´ bəl| *n.* Often **stables.** A building for the shelter of horses or other domestic animals.

Practice Write *1* or *2* to indicate which of the above homographs is used in each sentence.

1. Since the election, the dollar's value has been *stable*.
2. Frightened horses neighed within the smoldering *stable*.
3. Gluing the leg will make this chair more *stable*.
4. Rachel maintained a *stable* lead over the other runners.

Review: Spelling Spree

Word Field 5–20. Find the Basic and Review Words hidden in the rows of crops. Write the words correctly in the order in which you find them. Begin at the haystack and end at the fence gate.

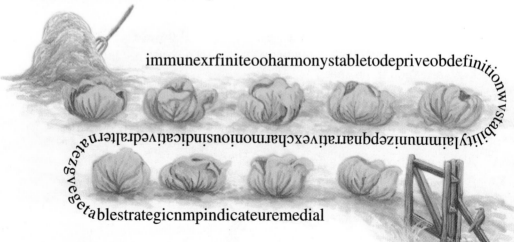

immunexrfiniteooharmonystabletodepriveobdefinitionwstability

laimmunizepgnarrativexcharmoniousindicativedraltern

atezgvegetablestrategicnmpindicateuremedial

Proofreading and Writing

Proofread for Spelling Find eight misspelled Basic or Review Words in this listing for a television program. Write each word correctly.

8:00 P.M. ❷ ⑩ Farming in America: Part 4

In this week's program, experts definne the problem of nutrient depravation in soil and explore various remedial techniques. One stratigy is to allternate regular crops with types of vegatation that restore nitrogen and other nutrients to the soil. Another alternetive is to use fertilizer. The experts warn, however, that we have a finnite supply of the raw materials used in fertilizer and indicate that this may create a fertilizer shortage. Dinah and Emery Williams narate this informative series.

Basic
1. vegetable
2. vegetation
3. strategy
4. strategic
5. stability
6. stable
7. alternative
8. alternate
9. definition
10. define
11. remedy
12. remedial
13. immunize
14. immune
15. deprivation
16. deprive
17. indicative
18. indicate
19. infinite
20. finite

Review
21. narrative
22. narrate
23. harmony
24. harmonious

Challenge
25. mandatory
26. mandate
27. initiative
28. initiate

Write a Help-Wanted Ad In summer, you work at a farmers' market. Business is brisk this year, and your boss has asked you to write a help-wanted ad for another worker. Write the ad, describing the position you need to fill. Try to use five spelling words.

Proofreading Marks
¶ Indent
∧ Add
⅄ Add a comma
∀ ∀ Add quotation marks
⊙ Add a period
⌿ Delete
≡ Capital letter
/ Small letter
∿ Reverse order

Expanding Vocabulary

Spelling Word Link

vegetable

Figurative Language When you use language literally, you create an image by describing how something actually looks, feels, or sounds. When you use **figurative language**, you create an image by comparing one thing with another thing that is completely different.

> LITERAL: The ripe **vegetable** was ready to be picked.

> FIGURATIVE: James was a **vegetable**, loafing the day away.

In the first example, *vegetable* refers to part of a plant. In the second one, James is not a beet or a carrot, but his behavior is compared to that of a vegetable, which is completely inactive.

Write *literal* or *figurative* to describe how the underlined word is used in each sentence.

1. Jacques is a walking encyclopedia.
2. Anne looked in the encyclopedia for facts about livestock.
3. The tornado touched down and destroyed the old barn.
4. Celia dashed through the room like a tornado.

TEST-TAKING TACTICS

Vocabulary-in-Context When a tested word in a vocabulary-in-context question is completely new to you, you may need to try several methods to figure out the word's meaning. First, look for context clues in the copy that surrounds the tested word. If you are still unsure of the word's meaning, try covering it up, substituting a word of your own that makes sense, and comparing your word with the answer choices. Finally, replace the tested word with each answer choice. Choose the one that seems to fit best.

Read the sample passage excerpt and question below. Then use one or more of the techniques given above to answer the question that follows.

Sample passage excerpt and question:

> In some underdeveloped countries, farm families are able to produce only enough food for their own subsistence. In a good year, when their
> *(20)* small plots yield more than the families need to feed themselves, they may be able to sell some of their surplus crops at local markets.

The word "subsistence" in line 19 means   (A) pleasure
(B) existence   (C) regions   (D) acreage   (E) cattle

5. Which meaning of "subsistence" is correct? Write its letter.

Real-World Connection

Careers: Agriculture All the words in the box relate to agriculture. Look up these words in your Spelling Dictionary. Then write the words to complete this paragraph.

Spelling Word Link

vegetable

agriculture
cultivate
pesticide
hybrid
reaper
scythe
thresher
fallow

Long ago, farmers learned that if they allowed a field to lie __(1)__ between crops, the field would be more fertile. Many farmers still do this. In other ways, however, the practice of __(2)__ has changed greatly over time. Farmers can now use a chemical __(3)__ to control harmful insects. They can also produce stronger crops by planting a __(4)__ variety, a cross between two different types of plants. In addition, most modern farmers rely on machines to __(5)__ and harvest crops. While grain was once cut by hand with a __(6)__, a mechanical __(7)__ now does the work. Another machine, the __(8)__, then separates the seeds from the rest of the plant.

TRY THIS!

True or False? Write *T* if the sentence is true and *F* if it is false.

9. Raising livestock is one type of agriculture.
10. Pesticide is a type of feed given to dairy cattle.
11. A scythe is driven by a gasoline-powered engine.
12. A fallow field is one in which several crops are grown.

Fact File

During the early 1900s, George Washington Carver made many contributions to agricultural research. In one major study, Carver used peanuts to create over three hundred products, including ink, paper, soap, and many food items.

Latin Roots I

Read and Say

Basic

READ the sentences. SAY each bold word.

1. reference — This **reference** book gives current facts.
2. transfer — I will **transfer** money from my bank to his.
3. abstract — The **abstract** painting was a colorful blur.
4. traceable — The tale was **traceable** back to one student.
5. disposal — Trash **disposal** is an expense for our town.
6. purpose — What is your **purpose** in telling me that?
7. differ — We share some opinions but **differ** on others.
8. proposal — I will offer a **proposal** on what we should do.
9. contract — We signed a **contract** detailing our agreement.
10. opposite — Heat is the **opposite** of cold.
11. preposition — Do not end a sentence with a **preposition**.
12. confer — I will **confer** with a partner about that idea.
13. distract — Loud music can **distract** you from studying.
14. exposure — It is wise to limit your **exposure** to the sun.
15. posture — Can good **posture** make my back stronger?
16. inference — An **inference** is a guess based on facts.
17. traction — Snow tires provide **traction** on ice and snow.
18. transpose — Did you **transpose** the order of these numbers?
19. fertile — Cotton needs **fertile** soil to grow.
20. preference — My **preference** is for comfort over style.

Spelling Strategy   Knowing the Latin roots *fer* ("to carry"), *pos* ("to put; place"), and *tract/trace* ("to draw; pull") can help you spell and understand words with these roots.

Think and Write   Write each Basic Word under its root.

fer	pos	tract/trace

Review	23. dictionary	**Challenge**	28. protractor
21. impose	24. encyclopedia	26. composite	29. decompose
22. disposition	25. bibliography	27. juxtapose	30. superimpose

Independent Practice

Vocabulary: Definitions Write the Basic Word that matches each definition.
Use your Spelling Dictionary.

1. a source of information
2. to reverse the order or change the positions of
3. a word that shows the relationship between a noun or pronoun and another word in a sentence
4. the friction that keeps a wheel from slipping
5. the way in which a person holds or carries his or her body
6. able to be followed back to its source
7. to consult with
8. favorable to the growth of crops
9. the act of throwing out or away
10. the act of revealing
11. to draw attention away from something
12. to move from one person, place, or thing to another

Vocabulary: Synonyms Write the Basic Word that has the same meaning as each word below. Use your Spelling Dictionary.

13. goal
14. summary
15. disagree
16. contradictory
17. conclusion
18. agreement
19. choice
20. suggestion

Challenge Words Write the Challenge Word that fits each clue. Use your Spelling Dictionary.

21. Many foods will do this if you leave them at room temperature for too long.
22. A face put together from different pictures would be this.
23. This could help you draw a perfect semicircle.
24. This is what you would do with tracing paper in order to trace something.
25. You could do this with twins to see if they were identical.

Review: Spelling Spree

Code Breaker The Basic and Review Words below are written in code. Use the following code key to figure out each word. Write the decoded words correctly.

CODE:	y	z	w	x	u	v	s	t	q	r	o	p	m	n	k	l	i	j	g	h	e	f	c	d	a	b
LETTER:	a	b	c	d	e	f	g	h	i	j	k	l	m	n	o	p	q	r	s	t	u	v	w	x	y	z

Example: pqzjyja   *library*

1. juvujunwu
2. xqglkgqhqkn
3. wknvuj
4. zqzpqksjylta
5. hjywuyzpu
6. xqwhqknyja
7. xqvvuj
8. unwawpkluxqy
9. udlkgeju

10. kllkgqhu
11. ljulkgqhqkn
12. xqghjywh
13. hjywhqkn
14. qmlkgu
15. lkgheju
16. hjynglkgu
17. lejlkgu

Root Riddles Answer each riddle with two Basic Words that share the same root.

Example: What is a conflicting goal?   *opposite*
purpose

18–19. What is a machine that gets rid of suggestions?
20–21. What do you do when you switch a choice?
22–23. What is a productive source of information?
24–25. What is a vague agreement?

How Are You Doing?

Write the spelling words in alphabetical order. Practice any misspelled words with a partner.

Proofreading and Writing

Proofread: Spelling and Negatives Negatives are words such as *no, not, none, never, nothing, hardly, barely,* or *scarcely*. A **double negative** is the incorrect use of two negative words to express one idea. Avoid double negatives.

INCORRECT: There **aren't scarcely** any books about that topic.
CORRECT: There **are scarcely** any books about that topic.
CORRECT: There **aren't** any books about that topic.

Find six misspelled Basic or Review Words and two double negatives in this computer listing of a library book. Write the listing correctly.

421.78   Watson, Kyle, 1943–   ed.

F407A   Legal Enciclopedia for Teenagers

Boston, Houghton Mifflin Co., 1999

The perpose of this referrence book is to give students

exsposure to the law in language they can understand.

Contains a dicshunary of legal terms. Includes hardly no

abstract arguments. Does not contain no bibleography.

Proofreading Marks
¶ Indent
∧ Add
⩜ Add a comma
ᵛᵛ ᵛᵛ Add quotation marks
⊙ Add a period
⟋ Delete
☰ Capital letter
╱ Small letter
↷ Reverse order

Write a Letter Which library do you use most often? Write a letter to the librarian there, telling what you like best about the library or suggesting a way to improve something you don't like. Try to use five spelling words, and express a negative idea at least once.

Unit 14 BONUS

Expanding Vocabulary

Multiple Meanings Many English words have more than one meaning.

> **con·tract** |kŏn´ trăkt´| *n.* **1.** A formal agreement between two or more persons or groups. **2.** A document stating the terms of such an agreement. —*v.* |kən **trăkt´**|. **1.** To make or become smaller. **2.** To arrange by a formal agreement. **3.** To get or acquire: *contract the mumps*.

Write a part-of-speech abbreviation and definition number to show which meaning of *contract* is used in each sentence below.

1. The lawyer witnessed the signing of the contract.
2. The flashes from the cameras made her pupils contract.
3. Children often contract the flu at school.
4. Did you contract with him to share the business?
5. The judge ruled that an oral contract existed between the parties.

Now write a sentence for each meaning of *contract* indicated below.

Spelling Word Link

contract

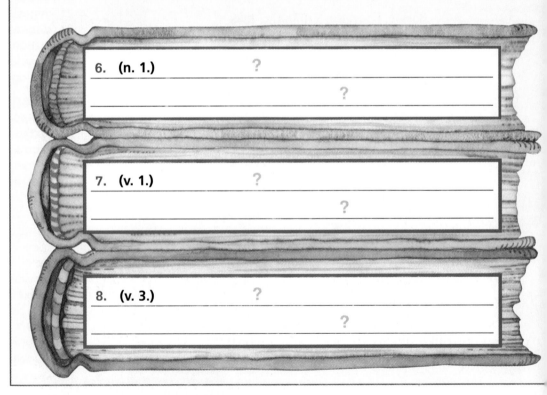

6. **(n. 1.)** ?
   ?

7. **(v. 1.)** ?
   ?

8. **(v. 3.)** ?
   ?

Real-World Connection

Language Arts: Library Skills All the words in the box relate to library skills. Look up these words in your Spelling Dictionary. Then write the words to complete this paragraph.

Spelling Word Link

reference

index
periodical
alphabetical
microfiche
carrel
circulation
fiction
nonfiction

C   B

Finding information in the library is not difficult, if you know where to look. All books are listed in the card catalog and/or on a computer database. Novels and other __(1)__ are listed in __(2)__ order by title and author. Most __(3)__ books are also listed by subject. If you cannot find a book on the shelves, the librarian at the __(4)__ desk can help you. Unlike books, magazine and newspaper articles are listed in a yearly __(5)__ showing everything published in a __(6)__ within that year. The library stores articles on film, called __(7)__. You can read the film with a magnifying viewer, usually kept on a table in a study __(8)__.

TRY THIS!

Yes or No? Write *yes* or *no* to answer each question.

9. Is an encyclopedia a periodical?
10. Can you check out a book at the circulation desk?
11. Can you study in a carrel?
12. Is a fairy tale an example of nonfiction?

Fact File

The Library of Congress, in Washington, D.C., is one of the world's largest libraries. It covers 71 acres of floor space and has over 100 million items in its collection, including maps, movies, photographs, and recordings, as well as books and pamphlets.

Noun Suffixes I

Read and Say

Basic

READ the sentences. **SAY** each bold word.

1. nationality — His **nationality** is noted on his passport.
2. hospitality — Their warm **hospitality** made us feel welcome.
3. agency — The **agency** charges a fee for its services.
4. society — Does the humane **society** rescue animals?
5. curiosity — Her **curiosity** led her to find some answers.
6. generosity — Your **generosity** has made all this possible.
7. familiarity — My **familiarity** with computers got me the job.
8. majority — We will do what the **majority** chooses.
9. privacy — I need some **privacy** to write in my diary.
10. frequency — What is the **frequency** of trucks on this road?
11. popularity — Having many friends is a sign of **popularity**.
12. accuracy — The **accuracy** of his foul shots was amazing.
13. minority — I lost because I got a **minority** of votes.
14. urgency — The **urgency** of her call alarmed us.
15. democracy — Our form of government is a **democracy**.
16. emergency — Call the police in an **emergency**.
17. personality — She has a cheerful **personality**.
18. maturity — We watched the kitten grow to **maturity**.
19. anxiety — Our **anxiety** grew as we saw the fire spread.
20. humidity — High **humidity** makes everything feel damp.

Spelling Strategy   The suffixes *-cy*, *-ty*, and *-ity* form nouns when added to base words or roots. Remember the spelling patterns for these suffixes.

Think and Write   Write each Basic Word under its suffix.

-cy   *-ty, -ity*

Review		Challenge	
	23. reality		28. consistency
21. opportunity	24. variety	26. prosperity	29. spontaneity
22. university	25. gravity	27. anonymity	30. eccentricity

Independent Practice

Vocabulary: Word Clues Write the Basic Word that fits each clue. Use your Spelling Dictionary.

1. This might be Mexican, French, or Hungarian.
2. Be sure to treat your guests with this if you want them to visit again.
3. A person gets this by being alone.
4. A firefighter or an ambulance driver must respond to this kind of situation.
5. A person might hire a detective from this type of place.
6. Best friends have this with each other.
7. If you do not agree with most of the people, you are in this.
8. This might cause someone to receive many party invitations.
9. This characteristic makes everyone unique.
10. You might feel this if you were lost in a strange place or if you were late for an important appointment.
11. This is determined by how often something occurs.
12. When there is a vote, this wins.
13. You feel this when a situation calls for immediate action.

Vocabulary: Analogies Write the Basic Word that completes each analogy. Use your Spelling Dictionary.

Example: few : many :: minority : _____ *majority*

14. desert : dryness :: jungle : _____
15. yell : anger :: question : _____
16. king : monarchy :: president : _____
17. childhood : youth :: adulthood : _____
18. recklessness : caution :: stinginess : _____
19. carelessness : error :: precision : _____
20. animal : herd :: person : _____

Challenge Words Write the Challenge Word that matches each definition. Use your Spelling Dictionary.

21. economic success
22. odd or unusual behavior
23. conforming to one way of thinking or behaving
24. the state of being unknown
25. impulsive behavior

Dictionary

Stress When you say a word with more than one syllable, you always accent one syllable more than the others. In the phonetic respelling next to a dictionary entry word, a stress mark (´) follows the accented syllable. If more than one syllable is stressed, a regular stress mark indicates the syllable that gets stronger, or **primary**, stress, and a lighter stress mark indicates **secondary** stress.

hospitality |hŏs´ pĭ tăl´ ĭ tē|

Practice Write each word in syllables. Underline the syllable with primary stress. Circle the syllable with secondary stress. Use your Spelling Dictionary.

1. opportunity
2. communication
3. personality
4. intercession

5. nationality
6. transportation
7. generosity
8. cafeteria

Review: Spelling Spree

Word Forms Add a noun suffix to create a Basic or Review Word. Write each word.

9. humid
10. hospital
11. frequent
12. accurate
13. national
14. minor
15. real
16. democrat
17. generous
18. major
19. vary
20. popular
21. universe

22. urgent
23. anxious
24. mature
25. emergent

Proofreading and Writing

Proofread for Spelling Find seven misspelled Basic or Review Words in this questionnaire for a student exchange program. Write each word correctly.

AGENSY FOR
INTERNATIONAL HOSPITALITY

1. Have you ever had the oportunity to travel

   overseas? If so, where?_____

2. What aspect of living in a foreign sociaty most

   provokes your curiousity? _____

   What aspect causes you the most anxiety?_____

3. With what language, other than English, do you

   have the most familarity?_____

4. How would you describe your personalty? _____

5. How important is privicy to you? Would you mind

   sharing a room with a host

   "brother" or "sister"?_____

Basic

1. nationality
2. hospitality
3. agency
4. society
5. curiosity
6. generosity
7. familiarity
8. majority
9. privacy
10. frequency
11. popularity
12. accuracy
13. minority
14. urgency
15. democracy
16. emergency
17. personality
18. maturity
19. anxiety
20. humidity

Review

21. opportunity
22. university
23. reality
24. variety
25. gravity

Challenge

26. prosperity
27. anonymity
28. consistency
29. spontaneity
30. eccentricity

Proofreading Marks

¶ Indent
∧ Add
⩓ Add a comma
ⅴⅴ Add quotation marks
⊙ Add a period
⌐ Delete
≡ Capital letter
/ Small letter
∿ Reverse order

Write a Persuasive Letter Would you like to become a foreign exchange student? Write a persuasive letter to a student exchange program. Explain why you want to study abroad and what you have to offer. Try to use five spelling words.

Unit 15 BONUS

Expanding Vocabulary

Spelling Word Link

anxiety

Connotation Is *anxiety* the same thing as *eagerness*? The **denotations**, or dictionary meanings, of the two words are similar; however, their **connotations** are quite different. The connotation of a word is the feeling or attitude that people generally associate with it. Connotations are frequently either positive or negative.

POSITIVE: Kari awaited the first day of school with **eagerness**.
NEGATIVE: Kari awaited the first day of school with **anxiety**.

Write the words in each pair. Label each word *P* for *Positive* or *N* for *Negative* to describe its connotation.

1. curiosity / nosiness
2. privacy / isolation
3. pathetic / touching

4. generosity / extravagance
5. aggressive / pushy

TEST-TAKING TACTICS

Analogies It is important to know that all of the word pairs in an analogy have parallel parts of speech. For example, if the first word in an analogy stem is a noun, then the first word in each answer choice will be a noun. If the second word in the stem is a verb, the second word in each answer choice will be a verb. Analogies can be tricky, though, when one word in a pair can be used as more than one part of speech. Study this sample analogy question.

ESCALATOR : TRANSPORT ::

(A) payment : balance   (B) roof : house   (C) chipmunk : burrow
(D) herb : season   (E) stereo : sound

In the sample, the first word in each pair is a noun, but the second word can be either a noun or a verb form. To discover how the paired words are related, you will have to write *two* test sentences for the stem words, such as these:

An ESCALATOR is a form of TRANSPORT. (TRANSPORT is a noun.)

An ESCALATOR is used to TRANSPORT. (TRANSPORT is a verb form.)

Then try each answer pair in *both* test sentences. An answer pair that makes sense in one of the test sentences will be the correct choice.

6. Which answer choice correctly completes the sample analogy? Write its letter.

Real-World Connection

Social Studies: Student Exchange Programs All the words in the box relate to student exchange programs. Look up these words in your Spelling Dictionary. Then write the words to complete this paragraph.

Spelling Word Link

nationality

scholarship
recipient
abroad
visa
reciprocate
semester
cultural
tuition

The main idea behind student exchange programs is that by studying __(1)__ for a year or even for just one __(2)__, students will gain __(3)__ awareness of other parts of the world. Once students are selected to participate, program officials assist them in many ways, from obtaining travel documents, such as a __(4)__, to teaching them a language, to helping them apply for financial assistance. A student who is unable to pay for travel or for __(5)__ at the foreign school might be the __(6)__ of a __(7)__ to help cover expenses. Upon their return, students and their families often __(8)__ by becoming host families themselves.

TRY THIS!

Yes or No? Write *yes* if the underlined word is used correctly. Write *no* if it is not.

9. Joan received a <u>scholarship</u> for one thousand dollars.
10. Fernando filled out the <u>recipient</u> for study in Peru.
11. Ms. Metzer wrote a check for her son's <u>tuition</u>.
12. We learned about festivals and other <u>cultural</u> events.

Fact File

Many students have realized the dream of studying overseas. Since 1914, the American Field Service (AFS) has sent American students to sixty-four countries and brought students from eighty countries to the United States.

101

Words from French

Read and Say

READ the sentences. SAY each bold word.

1. chef — Will the **chef** prepare my favorite dish?
2. gourmet — She is a **gourmet** who writes about fine food.
3. buffet — You can serve your own meal at a **buffet**.
4. sauté — Please **sauté** the onions in a little oil.
5. fillet — A fish **fillet** should not have bones in it.
6. parfait — A tall ice cream **parfait** is a great dessert.
7. omelet — Do we have enough eggs to make an **omelet**?
8. foyer — The front door opens into a large **foyer**.
9. brochure — This travel **brochure** describes the city.
10. suite — Our hotel **suite** had two bedrooms and a bath.
11. etiquette — Dining **etiquette** demands clean hands.
12. mustache — Dad shaved off his beard and **mustache**.
13. memoir — I wrote a **memoir** of my childhood years.
14. souvenir — Save your ticket as a **souvenir** of your trip.
15. camouflage — The enemy won't spot you in your **camouflage**.
16. chauffeur — Did they hire a **chauffeur** to drive them?
17. opaque — You cannot see through **opaque** glass.
18. intrigue — The spy told stories of secrets and **intrigue**.
19. rendezvous — All hikers will **rendezvous** back at the camp.
20. elite — The **elite** of the kingdom lived at the palace.

Spelling Strategy Remember that words from French often contain silent letters, especially the final *t*. Also, French words often spell the |ē| sound with *i*, the |ā| sound with *e*, and the |sh| sound with *ch*.

Think and Write   Write the Basic Words.

Review		Challenge	
	23. antique		28. liaison
21. technique	24. boulevard	26. hors d'oeuvre	29. genre
22. amateur	25. portrait	27. connoisseur	30. détente

Independent Practice

Vocabulary: Using Context Write the Basic Word that completes each sentence. Use your Spelling Dictionary.

1. Be careful when you eat the fish _____; it may contain tiny bones.
2. Jim ordered a ham and cheese _____ for breakfast.
3. Susan's favorite dessert is a strawberry _____.
4. The holiday party was held in a large _____ at the Lakeview Hotel, with food catered by the hotel's restaurant.
5. On the walls of the restaurant's _____ were photographs of its most famous patrons.
6. The _____ waited in the limousine outside the entrance to the restaurant.
7. Delicate sauces are the specialty of the restaurant's head _____.
8. In her _____, the actor wrote about spending a summer washing dishes at a resort.
9. The _____ from the ski lodge promises brunch on Sunday.
10. The French restaurant is offering a course in _____ cooking.
11. The two spies arranged to _____ at Joe's cafe at midnight.
12. The restaurant serves an all-you-can-eat _____ for ten dollars.

Vocabulary: Question Clues Write the Basic Word that answers each question. Use your Spelling Dictionary.

13. What kind of rules do you practice at a fancy dinner?
14. What do you buy in order to remember a vacation?
15. Who are the cream of the crop?
16. What is a common way to cook onions?
17. What kind of glass is hard to see through?
18. What does a good mystery story contain?
19. What often goes with a beard?
20. What allows many animals to blend in with the scenery?

Challenge Words Write the Challenge Word that matches each definition. Use your Spelling Dictionary.

21. a relaxing or easing of tension, especially between nations
22. one who knows about and has good taste in art or food
23. an appetizer served before a meal
24. a channel or means of communication; a communication link
25. a type or style of literature, music, or art

Review: Spelling Spree

Word Combination In each item, add the beginning letters of the first word to the last letters of the second word to form a Basic or Review Word. Write the words.

Example: omit + bracelet   *omelet*

1. portion + strait
2. chilly + thief
3. memory + reservoir
4. follow + destroyer
5. suit + bite
6. intramural + fatigue
7. technology + unique
8. sausage + rate

9. elder + cite
10. filthy + skillet
11. antonym + physique
12. mustard + microfiche
13. gourd + comet
14. buffalo + ballet
15. opal + boutique

Puzzle Play Write the Basic or Review Word that fits each clue. Circle the letter that would appear in the box.

Example: a cook _ _ _ ☐   che(f)

16. a dessert _ _ ☐ _ _ _ _
17. a pamphlet _ _ _ _ _ _ _ ☐
18. a memento ☐ _ _ _ _ _ _ _
19. an egg dish _ _ _ _ _ ☐
20. a driver _ _ ☐ _ _ _ _ _ _
21. a nonprofessional _ _ _ _ _ ☐ _
22. a broad street _ _ _ _ _ _ _ ☐ _
23. concealment _ ☐ _ _ _ _ _ _ _ _
24. a prearranged meeting _ _ ☐ _ _ _ _ _ _ _
25. manners _ ☐ _ _ _ _ _ _ _

Now write the circled letters in sequence. They will spell a mystery word that names a place to eat.

Mystery Word: _ _ _ _ _ ? _ _ _ _ _

How Are You Doing?
Write each spelling word in a sentence. Practice any misspelled spelling words with a partner.

Proofreading and Writing

Proofread: Spelling, Usage of Adjectives and Adverbs

Remember that *good, bad, sure,* and *real* are adjectives, which modify nouns or pronouns and may follow linking verbs. *Well, badly, surely,* and *really* are adverbs, which modify verbs, adjectives, and other adverbs.

ADJECTIVE: Chef Chang makes **good** vegetable dishes.
His vegetable dishes taste **good**.

ADVERB: Chef Chang cooks everything **well**.

Find five misspelled Basic or Review Words and two incorrect adjectives or adverbs in this excerpt from a menu. Write the menu correctly.

Gormet hamburger *Beef up this burger with your choice of fine cheeses and rich sauces.*

Vegetable suaté *Crunchy garden vegetables in a real light dressing of lemon and herbs.*

Heavenly omlet *A specialty of our chef—it tastes as well as it looks.*

Fillet of sole *Prepared with a secret tecnique.*

Perfect parfet *A wickedly rich creation.*

Write a Story   Write a story set in a restaurant. Tell about the staff, customers, or even the food. Try to use five spelling words. Also, try to use one of these adjective or adverb modifiers correctly: *good, bad, sure, real, well, badly, surely,* or *really.*

Basic

1. chef
2. gourmet
3. buffet
4. sauté
5. fillet
6. parfait
7. omelet
8. foyer
9. brochure
10. suite
11. etiquette
12. mustache
13. memoir
14. souvenir
15. camouflage
16. chauffeur
17. opaque
18. intrigue
19. rendezvous
20. elite

Review
21. technique
22. amateur
23. antique
24. boulevard
25. portrait

Challenge
26. hors d'oeuvre
27. connoisseur
28. liaison
29. genre
30. détente

Proofreading Marks
¶ Indent
∧ Add
⅄ Add a comma
∨ ∨ Add quotation marks
⊙ Add a period
ᵍ Delete
≡ Capital letter
/ Small letter
∩ Reverse order

105

Expanding Vocabulary

Spelling Word Link

etiquette

Context Clues A sentence containing an unfamiliar word might also contain clues to its meaning. Synonyms are excellent context clues. Suppose you did not know the word *etiquette*. In this sentence, the synonym might help.

My etiquette book covers **manners** for all dining occasions.

Write the word that is a synonym for the underlined word in each sentence.

1. The Hill House's <u>ambiance</u> is wonderful, but the food is only fair, while Tony's has great food but no atmosphere.
2. Normally <u>bland</u> foods are even more tasteless at Mel's.
3. This restaurant offers an <u>eclectic</u> selection of dishes that will satisfy many diverse tastes.
4. Knowing that <u>aesthetic</u> appeal is as important as taste, the chef made each dish an artistic presentation.

1. _____ ?
2. _____ ?
3. _____ ?
4. _____ ?

Now write two sentences of your own. In each one, include a synonym pair from items 1–4. Use one word in the pair as a context clue to the meaning of its synonym.

5. _____ ?
_____ ?
6. _____ ?
_____ ?

Real-World Connection

Business: Restaurant Management All the words in the box relate to restaurant management. Look up these words in your Spelling Dictionary. Then write the words to complete this paragraph.

Students in restaurant management programs learn a variety of skills. They practice communication skills, such as taking a __(1)__ over the telephone or dealing tactfully with a difficult __(2)__. They learn to plan a formal __(3)__, choosing an appetizer, salad, __(4)__, and dessert that complement one another. They also learn how to create an attractive __(5)__, from which guests serve themselves. Students are introduced to a variety of __(6)__ styles, from elegant French __(7)__ to regional American cooking. Finally, students study business principles necessary for operating anything from a __(8)__ in a fast-food chain to a four-star restaurant.

Spelling Word Link

chef

franchise
cuisine
menu
customer
entrée
reservation
smorgasbord
culinary

TRY THIS!

Yes or No? Write *yes* or *no* to answer each question.

9. Can a restaurant chain have more than one franchise?
10. Are culinary skills important to being a good waiter?
11. Is an entree the main course served at a restaurant?
12. Does a smorgasbord contain a variety of dishes?

Fact File

Cooks from all over the world attend the Cordon Bleu, a famous school of cooking in Paris. Its name, meaning "blue ribbon," came from the ribbons worn by an order of knights known for their excellent cuisine.

Words Often Misspelled I

Read and Say

Basic	READ the sentences. SAY each bold word.

1. playwright — This **playwright** won awards for two plays.
2. tragedy — Must someone always die in a **tragedy**?
3. metaphor — This **metaphor** compares doubt to fog.
4. melancholy — Rainy days make me sad and **melancholy**.
5. propaganda — Some **propaganda** makes false claims.
6. subtle — I barely noticed her **subtle** movement.
7. pageant — What role will you play in the **pageant**?
8. unanimous — Can we agree to make the vote **unanimous**?
9. extraordinary — I admire her **extraordinary** courage.
10. enthusiastic — An **enthusiastic** fan leaped onto the field.
11. outrageous — I am shocked by his **outrageous** comment.
12. pneumonia — A serious cold can turn into **pneumonia**.
13. khaki — The guide wore a **khaki** shirt and shorts.
14. adjourn — Plan to **adjourn** the meeting for lunch.
15. minuscule — A flea is a **minuscule** insect.
16. siege — The **siege** led to the capture of the city.
17. endeavor — I will **endeavor** to do my best on the test.
18. prominent — His **prominent** jaw is square and broad.
19. wretched — I feel **wretched** about losing your book.
20. flourish — Roses **flourish** with sun and plant food.

Spelling Strategy   Knowing a word's origin, thinking about the meanings of its parts, and practicing the word can often help you spell the word correctly.

Think and Write   Write the Basic Words. Underline any part of a word that you have trouble spelling.

Review	23. miniature
21. tongue	24. campaign
22. consequence	25. vacuum

Challenge	28. hypocrite
26. soliloquy	29. queue
27. rhetoric	30. susceptible

Independent Practice

Vocabulary: Analogies Write the Basic Word that completes each analogy.
Use your Spelling Dictionary.

Example: elephant : huge :: flea : _____   *minuscule*

1. giving : generous :: hateful : _____
2. class : dismiss :: court : _____
3. medication : penicillin :: disease : _____
4. fiction : novelist :: drama : _____
5. festivity : party :: ceremony : _____
6. defeat : conquer :: attempt : _____
7. fort : attack :: castle : _____
8. nurse : white :: soldier : _____
9. literal : fact :: figurative : _____
10. cure : medicine :: persuade : _____
11. drought : wilt :: rain : _____
12. amuse : funny :: shock : _____

Vocabulary: Antonyms Write the Basic
Word that means the opposite of each word.
Use your Spelling Dictionary.

Mr. WILLIAM
SHAKESPEARES
COMEDIES,
HISTORIES, &
TRAGEDIES.
Published according to the True Originall Copies.

LONDON
Printed by Isaac Iaggard, and Ed. Blount. 1623

13. comedy
14. disinterested
15. unnoticeable
16. happy
17. divided
18. enormous
19. obvious
20. usual

Challenge Words Write the Challenge Word that completes each sentence.
Use your Spelling Dictionary.

21. The eager fans did not mind standing in a _____ at the theater box office.
22. The scene was ruined when Emma forgot her lines in the middle of her
    _____.
23. The unconvincing actor made the speech sound like _____.
24. Steve plays the part of a _____ who never follows his own advice.
25. Some sensitive actors are too _____ to criticism.

Review: Spelling Spree

Rhyming Clues Write the Basic or Review Word that rhymes with the underlined word in each sentence.

1. When a play is this <u>fantastic</u>, the audience is always _____.
2. If you are wise as well as <u>clever</u>, you will succeed in your_____.
3. A person who behaves without any <u>sense</u> will eventually face the _____.
4. Although I am often <u>jolly</u>, sometimes I feel _____.
5. The long hours can be a <u>strain</u>, working on a political _____.
6. Floating in a swimming <u>pool</u>, the tiny toad looked _____.
7. Everyone will have a <u>turn</u>; then the meeting will _____.
8. This article about the <u>panda</u> is an example of _____.
9. If you took the time to <u>nourish</u>, your plants would probably grow and _____.
10. Don't close your mouth or you'll be <u>stung</u>; a bee has landed on your _____.

Invisible Letters Decide which letters should be added to complete each Basic or Review Word. Write the words correctly.

11. o _ t r a _ _ o u _
12. e _ t r _ _ r d _ n _ _ y
13. p a _ _ a _ t
14. p l _ y _ _ i _ _ t
15. m _ t a _ _ o r
16. m i n _ _ t _ r e
17. s u _ _ l _
18. s _ _ g _
19. _ n _ n _ m _ _ s
20. v a _ _ u m
21. t r _ g _ d _
22. w r _ t _ h _ d
23. k _ a k _

24. p _ _ _ m o n _ a
25. p r _ m _ n _ n t

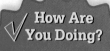

How Are You Doing?

Write each spelling word as a partner reads it aloud. Did you misspell any words?

Proofreading and Writing

Proofread: Spelling, Proper Nouns and Proper Adjectives
A **proper noun** names a specific person, place, or thing. A **proper adjective** is formed from a proper noun. Capitalize each important word in a proper noun or proper adjective.

The Taming of the Shrew stars the **Canadian** actor **Paul Dunn**.

Find five misspelled Basic or Review Words and two capitalization errors in this excerpt from a theater program. Write the program correctly.

About the Players

THEO THESPIAN is a prominant

Shakespearean actor. Although his comic

performances have won unanamous praise, he

is best known for his extrordinary work in

tragedy. His first role of consequance was that

of Hamlet, the melancoly danish prince. In the

current production, Mr. Thespian again plays a

prince—this time Henry, Prince of wales. Once

again, he is receiving enthusiastic applause.

Basic
1. playwright
2. tragedy
3. metaphor
4. melancholy
5. propaganda
6. subtle
7. pageant
8. unanimous
9. extraordinary
10. enthusiastic
11. outrageous
12. pneumonia
13. khaki
14. adjourn
15. minuscule
16. siege
17. endeavor
18. prominent
19. wretched
20. flourish

Review
21. tongue
22. consequence
23. miniature
24. campaign
25. vacuum

Challenge
26. soliloquy
27. rhetoric
28. hypocrite
29. queue
30. susceptible

Proofreading Marks
¶   Indent
∧   Add
⋏   Add a comma
∀ ∀   Add quotation marks
⊙   Add a period
_ɡ_   Delete
≡   Capital letter
／   Small letter
∿   Reverse order

Write a Summary of a Play   What especially memorable play have you seen or read? Was it memorable because it was good or because it was terrible? Write a brief summary of that play. Try to use five spelling words and at least one proper noun or proper adjective.

Expanding Vocabulary

Spelling Word Link

playwright

Compound Words The word *playwright* is a combination of the words *play* ("a literary work written for performance on the stage") and *wright* ("a person who constructs something"). A word created by combining two or more smaller words is called a **compound word**. Some compound words are written as one word, some as hyphenated words, and some as separate words.

extra + ordinary = extraordinary

old + fashioned = old-fashioned

word + processor = word processor

By combining two words below, write a compound word to fit each clue. Use your Spelling Dictionary.

disc	print	product	jockey
blue	ware	by	hard

1. a side effect
2. a radio announcer
3. an architectural plan
4. tools, nails, and bolts

Now write the six new compound words you find in the speech balloons below. Use your Spelling Dictionary.

Real-World Connection

Language Arts: Shakespeare All the words in the box relate to Shakespeare. Look up these words in your Spelling Dictionary. Then write the words to complete this paragraph.

Spelling Word Link

playwright

dramatist
Elizabethan
sonnet
prose
blank verse
theatrical
apprentice
repertory

William Shakespeare was an English playwright and poet during the __(1)__ era. Although he is considered the greatest __(2)__ of all time, little is known about him. He was born in Stratford-upon-Avon in 1564. When he was eighteen, he left to seek his fortune in London's __(3)__ world. It is likely that he began as an __(4)__ member of a __(5)__ theater but soon became a leading actor. Shakespeare wrote at least thirty-seven plays, containing both __(6)__ and poetry. His poetry included rhyming forms, such as the __(7)__, and also an unrhymed form called __(8)__. Shakespeare had an enormous influence on the English language and actually invented many of the words we use today.

TRY THIS!

True or False? Write *T* if the sentence is true and *F* if it is false.

9. The Elizabethan era was named after a queen.
10. In blank verse, every other line rhymes.
11. A sonnet contains only five lines.
12. A repertory company performs a variety of plays.

Fact File

Many of Shakespeare's plays were first performed at the Globe Theatre. Built in 1599, the Globe had eight sides that surrounded a roofless courtyard. It held 1,200 people, who stood in the yard or sat in one of two galleries.

113

18 Review: Units 13–17

Unit 13 Vowel Changes I   pages 84–89

strategy	alternative	definition	immunize	remedy
strategic	alternate	define	immune	remedial

💡 **Spelling Strategy**   To remember the spelling of |ə| in some words, think of a related word in which the pronunciation and spelling of the vowel are more obvious.

Write the word that is a synonym for each word.
1. planned
2. vaccinate
3. helpful
4. safe
5. choice
6. specify

Write a word to replace the underlined word or words below.
7. We had one pen between us, so we chose to <u>take turns</u> writing.
8. A warm bath is sometimes the best <u>cure</u> for sore muscles.
9. Does your dictionary give the <u>meaning</u> of *revelation*?
10. The team met to discuss a <u>plan of action</u> for the next game.

Unit 14 Latin Roots I   pages 90–95

reference	abstract	traceable	proposal	opposite
confer	exposure	inference	traction	posture

💡 **Spelling Strategy**   Knowing the Latin roots *fer* ("to carry"), *pos* ("to put; place"), and *tract/trace* ("to draw; pull") can help you spell and understand words with these roots.

Write the word that fits each clue.
11. If something is this it can be located.
12. This type of book is used for information.
13. This is the way someone stands.
14. The word *honor* is this kind of noun.

Write the word that is a synonym for each word.
15. friction
16. discuss
17. uncovering
18. contrary
19. conclusion
20. plan

Unit 15   Noun Suffixes I   pages 96–101

agency	society	curiosity	privacy	frequency
accuracy	maturity	emergency	anxiety	humidity

💡 **Spelling Strategy**   The suffixes -*cy*, -*ty*, and -*ity* form nouns when added to base words or roots. Remember the spelling patterns for these suffixes.

Write the word that is an antonym for each word.

21. indifference
22. calmness
23. dryness
24. childishness
25. openness
26. inexactness

Write the word that completes each sentence.

27. Car accidents occurred at the dangerous intersection with alarming _____.
28. He is a doctor in the _____ room of the hospital.
29. Mary belongs to her high school's honor _____.
30. If you need a job, consult an employment _____.

Unit 16   Words from French   pages 102–107

gourmet	sauté	parfait	omelet	foyer
etiquette	souvenir	camouflage	chauffeur	intrigue

💡 **Spelling Strategy**   Remember that words from French often contain silent letters, especially the final *t*. Also, French words often spell the |ē| sound with *i*, the |ā| sound with *e*, and the |sh| sound with *ch*.

Write the words that complete the paragraph.

As soon as you step into the __(31)__ of my aunt's apartment, you will smell something delicious. Aunt Carol is a __(32)__ cook, and today she is making an __(33)__ from eggs and fresh vegetables. Her secret is to __(34)__ the vegetables before adding the eggs.

Write the word that matches each definition.

35. a person hired to drive a car
36. a layered dessert in a tall glass
37. coloring that blends with the background
38. a memento
39. a secret plot
40. rules of conduct

Unit 17 Words Often Misspelled I
pages 108–113

playwright	propaganda	pageant	unanimous	extraordinary
pneumonia	khaki	siege	endeavor	prominent

Spelling Strategy Knowing a word's origin, thinking about the meanings of its parts, and practicing the word can often help you spell the word correctly.

Write the word that completes each sentence.
41. The invaders held the city under _____.
42. The Fourth of July _____ included skits about Colonial heroes.
43. One person opposed the plan, so the vote was not _____.
44. The leader's fiery speeches served as _____ for the government.

Write the word that belongs in each group.
45. well-known, important, _____
46. bronchitis, influenza, _____
47. gray, blue, _____
48. attempt, strive, _____
49. unusual, remarkable, _____
50. novelist, poet, _____

Challenge Words   Units 13–17
pages 84–113

initiative	eccentricity	connoisseur	consistency	rhetoric
initiate	hors d'oeuvre	decompose	soliloquy	composite

Write the word that fits each clue.
51. cheese on crackers
52. an expert in art and matters of taste
53. an odd personal habit
54. a speech to oneself

Write the word that completes each analogy.
55. end : begin :: finish : _____
56. rot : decay :: crumble : _____
57. mixture : blend :: combination : _____
58. performance : music :: speech : _____
59. ability : talent :: leadership : _____
60. steadiness : stability :: sameness : _____

Spelling-Meaning Strategy

The Latin Root *fin*

You know that the words *define* and *definition* are related in spelling and meaning. You also know that the words *finite* and *infinite* are related in spelling and meaning. Did you know, however, that *define* and *definition* are related to *finite* and *infinite*? All four words contain the Latin root *fin*, meaning "end." To define something is to specify or set limits or ends. Something that is finite has a defined end, while something that is infinite has no end at all.

Below are more words that contain the root *fin*.

finalist	definite	infinitive
confine	definitive	infinitesimal

define
definition
finite
infinite

Think

- How does the root *fin* contribute to the meaning of each word? Look up the words in your Spelling Dictionary.

- In Unit 13, you learned that the |ī| sounds in *define* and *finite* can help you remember how to spell the |ə| sounds in *definition* and *infinite*. How is the *i* in *fin* pronounced in each of the words in the box above?

Apply and Extend

Complete these activities on a separate piece of paper.

1. Write six sentences. Use one word from the word box above in each sentence.

2. What other words belong to the same family as *define*, *definition*, *finite*, and *infinite*? With a partner, make a list of related words. Then look up the Latin root *fin* in your Spelling-Meaning Index. Add to your list any other related words that you find.

Summing Up

The Latin root *fin* means "end." Words that contain the same root are often related in spelling and meaning. Knowing some of the words in a family can help you to use and spell the others correctly.

Two young runners are discussing their competitors in an upcoming Olympic race. Are the runners modern athletes? Where and when do you think their race is taking place?

from

Heather, Oak, and Olive: Three Stories

by Rosemary Sutcliff

They were down by the river one hot noontide something over a week after they had first arrived at Olympia; Amyntas lying on his back, his hands behind his head, squinting up into the dark shadow-shapes of the oleander branches against the sky; Leon sitting beside him with his arms round his updrawn knees, staring out into the dazzle of sunlight over the open riverbed. They had been talking runners' talk, and suddenly Amyntas said, "I was watching the Corinthian making his practice run this morning. I don't *think* we have either of us much to fear from him."

"The Rhodian runs well," said Leon, not bringing back his gaze from the white dance of sunlight beyond the oleanders.

"But he uses himself up too quickly. . . . I'd say that redhead from Macedon had the better chance."

. . . Then Amyntas said, "I think you are the one I have most to fear."

Leon turned his head slowly and looked down at him, and said, "Have you only just woken to that? I knew the same thing of *you*, three days ago."

They were both silent again and suddenly a little shocked. You might think that kind of thing, but it is best not to put it into words.

Think and Discuss

1. What is the setting of this story?
2. What do you know about the two characters in the story?
3. In a good story, events build to a climax, or high point. Given the way this story begins, what do you think the climax will be?

The Writing Process
Story

Have you ever wanted to write an adventure story, a mystery, or a true story? Choose an idea and write a story about it. Keep the guidelines in mind, and follow the Writing Process.

Guidelines for Writing a Story

✓ Design a plot that has a conflict, a climax, and a resolution.
✓ Use details about your setting to create a mood for the story.
✓ Use dialogue to enliven your characters.

1 ▶ Prewriting
- Make story plans for a few ideas. For each idea, outline the setting, characters, and plot of a potential story.
- Choose one story plan and fill out the details.

2 ▶ Draft
- Using your story plan, start to write. Correct errors later.
- Build a conflict, a climax or high point, and a resolution into your plot. Use details and dialogue to *show* what your setting and characters are like.

3 ▶ Revise
- Add dialogue, details, or actions to paint clearer pictures of your characters and setting.
- Use your Thesaurus to find words that convey your exact meaning.
- Have a writing conference.

Composition Words

strategy
curiosity
anxiety
extraordinary
distract
intrigue
pageant
outrageous

4 ▶ Proofread
- Did you spell each word correctly?
- Did you use negatives, adjectives, and adverbs correctly?
- Did you capitalize all proper nouns and proper adjectives?

5 ▶ Publish
- Copy your story neatly and add an appropriate and catchy title.
- Practice reading your story aloud. Then read it to the class.

Vowel Changes II

Read and Say

Basic

READ the sentences. SAY each bold word.

1. restoration — Can **restoration** save the old building?
2. restore — Experts tried to **restore** the damaged art.
3. original — Keep the **original** form and send me a copy.
4. origin — They traced the river back to its **origin**.
5. illustrate — Can you **illustrate** the plan with a drawing?
6. illustrative — This painting is **illustrative** of her style.
7. sequence — Follow the **sequence** of steps in the guide.
8. sequential — Tell the story events in **sequential** order.
9. punctual — I will miss the train if I am not **punctual**.
10. punctuality — Will wearing a watch improve his **punctuality**?
11. symbolism — Some artists use **symbolism** to express ideas.
12. symbolic — Why is the dove **symbolic** of peace?
13. tranquil — I feel calm and **tranquil** after a warm bath.
14. tranquility — Peaceful scenes fill me with **tranquility**.
15. syllable — Say each **syllable** of the word after me.
16. syllabication — Use **syllabication** to divide a word.
17. neutral — I try to stay **neutral** when they argue.
18. neutrality — Declare **neutrality** if you won't take sides.
19. trivial — Do not waste time on such a **trivial** matter.
20. triviality — Cost is a **triviality** when a life is at risk.

Spelling Strategy   To remember the spelling of |ə| in some words, think of a related word in which the pronunciation and spelling of the vowel are more obvious.

Think and Write   Write the pairs of Basic Words. Underline the vowels that change from |ə| to the short vowel sound.

Review		Challenge	
	23. adaptation		27. economy
21. excellence	24. adapt	25. emphasis	28. economics
22. excel		26. emphatic	

Independent Practice

Vocabulary: Definitions Write the Basic Word that matches each definition.
Use your Spelling Dictionary.

1. the act or process of bringing something back into existence or to its previous condition
2. serving as an explanation, clarification, or decoration
3. to explain or clarify using pictures or examples
4. not favoring any side in a war, dispute, or contest
5. the use of one thing to represent another
6. the act or quality of being on time
7. a single sound that forms a word or part of a word
8. a policy of not taking sides in a dispute, war, or contest
9. to bring back into existence or to a previous condition
10. an unimportant point, fact, or issue
11. the division of a word into smaller units
12. characterized by a particular order
13. a state of peace

Vocabulary: Synonyms in Context Write the Basic Word that is a synonym
for the underlined word. Use your Spelling Dictionary.

14. a meaningful gesture
15. her prompt arrival
16. traced to its source
17. the peaceful surface of the lake
18. the order of events
19. the first edition
20. an unimportant detail

Challenge Words Write the Challenge
Word that matches each clue. Use your
Spelling Dictionary.

21. This kind of person comes across loud and clear.
22. This is the management of a country's money and other resources.
23. To show this you could shout, underline, or use exclamation points.
24. Studying this science helps you make sense of dollars and cents.

Dictionary

Parts of Speech One of the first facts given in a dictionary entry is the **part of speech** of the entry word.

> **re·store** |rĭ stôr´| v. **1.** to bring back to prior condition

The abbreviation *v.* means that *restore* is a verb. On page 283 is a key to the abbreviations used in your Spelling Dictionary.

Some words can be more than one part of speech. In the entries for those words, the numbering of the definitions begins over again each time a new part of speech is introduced.

Practice Use your Spelling Dictionary to look up the following words. Write the parts of speech listed for each one.

1. succumb
2. produce
3. pedestrian
4. manual
5. buttress
6. alternate

1. _____ ?
2. _____ ?
3. _____ ?
4. _____ ?
5. _____ ?
6. _____ ?

Review: Spelling Spree

Invisible Vowels Decide which vowels should be added to complete each Basic or Review Word. Write the words correctly.

7. s y m b _ l _ c
8. _ l l _ s t r _ t _
9. r _ s t _ r _
10. _ d _ p t _ t _ _ n
11. _ l l _ s t r _ t _ v _
12. s _ q _ _ n c _
13. s y l l _ b l _
14. n _ _ t r _ l _ t y
15. t r _ n q _ _ l _ t y
16. p _ n c t _ _ l
17. t r _ v _ _ l _ t y
18. n _ _ t r _ l

19. s y l l _ b _ c _ t _ _ n
20. _ d _ p t
21. s _ q _ _ n t _ _ l
22. p _ n c t _ _ l _ t y

Proofreading and Writing

Proofread for Spelling Find seven misspelled Basic or Review Words in this paragraph. Write each word correctly.

In his tranqual studio, the old man thought about the oregin of the faded painting that stood before him. Each seemingly triviel detail had been deliberately included to contribute to the overall symbelism of the work. In his own symbolic gesture, the man kept beside him an empty stool, a reminder of the master whose work he was to restore. The resteration expert never painted over origanal strokes. Instead he worked around them, matching colors and filling gaps. He had achieved a reputation for excellance by making his own work impossible to detect. "No painting," he often said, "should look as if it has been taken to the cleaners."

Proofreading Marks
¶ Indent
∧ Add
⋏ Add a comma
∀ ∀ Add quotation marks
⊙ Add a period
↗ Delete
≡ Capital letter
/ Small letter
∿ Reverse order

Write a Description If you were to paint a portrait, who would your subject be? Write a description of the person and tell why you would paint him or her. Try to use five spelling words.

Unit 19 BONUS

Expanding Vocabulary

Spelling Word Link

punctual

Language Change The meaning of a word often changes over time. Some words take on narrower or more specific meanings. Others become broader or more general. Meanings can also become more positive or more negative.

WORD	OLD MEANING	NEW MEANING	CHANGE
punctual	careful; exact	on time	narrower
realm	land of a king	area of interest	broader
mansion	simple dwelling	large house	more positive
trivial	ordinary	unimportant	more negative

Write *narrower* or *broader* to describe how each meaning has changed.

1. success: an outcome (old) → a favorable outcome (new)
2. lady: wife of a lord (old) → a female adult (new)
3. century: group of 100 (old) → 100 years (new)

Write *positive* or *negative* to describe how each meaning has changed.

4. fond: foolish (old) → affectionate (new)
5. counterfeit: a likeness (old) → a deceptive copy (new)
6. propaganda: opinion (old) → misleading information (new)

TEST-TAKING TACTICS

Sentence Completion Some sentence completion test questions contain cause and effect signals that can help lead you to the correct answer choice. Words and phrases such as *because, consequently, as a result, therefore,* and *since* signal that one thing causes another.

Read the sentence completion question below, and then write the answers to the questions that follow.

The work of a painting restorer is quite _____; consequently, people who want to be restorers must have excellent vision and fine manual dexterity.

(A) time-consuming   (B) repetitive   (C) detailed

(D) exhausting   (E) valuable

7. Which word serves as the cause and effect signal in the sentence completion question above?
8. Which answer choice makes the most sense in the sentence? Write its letter.

Real-World Connection

Art: Painting Restoration All the words in the box relate to painting restoration. Look up these words in your Spelling Dictionary. Then write the words to complete this paragraph.

Five centuries ago, Michelangelo decorated the ceiling of Rome's Sistine Chapel with a spectacular __(1)__, a painting created in wet __(2)__. Over time, dirt collected on the painting, and layers of protective __(3)__ and glue began to darken and __(4)__. These problems were recently addressed by a restoration team that drew on historical and technical __(5)__ from all over the world. Daily, members of the team climbed a __(6)__ to work on the vast ceiling, a square foot at a time. With __(7)__ care, they removed only unwanted layers, analyzing each __(8)__ and leaving intact any that could have been applied by Michelangelo himself. As a result, vivid colors and details long veiled in darkness have reappeared.

Spelling Word Link

restoration

fresco
varnish
deteriorate
expertise
plaster
pigment
scaffold
meticulous

▶ TRY THIS!

True or False? Write *T* if the statement is true. Write *F* if it is false.

9. A pigment is found in paint.
10. Plaster is a type of paint.
11. A fresco covers a wall or a ceiling.
12. A scaffold is a type of knife.

Fact File

Michelangelo was one of the greatest artists of all time. Although an accomplished painter, he thought of himself as a sculptor. His marble statues are so beautiful that they often have a powerful impact on their viewers.

Latin Roots II

Read and Say

Basic	READ the sentences. SAY each bold word.
1. *conspiracy*	They formed a **conspiracy** to steal the jewels.
2. *diversion*	Use a **diversion** to draw away the angry dog.
3. *transpire*	What do you think will **transpire** tomorrow?
4. *convert*	We plan to **convert** the house into an inn.
5. *expire*	Coupons must be used before they **expire**.
6. *advertisement*	Which product is shown in the **advertisement**?
7. *universal*	Curing this disease is a **universal** goal.
8. *reverse*	Put the car in **reverse** and back up.
9. *perspiration*	His face was dripping with **perspiration**.
10. *extrovert*	A true **extrovert** loves having company.
11. *diverse*	Our store carries a **diverse** range of goods.
12. *respiration*	Lungs play a big role in **respiration**.
13. *vertical*	Raise the pole to a **vertical** position.
14. *controversy*	Both sides agreed to end the **controversy**.
15. *versus*	Her story is about good **versus** evil.
16. *anniversary*	Is today the **anniversary** of their marriage?
17. *aspire*	I **aspire** to be the next class president.
18. *versatile*	You can use this **versatile** tool in many ways.
19. *introvert*	An **introvert** enjoys being alone.
20. *invert*	Just **invert** the box to use it as a table.

Spelling Strategy   Knowing the Latin roots *ver* ("to turn") and *spir/pir* ("to breathe") can help you spell and understand words with these roots.

Think and Write   Write each Basic Word under its root.

ver   *spir/pir*

Review		**Challenge**	
	23. assignment		28. vice versa
21. inspiration	24. investigate	26. adversary	29. inverse
22. intelligence	25. suspense	27. revert	30. vertebra

Independent Practice

Vocabulary: Word Clues Write the Basic Word that fits each clue. Use your Spelling Dictionary.

1. This may say "for sale" or "help wanted."
2. You do this to yourself when you stand on your head.
3. Coupons and magazine subscriptions do this.
4. This takes your mind off things.
5. An event, a conversation, or a deal might do this.
6. A hot, humid day or strenuous exercise might increase this.
7. This separates the names of opposing teams at a sports event.
8. This fills the lungs with air.
9. Sofas that can become beds do this.
10. This causes a lot of debate.
11. When you stand up, you are in this position.
12. This might describe people, tastes, or opinions.

Vocabulary: Using Context Write the Basic Word that completes each sentence. Use your Spelling Dictionary.

13. C.W. marked his tenth _____ as secret service chief by learning of a shocking betrayal.
14. The news concerned the McCoy twins, whose combined talents and identical faces made them _____ "double agents."
15. Though the twins looked exactly alike, their personalities were the _____ of each other.
16. Preferring to be alone, Kara was a shy, serious _____.
17. In contrast, her sister Kyla was a crowd-loving _____.
18. Neither twin seemed to _____ to anything more than doing her job, and together they completed many successful missions.
19. Throughout the international spy network, the name McCoy stood for the _____ ideals of sisterhood and loyalty.
20. Now one twin was part of an enemy _____.

Challenge Words Write the Challenge Word that matches each definition. Use your Spelling Dictionary.

21. one of the bones that form the spinal column
22. an opponent, enemy, or rival
23. to return to a former condition
24. opposite
25. the other way around

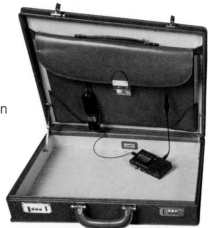

Review: Spelling Spree

Secret Message Decoder Each secret message below contains a Basic or Review Word written in code. Your objective is to use the code key to figure out the words. Write each one correctly.

CODE:	e	f	g	h	i	j	k	l	m	n	o	p	q	r	s	t	u	v	w	x	y	z	a	b	c	d
LETTER:	a	b	c	d	e	f	g	h	i	j	k	l	m	n	o	p	q	r	s	t	u	v	w	x	y	z

1. To Agents 073 and 074: mrziwxmkexi Dr. Maybee.
2. Look for mrxippmkirgi reports in potted ferns.
3. Tune cuff-link radio to 55.4 for new ewwmkrqirx.
4. Beware of the mysterious mrxvszivx in the black robe.
5. In Budapest, use the yrmzivwep password *Open Sesame*.
6. There is a gsrwtmvegc to unseat the dictator.
7. Look in a newspaper ehzivxmwiqirx for further instructions.
8. The agent, an ibxvszivx, has many acquaintances.
9. Your contact will be wearing a sweater with zivxmgep stripes.
10. Wanted: zivwexmpi agent who can adopt many disguises.
11. Check the trenchcoat for smoke and tivwtmvexmsr stains.
12. Keep a low profile and avoid gsrxvszivwc.
13. The subject will be at the ambassador's errmzivwevc party.

Words in Disguise Change one or two letters in each word to form a Basic or Review Word. Write the words correctly.

14. verses (1 letter)
15. dispense (2 letters)
16. transport (2 letters)
17. instigation (2 letters)
18. diverge (1 letter)
19. attire (2 letters)
20. entire (2 letters)
21. insert (1 letter)
22. desperation (2 letters)
23. concert (1 letter)
24. remorse (2 letters)
25. diversity (2 letters)

How Are You Doing?
Write the spelling words in alphabetical order. Practice any misspelled words with a partner.

Proofreading and Writing

Proofread: Spelling and Uses for Commas Use commas to separate three or more items in a series. Also use a comma between two or more adjectives that come before a noun.

> Spies communicate with **passwords, codes,** and **signals**.
> John le Carré is a **respected, successful** writer.

Some adjectives should not be separated with commas. To decide whether or not to use one, replace the comma with the word *and*. If *and* makes the sentence awkward, do not use a comma.

> George Smiley is his **famous main** character.

Find six misspelled Basic or Review Words and two missing commas in this book report. Write the report correctly.

Spy School, by Kim Ky, is about a virsatile clever agent whose assigment is to investagate a spy ring at a small college. Through intelligence sources, agent P. D. Carr learns of a consperacy to sell government secrets. Suspence mounts as Carr unveils the plot, using a coded advetisement a student's research report, and the school newspaper. The book is an entertaining diversion.

Write a Plot Outline What might make a great plot for a spy novel? Write an outline of the plot. List the story's key events, and identify the characters' central problem. Tell how the problem is solved. Try to use five spelling words. Also, try to use three or more items in a series or two or more adjectives before a given noun.

Basic

1. conspiracy
2. diversion
3. transpire
4. convert
5. expire
6. advertisement
7. universal
8. reverse
9. perspiration
10. extrovert
11. diverse
12. respiration
13. vertical
14. controversy
15. versus
16. anniversary
17. aspire
18. versatile
19. introvert
20. invert

Review

21. inspiration
22. intelligence
23. assignment
24. investigate
25. suspense

Challenge

26. adversary
27. revert
28. vice versa
29. inverse
30. vertebra

Proofreading Marks
- ¶ Indent
- ∧ Add
- ⌄ Add a comma
- ⌄⌄ Add quotation marks
- ⊙ Add a period
- ⸜ Delete
- ≡ Capital letter
- / Small letter
- ∾ Reverse order

Expanding Vocabulary

Spelling Word Link

introvert
extrovert

The Prefixes *intro-* and *extra-* Introverts turn inside themselves, away from other people, and extroverts turn outside themselves, toward others. What does this tell you about the prefixes *intro-* and *extra-*?

> intro = inside   extra (extro) = outside

Write the word that matches each definition. Use your Spelling Dictionary.

> extracurricular   introspection   extraordinary   extraterrestrial

1. beyond the usual or commonplace
2. outside the earth or its atmosphere
3. the act of looking inward to examine your feelings
4. carried on outside the classroom

TEST-TAKING TACTICS

Vocabulary-in-Context When trying to answer a vocabulary-in-context test question, always keep in mind that words can have multiple meanings. Don't automatically assume that a familiar meaning of a tested word is correct just because it appears among the answer choices. Instead, pay careful attention to the context clues given in the sentence in which the tested word appears as well as in the surrounding sentences. Then use logic to find the answer choice that makes the most sense in the passage.

Study the following sample. Then answer the questions that follow.

Sample passage excerpt and question:

(35)   At the conclusion of a harrowing time spent in the field, the main character in a spy novel often spends time in a safe house. The secret location of this sanctuary is known to only a few people. While in hiding, the spy is usually debriefed, protected, and allowed to rest.

The word "sanctuary" in line 37 most nearly means

(A) bank   (B) sacred place   (C) gated estate
(D) prison   (E) place of refuge

5. Which answer choice, although incorrect, might you be tempted to choose because it is a familiar meaning of "sanctuary"? Write its letter.
6. Which answer choice is correct because the passage's context clues led you to it? Write its letter.

Real-World Connection

Language Arts: Spy Novels All the words in the box relate to spy novels. Look up these words in your Spelling Dictionary. Then write the words to complete this paragraph.

File 10382

TOP SECRET

Agent 8 paused at the door. Inside, SyNerg engineers were designing a spy satellite for constant __(1)__ of foreign countries. Agent 8 knew that one of those engineers was actually a double agent from M.E.S.S., the sinister __(2)__ organization. Working __(3)__, the double agent had gained Top Secret __(4)__ at SyNerg, had photographed their designs with his key-ring camera, and was about to hand off the designs on a tiny piece of __(5)__. Earlier, at __(6)__ headquarters, Agent 8 had read the __(7)__ detailing every chapter in the spy's career. Now, before the double agent could __(8)__ SyNerg's secrets, Agent 8 would close the book on that career.

Spelling Word Link

conspiracy

espionage
divulge
incognito
dossier
microfilm
clearance
surveillance
Interpol

TRY THIS!

Possible or Impossible? Write *possible* if the activity described is possible. Write *impossible* if it is not.

9. to divulge a code
10. to eat a dossier
11. to see microfilm
12. to travel incognito

Fact File

The number *007* is well known to fans of espionage fiction. It is the code name of James Bond, the popular spy hero created by British novelist Ian Fleming. A series of movies based on the novels has given Fleming's secret agent even greater fame.

Noun Suffixes II

Read and Say

Basic

READ the sentences. SAY each bold word.

1. *historian*	A noted **historian** will speak on the last war.
2. *politician*	Which **politician** do you want to be elected?
3. *comedian*	That **comedian** writes all her own jokes.
4. *pianist*	A famous **pianist** is giving a concert tonight.
5. *librarian*	Ask the **librarian** to help you find the book.
6. *novelist*	That **novelist** writes the best stories!
7. *pharmacist*	A **pharmacist** must count pills carefully.
8. *custodian*	Does the **custodian** lock the school at night?
9. *criticism*	I don't mind **criticism** that helps me improve.
10. *idealism*	His **idealism** led him to work with the poor.
11. *guitarist*	Who is the new **guitarist** in your rock group?
12. *soloist*	The band sat down while the **soloist** played.
13. *realism*	His use of **realism** made the story come alive.
14. *civilian*	That retired general is now a **civilian**.
15. *conformist*	A **conformist** tries not to be different.
16. *perfectionist*	Mistakes drive a **perfectionist** crazy.
17. *mannerism*	Tapping your foot is a nervous **mannerism**.
18. *pedestrian*	The **pedestrian** crossed at the green light.
19. *guardian*	Should a parent or **guardian** sign the report?
20. *individualist*	An **individualist** does not follow the crowd.

Spelling Strategy Remember the meanings of the noun suffixes *-ian* and *-ist* ("one who does or studies") and of the noun suffix *-ism* ("the act, profession, or theory of").

Think and Write   Write each Basic Word under its suffix.

-ian   -ist   -ism

Review   23. veterinarian
21. physician 24. reporter
22. columnist 25. secretary

Challenge   28. optimism
26. linguist   29. pessimism
27. equestrian 30. skepticism

Independent Practice

Vocabulary: Definitions Write the Basic Word that matches each definition. Use your Spelling Dictionary.

1. the act of forming and expressing judgments about the worth of something
2. the practice of seeing or representing things as being better than they actually are
3. a person traveling on foot, especially on city streets
4. the practice of seeing or representing things as they really are
5. a person who is independent in action and thought
6. one who always agrees with the opinions or follows the behaviors of the majority
7. a person who sets extremely high standards and is dissatisfied with anything less
8. a personal habit
9. a person who performs alone
10. a person who protects or defends, or a person who is responsible for another person
11. a person not serving in the military
12. a person who takes care of a building

Vocabulary: Categorizing Write the Basic Word that names a career associated with each pair of items. Use your Spelling Dictionary.

13. names, dates
14. jokes, laughter
15. plots, publishers
16. votes, campaigns
17. books, card catalog
18. prescriptions, medication
19. strings, picks
20. keys, music

Challenge Words Write the Challenge Word that fits each clue. Use your Spelling Dictionary.

21. This person spends a lot of time horsing around.
22. This is a belief that something will go wrong.
23. This person might speak English, Spanish, and French.
24. This is a belief that something cannot quite be believed.
25. This is the belief that every cloud has a silver lining.

Review: Spelling Spree

Rhyming Role Call Write the Basic or Review Word that fits each rhyming clue.

1. one who gives medical care to a bear, a hare, or a mare
2. one who tells jokes to folks
3. one who performs alone with a microphone
4. one who arranges a file with style
5. one who lives by the sales of tales
6. one who often finds nooks for books
7. one who lives in terror of error
8. one who regularly writes views about news
9. one who fills a prescription with pills
10. one who would rather stride than ride
11. one who can make a string almost sing
12. one whose cure should be quick when you're sick
13. one who writes facts about news-making acts

Word Forms Add a noun suffix to create a Basic or Review Word. Write each word.

14. history
15. custody
16. piano
17. civil
18. politic
19. real
20. conform

21. guard
22. ideal
23. manner
24. critic
25. individual

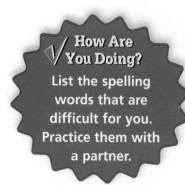

How Are You Doing?

List the spelling words that are difficult for you. Practice them with a partner.

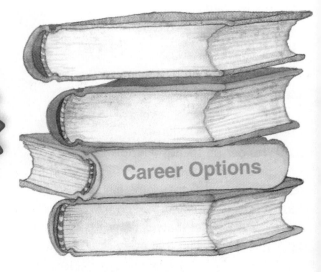

Career Options

Proofreading and Writing

Proofread: Spelling, Dates and Addresses In a date, use commas to separate the month and the day from the year, and the year from the rest of the sentence. In an address, use a comma to separate the city and the state, and the state from the rest of the sentence.

> On September 6, 1985, Ms. Ryan began her first teaching job. She taught in Provo, Utah, in a junior high school.

Find five misspelled Basic or Review Words and two missing commas in this letter. Write the letter correctly.

Dear Dr. Rollins:

On May 5, 2000 our school will hold a career day. Could you come and speak to us about being a phisician? The other speakers will be a novelist from Columbus Ohio, and a reportor, a gitarist, a pharmasist, and a librarian, all from Chicago.

Sincerely,

Alex Gediman

Alex Gediman, Class Secretery

Write a Career Plan Choose a career that you might like to follow. Then write a career plan that answers these questions: How is my personality suited to this career? Which of my skills would be useful in this career? When do I expect to begin working? In what city and state would I like to work? Try to use five spelling words and at least one date or address.

Dr. Scott Ro...
2093 North Place
...llinois 60161

Basic

1. historian
2. politician
3. comedian
4. pianist
5. librarian
6. novelist
7. pharmacist
8. custodian
9. criticism
10. idealism
11. guitarist
12. soloist
13. realism
14. civilian
15. conformist
16. perfectionist
17. mannerism
18. pedestrian
19. guardian
20. individualist

Review

21. physician
22. columnist
23. veterinarian
24. reporter
25. secretary

Challenge

26. linguist
27. equestrian
28. optimism
29. pessimism
30. skepticism

Proofreading Marks

¶ Indent
∧ Add
⋏ Add a comma
⦙ Add quotation marks
⊙ Add a period
⤵ Delete
≡ Capital letter
／ Small letter
∿ Reverse order

Expanding Vocabulary

Spelling Word Link

criticism

Context Clues A sentence that contains an unfamiliar word might also contain an antonym for the word. Like synonyms, antonyms are helpful context clues. Words such as *but, not, however, except,* and *although* can help you identify antonyms in a sentence. Look at the context clue for the word *criticism*.

Cait often gives criticism, but she rarely offers **praise**.

Write the meaning of each underlined word. Then write the antonym that gives a clue to the meaning of the underlined word.

1. Except for the lazy pianist, the band was quite <u>diligent</u>.
2. The comedian is <u>audacious</u> on stage but timid in reality.
3. That novelist is usually <u>prolific</u>; however, she has been somewhat unproductive lately.
4. Although the other politicians gave lengthy speeches, the mayor's remarks were <u>terse</u>.

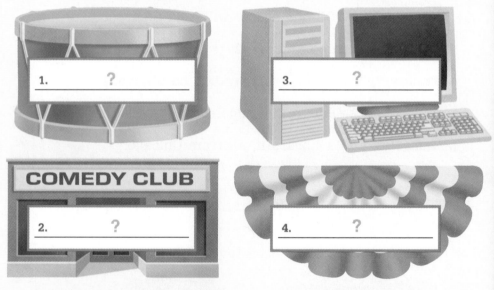

1.   ?

3.   ?

COMEDY CLUB

2.   ?

4.   ?

Now choose two antonym pairs from items 1–4. Write a sentence for each pair, using one antonym as a context clue to the meaning of the other.

5.   ?

   ?

6.   ?

   ?

Real-World Connection

Life Skills: Choosing a Career All the words in the box relate to choosing a career. Look up these words in your Spelling Dictionary. Then write the words to complete this paragraph.

> How do you choose a career? Start by thinking about what you enjoy doing. Do you like to cook or give parties? You could do that as a __(1)__ . Do you like to collect and display things? If so, you could be a museum __(2)__ . If you enjoy taking pictures, you might choose to be a __(3)__ . Are you interested in drawing or geography? Perhaps you could be a mapmaker, or __(4)__ . Do you manage money well? Be a __(5)__ and invest money for others. If science interests you, you might be a __(6)__ and relieve people's backaches or an __(7)__ , who helps to correct people's vision. Maybe you would prefer to work with wiring and switches as an __(8)__ . The more you enjoy what you do, the more likely you will be able to do it well.

Spelling Word Link

historian

electrician
curator
photographer
stockbroker
optometrist
caterer
chiropractor
cartographer

TRY THIS!

True or False? Write *T* if the statement is true. Write *F* if it is false.

9. A caterer sells maps.
10. A curator sells food.
11. An optometrist examines eyes.
12. An electrician fixes wiring.

Fact File

What do forest rangers, air traffic controllers, and mail carriers have in common? They all work for the government as part of the civil service. With three million workers, the civil service is the nation's largest employer.

Words from Other Languages

Read and Say

Basic

READ the sentences. SAY each bold word.

1. villa — The grand **villa** had too many rooms to count.
2. pizza — I like cheese **pizza** with a thin crust.
3. spaghetti — Twirl the **spaghetti** strings around your fork.
4. gondola — We floated down the canal in a **gondola**.
5. accordion — An **accordion** has a keyboard like a piano.
6. balcony — The **balcony** of our room looked over the bay.
7. opera — A dramatic story told in song is an **opera**.
8. waltz — Can you teach me how to dance the **waltz**?
9. macaroni — May I have some sauce on my **macaroni**?
10. tycoon — The **tycoon** made his fortune in stocks.
11. finale — We had to leave before the **finale** of the show.
12. violin — Always tune your **violin** before playing it.
13. confetti — We tossed **confetti** at the bride and groom.
14. pretzel — Each **pretzel** is rolled in salt and baked.
15. kindergarten — Children enter **kindergarten** at age five.
16. kimono — Her long silk robe looked like a **kimono**.
17. influenza — My fever and pain were due to **influenza**.
18. umbrella — Take your **umbrella** if you want to stay dry.
19. sauerkraut — Shall we use this cabbage to make **sauerkraut**?
20. graffiti — Please scrub the **graffiti** off the walls.

Spelling Strategy   Remember that English has borrowed words from many languages.

Think and Write   Write the Basic Words.

Review
21. landscape
22. easel
23. sketch
24. squash
25. mammoth

Challenge
26. pistachio
27. tempera
28. wanderlust
29. hibachi
30. delicatessen

Independent Practice

Vocabulary: Word Clues Write the Basic Word that fits each clue. Use your Spelling Dictionary.

1. This pie is not for dessert.
2. This is a tangy way to eat cabbage.
3. This is usually worn with a sash.
4. These hollow tubes are often in hot water.
5. This ending is often grand.
6. This comes between nursery school and first grade.
7. This stringy dish is often eaten with tomato sauce, cheese, and meatballs.
8. This person usually means big business.
9. This keeps you dry on a rainy day.
10. This musical instrument uses air, but a musician does not blow into it.
11. This section of a theater gives you a lift.
12. These messages are the handwriting on the wall.

Vocabulary: Classifying Write the Basic Word that fits each group. Use your Spelling Dictionary.

13. concert, ballet, play, _____
14. ribbons, balloons, streamers, _____
15. canoe, rowboat, raft, _____
16. mansion, cottage, lodge, _____
17. guitar, cello, banjo, _____
18. polka, jitterbug, tango, _____
19. cracker, chip, popcorn, _____
20. mumps, chicken pox, measles, _____

Challenge Words Write the Challenge Word that matches each definition. Use your Spelling Dictionary.

21. a small, charcoal-burning grill
22. the strong and irresistible urge to travel
23. a painting method in which pigments are mixed with glue or egg yolk
24. a small, edible, green nut that is often dyed red, or the tree from which it comes
25. a store that sells foods already cooked or prepared, such as cheeses, sliced meats, pickles, and relishes

Dictionary

Pronunciation The phonetic respelling next to each dictionary entry includes special symbols that tell you how to pronounce the entry word. If you do not understand a symbol in the respelling, check the pronunciation key that appears regularly throughout the dictionary. The pronunciation key explains what sound each symbol stands for by giving an example of a familiar word that contains the sound.

ă	pat	ŏ	pot	û	fur
ā	pay	ō	go	*th*	**the**
â	care	ô	paw, for	th	thin
ä	father	oi	oil	hw	which
ĕ	pet	ŏŏ	book	zh	usual
ē	be	ōō	boot	ə	ago, item,
ĭ	pit	yōō	cute		pencil, atom,
ī	ice	ou	out		circus
î	near	ŭ	cut	ər	butter

Practice Look up each of the following words in your Spelling Dictionary. Write the example word from the pronunciation key that has the same sound as the underlined letter or letters in each word.

1. spaghett<u>i</u>
2. m<u>a</u>caroni
3. final<u>e</u>
4. tyc<u>oo</u>n
5. kim<u>o</u>no
6. sauerkr<u>au</u>t
7. calculat<u>or</u>
8. scy<u>the</u>

Review: Spelling Spree

Word Canals 9–25 Find the Basic and Review Words that are hidden in the canals. Write the words correctly in the order in which you find them. Begin at the gondola and end at the footbridge.

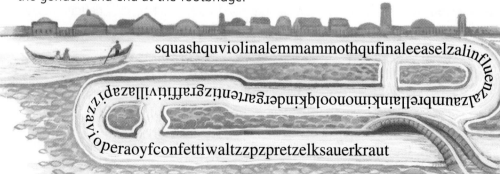

Proofreading and Writing

Proofread for Spelling Find seven misspelled Basic or Review Words in this journal entry. Write each word correctly.

May 20

We arrived in Venice yesterday. The lanscape is so unusual! I drew a skech from our balcuny. There are canals instead of streets and boats instead of cars. Even the taxis are boats! Last night as I was lying in bed, I heard acordian music and people singing. The sounds came from a gondala that floated by our window. The food here is unusual, too. People eat several courses for dinner. First they have some kind of spagetti or macaronni.

Then they have a meat course.

My favorite food is the pizza.

The crust is so thin you can

eat a whole one by yourself.

Proofreading Marks

¶ Indent
∧ Add
⩘ Add a comma
⸌⸍ Add quotation marks
⊙ Add a period
⸜ Delete
≡ Capital letter
/ Small letter
∽ Reverse order

Write a Travel Brochure What foreign country or city especially interests you? Write a travel brochure about that place. Describe the area, its food, and things to do there. Make it sound so appealing that everyone will want to visit it. Try to use five spelling words.

Expanding Vocabulary

Informal Words Although the words *violin* and *fiddle* have the same meaning, *fiddle* is a more informal word than *violin*. An **informal word** is one that is used mainly in casual speaking or writing.

Write the informal word in each pair.

1. sleep, snooze
2. twister, tornado
3. nerve, boldness
4. child, kid

Spelling Word Link

violin

1. _____ ?   3. _____ ?

2. _____ ?   4. _____ ?

TEST-TAKING TACTICS

Analogies As you have learned, being knowledgeable of the types of relationships found in analogy test questions can help you recognize those types quickly when you see them. Sometimes, though, because of a similarity among the kinds of relationships covered in a test question, you must analyze each word pair very carefully in order to distinguish between them. Three types of analogy relationships that can be confusing are *worker* and *action*, *worker* and *tool*, and *worker* and *creation*.

Study this analogy question. Then write the answers to the questions that follow.

PROGRAMMER : SOFTWARE ::

(A) surgeon : operation   (B) florist : bouquet   (C) weaver : loom
(D) actor : role   (E) logger : chainsaw

5. Which of the three types of relationships noted above exists between the stem words?
6. Which answer choice correctly completes the analogy because its word pair has the same relationship as the stem words? Write its letter.
7. What type of relationship exists between the word pairs in answer choices A and D?
8. What type of relationship exists between the word pairs in answer choices C and E?

Real-World Connection

Social Studies: Italy All the words in the box relate to Italy. Look up these words in your Spelling Dictionary. Then write the words to complete this paragraph.

Spelling Word Link

villa

pasta
cathedral
tomb
café
forum
catacombs
carnival
regatta

Italy offers much to see and do. Walk down a modern street in Rome, and you may find the ruins of a __(1)__, once a public gathering place. Along the Appian Way, a road leading out of Rome, you might see an old __(2)__, or burial place. You can even take a tour of one of the __(3)__, underground cemeteries with miles of tunnels. Almost every Italian city or town has a __(4)__, each offering unique architecture or a breathtaking view from its dome or bell tower. In Venice, join the crowds who line the shores of the Grand Canal to watch a __(5)__ or don elaborate masks to attend a __(6)__. No matter where in Italy you are, sample the food—whether it be a snack at an outdoor __(7)__ or a plate of homemade __(8)__ in one of the country's many fine restaurants.

TRY THIS!

Yes or No? Write *yes* if the objects are listed with their proper use. Write *no* if they are not.

9. boats for a regatta
10. flour for pasta
11. snacks for a cathedral
12. masks for a carnival

Fact File

In 1174 construction began on a bell tower in Pisa, Italy. The ground beneath it began to sink, however, causing the tower to tilt. The Tower of Pisa leans about one inch farther every four years.

Words Often Misspelled II

Read and Say

Basic

1. mortgage	Which bank carries the **mortgage** on your home?
2. acreage	Buying more land will increase our **acreage**.
3. vacancy	When does she plan to fill the job **vacancy**?
4. license	You must have a **license** to drive a car.
5. pamphlet	This free **pamphlet** describes the old mill.
6. acquaintance	He is an **acquaintance** of a close friend.
7. drought	Did the stream dry up in the summer **drought**?
8. conscientious	A **conscientious** student studies for exams.
9. miscellaneous	Our junk box is full of **miscellaneous** items.
10. exquisite	Pearls covered her **exquisite** silk gown.
11. aerial	The planes did an **aerial** dance in the sky.
12. catastrophe	That awful fire was a **catastrophe** for us.
13. inevitable	Death is **inevitable** for all living things.
14. forfeit	Will we **forfeit** the game if we don't show up?
15. lieutenant	The **lieutenant** reports to the captain.
16. abundant	Fine weather gave us an **abundant** harvest.
17. colossal	A **colossal** wave washed over the village.
18. quarantine	Please stay indoors during the **quarantine**.
19. succumb	I worry that he will **succumb** to old habits.
20. anxious	We were **anxious** when the baby wandered off.

Spelling Strategy Knowing a word's origin, thinking about the meanings of its parts, and practicing the word can often help you spell the word correctly.

Think and Write Write the Basic Words. Underline any parts that you have trouble spelling.

Review		**Challenge**	
21. guarantee	23. beige	26. aesthetic	28. continuum
22. livelihood	24. nuisance	27. bureaucrat	29. disheveled
	25. prior		30. bouillon

Independent Practice

Vocabulary: Using Context Write the Basic Word that completes each sentence. Use your Spelling Dictionary.

1. Amos bought land with lots of _____ for planting an orchard.
2. The apartment building manager advertised to fill the _____.
3. Ms. Cox signed a _____ agreement for a loan to buy her house.
4. The pilot took an _____ picture of the property.
5. After years of living on military bases, the _____ was finally going to buy a house.
6. The ad lists _____ features, such as closets and a fireplace.
7. The colorful _____ contained photographs of vacation homes.
8. Ace Realty was recommended to Marcy by a casual _____.
9. A person must have a _____ to sell real estate.
10. The _____ stained-glass window increased the house's value.
11. Because he was still contagious, the real estate agent was under _____ and could not show any property to his clients.
12. When Laura broke her agreement to buy the house, she had to _____ the deposit she had put down on it.
13. When the flood destroyed our new home, we were glad that our home insurance covered that kind of _____.

Vocabulary: Antonyms Write the Basic Word that means the opposite of each word. Use your Spelling Dictionary.

14. flood
15. calm
16. tiny
17. scarce
18. overcome
19. preventable
20. careless

Challenge Words Write the Challenge Word that completes each analogy. Use your Spelling Dictionary.

21. charming : pleasing ::
    artistic : _____
22. sauce : gravy ::
    broth : _____
23. corporation : executive ::
    government : _____
24. part : section ::
    range : _____
25. clean : dirty ::
    neat : _____

FOR SALE
BY OWNER

Review: Spelling Spree

Words Within Words Each word below can be found within a Basic or Review Word. Find the word and write it correctly.

1. cell
2. tenant
3. bun
4. loss
5. quaint
6. hood

Letter Math Add and subtract letters from the words below to make a Basic or Review Word. Write the new words.

Example: a + but – t + pendant – pe = *abundant*

7. con + scientific – fic + ous =
8. guard – d + an + tee =
9. be + ignore – nor =
10. for + counterfeit – counter =
11. pamper – er + h + let =
12. age – g + trial – t =
13. vacate – ate + fancy – f =
14. lick – k + dense – d =
15. such – h + crumb – r =
16. an + x + furious – fur =
17. superior – su – e =

18. nut – t + is + dance – d =
19. quart – t + ant + fine – f =
20. sacred – s – d + age =
21. mortal – al + gag + e =
22. in + evil – l + table =
23. ex + quiz – z + site =
24. cat + astro + phone – on =
25. dry – y + ought =

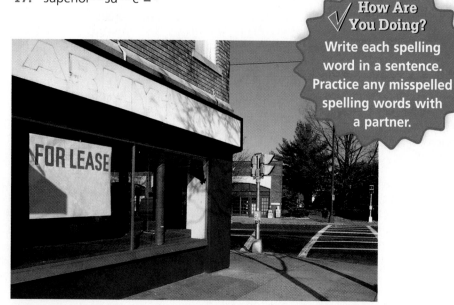

How Are You Doing?
Write each spelling word in a sentence. Practice any misspelled spelling words with a partner.

Proofreading and Writing

Proofread: Spelling and Direct Quotations Use quotation marks and commas to set off a **direct quotation** from the rest of a sentence. If a quotation is divided, or interrupted by other words, enclose each part in quotation marks. If the second part continues the sentence, begin it with a small letter. If it starts a new sentence, begin it with a capital letter.

> "You can have the house," the agent said, "in three weeks."
> "That's good," said Dad. "It will give us time to pack."

Find five misspelled Basic or Review Words, one missing quotation mark, and one capitalization error in this letter excerpt. Write the excerpt correctly.

Dear Jeannie,

My new room is esquisite. It's biege and rose.

Unpacking is a nusance, however. There are still

boxes of misellaneous things all over my room.

I'm anxious to make some friends. I have made

one aquaintance—the girl next door. "All my

friends," she said, "Want to meet you." So far, I

haven't met one of them. "Be patient, Dad said.

That's his answer for everything!

Write the Script of a Conversation A real estate agent is showing you and your family a house. Write the script of a humorous conversation that takes place between one of your family members and the agent. Try to use five spelling words, and remember to write the dialogue correctly.

Basic

1. mortgage
2. acreage
3. vacancy
4. license
5. pamphlet
6. acquaintance
7. drought
8. conscientious
9. miscellaneous
10. exquisite
11. aerial
12. catastrophe
13. inevitable
14. forfeit
15. lieutenant
16. abundant
17. colossal
18. quarantine
19. succumb
20. anxious

Review

21. guarantee
22. livelihood
23. beige
24. nuisance
25. prior

Challenge

26. aesthetic
27. bureaucrat
28. continuum
29. disheveled
30. bouillon

Proofreading Marks

¶ Indent
∧ Add
⩓ Add a comma
⩒⩒ Add quotation marks
⊙ Add a period
⟋ Delete
≡ Capital letter
╱ Small letter
∿ Reverse order

Expanding Vocabulary

Spelling Word Link

abundant

Synonyms You know that synonyms are words with the same or nearly the same meaning.

abundant = plentiful   guarantee = promise

Write the word that is a synonym for each underlined word. Use your Thesaurus.

1.	nuisance	noise	bother	disease	benefit
2.	catastrophe	sadness	flood	fortune	disaster
3.	succumb	yield	leave	survive	give
4.	colossal	sad	huge	dangerous	cold

1. ___?___

2. ___?___

3. ___?___

4. ___?___

Now review the Thesaurus entries for *nuisance, catastrophe, succumb,* and *colossal.* From the subentries for each word, choose one synonym to use in a sentence. Do not choose any of the synonyms that you wrote as answers to items 1–4. Write a sentence, on any topic, for each of your chosen synonyms.

5. ___?___

6. ___?___

7. ___?___

8. ___?___

Real-World Connection

Careers: Real Estate All the words in the box relate to real estate. Look up these words in your Spelling Dictionary. Then write the words to complete this paragraph.

When Mr. Craner decided to sell his house, he hired a __(1)__ to arrange the sale and a __(2)__ to measure the lot. The boundary measurements had to match those recorded on the __(3)__ to the house. Mr. Craner's bank did an __(4)__ of the property to determine its value. Dr. Frye wanted to buy the property because the town's __(5)__ laws allowed office space in the house; however, she found it too expensive. Mr. Craner agreed to __(6)__ the price, and the two reached a compromise. Mr. Craner's __(7)__, Liz, lived on the second floor. Dr. Frye did not __(8)__ Liz, but let her continue to rent her rooms.

Spelling Word Link

mortgage

Realtor
appraisal
zoning
surveyor
negotiate
deed
evict
tenant

TRY THIS!

Possible or Impossible? Write *possible* if the activity described is possible. Write *impossible* if it is not.

9. to read a deed
10. to rent an appraisal
11. to sell a tenant
12. to hire a surveyor

Fact File

In 1867 Secretary of State William H. Seward bought Alaska from Russia for $7,200,000, about two cents per acre. Thought to be a wasteland, Alaska was called Seward's Folly. The purchase proved wise, however, as Alaska is rich in oil, gas, timber, minerals, and wildlife.

149

24 Review: Units 19–23

Unit 19 Vowel Changes II   pages 120–125

illustrate	sequence	original	symbolism	syllable
illustrative	sequential	origin	symbolic	syllabication

💡 **Spelling Strategy** To remember the spelling of |ə| in some words, think of a related word in which the pronunciation and spelling of the vowel are more obvious.

Write the word that completes each sentence.
1. The teacher used _____ charts to make her explanation clearer.
2. To hyphenate a word properly, first check its _____.
3. A poet's use of a rose to represent love is an example of _____.
4. Directions are usually _____ and should be followed in order.

Write the word that fits each definition.
5. a source
6. first
7. the order of things
8. to explain by using examples
9. serving to represent something
10. an uninterrupted language sound

Unit 20 Latin Roots II   pages 126–131

conspiracy	diversion	transpire	advertisement	extrovert
respiration	versatile	diverse	controversy	aspire

💡 **Spelling Strategy** Knowing the Latin roots *ver* ("to turn") and *spir/pir* ("to breathe") can help you spell and understand words with these roots.

Write the words that complete the paragraph.
    A newspaper printed this __(11)__ for a new product: "If you __(12)__ to success in business, let the __(13)__ Do-It-All Computer write your reports, clean your office, take telephone messages, and water your plants. It can handle all your jobs, no matter how __(14)__ they are."

Write the word that matches each definition.
15. an outgoing person
16. the act of breathing
17. a distraction
18. a lengthy disagreement
19. a plan to do something illegal
20. to happen

Unit 21 Noun Suffixes II pages 132–137

politician	comedian	pianist	pharmacist	criticism
perfectionist	guardian	mannerism	pedestrian	individualist

💡 **Spelling Strategy** Remember the meanings of the noun suffixes *-ian* and *-ist* ("one who does or studies") and of the noun suffix *-ism* ("the act, profession, or theory of").

Write the word that names a person associated with each activity.

21. making music
22. refusing to accept mistakes
23. filling prescriptions
24. making people laugh
25. working in government
26. acting independently

Write the word that completes each analogy.

27. routine : regimen :: habit : _____
28. drive : motorist :: walk : _____
29. instruction : teacher :: protection : _____
30. positive : compliment :: negative : _____

Unit 22 Words from Other Languages pages 138–143

spaghetti	accordion	balcony	waltz	tycoon
sauerkraut	kindergarten	graffiti	kimono	finale

💡 **Spelling Strategy** Remember that English has borrowed words from many languages.

Write the word that matches each definition.

31. a powerful business person
32. a Japanese robe
33. long, thin noodles
34. a dish with shredded cabbage
35. a type of dance
36. a porchlike platform on the wall of a building

Write the word that completes each analogy.

37. strum : guitar :: squeeze : _____
38. junior high : high school :: nursery school : _____
39. beginning : introduction :: ending : _____
40. canvas : painting :: wall : _____

Unit 23 Words Often Misspelled II   pages 144–149

mortgage	license	drought	conscientious	miscellaneous
colossal	aerial	succumb	lieutenant	quarantine

 Spelling Strategy   Knowing a word's origin, thinking about the meanings of its parts, and practicing the word can often help you spell the word correctly.

Write the word that is a synonym for each word below.

41. yield
42. various
43. lofty
44. gigantic
45. careful
46. dryness

Write the word that matches each definition.

47. a military officer ranking below a captain
48. legal permission to do or own a specified thing
49. a pledge of property as security for the payment of a debt
50. the isolation of a person with a contagious disease

Challenge Words   Units 19–23   pages 120–149

emphasis	adversary	equestrian	delicatessen	disheveled
emphatic	vertebra	skepticism	hibachi	continuum

Write the word that completes each sentence.

51. The _____ was just big enough to grill four pieces of chicken.
52. The doctor examined my spine for a bruised _____.
53. The _____ events tested the skills of both horse and rider.
54. We stopped at the _____ to buy potato salad and cold cuts.
55. On gray days, the gray ocean seems to form a _____ with the sky.

Write the word that is either a synonym or an antonym for each word below.

56. neat
57. opponent
58. forceful
59. doubt
60. stress

Spelling-Meaning Strategy

The Latin Root *sol*

As you have learned, a soloist is a person who performs alone. The word *solo* means "a performance by a single person." One kind of solo is a soliloquy, a speech a character in a play makes to him- or herself. The words *solo* and *soliloquy* are related in spelling and meaning because both contain the Latin root *sol*, meaning "alone."

Below are more words that contain the root *sol*.

solo
soloist
soliloquy

sole	de**sol**ate	**sol**itude
solitary	de**sol**ation	**sol**itaire

Think

- How does the root *sol* contribute to the meaning of each word? Look up the words in your Spelling Dictionary.

- In Unit 19, you learned that one way to remember how to spell |ə| in a word is to think of a related word in which the vowel is more obvious. How is the *o* in *sol* pronounced in each word above?

Apply and Extend
Complete these activities on a separate piece of paper.

1. Write six sentences. Use one word from the word box above in each sentence.
2. Be careful not to confuse the root *sol* meaning "alone" with the roots *sol* meaning "sun," as in *solar*, and "whole," as in *solid*. Though they are spelled the same, the roots have different meanings because they come from different Latin words. Write *sun* and *whole* at the top of a piece of paper. With a partner, think of words in which *sol* has these meanings. List each word under the appropriate meaning. Then look up the Latin root *sol* in your Spelling-Meaning Index. Add to your list any other related words that you find.

Summing Up
The Latin root *sol* means "alone." Words that contain the same root are often related in spelling and meaning. Knowing some of the words in a family can help you to use and spell the others correctly.

Hank, a city boy visiting cowhand country, was about to ride his horse, Babe, up to the top of a butte and into a different world. What was that world like?

from

"The Slim Butte Ghost"

by Virginia Driving Hawk Sneve

The men and boys moved quickly to saddle and bridle the horses, mounted, and followed the stallion's trail up the butte. Babe stayed in her end place as the single file traversed the slope, but Hank was content to let her follow. He felt as though he were in a dreamworld as the other riders blended into the fog blanketing the butte. At times his head broke through the cloud into blinding sunlight, and he could see only the tips of Babe's ears; the rest of her was in the fog.

Babe stumbled up the steep trail and then walked above the fog onto the sunlit summit. Hank gasped at the vista about him; the flat summit was an enchanted island in a fluffy sea of cloud. He sat, reins slack, open-mouthed, enthralled, until, abruptly, it all changed and the fog dispersed into tattered ribbons and the rough slope of the butte emerged.

"Hey!" Hank was jolted out of his dreamworld by Joe's call.

Think and Discuss

1. What details does the author give to describe what Hank saw?
2. What details tell you that Hank has never seen this view before?
3. In what ways is dispersing fog like "tattered ribbons"? What else could you compare the fog to in order to create a less dreamlike impression?

The Writing Process
Description

When you write a description, you relay your observations to others. Write a description of a person, place, or thing that you find interesting. Use the guidelines, and follow the Writing Process.

Guidelines for Writing a Description

✓ Open with an interesting topic sentence.
✓ Use exact words and imagery to paint a vivid picture of your subject.
✓ Make comparisons by using figurative language such as similes and metaphors.
✓ Organize your details clearly.

1 ▶ Prewriting
- For topic ideas, list people, places, and objects that you can recall clearly and describe in detail. Select a topic that you will enjoy writing about.
- Choose a point of view and decide what impression you want to make. List details that help to create that impression.

2 ▶ Draft
- Start writing. Don't worry now about making mistakes.
- Include details that support your purpose and point of view.

3 ▶ Revise
- Review your description to see where you can create clearer pictures. Add exact words, figurative language, and sensory details.
- If necessary, rearrange your details so that their order is easy to follow.
- Have a writing conference.

4 ▶ Proofread
- Did you spell each word correctly?
- Did you use commas correctly?

5 ▶ Publish
- Copy your description neatly. Add an interesting title.
- Add a drawing or diagram. Share your description.

Composition Words

original
exquisite
tranquil
abundant
vertical
waltz
colossal
realism

Vowel Changes III

Read and Say

Basic

READ the sentences. SAY each bold word.

1. *produce*	Will these trees **produce** apples?
2. *production*	Auto **production** drops during a strike.
3. *consume*	Can a bird **consume** its own weight in food?
4. *consumption*	Driving fast increases gas **consumption**.
5. *reduce*	He is dieting to **reduce** his weight.
6. *reduction*	She worried about a **reduction** in her pay.
7. *retain*	This cream helps skin **retain** its moisture.
8. *retention*	His mental **retention** of facts is amazing!
9. *detain*	Traffic will **detain** us and make us late.
10. *detention*	The police held the thief in **detention**.
11. *introduce*	I want to **introduce** our new student to you.
12. *introduction*	Is the book as good as its **introduction**?
13. *resume*	Can we **resume** our lesson where we left off?
14. *resumption*	We awaited the **resumption** of the game.
15. *induce*	Nothing could **induce** me to jump from a plane.
16. *induction*	I used **induction** to prove my answer.
17. *abstain*	Her dentist told her to **abstain** from sweets.
18. *abstention*	My **abstention** led to the defeat of the bill.
19. *presume*	I **presume** you are hungry after missing lunch.
20. *presumption*	The **presumption** of guilt proved to be wrong.

Spelling Strategy   Knowing how the vowels change in one pair of related words can help you predict changes in other pairs with the same root.

Think and Write   Write the pairs of Basic Words.

Review	23. grateful
21. revise	24. gratitude
22. revision	

Challenge	27. ferocious
25. atrocious	28. ferocity
26. atrocity	

Independent Practice

Vocabulary: Definitions Write the Basic Word that matches each definition. Use your Spelling Dictionary.

1. to assume to be true; take for granted
2. to begin again after a break
3. the act of using up
4. the act of making or manufacturing
5. the act of keeping confined
6. the act of choosing to hold back from something, especially from voting in an election
7. the act of arriving at a general conclusion based on particular facts
8. the act of keeping something
9. the act of beginning again after an interruption
10. the act or process of presenting information or products to the public or of acquainting people with one another
11. the act of decreasing something
12. the act of accepting something as true before the actual truth is known

Vocabulary: Synonyms in Context Write the Basic Word that is a synonym for the underlined word. Use your Spelling Dictionary.

13. fabrics that <u>hold</u> their original shapes
14. <u>present</u> new ideas
15. <u>use</u> goods and services
16. to <u>lower</u> prices
17. <u>refrain</u> from sweets
18. <u>delay</u> the shipment
19. factories that <u>make</u> plastic tableware
20. to <u>conclude</u> from the information

Challenge Words Write the Challenge Word that is an antonym for each word below. Use your Spelling Dictionary.

21. kindness
22. tame
23. wonderful
24. gentleness

Review: Spelling Spree

Word Graph 1–10. Find the Basic and Review Words hidden in this graph. Write the words in the order in which you find them.

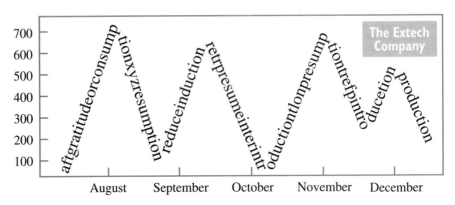

The Extech Company

aftgratitudeorconsumptionxyzresumption reduceinduction retpresumeinterintroductiontlonpresumptiontrefpintroducetion production

700
600
500
400
300
200
100

August   September   October   November   December

Word Combination In each item, add the beginning letters of the first word to the last letters of the second word to form a Basic or Review Word. Write the words.

Example: press + costume   *presume*

11. indicate + truce
12. reserve + plume
13. remember + stain
14. product + lettuce
15. conserve + fume
16. revolve + precision
17. detail + pain
18. abstract + rain
19. defect + attention
20. retire + mention
21. absent + intention
22. redden + auction
23. grasp + hateful
24. rescue + advise

How Are You Doing?

Write each spelling word as a partner reads it aloud. Did you misspell any words?

Proofreading and Writing

Proofread: Spelling and Titles Use quotation marks around the titles of short works. Underline the titles of long works. In both types of titles, capitalize the first, last, and all important words.

SHORT STORY:	"The Outcasts of Poker Flat"
POEM:	"Stopping by Woods on a Snowy Evening"
BOOK:	Of Mice and Men
MOVIE:	The Sound of Music

Find five misspelled Basic or Review Words and two errors in titles in this book review. Write the review correctly.

In the revizion of their book <u>Students and money</u>, Hall and Ryan introduce students to economics. The authors prisume that readers know little about the subject and present information in a simple yet sophisticated way. The chapter called Meeting People's Needs gives a clear introduction to the produktion and consumtion of goods and services. In another chapter, the authors analyze a student's earnings and expenses and provide an example of sound budgeting, for which many students will be gratful.

Write a Personal Budget Make a budget for next week. Note how much money you will earn and how much you will spend. Itemize each expense, including the title and cost of a video rental or of a book you will buy. Then write a plan telling how you can cut your spending. Try to use five spelling words, and remember to write the movie or book title correctly.

Basic

1. produce
2. production
3. consume
4. consumption
5. reduce
6. reduction
7. retain
8. retention
9. detain
10. detention
11. introduce
12. introduction
13. resume
14. resumption
15. induce
16. induction
17. abstain
18. abstention
19. presume
20. presumption

Review

21. revise
22. revision
23. grateful
24. gratitude

Challenge

25. atrocious
26. atrocity
27. ferocious
28. ferocity

Proofreading Marks

¶	Indent
∧	Add
⁁	Add a comma
ⱽⱽ	Add quotation marks
⊙	Add a period
⌐	Delete
≡	Capital letter
/	Small letter
∿	Reverse order

Unit 25
BONUS

Expanding Vocabulary

Spelling Word Link

resume

The Latin Root *sume* The Latin root *sume* means "to take or obtain." The word *resume*, meaning "to take up again," is one of many English words formed from this root.

assume   subsume   consumer   sumptuous

Write a word from the list above to complete each sentence. Use your Spelling Dictionary.

1. The supporters enjoyed a _____ meal at the fundraiser.
2. An interviewer asked the _____ to rate the new cereal.
3. General categories, such as literature, _____ more specific ones, such as poetry.
4. I _____ this report is accurate.

Now complete this crossword puzzle. Write a definition clue for each word in the puzzle. Refer to your Spelling Dictionary again if necessary.

```
 5              6
 C  O  N  S  U  M  E  R
             U
             B        7
             S        A
             U        S
 8                    S
 S  U  M  P  T  U  O  U  S
             E        M
                      E
```

Down

6. _____ ?
_____ ?
7. _____ ?

Across

5. _____ ?
8. _____ ?
_____ ?

Vocabulary Enrichment

Real-World Connection

Social Studies: Economics All the words in the box relate to economics. Look up these words in your Spelling Dictionary. Then write the words to complete this paragraph.

> ### Spelling Word Link
>
> production
>
> income
> gross
> net
> per capita
> scarcity
> surplus
> inflation
> unemployment

NO. 38-5947-65   **SAVINGS PASSBOOK**

Mr. Winter's social studies class learned about economics by studying the summer __(1)__ of the class. Of the twenty students, seven baby-sat and nine mowed lawns. Four did not work, giving the class a 20% rate of __(2)__. The baby sitters earned $5 an hour. Those who mowed lawns averaged __(3)__ earnings of $6 per hour, minus $1 for gasoline, leaving __(4)__ earnings of $5 per hour. In July many students went to camp, causing a __(5)__ of workers. Because lawns still needed tending, the remaining students were able to raise their prices. In August, the return of the campers created a __(6)__, which drove the prices down to what they had been before the July price __(7)__. The __(8)__ summer earnings of the class was $400.

TRY THIS!

Yes or No? Write *yes* if the underlined word is used correctly. Write *no* if it is not.

9. Because of <u>inflation</u>, most products were cheaper.
10. The product's <u>scarcity</u> made it hard to find in stores.
11. After taxes, my <u>net</u> income was alarmingly small.
12. The long drought caused a <u>surplus</u> of corn.

Fact File

A country's gross domestic product (GDP) is the total value of the goods and services it produces in a year. The GDP of the United States has doubled about every 20 years since 1900. Today it is over six trillion dollars.

Latin Roots III

Read and Say

Basic

READ the sentences. SAY each bold word.

1. structure — Is that large **structure** a hotel or a school?
2. complexity — This puzzle has a high level of **complexity**.
3. reconstruct — Can you **reconstruct** the damaged tower?
4. complication — A power failure was yet another **complication**.
5. sensible — It is **sensible** to wear boots in the snow.
6. obstruct — Does this post **obstruct** your view?
7. imply — Your yawns **imply** that I am boring you.
8. pliers — Use a pair of **pliers** to loosen the bolt.
9. sentry — Is a **sentry** standing guard at the gate?
10. sensation — The first car created quite a **sensation**.
11. accomplice — She was always my **accomplice** in mischief.
12. destruction — Hurricanes leave paths of **destruction**.
13. resent — I **resent** that mean remark about my drawing.
14. sentimental — The film's **sentimental** ending made me cry.
15. applicable — School rules are **applicable** to all students.
16. sensor — A **sensor** keeps the room temperature constant.
17. perplex — You **perplex** me by always changing your mind.
18. multiplication — Think of **multiplication** as fast addition.
19. instructor — My driving **instructor** taught me how to park.
20. sensitivity — A **sensitivity** to cat hair makes me sneeze.

Spelling Strategy   Knowing the Latin roots *plic/plex/ply/pli* ("to fold"), *sens/sent* ("to feel"), and *struct* ("to build") can help you spell and understand words with these roots.

Think and Write   Write each Basic Word under its root.

plic/plex/ply/pli	*sens/sent*	*struct*

Review
21. application
22. duplicate
23. architecture
24. column
25. design

Challenge
26. replica
27. consensus
28. explicit
29. implicit
30. pliable

Independent Practice

Vocabulary: Using Context Write the Basic Word that completes each sentence. Use your Spelling Dictionary.

1. The Roman bridge was the oldest _____ in the village.
2. Residents consider the ugly city hall to be an architectural crime, and the mayor to be an _____ of the designer.
3. As experts prepared to set off the explosives, fascinated crowds gathered to watch the _____ of the old building.
4. The bright pink restaurant caused a _____ among passersby.
5. Using the ruins, architects were able to _____ the building.
6. The architects concealed the electronic _____ for the alarm system in the decorative door frame.
7. Critics say the office tower does nothing but _____ the view.
8. New houses often imitate old styles to appeal to buyers' _____ longing for the past.
9. A _____ once guarded the entrance to the palace.
10. The _____ of the museum's design challenged the builders.
11. Did the clients' silence _____ that they were not pleased with the design for their house?
12. A _____ with the wiring will delay the building's completion.
13. Architects must show _____ to the needs of their clients.

Vocabulary: Word Clues Write the Basic Word that fits each clue. Use your Spelling Dictionary.

14. This person teaches you a lesson.
15. You might do this to someone if you are angry or hurt.
16. A confusing message might do this to you.
17. These can help you pull, twist, or break.
18. Your elders may have urged you to be this.
19. This goes with addition, subtraction, and division.
20. Information that is useful in a particular situation is this.

Challenge Words Write the Challenge Word that fits each definition. Use your Spelling Dictionary.

21. easily bent without breaking
22. clearly stated
23. a copy or reproduction of something
24. understood without being directly expressed
25. general agreement

Dictionary

Word Forms Following the part of speech in a dictionary entry are the **inflected forms** of the entry word. Inflected forms usually include the plural forms of nouns, the -ed and -ing forms of verbs, and the -er and -est forms of adjectives. Many dictionaries list inflected forms only if they change the spelling of the entry word.

> **im·ply** |ĭm plī′| *v.* **implied, implying, implies**

At the end of a dictionary entry are **run-ons**, words formed by adding suffixes to the entry word. Run-ons are different parts of speech than the entry word and do not have their own entries.

Practice Write the inflected forms listed in your Spelling Dictionary for each word.

1. atrium _____?_____

2. excel _____?_____

3. stable _____?_____

Write a run-on for each word. Use your Spelling Dictionary.

4. grateful _____?_____

5. sentimental _____?_____

6. duplicate _____?_____

Review: Spelling Spree

Letter Math Add and subtract letters from the words below to make Basic or Review Words. Write the new words.

Example: due – e + p + delicate – de =   *duplicate*

7. col + autumn – aut =
8. simplify – s – if =
9. ply – y + piers – p =
10. read – ad + sent =
11. deal – al + sign =
12. sense – e + nor – n =
13. per + duplex – du =
14. accomplish – sh + ce =
15. seen – e + try =

16. apple – e + i + cable =
17. sends – d + ration – r =
18. com + publication – ub =
19. applied – ed + vacation – va =
20. mobs – m + truck – k + t =
21. sense – e + legible – leg =
22. mul + triplicate – r – e + ion =
23. struck – k + mature – ma =
24. sent + pimento – p – o + al =

Proofreading and Writing

Proofread for Spelling Find seven misspelled Basic or Review Words in this paragraph. Write each word correctly.

1. structure
2. complexity
3. reconstruct
4. complication
5. sensible
6. obstruct
7. imply
8. pliers
9. sentry
10. sensation
11. accomplice
12. destruction
13. resent
14. sentimental
15. applicable
16. sensor
17. perplex
18. multiplication
19. instructor
20. sensitivity

Review

21. application
22. duplicate
23. architecture
24. column
25. design

Challenge

26. replica
27. consensus
28. explicit
29. implicit
30. pliable

Irma stared at her drawing. Her presentation was scheduled for the next day, but her design was still not finished. The project, to reconstruck Town Hall, presented a degree of compleksity Irma had not encountered in thirty years as an instructer at the school of archetecture. She knew she could not simply duplecate the outdated hall, but neither could she justify the complete distruction of a historical structure. Was it possible to meet current needs and show sensativity to the past? Irma hoped her plan would.

Write a Letter to the Editor A historic building in your area will soon be torn down. Unfortunately, it's your favorite building! Write a letter to the editor of your local paper, explaining why you think the building should be saved. Try to use five spelling words.

Proofreading Marks

¶ Indent
∧ Add
⩟ Add a comma
ⱽⱽ Add quotation marks
⊙ Add a period
⌐ Delete
☰ Capital letter
∕ Small letter
∿ Reverse order

Expanding Vocabulary

**Spelling
Word Link**

sensible

Idioms An **idiom** is an expression that has a different meaning from the combined meanings of its individual words.

> The spaceship came **down to earth**.
> Alice is a **down-to-earth** person.

Knowing the meaning of each word helps you understand the first sentence, but not necessarily the second one. The second sentence does not mean that Alice is descending to this planet. In that sentence, *down-to-earth* is an idiom meaning "sensible." An idiom is usually listed in the dictionary under the entry for one of its main words.

Write a word or words that mean the same thing as each underlined idiom. Use your Spelling Dictionary.

1. A good diver, Cleon is, <u>by the same token</u>, a strong swimmer.
2. You should <u>hold your tongue</u> in the principal's office.
3. Keith and Mimi never did <u>see eye to eye</u>.
4. "I will give her a <u>piece of my mind</u>," said Ana.

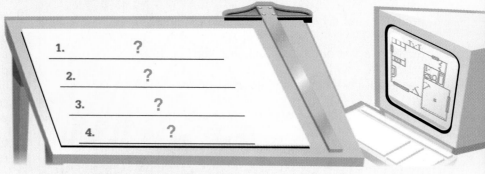

1. _____ ?
2. _____ ?
3. _____ ?
4. _____ ?

Now write your own sentence for each of the four idioms given above.

5. _____ ?
_____ ?
6. _____ ?
_____ ?
7. _____ ?
_____ ?
8. _____ ?
_____ ?

Real-World Connection

Careers: Architecture All the words in the box relate to architecture. Look up these words in your Spelling Dictionary. Then write the words to complete this paragraph.

Spelling Word Link

structure

blueprint
renovate
colonnade
facade
pilaster
atrium
turret
buttress

An architect's task may be to draw a __(1)__ for a new building or __(2)__ an old one. In either case, he or she might draw on features from various styles and periods, such as a supporting __(3)__ from the Gothic period or a towerlike __(4)__ similar to those used on castles in the Middle Ages. To create a __(5)__ for the front of a modern structure that recalls ancient Rome, an architect might use columns in a __(6)__. The __(7)__, or courtyard, as well as the ornamental __(8)__ set into a wall, are also design features that appeared in ancient Rome. These features have been revived in many contemporary buildings.

TRY THIS!

Yes or No? Write *yes* if the underlined word is used correctly. Write *no* if it is not.

9. The prince climbed to the top of the <u>turret</u>.
10. The <u>atrium</u> contained a fountain and a lovely garden.
11. The <u>facade</u> was the interior's most striking feature.
12. Open the window in the <u>colonnade</u>.

Fact File

Gothic architecture was popular in Europe during the Middle Ages. Gothic structures feature pointed arches, supports called flying buttresses, and waterspouts called gargoyles. Gargoyles were sculpted in strange human or animal shapes and were used to drain rain from the roof.

Adjective Suffixes

Read and Say

Basic

READ the sentences. **SAY** each bold word.

1. mountainous — People go to **mountainous** regions to ski.
2. gradual — A **gradual** slope is easy after a steep climb.
3. agile — The deer is an **agile** and graceful animal.
4. cautious — Be alert and **cautious** crossing the road.
5. strenuous — Running three miles is **strenuous** exercise.
6. crucial — Food aid is **crucial** if they are to survive.
7. mobile — Has her wheelchair made her more **mobile**?
8. horizontal — I think of **horizontal** as east to west.
9. disastrous — Were you sick after that **disastrous** meal?
10. tremendous — That **tremendous** bear is taller than the bus!
11. occasional — Our daily visits are now only **occasional**.
12. artificial — Some **artificial** grass looks almost real.
13. fragile — Thin and **fragile** glass breaks easily.
14. precious — Water is rare and **precious** in dry areas.
15. juvenile — He is too old for such a **juvenile** prank.
16. ridiculous — We laughed at her **ridiculous** duck costume.
17. impartial — A judge must be fair and **impartial**.
18. social — We studied the **social** life of wolf packs.
19. hysterical — He was so upset that he became **hysterical**.
20. contagious — Avoid people who have **contagious** illnesses.

Spelling Strategy The suffixes *-al*, *-ile*, and *-ous* ("of; relating to; capable of; characterized by; full of") form adjectives when added to base words or roots. Remember the spelling patterns for these suffixes.

Think and Write Write each Basic Word under its suffix.

-al	-ile	-ous

Review		Challenge	
21. thermal	23. abnormal	26. notorious	28. volatile
22. continuous	24. various	27. simultaneous	29. ambiguous
	25. hostile		30. intellectual

Independent Practice

Vocabulary: Analogies Write the Basic Word that completes each analogy.
Use your Spelling Dictionary.

Example: chilly : freezing :: hilly : _____   *mountainous*

1. school : academic :: party : _____
2. armchair : stationary :: wheelchair : _____
3. school : usual :: vacation : _____
4. thirty : adult :: ten : _____
5. wood : natural :: plastic : _____
6. longitude : vertical :: latitude : _____
7. eager : hesitant :: careless : _____
8. tired : exhausted :: upset : _____
9. heavy : light :: sturdy : _____
10. delightful : enchanting :: absurd : _____
11. cheap : inexpensive :: valuable : _____
12. small : immense :: easy : _____
13. honest : truthful :: fair : _____

Vocabulary: Using Context Write the
Basic Word that completes each sentence.
Use your Spelling Dictionary.

14. A guide led the climbers over the _____ region.
15. The skilled climber was as _____ as a cat as she leaped from the rock face to the ledge below.
16. The leader's enthusiasm upon reaching the peak was _____.
17. Ted hiked the _____ slopes of the foothills before attempting a steeper climb.
18. One _____ peak towered above the rest of the range.
19. Proper equipment is _____ to a safe climb.
20. Climbing in rough weather could have _____ consequences.

Challenge Words Write the Challenge Word that fits each clue. Use your
Spelling Dictionary.

21. When the race is a tie, the runners have this kind of finish.
22. A storm, a volcano, and a person's temper can all be this.
23. This kind of person is well known, but not for good reasons.
24. Being this is all in the mind.
25. This kind of statement is bound to confuse.

Review: Spelling Spree

Invisible Letters Decide which letters should be added to complete each Basic or Review Word. Write the words correctly.

1. f r a _ _ l _
2. t h _ r m _ _
3. m o _ n t _ i _ _ u _
4. h o _ _ i l _
5. i _ p a r _ _ _ l
6. c o _ t i n _ _ _ s
7. m _ b i _ _
8. t r _ m e n _ _ _ s
9. s o _ i _ l
10. g r a _ _ _ l
11. a r t _ f i _ _ _ l
12. c o n t a _ _ _ _ s
13. r _ d i c _ l _ _ s

Puzzle Play Write the Basic or Review Word that fits each clue. Circle the letter that would appear in the box.

Example: easily broken _ _ _ _ ☐ _ _   *frag i̇ le*

14. unusual _ _ _ _ _ ☐ _ _
15. not vertical _ ☐ _ _ _ _ _ _ _ _
16. causing great destruction _ _ _ _ _ _ _ _ _ ☐ _
17. requiring effort _ _ _ _ ☐ _ _ _ _
18. careful _ _ _ ☐ _ _ _ _
19. valuable _ ☐ _ _ _ _ _ _
20. of different kinds _ ☐ _ _ _ _ _
21. childish _ _ _ _ _ ☐ _ _
22. occurring sometimes _ _ _ _ _ _ _ ☐ _ _
23. extremely important _ _ _ _ ☐ _ _
24. able to move easily _ _ _ _ ☐
25. very upset _ _ _ _ _ ☐ _ _ _ _

Now write the circled letters in sequence.
They will spell two mystery words that name a famous mountain.

Mystery Words:

_ _ _ ? _ _   _ _ _ _ _ ? _ _ _

Proofreading and Writing

Proofread: Spelling and Pronoun Case Use a **subject pronoun** as the subject of a sentence or as a predicate pronoun. Use an **object pronoun** as a direct or indirect object. Be careful to use the correct pronoun case, especially in a compound subject or object.

SUBJECT:	**Sam** and **I** planned the climb together.
PREDICATE PRONOUN:	The lead climbers are **Sam** and **I**.
DIRECT OBJECT:	The climbers followed **Sam** and **me**.
INDIRECT OBJECT:	The climb gave **Sam** and **me** confidence.

Find five misspelled Basic or Review Words and two incorrect pronouns in this article from a school newspaper. Write the article correctly.

On Tuesday an open house was held by members of the Albion Climbing Club. Club president Lucy Valdez showed slides of the mountainus regions they have climbed. Then her and the club members demonstrated the strenuous exercises that keep them agile enough to conquer hostil environments. Ms. Valdez also displayed varyous pieces of the equipment crucal to safe climbing. The enthusiasm of the club members proved contagous; many people thanked they and Lucy and asked to join the club.

Write a Story Beginning Has anything unexpected ever happened while you and a friend were climbing, hiking, camping, or skiing? Compose the opening paragraph of a story about your experience. Try to use five spelling words and at least one subject or object pronoun.

Basic

1. mountainous
2. gradual
3. agile
4. cautious
5. strenuous
6. crucial
7. mobile
8. horizontal
9. disastrous
10. tremendous
11. occasional
12. artificial
13. fragile
14. precious
15. juvenile
16. ridiculous
17. impartial
18. social
19. hysterical
20. contagious

Review

21. thermal
22. continuous
23. abnormal
24. various
25. hostile

Challenge

26. notorious
27. simultaneous
28. volatile
29. ambiguous
30. intellectual

Proofreading Marks
¶ Indent
∧ Add
⋏ Add a comma
ⱽⱽ Add quotation marks
⊙ Add a period
˒ Delete
≡ Capital letter
/ Small letter
∩ Reverse order

171

Expanding Vocabulary

Spelling
Word Link

strenuous

Antonyms **Antonyms** are words that are opposite in meaning.

The climb was **effortless** for the guide; for the others it was a **strenuous** task.

Write the word that is the antonym of the underlined word. Use your Thesaurus.

1. juvenile	wise	adult	childish	young
2. gradual	abrupt	smooth	total	long
3. horizontal	straight	diagonal	vertical	flat
4. hysterical	upset	calm	happy	worried

TEST-TAKING TACTICS

Analogies You have already learned about several kinds of relationships that can exist between analogy word pairs. Here are some more types of analogy relationships:

TYPE	EXAMPLE
degree of intensity	rage : anger
time sequence	breakfast : lunch
spatial location	summit : mountain

Analyze the word pairs in the sample analogy test question below. Then write the answers to the questions that follow.

ENGAGEMENT : MARRIAGE ::

(A) canopy : rain forest
(B) inferno : fire
(C) calamity : mishap
(D) beacon : lighthouse
(E) examination : diagnosis

5. What kind of relationship exists between the word pairs in answer choices A and D?
6. What kind of relationship exists between the word pairs in answer choices B and C?
7. What kind of relationship exists between the stem words?
8. Which answer choice correctly completes the analogy? Write its letter.

Real-World Connection

Recreation: Mountain Climbing All the words in the box relate to mountain climbing. Look up these words in your Spelling Dictionary. Then write the words to complete this paragraph.

Spelling Word Link

mountainous

scale
rappel
summit
crevice
avalanche
piton
crampons
hypothermia

To those who are not mountain climbers, the desire to __(1)__ a mountain may be difficult to comprehend. The hardship is extreme, and the dangers are many. At high altitudes, mountains are typically covered with ice and snow. That means climbers must use ice axes and strap __(2)__, or spikes, to their boots. Often the only foothold is a narrow __(3)__ in an otherwise smooth surface. Sometimes the only way to descend safely is to __(4)__ down, depending for survival on a rope attached to a __(5)__, which is hammered into the rock. Climbers also face the danger of being buried by an __(6)__ or of losing body temperature and suffering from __(7)__. To serious climbers, reaching the __(8)__ makes the hardship worthwhile.

TRY THIS!

True or False? Write *T* if a sentence is true and *F* if it is false.

9. Hypothermia is caused by heat at a mountain's peak.
10. Crampons give hiking boots a better grip on ice.
11. One way to climb a mountain is to rappel.
12. An avalanche is a welcome climbing companion.

Fact File

At 29,028 feet, Mount Everest is the world's highest mountain. It towers over Tibet and Nepal as part of the Himalaya range. In 1953 Edmund Hillary of New Zealand and Tenzing Norgay of Nepal became the first to reach Everest's summit.

Words from Places

Read and Say

READ the sentences. SAY each bold word.

1. denim   Most jeans are made of blue **denim**.
2. jersey   Each player wears a **jersey** with a number.
3. satin   The bride wore a white dress of shiny **satin**.
4. suede   I prefer soft **suede** over other leathers.
5. cashmere   Is **cashmere** the finest and warmest wool?
6. gauze   A **gauze** bandage lets in air but not dirt.
7. calico   Many settlers wore clothes made of **calico**.
8. turquoise   The stone in my ring is a greenish **turquoise**.
9. dungarees   Wear sturdy **dungarees** to clean the barn.
10. italics   The book title was printed in **italics**.
11. tuxedo   My brother wore a black **tuxedo** to the prom.
12. muslin   Curtains are often made of printed **muslin**.
13. rhinestone   Is that gem a diamond or just a **rhinestone**?
14. magenta   The red sky ranged from pink to deep **magenta**.
15. damask   Our **damask** drapes have a woven leaf pattern.
16. duffel   Pack the gear in a strong **duffel** bag.
17. limousine   The bride and groom left in a **limousine**.
18. spa   Did you take a mud bath at the health **spa**?
19. Rugby   Football resembles **Rugby** in some ways.
20. geyser   Steam and water sprayed from the **geyser**.

Spelling Strategy   Knowing the origin of words that come from the names of places can help you spell and understand the meanings of the words.

Think and Write   Write the Basic Words.

Review
21. cologne
22. seltzer
23. Cheddar
24. mayonnaise
25. badminton

Challenge
26. jodhpurs
27. laconic
28. serendipity
29. frieze
30. sardonic

Independent Practice

Vocabulary: Definitions Write the Basic Word that matches each definition.
Use your Spelling Dictionary.

1. a cotton cloth of plain weave used for sheets or curtains
2. a coarse, heavy cloth used for work clothes and sport clothes
3. a wool yarn or cloth made from the soft coat of a Himalayan goat
4. cloth that is thin enough to see through
5. a soft, elastic, knitted fabric usually made of wool or cotton
6. a rich, glossy fabric woven to produce patterns on both sides
7. a coarse cotton cloth printed with bright designs
8. a smooth fabric, often of silk, woven with a glossy finish on one side
9. a coarse woolen cloth with a fuzzy surface on both sides
10. leather with a soft, fuzzy surface
11. a resort area having mineral springs
12. a colorless artificial gem that looks like a diamond but is made of glass
13. a printing type with letters slanted to the right

Vocabulary: Analogies Write the Basic Word that completes each analogy.
Use your Spelling Dictionary.

Example: real : diamond :: imitation : _____   *rhinestone*

14. red : ruby :: aqua : _____
15. dress : gown :: suit : _____
16. jacket : blazer :: pants : _____
17. United States : football :: England : _____
18. red : scarlet :: purple : _____
19. pilot : jet :: chauffeur : _____
20. puddle : pond :: fountain : _____

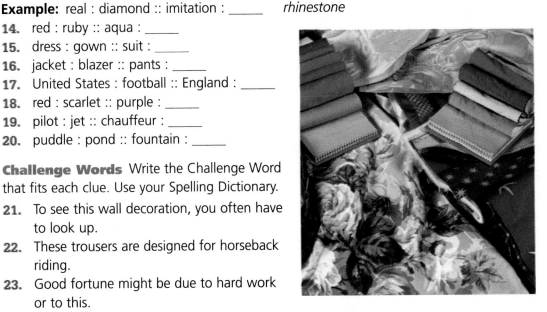

Challenge Words Write the Challenge Word
that fits each clue. Use your Spelling Dictionary.

21. To see this wall decoration, you often have to look up.
22. These trousers are designed for horseback riding.
23. Good fortune might be due to hard work or to this.
24. This kind of person answers questions with a simple *yes* or *no*.
25. This kind of person scoffs, scorns, or mocks.

Review: Spelling Spree

Code Breaker The Basic and Review Words below are written in code. Use the following code key to figure out each word. Write the decoded words correctly.

CODE:	j	k	l	m	n	o	p	q	r	s	t	u	v	w	x	y	z	a	b	c	d	e	f	g	h	i
LETTER:	a	b	c	d	e	f	g	h	i	j	k	l	m	n	o	p	q	r	s	t	u	v	w	x	y	z

1. lxuxpwn
2. cdazdxrbn
3. lqnmmja
4. bdnmn
5. cdgnmx
6. mdwpjannb
7. pjdin
8. vdburw
9. urvxdbrwn
10. byj

11. vjpnwcj
12. bnucina
13. vjhxwwjrbn
14. rcjurlb
15. mdoonu
16. snabnh
17. mnwrv
18. bjcrw
19. pnhbna

Rebuses Write the Basic or Review Word that matches each rebus puzzle.

20. ca +  + o

21.  +

22. r +  + n +

23.  +

24. b +  + min +

25.  + m +

√ **How Are You Doing?**
List the spelling words that are difficult for you. Practice them with a partner.

Proofreading and Writing

Proofread: Spelling and Agreement with Indefinite Pronouns An **indefinite** pronoun refers to a person or thing that is not identified. When an indefinite pronoun is the subject of a sentence, the verb must agree with it.

SINGULAR: **Somebody is** in charge of the fabric samples.
PLURAL: **Many are** working in the knitwear division.

An **antecedent** usually goes before a pronoun and names the person or thing to which the pronoun refers. If an indefinite pronoun is the antecedent of a personal pronoun, the personal pronoun must agree with it.

SINGULAR: **Each** of the workers cleaned **his** sewing machine.
PLURAL: **All** of the store owners ordered **their** fabrics.

Find six misspelled Basic or Review Words and two mistakes in agreement with indefinite pronouns in this label. Write the label correctly.

CONTENTS: All of the designers in Design Group make her garments from 100% cotton. Each of the garments are prewashed.

CARE INSTRUCTIONS: Machine wash jersie and dennim in warm or cold water, regular cycle. Tumble dry low. For stubborn stains such as grass, mayonaise, or berry juice, presoak in seltser water. Wash bright colors, such as turqoise or majenta, separately.

Write a Description
Think of a piece of clothing you love to wear. What fabric is it made of? What do you like about the fabric? Write a description of it. Try to use five spelling words. Also, try to use at least one indefinite pronoun as the subject of a sentence or as the antecedent of a personal pronoun.

Basic
1. denim
2. jersey
3. satin
4. suede
5. cashmere
6. gauze
7. calico
8. turquoise
9. dungarees
10. italics
11. tuxedo
12. muslin
13. rhinestone
14. magenta
15. damask
16. duffel
17. limousine
18. spa
19. Rugby
20. geyser

Review
21. cologne
22. seltzer
23. Cheddar
24. mayonnaise
25. badminton

Challenge
26. jodhpurs
27. laconic
28. serendipity
29. frieze
30. sardonic

Proofreading Marks
¶	Indent
∧	Add
⩓	Add a comma
⩔ ⩔	Add quotation marks
⊙	Add a period
⤴	Delete
≡	Capital letter
/	Small letter
∾	Reverse order

Expanding Vocabulary

Spelling
Word Link

denim

Regional Differences Do you wear dungarees, blue jeans, or denims? Although all of the words refer to the same thing, some may be more common than others where you live. The form of a language spoken in a particular region is called a **dialect**.

From each list, write the word or words commonly used where you live.

1. sofa, davenport, couch
2. grinder, submarine, hero
3. stoop, veranda, porch
4. expressway, freeway, highway

1. _____ ? _____
2. _____ ? _____
3. _____ ? _____
4. _____ ? _____

TEST-TAKING TACTICS

Sentence Completion Sometimes a sentence completion test question will contain two blanks in the given sentence. You can approach a question like this one in three steps.

Step One: Read the entire sentence.

Step Two: Try the first word in each answer choice in the first blank of the sentence. If the word doesn't make sense, eliminate that answer choice.

Step Three: Test both words of the remaining answer choices in the blanks. Only one answer choice will contain a pair of words that *both* make sense in the sentence.

Study this sample sentence completion question.

The straight, fine wool _____ by the alpaca, a grazing animal related to the llama, is sought after by many _____ of woolen textiles.

(A) trampled...collectors (B) produced...manufacturers
(C) sheared...lovers (D) shed...growers (E) cultivated...tailors

5. Which answer choices can you eliminate because the first word in the answer choice pair does not make sense in the sentence? Write the letters of the eliminated answer choices.

6. Which of the remaining answer choices contains a pair of words that *both* make sense in the sentence? Write its letter.

Real-World Connection

Home Economics: Textiles All the words in the box relate to textiles. Look up these words in your Spelling Dictionary. Then write the words to complete this paragraph.

Spelling Word Link

satin

textile
polyester
acrylic
corduroy
flax
cellulose
dyeing
apparel

The fabrics used to make our shirts, dresses, coats, and other __(1)__ are produced in __(2)__ mills. The production of the fabrics begins with the processing of material fibers. These include natural fibers, such as linen, which comes from __(3)__ ; manufactured fibers, which are made from the __(4)__ in wood pulp; and synthetic fibers made from chemicals. The last group includes __(5)__ , a wrinkle-resistant fiber used in permanent-press items, and __(6)__ , a bulky but lightweight fiber used in blankets and sweaters. Fibers are made into yarn or thread that is woven or knitted into fabric. Cotton yarn, for example, can be woven into a smooth, flat fabric or a ribbed fabric such as __(7)__ . The last step in the process is __(8)__ the uncolored cloth.

TRY THIS!

True or False? Write *T* if the sentence is true and *F* if it is false.

9. Flax comes from a tree.
10. Polyester is a synthetic fiber.
11. Cellulose is a knitting method.
12. Acrylic is a natural fiber.

Fact File

A silkworm spins a cocoon of one long silk thread. Silk workers unwind the thread and spin it onto reels. Then it is woven into fabric. Though the individual threads are delicate, woven silk is one of the strongest of all fabrics.

Single or Double Consonants

Read and Say

Basic

READ the sentences. SAY each bold word.

1. personnel — The **personnel** on my staff are well trained.
2. applicant — She will interview each job **applicant**.
3. referral — A **referral** can help you get a job.
4. occupation — Have you always worked in this **occupation**?
5. recommend — I **recommend** that you avoid that dumb movie.
6. occurrence — Snow is a rare **occurrence** in warm areas.
7. committee — We formed a **committee** to solve the problem.
8. essential — Exercise is **essential** to good health.
9. broccoli — Her favorite green vegetable is **broccoli**.
10. summary — Does your **summary** include the main ideas?
11. tariff — They had to pay a **tariff** on imported tea.
12. trespass — Is it unlawful to **trespass** on private land?
13. possession — He took **possession** of the ball and scored.
14. opossum — The **opossum** hung by its tail from a limb.
15. accommodate — Can this small room **accommodate** a piano?
16. embarrass — I **embarrass** my brother when I hug him.
17. paraffin — Dip each candle into the melted **paraffin**.
18. affectionate — An **affectionate** puppy will lick you.
19. shrubbery — We planted trees and **shrubbery** in the yard.
20. harass — Fans began to mob and **harass** the actor.

Spelling Strategy   Remember that double consonants can occur when a prefix is absorbed or before a suffix beginning with a vowel. Double consonants in other words must be remembered.

Think and Write   Write the Basic Words.

Review
21. bulletin
22. cancellation
23. possibility
24. necessary
25. challenge

Challenge
26. succinct
27. renaissance
28. irrevocable
29. collateral
30. reconnaissance

Independent Practice

Vocabulary: Word Clues Write the Basic Word that fits each clue. Use your Spelling Dictionary.

1. This can be anything that takes place.
2. You might show fondness with this kind of behavior.
3. This duty is a tax, not a task.
4. If you do this to a person, he or she might turn red.
5. If you planted a group of low bushes, you would have this.
6. This is to bother again and again.
7. If something is necessary, it is this.
8. You do this when you walk on someone's property without permission.
9. This wraps things up, but it is not paper, string, or tape.
10. Candles, wax paper, and oil are made of this.
11. This animal has a pouch and lives in a tree.
12. A piece of this green vegetable is shaped like a tree.

Vocabulary: Using Context Write the Basic Word that completes each sentence. Use your Spelling Dictionary.

13. The interviewer felt that only one job _____ was qualified.
14. Seymour could offer a wide range of job experience, having switched from one _____ to another.
15. When the missing files were found in Nick's _____, he was fired.
16. Ruth served on a _____ to review company policies.
17. Ms. Velázquez explained that it was impossible to _____ each employee's request for a private office.
18. Sean learned about the Intex Corporation when he was given a _____ by the employment agency.
19. Many experts _____ that supervisors meet with employees at least twice a year to discuss their performance.
20. The ad says to contact Erica Sandler in the _____ department.

Challenge Words Write the Challenge Word that matches each definition. Use your Spelling Dictionary.

21. an inspection or exploration of an area
22. something pledged as security for a loan
23. brief and clear
24. a rebirth or revival
25. not able to be reversed

Dictionary

Usage Notes If you use the word *committee* as the subject of a sentence, should you use a singular or plural verb? The answer can be found in the usage note for that word. **Usage notes** follow the dictionary entries for certain words that might be confusing and explain how those words should be used.

> *Usage:* **Committee.** *Committee* takes a singular verb when it refers to the committee as a whole and a plural verb when it refers to the members of the committee as separate persons: *The committee votes every third Wednesday. The committee vote as they see fit.*

Practice Write *yes* if the underlined word is used correctly. Write *no* if it is not. Use your Spelling Dictionary.

1. Six personnel were present.
2. Mint sauce is a good complement to lamb.
3. Kai wanted to immigrate to the United States.
4. The continuous roaring of the waterfall made Don sleepy.

Review: Spelling Spree

Syllable Scramble Rearrange the syllables in each item to form a Basic or Review Word. Write the words correctly.

5. pos o sum
6. ber y shrub
7. lenge chal
8. rass bar em
9. pass tres
10. tion can la cel
11. pli cant ap
12. i bil pos ty si
13. rence oc cur
14. li co broc
15. sar nec y es
16. par fin af
17. iff tar
18. rass ha
19. com ac date mo

20. ses pos sion
21. ate fec tion af
22. bul tin le

Proofreading and Writing

Proofread for Spelling Find seven misspelled Basic or Review Words in this applicant evaluation form. Write each word correctly.

Applicant Evaluation Form

1. Does the person possess the esential skills for the job?

_____

2. What was the person's previous ocupation? _____

3. Did the person receive a refferal to the company? _____

4. Will it be necessary to enroll the person in a training

   program? _____

5. Do you reccommend that the person be hired? On the

   back of this form, give a brief summery of your reasons.

   PLEASE SIGN AND RETURN

   TO THE PERSONELL COMITEE.

Proofreading Marks
¶ Indent
∧ Add
⩘ Add a comma
`❝❞` Add quotation marks
⊙ Add a period
⟋ Delete
≡ Capital letter
╱ Small letter
∽ Reverse order

Write a Thank-You Letter Write a thank-you letter to someone who recently interviewed you for a summer or part-time job. Thank the person for the interview and restate your interest in the position. Try to use five spelling words.

Expanding Vocabulary

Spelling Word Link

personnel
broccoli

Context Clues If you encounter an unfamiliar word in a list, the other words in the list might provide clues to its meaning. The words in a list can also help you figure out the general meaning of a word that summarizes the list. Suppose you did not know the words *personnel* and *broccoli*. The lists in the sentences below would provide context clues.

The personnel included **designers, artists,** and a **secretary**.

Vegfro packages frozen **peas, carrots,** and broccoli.

Use context clues to figure out the general meaning of each underlined word. Write your answers.

1. One job applicant speaks French, Latin, and <u>Latvian</u>.
2. <u>Perquisites</u> for company executives include a car, an athletic club membership, and travel expenses.
3. The company encourages employees to attend classes, workshops, and <u>seminars</u>.
4. Rick received <u>remuneration</u> in the form of a salary, overtime pay, and a yearly bonus.

1. ?
2. ?
3. ?
4. ?

Now write one sentence that uses the word *trespass* and a second sentence that uses the word *opossum*. Each sentence should include a list that gives context clues to the meaning of *trespass* or *opossum*.

5. ?
?
6. ?
?

Real-World Connection

Business: Personnel Management All the words in the box relate to personnel management. Look up these words in your Spelling Dictionary. Then write the words to complete this paragraph.

Many companies hire specialists to manage personnel effectively. These personnel managers oversee hiring practices to protect job applicants from __(1)__ . They take new employees through an __(2)__ session to inform them of the firm's procedures and benefits. They administer plans for health and life __(3)__ and develop __(4)__ programs to encourage workers to work productively. On occasion, they may circulate a __(5)__ telling employees of new company policies or developments. An employee with a work-related complaint may discuss the __(6)__ with a personnel manager, who will keep the matter strictly __(7)__ . If someone is fired, the personnel manager makes sure that the __(8)__ is fair and legal.

Spelling Word Link

personnel

orientation
dismissal
memorandum
discrimination
insurance
incentive
grievance
confidential

TRY THIS!

Yes or No? Write *yes* or *no* to answer each question.

9. Is an orientation given to someone who is fired?
10. Could a bonus be an incentive for a salesperson?
11. Is a dismissal given as a reward for good work?
12. Is confidential information open to the public?

Fact File

Recruiting, also known as headhunting, matches people to jobs. Headhunters often lure workers from one company and place them in another. Headhunters are paid by either the new employer or the new employee.

30 Review: Units 25–29

Unit 25 Vowel Changes III
pages 156–161

consume	reduce	detain	induce	presume
consumption	reduction	detention	induction	presumption

Spelling Strategy Knowing how the vowels change in one pair of related words can help you predict changes in other pairs with the same root.

Write the word that is a synonym for each word below.

1. confinement
2. diminish
3. eat
4. belief
5. conclusion
6. persuade

Write the word that completes each analogy.

7. cooking : preparation :: eating : _____
8. bigger : enlargement :: smaller : _____
9. want : desire :: suppose : _____
10. free : release :: hold : _____

Unit 26 Latin Roots III
pages 162–167

structure	complication	obstruct	pliers	sensible
accomplice	sentimental	instructor	perplex	sensitivity

Spelling Strategy Knowing the Latin roots *plic/plex/ply/pli* ("to fold"), *sens/sent* ("to feel"), and *struct* ("to build") can help you spell and understand words with these roots.

Write the word that belongs in each group.

11. reasonable, rational, _____
12. confuse, puzzle, _____
13. partner, helper, _____
14. teacher, trainer, _____
15. hammer, wrench, _____
16. block, hinder, _____

Write the word that matches each definition.

17. something that increases confusion or difficulty
18. influenced by emotions
19. something that is built, such as a bridge or a building
20. the quality of being responsive to the feelings of others

Unit 27 Adjective Suffixes

pages 168–173

agile	strenuous	crucial	horizontal	disastrous
juvenile	contagious	impartial	ridiculous	occasional

Spelling Strategy The suffixes *-al*, *-ile*, and *-ous* ("of; relating to; capable of; characterized by; full of") form adjectives when added to base words or roots. Remember the spelling patterns for these suffixes.

Write the word that is an antonym for each word below.
21. easy   22. adult   23. unimportant   24. unfair   25. vertical

Write the word that fits each clue.
26. Someone who is quick and graceful is this.
27. This kind of event happens from time to time.
28. This type of behavior is really silly.
29. The effects of a flood or fire can be this.
30. Measles or chicken pox are this type of disease.

Unit 28 Words from Places

pages 174–179

suede	cashmere	calico	turquoise	italics
duffel	rhinestone	geyser	limousine	magenta

Spelling Strategy Knowing the origin of words that come from the names of places can help you spell and understand the meanings of the words.

Write the word that fits each clue.
31. This makes a cotton dress.   34. This makes soft shoes.
32. This sprays steam.   35. This makes a sturdy bag.
33. These letters show emphasis.   36. This makes a soft sweater.

Write the words that complete the paragraph.
The long __(37)__ glided to a stop in front of the hotel. Out stepped a famous movie actor. She wore an outfit in a brilliant shade of __(38)__ that matched her lipstick. Her sunglasses were the __(39)__ color of the tropical sea, and on each finger she displayed an enormous, glittering __(40)__ ring.

Unit 29 Single or Double Consonants pages 180–185

personnel	recommend	occurrence	broccoli	summary
affectionate	embarrass	accommodate	trespass	opossum

 Spelling Strategy Remember that double consonants can occur when a prefix is absorbed or before a suffix beginning with a vowel. Double consonants in other words must be remembered.

Write the word that can replace the underlined words.

41. The dog will scare anyone who might <u>enter without permission</u>.
42. Here is a <u>condensed version</u> of the report.
43. We can <u>make room for</u> another person in our car pool.
44. On my hike I saw an <u>animal that carries its young in a pouch</u>.

Write the word that belongs in each group.

45. tender, loving, _____
46. incident, happening, _____
47. employees, staff, _____
48. advise, suggest, _____
49. shame, humiliate, _____
50. spinach, green beans, _____

Challenge Words Units 25–29 pages 156–185

atrocious	simultaneous	renaissance	explicit	consensus
atrocity	serendipity	irrevocable	jodhpurs	volatile

Write the words that complete the paragraph.

In the kingdom of Klodd, an __(51)__ crime had been committed. Someone had stolen the king's favorite pair of __(52)__ . The king, who had a __(53)__ temper, was enraged by the __(54)__ . He feared his loss was __(55)__ . Still, he offered a reward, giving __(56)__ instructions to a servant about the wording of the reward notice.

Write the word that matches each definition.

57. the accidental or unexpected discovery of something good
58. a rebirth or revival
59. a general agreement
60. happening at the same time

Spelling-Meaning Strategy

The Latin Root *duc*

In Unit 25, you studied several pairs of words containing the Latin root *duc*. Because *duc* means "to lead or bring," all of the words containing the root have something to do with leading or bringing. To produce something is to bring it into existence. To induce is to lead or influence someone into doing something. The word *reduce* originally meant "to bring back or down" and later came to mean "to decrease." *Introduce* was first used to mean "to bring into notice or knowledge" and now has the additional meaning "to bring into personal acquaintance."

The words below also contain the root *duc*.

pro**duc**e
in**duc**e
re**duc**e
intro**duc**e

duct	de**duct**ion	con**duc**ive
ab**duct**	e**duc**ate	aque**duct**

Think

- How does the root *duc* contribute to the meaning of each word? Look up the words in your Spelling Dictionary.
- How is the *u* in *duc* pronounced in each word above?
- What other spelling for *duc* occurs in the words above?

Apply and Extend
Complete these activities on a separate piece of paper.

1. Write six sentences. Use one word from the word box above in each sentence.
2. Can you think of other words that belong to the same family as *produce*, *induce*, *reduce*, and *introduce*? With a partner, make a list of related words. Then look up the Latin root *duc* in your Spelling-Meaning Index. Add to your list any other related words that you find.

Summing Up
The Latin root *duc* means "to lead or bring." Words that contain the same root are often related in spelling and meaning. Knowing some of the words in a family can help you to use and spell the others correctly.

Literature and Writing

In 1965 Luis
Valdez founded
a California
theater group
for campesinos,
farmworkers of
Mexican origin.
Within two
years, the group
was performing
nationally to
great acclaim.

Persuasive Letter

After reading "El Teatro Campesino: From Thin Air to Theatrics"
by Stephen Tracy with Maria Guerrero, one student wrote this
letter to Luis Valdez. If you were Valdez, how would you react?

Dear Mr. Valdez:

I read about your theater group in "El Teatro Campesino:
From Thin Air to Theatrics," by Stephen Tracy with Maria
Guerrero. I think that I could be valuable to you as a
summer apprentice.

I am a high school junior in Chino, California. Although
I am young, I am hard working, creative, and enthusiastic,
as the enclosed letters from teachers and a local theater
director show.

Since third grade, I have been active in school plays and
in the Chino Youth Theater. I act, sing, and dance and also
work on scenery and costumes, as all of your members do. I
have enclosed a résumé showing my experience.

I have a special interest in your group because my
grandparents, like your parents, were *campesinos*. All my
life I have heard their stories and songs. I am fluent in both
English and Spanish, so your bilingual performances would
not be a problem for me.

While your workshops would provide me with the best
training I can imagine, I believe that my experience,
background, and enthusiasm would also provide you with a
useful new member.

Sincerely,

Ana Ruiz

Think and Discuss

1. If you were Luis Valdez, would you hire the writer? Why
   or why not?
2. What opinion does Ana express?
3. What reasons does she give to support her opinion?

The Writing Process

Persuasive Letter

Would you like to convince someone to do something? Write a persuasive business letter to that person. Use the Guidelines for Persuading, and follow the Writing Process.

1 Prewriting

- List some things you would like to persuade someone to do. For each topic, note your audience, opinion, reasons and examples, and possible objections or consequences.
- Choose a topic and expand your notes on it.

2 Draft

- Begin to write, using proper letter form. Correct errors later.
- State your opinion in a topic sentence; support it with reasons and factual examples.
- Use a persuasive strategy: offer a precedent, appeal to your reader's sense of fairness, answer possible objections, or explore your argument's consequences.
- End with a strong summary statement.

3 Revise

- If necessary, restate your opinion more clearly.
- Add reasons and examples. Arrange them in order of importance.
- Have a writing conference. Is your persuasive argument successful?

4 Proofread

- Did you spell each word correctly?
- Did you use pronouns correctly?

5 Publish

- Copy your letter neatly.
- Share your letter. Have a classmate write a response.

Guidelines for Persuading

✓ Clearly state your goal and opinion in a topic sentence.
✓ Provide strong reasons and factual examples to support your argument. Answer objections.
✓ Encourage an action in your conclusion.

Composition Words

introduce
impartial
applicant
recommend
sensible
crucial
essential
summary

Vowel Changes IV

Read and Say

READ the sentences. SAY each bold word.

1. proclaim — I **proclaim** this date a holiday forever!
2. proclamation — The mayor stood to make his **proclamation**.
3. deceive — Do not **deceive** me again by lying.
4. deception — A spy is an expert at **deception**.
5. acclaim — We all cheered to **acclaim** the winners.
6. acclamation — Her design won awards and **acclamation**.
7. pertain — To what does this vague note **pertain**?
8. pertinent — The judge weighed all the **pertinent** facts.
9. maintain — I **maintain** their yard when they are away.
10. maintenance — Good **maintenance** helps tools last longer.
11. exclaim — I heard him **exclaim** in terror at the sight.
12. exclamation — Her loud **exclamation** told me she was hurt.
13. perceive — I could barely **perceive** the faint tapping.
14. perception — Give your **perception** of the poem's meaning.
15. conceive — We must **conceive** a plan to stop him!
16. conception — Here is my **conception** of what we should do.
17. prevail — Will the hero **prevail** over the villain?
18. prevalent — This disease is **prevalent** in poor countries.
19. sustain — How much weight can the bridge **sustain**?
20. sustenance — The animals will starve without **sustenance**.

Spelling Strategy   Knowing how the vowels change in one pair of related words can help you predict changes in other pairs with the same root.

Think and Write   Write the pairs of Basic Words.

Review
21. precise
22. precision
23. humane
24. humanity

Challenge
25. pronounce
26. pronunciation
27. denounce
28. denunciation

Independent Practice

Vocabulary: Replacing Words Write the Basic Word that means the same as the underlined word or words. Use your Spelling Dictionary.

1. If you read and listen critically, you may <u>become aware</u> that many political speeches are based on propaganda.
2. The debate changed Ron's <u>understanding</u> of the issues.
3. The mayor will <u>officially announce</u> that May is Workers' Month.
4. Maria couldn't help but <u>cry out</u> in anger at the advertisement's false promises.
5. "Truth will <u>triumph</u> over falsehood," the poet wrote.
6. Many ads purposely <u>mislead</u> people by twisting the facts.
7. Senator Rourke will <u>suffer</u> a defeat if she loses the debate.
8. Critics were quick to <u>praise</u> the book *Persuasive Power*.
9. Include only ideas that directly <u>relate</u> to the issue.
10. The mayor's inability to <u>keep up the condition of</u> the streets became a campaign issue.
11. The leader met with <u>enthusiastic praise</u> when she spoke.
12. Many were surprised to find propaganda so <u>widespread</u>.

Vocabulary: Definitions Write the Basic Word that matches each definition. Use your Spelling Dictionary.

13. an abrupt, sudden utterance
14. the act of keeping in good condition
15. to grasp or understand an idea
16. an official, public announcement
17. the process of becoming aware, especially through the senses
18. related to a specific matter
19. something that supports life or health
20. the act of tricking someone

Challenge Words Write the Challenge Word that completes each sentence. Use your Spelling Dictionary.

21. Senator Lai's disapproving speech contained a strong _____ of the press.
22. The speaker gave an incorrect _____ of the general's name.
23. Sign this petition to _____ the unfair bill.
24. The bumper stickers saying "Reuth rhymes with truth" helped voters to remember as well as to _____ the candidate's name.

Review: Spelling Spree

Word Combination In each item, add the beginning letters of the first word to the last letters of the second word to form a Basic or Review Word. Write the words.

Example: percent + active   *perceive*
1. person + fountain
2. humid + insanity
3. detect + receive
4. suspect + mountain
5. prepare + decision
6. precede + equivalent
7. account + declaim
8. mainland + retain
9. detail + reception
10. perhaps + exception
11. preheat + concise
12. expert + reclaim
13. perfect + continent
14. humor + insane
15. press + avail

> **How Are You Doing?**
> Write each spelling word in a sentence. Practice any misspelled spelling words with a partner.

Puzzle Play Write the Basic Word that fits each clue. Circle the letter that would be boxed.

Example: to mislead _ _ _ _ □ _ _   *dece(i)ve*
16. preservation _ _ _ _ _ _ _ _ _ _ □ _
17. an announcement _ _ □ _ _ _ _ _ _ _ _ _ _
18. an idea _ _ □ _ _ _ _ _ _ _
19. to form in the mind _ _ _ _ _ _ _ □ _
20. to declare _ _ _ _ _ _ □ _
21. praise _ _ _ _ _ _ _ _ _ _ _ □
22. an outcry _ _ □ _ _ _ _ _ _ _ _
23. to understand _ _ _ _ _ _ _ □
24 the act of keeping alive □ _ _ _ _ _ _ _ _ _ _

Now write the circled letters in sequence. They will spell a mystery word that tells what propaganda sometimes does.

Mystery Word: _ _ _ _ ? _ _ _ _

Proofreading and Writing

Proofread: Spelling and Commas with Participial Phrases
Use a comma after a **participial phrase** that introduces a sentence.

Grinning at the crowd, the victorious candidate waved.

Use commas to set off a participial phrase following the subject if the phrase is not necessary to the meaning of the sentence.

NECESSARY: We saw the president **casting his vote**
NOT NECESSARY: Lee Ames, **stunned by her loss,** left the hall.

Find five misspelled Basic or Review Words and two incorrectly punctuated participial phrases in this excerpt from a campaign speech. Write the excerpt correctly.

I cannot concieve of a greater honor than to be your president. Under my leadership, class spirit will prevale at Kittle Junior High. Judging from her lack of interest in class events my opponent cannot mantain that claim. Sherri Garth may proclame herself to be a leader, but that is not my perception. To be presise, I care more about the issues, raised by this class, than Sherri does.

JR. HIGH

Write an Opinion   You have just heard a campaign speech. What did you think of it? Is that candidate the right person for the job? Write your opinion of the speech and of the person running for office. Try to use five spelling words and at least one participial phrase.

Basic
1. proclaim
2. proclamation
3. deceive
4. deception
5. acclaim
6. acclamation
7. pertain
8. pertinent
9. maintain
10. maintenance
11. exclaim
12. exclamation
13. perceive
14. perception
15. conceive
16. conception
17. prevail
18. prevalent
19. sustain
20. sustenance

Review
21. precise
22. precision
23. humane
24. humanity

Challenge
25. pronounce
26. pronunciation
27. denounce
28. denunciation

Proofreading Marks
¶ Indent
∧ Add
⩘ Add a comma
ᕯ ᕯ Add quotation marks
⊙ Add a period
ℐ Delete
≡ Capital letter
／ Small letter
∩ Reverse order

Expanding Vocabulary

The Latin Root *ceive/cept* *Deceive* and *deception* come from the Latin root *ceive* (or *cept*), meaning "to take." Other English words that share this root are related in meaning.

except   intercept   receive   susceptible

Write a word from the list above to complete each sentence. Use your Spelling Dictionary.

Spelling Word Link

deceive
deception

1. You will _____ the gift you ordered in next week's mail.
2. Andy is so _____ to ads that he will buy almost anything.
3. I tried to _____ the telegram by stopping the messenger.
4. Yoko is a good speaker _____ when she is nervous.

Now look up these words in your Spelling Dictionary: *receptive*, *acceptance*, *misconception*, and *perceptible*. Write the word that completes each speech balloon below.

One tiny taste of a Chocoholic Delite, with its barely __(5)__ flavor of raspberries, will send you into orbit!

The senator is known for not being __(6)__ to the wishes of the voters. Don't send her back to Washington!

Any __(7)__ speech I make for this award must include a mention of Vitavim, the product that puts the sizzle in my sneakers.

Don't labor under the __(8)__ that you can't afford to travel. Adventure and exotic destinations await you! Call Terrific Travel Thrills today!

Real-World Connection

Language Arts: Propaganda All the words in the box relate to propaganda. Look up these words in your Spelling Dictionary. Then write the words to complete this paragraph.

Although you may not realize it, you face propaganda daily. This __(1)__ information is used in everything from soap advertisements to political slogans. One type uses __(2)__, or overstatement. Another, called __(3)__, uses sweeping statements that oversimplify an idea. Another is based on a __(4)__ by a celebrity who claims to support a certain product. Does the celebrity really use the product? There is no way to obtain __(5)__. Learning to recognize propaganda techniques is important, because they often __(6)__ the truth. Watch for statements that contain a __(7)__, two ideas that cannot both be true. Above all, beware of ideas presented without facts to __(8)__ them.

Spelling Word Link

deception

generalization
persuasive
distort
exaggeration
contradiction
substantiate
testimonial
verification

▶ **TRY THIS!**

Yes or No? Write *yes* if the underlined word is used correctly. Write *no* if it is not.

9. Saying Ace Soap cleans everything is an <u>exaggeration</u>.
10. The senator criticized the bill in a long <u>testimonial</u>.
11. These pamphlets <u>distort</u> the truth by omitting key facts.
12. The perfume ad was so <u>persuasive</u> that I bought some.

Fact File

In 1898 newspaper publisher William Randolph Hearst wanted the United States to fight Spain. In a classic case of propaganda, he ran a headline claiming, without proof, that Spain had sunk the American ship *Maine*. Soon after, the United States went to war.

Latin Roots IV

Read and Say

Basic	READ the sentences. SAY each bold word.
1. manufacture	We **manufacture** tires at this plant.
2. factory	Is furniture made in that **factory**?
3. management	Hiring is done by people in **management**.
4. efficient	An **efficient** engine uses less fuel.
5. manual	Read the instruction **manual** for the camera.
6. profit	Will your business earn a **profit** this year?
7. convenient	Having a market on the corner is **convenient**.
8. benefit	One company **benefit** is free child care.
9. defect	The operation is to repair her heart **defect**.
10. inventive	His **inventive** thinking solved the problem.
11. effect	What **effect** has practice had on your game?
12. manipulate	My stiff hands could not **manipulate** the key.
13. factor	What was the main **factor** in your choice?
14. convention	Hundreds of doctors attended the **convention**.
15. eventually	I'll get around to it **eventually**.
16. maneuver	Cars had to **maneuver** around cows in the road.
17. feat	Swimming across the channel is a major **feat**.
18. sacrifice	I **sacrifice** my spare time to study more.
19. manicure	My nails always look better after a **manicure**.
20. preventive	Exercising daily is **preventive** health care.

Spelling Strategy   Knowing the Latin roots *fac/fic/fit/fec/feat* ("to make or do"), *man* ("hand"), and *ven* ("to come") can help you spell and understand words with these roots.

Think and Write   Write the Basic Words. Underline the Latin root or roots in each word.

Review			Challenge	
Review	23. manuscript		**Challenge**	28. circumvent
21. satisfactory	24. magnificent		26. deficit	29. facsimile
22. significant	25. machinery		27. manifest	30. artifact

Independent Practice

Vocabulary: Using Context Write the Basic Word that completes each sentence. Use your Spelling Dictionary.

1. Sole stitchers at the shoe _____ are on strike.
2. Because Craig is so _____, he often finishes first.
3. The secret to Lee Industry's success has been its unwillingness to _____ quality.
4. Although many new businesses lose money at first, the successful ones will _____ come out ahead.
5. Brandex Company performed an amazing _____ when it doubled its rate of production.
6. The plant advertised for workers to perform _____ labor.
7. Fancy Fingernails, Inc. produces a variety of _____ products.
8. Managers from the regional plants met at a _____ in Dallas.
9. In order to back up to the loading dock, the driver had to _____ the huge truck carefully.
10. Ella Nye owns two companies that _____ and distribute radios.
11. A floor supervisor must have good _____ skills.
12. To avoid injuries on the job, take _____ safety measures.

Vocabulary: Synonyms Write the Basic Word that has the same meaning as each word below. Use your Spelling Dictionary.

13. handle
14. flaw
15. handy
16. consideration
17. creative
18. earnings
19. result
20. advantage

Challenge Words Write the Challenge Word that fits each clue. Use your Spelling Dictionary.

21. A photocopy is an example of this.
22. Do this to a problem to avoid it.
23. If you have this, you need more money.
24. This could be a Bronze Age tool or an arrowhead.
25. Something may do this to reveal itself.

Review: Spelling Spree

Rhyming Words Write a Basic or Review Word that rhymes with the underlined word.

1. I'm sure I cannot <u>beat</u> that hero's amazing _____.
2. This bike is really quite a <u>mover</u>—easy to handle and _____.
3. The price of this <u>tractor</u> is a discouraging _____.
4. A car's checkup should be <u>annual</u>; look for details in the _____.
5. Kindly direct your <u>attention</u> to the chairperson of the _____.
6. Our company rules are relaxed and <u>lenient</u>, which workers say is quite _____.
7. Don't tear up the <u>greenery</u> with the blades of your _____.
8. Expensive vacations are very <u>nice</u>, but may require a _____.
9. Polish may help your nails to <u>endure</u>; why not try a _____?

Word Assembly Line 10–25. Find the Basic and Review Words that are hidden in the assembly line. Write the words correctly in the order in which you find them.

How Are You Doing?
Write each spelling word as a partner reads it aloud. Did you misspell any words?

Proofreading and Writing

Proofread: Spelling, Essential and Nonessential Clauses
An **essential** clause is a clause that is necessary to the meaning of a sentence. A **nonessential clause** adds optional information not necessary to the meaning of a sentence. Use commas to set off a nonessential clause. Do not set off an essential clause.

ESSENTIAL: This is the blade **that comes with the saw**.
NONESSENTIAL: That blade**, which is on sale,** fits many saws.

Find five misspelled Basic or Review Words and two incorrectly punctuated clauses in these industrial safety rules. Write the rules correctly.

1. Read the manule which contains important safety information before using any machinary.
2. Be sure that tools are in satisfactry condition; check for missing parts or any other defect.
3. When operating a factory vehicle, obey the traffic rules, that are posted on walls and entrances.
4. Use warning beepers if you must manuver a vehicle in an area with poor visibility.

TAKING PRAVENTIVE STEPS KEEPS JOB ACCIDENTS OFF THE JOB!

Write a Letter Think of a product that you use often. Write a letter to the manufacturer, telling what you like about the product or suggesting a way to improve it. Try to use five spelling words and at least one sentence containing an essential or a nonessential clause.

Basic

1. manufacture
2. factory
3. management
4. efficient
5. manual
6. profit
7. convenient
8. benefit
9. defect
10. inventive
11. effect
12. manipulate
13. factor
14. convention
15. eventually
16. maneuver
17. feat
18. sacrifice
19. manicure
20. preventive

Review

21. satisfactory
22. significant
23. manuscript
24. magnificent
25. machinery

Challenge

26. deficit
27. manifest
28. circumvent
29. facsimile
30. artifact

Proofreading Marks

- ¶ Indent
- ∧ Add
- ∧ Add a comma
- ∨ ∨ Add quotation marks
- ⊙ Add a period
- Delete
- ≡ Capital letter
- / Small letter
- ∾ Reverse order

Expanding Vocabulary

Spelling Word Link

factory

The Verb Suffix *-ify* You have learned that the root *fac*, as in *factory*, means "to make or do." The suffix *-ify* is a form of *fac*. When added to a root or base word, *-ify* forms a verb.

false + ify = fals**ify** (to make false)

Write a word from the list below to complete each sentence. Use your Spelling Dictionary.

notify   qualify   verify   solidify

1. A product must pass a stress test to _____ for sale.
2. Stedcorp will _____ its employees of the plant closing.
3. The inspector wishes to _____ the plant's safety record.
4. The melted plastic began to _____ on the conveyor belt.

1. _____ ?

2. _____ ?

3. _____ ?

4. _____ ?

Now look up the words *justify* and *pacify* in your Spelling Dictionary. Choose the word that completes each picket sign. Write the words.

5. Can management _____ longer hours, with no increase in pay? NO! This is UNFAIR TO WORKERS!

6. Management cannot _____ us with empty promises. We need FAIR PAY NOW!

Real-World Connection

Business: Manufacturing All the words in the box relate to manufacturing. Look up these words in your Spelling Dictionary. Then write the words to complete this paragraph.

When Henry Ford received a __(1)__ for the Model T automobile, he altered the course of modern production. In 1903, he founded the Ford Motor Company and created a model, or __(2)__, of the car. The Model T was built according to __(3)__ designed to make it simple, dependable, and powerful. The car's most important __(4)__ was its twenty-horsepower engine. In an early use of __(5)__, Ford built an __(6)__ line on which cars moved along a conveyor belt from worker to worker. This mass-production process not only gave the cars a __(7)__ of appearance, but also enabled Ford to cut production costs and price his product at an affordable $850. Ford had to stock a large __(8)__ to meet the huge demand for the Model T.

Spelling Word Link

manufacture

automation
assembly
inventory
specifications
prototype
uniformity
component
patent

TRY THIS!

Yes or No? Write *yes* or *no* to answer each question.

9. Does an inventor work in an inventory?
10. Is a speaker a component of a stereo system?
11. Can you type a letter on a prototype?
12. Does a patent protect someone's invention?

Fact File

The assembly line was born in 1901 after a fire destroyed the Olds Motor Works in Detroit. Rather than making car parts, the new factory received them from several machine shops. Workers added the parts to car frames piece by piece.

Number Prefixes

Read and Say

Basic	READ the sentences. SAY each bold word.
1. monarch	Who will be the **monarch** when the queen dies?
2. duel	The enemies fought a **duel** with swords.
3. dilemma	Deciding which club to join was a **dilemma**.
4. century	Cars were rare a **century** ago.
5. monk	Each **monk** gives up all his worldly goods.
6. decade	A storm like this comes once in a **decade**.
7. monopoly	Is a **monopoly** always unfair to the consumer?
8. decimal	The **decimal** system is based on ten.
9. monotone	He read in a dull **monotone** that made me yawn.
10. duet	Shall the two of us sing a **duet**?
11. monotonous	Doing the same thing all day is **monotonous**.
12. diploma	My framed college **diploma** is on the wall.
13. decathlon	Can you name all ten **decathlon** events?
14. monologue	The actor gave her **monologue** alone on stage.
15. dual	My **dual** task is to sweep and wash the floor.
16. centigrade	What's the temperature in degrees **centigrade**?
17. monogram	There are often three letters in a **monogram**.
18. monorail	A **monorail** drops riders at various stations.
19. duplex	Each family rents one side of the **duplex**.
20. centennial	The **centennial** of our city is next year.

Spelling Strategy   Remember that *mon-/mono-* ("one"), *di-* ("two"), *du-* ("two"), *dec-* ("ten"), and *cent-* ("one hundred") are number prefixes.

Think and Write   Write each Basic Word under its prefix.

mon-/mono-   *di-*   *du-*   *dec-*   *cent-*

Review	23. bravery
21. centimeter	24. tournament
22. legendary	25. literature

Challenge	28. digraph
26. decibel	29. diphthong
27. centipede	30. monochrome

Independent Practice

Vocabulary: Completing Definitions Write the Basic Word that completes each statement below. Use your Spelling Dictionary.

1. A one-hundredth anniversary is a _____.
2. A period of ten years is a _____.
3. A design made up of one or more letters, usually the initials of a name, is a

    _____.
4. The temperature scale on which the freezing point of water is 0 degrees and the boiling point is 100 degrees is _____.
5. An athletic contest made up of ten events is a _____.
6. Sole possession or control of anything is a _____.
7. A numeral based on ten used to express a fraction is a _____.
8. Repetitiously dull is _____.
9. A situation that requires a person to choose between courses of action that are equally difficult is a _____.
10. Composed of two parts or double is _____.
11. A long speech made by one person is a _____.
12. A succession of sounds or words uttered in a single tone of voice is a _____.
13. A period of one hundred years is a _____.

Vocabulary: Classifying Write the Basic Word that fits each group. Use your Spelling Dictionary.

14. priest, nun, bishop, _____
15. solo, trio, quartet, _____
16. house, cottage, condominium, _____
17. subway, trolley, cable car, _____
18. license, certificate, document, _____
19. dictator, president, chief, _____
20. wrestling match, joust, prizefight, _____

Challenge Words Write the Challenge Word that answers each question. Use your Spelling Dictionary.

21. What is the *oy* in *boy*?
22. What painting is done in different shades of one color?
23. What animal has a wormlike body with many pairs of legs?
24. What unit is used to express the loudness of sounds?
25. What is the *ph* in *pheasant*?

Dictionary

Prefixes and Suffixes Dictionaries contain separate entries for many prefixes and suffixes. The entries below show the prefix and suffix in *monotonous*.

> **mono-.** A prefix meaning "one; single; alone": **monopoly.** [Middle English, from Old French, from Latin, from Greek, from *monos*, single, alone.]
>
> **-ous.** A suffix that forms adjectives and means "full of or having": **joyous.** [Middle English, from Old French, from *-ous, -eus, -eux*, from Latin, *-osus* and *-us*, adj. suffixes]

Practice Write the answer to each question below. Use your Spelling Dictionary.

1. From what language did *cent-* originally come?
2. Which meaning of *ex-* is used in *ex-president*?
3. From what language did *-ance* most recently come?
4. What does the prefix *bi-* mean in *binoculars*?
5. Which definition of *-ish* is used in the sentence *Jan's mother is Scottish*?

Review: Spelling Spree

Code Breaker The Basic and Review Words below are written in code. Use the following code key to figure out each word. Write the decoded words correctly.

CODE:	m	l	k	j	i	h	t	f	e	d	c	b	a	z	y	x	w	v	u	g	s	r	q	p	o	n
LETTER:	a	b	c	d	e	f	g	h	i	j	k	l	m	n	o	p	q	r	s	t	u	v	w	x	y	z

Example: lvmrivo   *bravery*

6. kizgetvmji
7. jsig
8. jikeamb
9. begivmgsvi
10. ayzyvmeb
11. kizgeaigiv
12. jsxbip

13. ayzc
14. ayzygyzysu
15. jsmb
16. ayzyxybo
17. jikmji
18. kizgizzemb
19. ayzybytsi

20. gysvzmaizg
21. ayzytvma
22. jexbyam
23. ayzygyzi
24. jikmgfbyz

Proofreading and Writing

Proofread for Spelling Find six misspelled Basic or Review Words in this paragraph. Write each word correctly.

In one of the great stories from medieval literature, King Arthur returned from a conquest to find that a knight called Modred had seized his kingdom. Arthur faced a dillema. Though Modred was Arthur's son, he refused to give up his kingdom. In a show of bravary, the legendery monarck challenged his son to a dual. Although he killed Modred, Arthur also died of battle wounds. The king's subjects greatly mourned Arthur's death, but many believed he would return in another censhury.

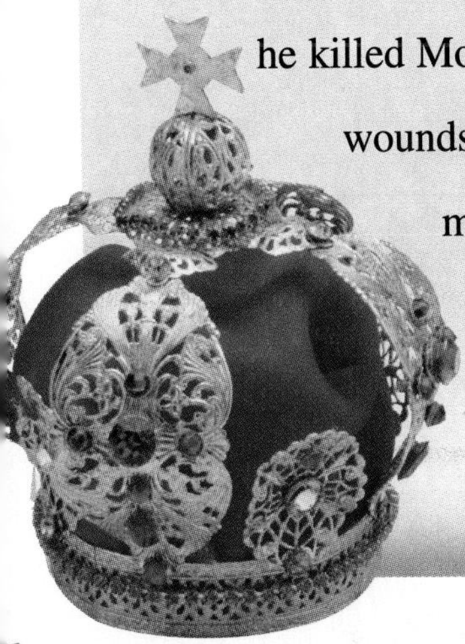

Basic

1. monarch
2. duel
3. dilemma
4. century
5. monk
6. decade
7. monopoly
8. decimal
9. monotone
10. duet
11. monotonous
12. diploma
13. decathlon
14. monologue
15. dual
16. centigrade
17. monogram
18. monorail
19. duplex
20. centennial

Review

21. centimeter
22. legendary
23. bravery
24. tournament
25. literature

Challenge

26. decibel
27. centipede
28. digraph
29. diphthong
30. monochrome

Write a Description Legends about kings, queens, and knights formed an important part of medieval literature. If you were to write a legend about someone living today, who would your subject be? Write a description of your subject, and explain why you chose that person. Try to use five spelling words.

Proofreading Marks

- ¶ Indent
- ∧ Add
- ∧, Add a comma
- “ ” Add quotation marks
- ⊙ Add a period
- Delete
- ≡ Capital letter
- / Small letter
- ∿ Reverse order

Expanding Vocabulary

Context Clues You have learned about a variety of context clues.

APPOSITIVE: I entered the *decathlon*, **an athletic contest**.

SYNONYM: As the **king** arrived, we greeted our *monarch*.

ANTONYM: Although the first act was *monotonous*, the others were more **varied**.

LIST: Please mark a *centimeter*, an **inch**, and a **foot**.

Write the meaning of the underlined word in each sentence below. Then write the word or words in the sentence that provide clues to the meaning of the underlined word.

1. The prince pretends to be brave but is really <u>pusillanimous</u>.
2. Knights wore <u>gauntlets</u>, metal gloves, in combat.
3. Is that a guitar, a harp, or a <u>lute</u>?
4. As I drew the sword from its <u>scabbard</u>, the case rattled.

Spelling Word Link

decathlon
monarch
monotonous

1.	?
2.	?
3.	?
4.	?

Now write a sentence of your own. In your sentence, include a word that might be unfamiliar to others and a context clue to that word's meaning. Your clue can be an appositive, a synonym, an antonym, or a list.

Real-World Connection

Language Arts: The Legends of King Arthur All the words in the box relate to the legends of King Arthur. Look up these words in your Spelling Dictionary. Then write the words to complete this paragraph.

Spelling Word Link

monarch

medieval
chronicle
chivalry
usurp
betrayal
sovereign
valor
conquest

The character of King Arthur is probably based on a British __(1)__ who ruled in the sixth century. However, most of the stories that __(2)__ Arthur's deeds were written in the later Middle Ages. According to these __(3)__ legends, King Arthur and his knights lived by a code of __(4)__ , rules of behavior based upon gallantry and honor. In the tales, Arthur performs many courageous feats of __(5)__ and achieves the __(6)__ of most of western Europe. Ultimately, however, Arthur's son Modred causes his downfall. In an act of __(7)__ , Modred attempts to __(8)__ Arthur's kingdom. Arthur vows to regain that which is rightfully his, and father and son battle to their deaths.

TRY THIS!

Yes or No? Write *yes* or *no* to answer each question.

9. Could a sovereign wear a crown?
10. Was the nineteenth century medieval?
11. Is a conquest a type of peace treaty?
12. Would someone with valor avoid danger?

Fact File

In the Arthurian legends, Merlin was an aged magician who could see into the future. He is said to have created the Round Table used in King Arthur's court. Because this table had no head, the knights around it sat in positions of equal importance.

Words New to English

Basic	READ the sentences. SAY each bold word.
1. software	All computers need **software** to run.
2. word processor	I typed my report on a **word processor**.
3. diskette	How much data can that **diskette** store?
4. robotics	Robots are built by experts in **robotics**.
5. android	Didn't the **android** in that movie seem human?
6. digital	The numbers on my **digital** clock are large.
7. transistor	I need a new **transistor** for my radio.
8. photocopy	Make a **photocopy** of the document for me.
9. smog	Brown **smog** pollutes the city's air.
10. antibiotic	Will this **antibiotic** cure my infection?
11. laser	A **laser** has a powerful light beam.
12. calculator	Use a **calculator** to check your math answers.
13. space shuttle	When will the **space shuttle** lift off?
14. sonar	Boats use **sonar** to locate schools of fish.
15. discotheque	Dancers crowded into the **discotheque**.
16. microwave	May I pop some corn in the **microwave** oven?
17. amplifier	Loud music screamed from the **amplifier**.
18. brunch	We start serving **brunch** at noon.
19. supersonic	A **supersonic** jet can break the sound barrier.
20. scuba	The **scuba** gear of a diver includes flippers.

Spelling Strategy Knowing whether a word new to English was formed by combining word parts from other languages or by creating a **compound word**, a **blend**, or an **acronym** can help you spell the word correctly.

Think and Write Write the Basic Words.

Review		Challenge	
	23. condominium		28. synthesizer
21. video	24. telecast	26. semiconductor	29. aerospace
22. aerobics	25. miniseries	27. simulation	30. hologram

Independent Practice

Vocabulary: Using Context Write the Basic Word that completes each sentence. Use your Spelling Dictionary.

1. Rick designs computer _____ for government use.
2. Computers measure the rate of objects moving at _____ speed.
3. Sharon wrote her report on a _____.
4. At the Duplicating Center, Carlo made a _____ of the printout.
5. Unlike a hard disk, a _____ is flexible.
6. While his computer was being serviced, Myles had to add the figures on a _____.
7. Manufacturers commonly use short bursts of intensified light from a _____ to weld together the small parts of a computer.
8. Modern communications rely on the tiny _____, which controls the flow of electric current in many electronic devices.
9. The hero of this science fiction movie is an _____.
10. Like most rockets, the _____ uses computers extensively.
11. Experiments in _____ may someday lead to a remote control machine that can cook, clean house, and even drive a car.
12. A _____ watch displays the time in numbers, not with hands.

Vocabulary: Word Clues Write the Basic Word that fits each clue. Use your Spelling Dictionary.

13. Undersea treasure hunters might use this to locate objects.
14. Some ovens use this type of radiation to cook foods quickly.
15. This can cure many types of infection.
16. This can be used to turn up the music.
17. This is usually a weekend meal.
18. Wear your dancing shoes to this place.
19. Filled with air, this tank travels underwater.
20. This often hangs over a city.

Challenge Words Write the Challenge Word that fits each definition. Use your Spelling Dictionary.

21. related to the science or technology of flight
22. a machine that duplicates the sounds of musical instruments
23. a substance that conducts electricity more easily than an insulator but less easily than a conductor
24. an imitation
25. a three-dimensional image produced by a laser

Review: Spelling Spree

Compound Clues Each item includes two definitions, one for each part of a Basic or Review Word. Write each word.

Example: above + related to sound = *supersonic*

1. an empty area + regular travel back and forth =
2. picture + mimic =
3. a sound that has meaning + a thing that performs a task =
4. fluffy + articles of the same general kind =
5. small + several related things in a row =
6. small + to flutter =

Invisible Letters Decide which letters should be added to complete each Basic or Review Word. Write the words correctly.

7. d i _ _ t _ l
8. c a l _ _ l a t _ r
9. _ r _ n _ h
10. a n t _ b _ _ t i c
11. _ m _ l _ f _ _ r
12. _ _ o t _ c _ p _
13. _ _ r _ b i _ s
14. _ m _ g
15. c _ n d _ _ _ n _ _ m
16. _ u p _ r s _ n _ _
17. d i _ _ o _ _ e _ _ e
18. t _ l _ _ _ _ s t
19. t r _ n _ _ s t _ r
20. s _ n _ r

21. _ i d _ _
22. d _ s _ e _ t _
23. a n _ r _ _ d
24. l a _ _ r
25. s _ _ b _

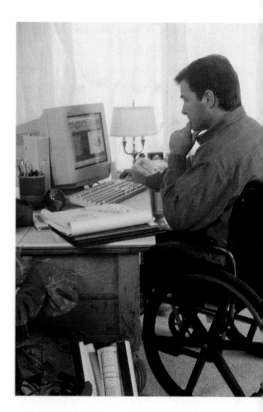

How Are You Doing?
Write the spelling words in alphabetical order. Practice any misspelled words with a partner.

Proofreading and Writing

Proofread: Spelling and Usage of *who* or *whom* Whether to use *who* or *whom* is determined by how the pronoun is used within a noun clause. When the pronoun is the subject, use *who* or *whoever*; when it is an object, use *whom* and *whomever*.

SUBJECT: **Whoever used the computer** forgot to turn it off.

OBJECT: Do you know **whom this printout belongs to**?

Find five misspelled Basic or Review Words and one error in using *who* or *whom* in this excerpt from a computer user's guide. Write the excerpt correctly.

The Supersonic Softwear System is designed for whoever has a need for a home word proccessor and calculater. To learn the system, follow the steps below.

1. Insert the training diskete in Drive A of the computer.

2. When you see the message DIJITAL CODE on your monitor, type in three numbers between 0 and 9.

3. The computer will ask whom is using the program. Type your name.

4. Wait for the next message to appear.

Single Sided
MICRO FLOPPY DISK
MFD-1DD

Write a List What features would the world's most advanced computer have? What could it do for its users? Write a list of sentences itemizing this remarkable computer's features. Try to use five spelling words and at least one of these pronouns: *who, whom, whoever,* or *whomever.*

Basic

1. software
2. word processor
3. diskette
4. robotics
5. android
6. digital
7. transistor
8. photocopy
9. smog
10. antibiotic
11. laser
12. calculator
13. space shuttle
14. sonar
15. discotheque
16. microwave
17. amplifier
18. brunch
19. supersonic
20. scuba

Review
21. video
22. aerobics
23. condominium
24. telecast
25. miniseries

Challenge
26. semiconductor
27. simulation
28. synthesizer
29. aerospace
30. hologram

Proofreading Marks

¶	Indent
∧	Add
⩘	Add a comma
ᵛᵛ ᵛᵛ	Add quotation marks
⊙	Add a period
ℐ	Delete
≡	Capital letter
/	Small letter
∩	Reverse order

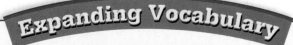

Expanding Vocabulary

Spelling Word Link

smog
sonar

Blends and Acronyms You have learned that a blend combines parts of two existing words and that an acronym is a combination of the first letter or two from a series of words.

BLEND: **sm**oke + f**og** = **smog**
ACRONYM: **so**und **na**vigation **r**anging = **sonar**

Write the words from which each blend is formed. Use your Spelling Dictionary.

1. brunch   2. transistor   3. motel

Write the acronym that is formed from each group of words.

4. self contained underwater breathing apparatus
5. radio detecting and ranging
6. light amplification by stimulated emission of radiation

TEST-TAKING TACTICS

Vocabulary-in-Context Vocabulary-in-context passages can contain a number of different types of clues to the meaning of the tested word. For example, words such as *but, however,* and *nonetheless* can alert you to look for an antonym of the tested word. Words and phrases such as *in addition, and, in other words,* and *also* can direct you to look for a synonym of the tested word. Study the following sample.

Sample passage excerpt and question:

A century ago, few people could have imagined the broad
(40) impact the computer would have on society. Early computers
were developed for discrete uses; in other words, they had specific
purposes. Today's systems, though, can perform many functions.

The word "discrete" in line 41 most nearly means
(A) distinct   (B) scientific   (C) various   (D) personal   (E) illegal

Now write the answers to the following questions.

7. What phrase contained in the passage alerts you to the fact that you should be looking for a synonym of the tested word?
8. Which answer choice is correct? Write its letter.

Real-World Connection

Science: Computers All the words in the box relate to computers. Look up these words in your Spelling Dictionary. Then write the words to complete this paragraph.

> To use a computer, you do not have to be an expert in __(1)__. Computer software is designed to be easy to learn. Many programs include a __(2)__ to explain how they work. Most software imitates things people already know how to use. Just as a file cabinet stores information on paper, a __(3)__ stores information in a computer. A __(4)__ is a computer version of an accountant's bookkeeping system. Every computer comes with a set of __(5)__ software. These programs control the __(6)__, or physical parts of the computer, and allow you to communicate with the computer by typing commands on the __(7)__. All of the software contained in a computer is listed in the computer's __(8)__.

Spelling Word Link

software

electronics
hardware
database
spreadsheet
directory
tutorial
utility
keyboard

TRY THIS!

True or False? Write *T* if a sentence is true and *F* if it is false.

9. The physical equipment of a computer is its hardware.
10. A database enables a user to store information.
11. A computer's memory is its spreadsheet.
12. A tutorial is a teaching program.

Fact File

ENIAC, the first fully electronic digital computer, was built in 1946. This machine worked quickly—about 5,000 arithmetic operations per second. It took up more space than today's computers, however; in fact, it filled an entire room.

Words Often Mispronounced

Read and Say

| Basic | READ the sentences. SAY each bold word. |

1. *algebra* — My math teacher helps me with **algebra**.
2. *mathematics* — Geometry is one branch of **mathematics**.
3. *probably* — I will **probably** be late because of traffic.
4. *nuclear* — Study **nuclear** science to learn about atoms.
5. *identity* — The spy kept her real **identity** a secret.
6. *liberal* — Be **liberal** with praise but not with blame.
7. *recognition* — The award was in **recognition** of his courage.
8. *laboratory* — Please do your experiments in the **laboratory**.
9. *mischievous* — My **mischievous** puppy chewed my shoes.
10. *temperamental* — The **temperamental** child cried easily.
11. *candidate* — Will he make a good **candidate** for mayor?
12. *dinghy* — A little **dinghy** trailed the larger boat.
13. *hindrance* — Heavy packs were a **hindrance** on our climb.
14. *privilege* — It was a **privilege** to sit at the head table.
15. *monstrous* — Her **monstrous** mask scared the other children.
16. *grievous* — His death was a **grievous** loss to all of us.
17. *preferable* — I think walking is **preferable** to riding a bus.
18. *arctic* — We nearly froze in the **arctic** weather.
19. *similarly* — The twins dressed **similarly**.
20. *sophomore* — A **sophomore** helped the freshman find her way.

Spelling Strategy Knowing the correct pronunciation of a word will help you spell it correctly.

Think and Write Write the Basic Words.

Review		Challenge	
21. quantity	23. environment	26. prerequisite	28. paraphernalia
22. comparable	24. governor	27. asterisk	29. forte
	25. restaurant		30. posthumous

Independent Practice

Vocabulary: Question Clues Write the Basic Word that answers each question. Use your Spelling Dictionary.

1. What field of study involves solving problems in which letters represent numbers?
2. What is similar to a right but is granted only to particular people?
3. What can you prevent by wearing a disguise?
4. What is an apple if you like it more than a banana?
5. What is a person who runs for class president?
6. What kind of person likes to play pranks?
7. What kind of wind is cold and icy?
8. What makes you different from everyone else?
9. What kind of politician is the opposite of conservative?
10. What kind of a loss causes sorrow?
11. What kind of energy comes from the center of an atom?
12. What kind of person changes moods quickly?

Vocabulary: Analogies Write the Basic Word that completes each analogy. Use your Spelling Dictionary.

Example: hot : tropical :: cold : _____   *arctic*
13. junior : senior :: freshman : _____
14. certain : likely :: definitely : _____
15. exercise : gymnasium :: experiment : _____
16. light : dark :: differently : _____
17. limousine : wagon :: yacht : _____
18. great : fantastic :: horrible : _____
19. gain : loss :: help : _____
20. biology : science :: geometry : _____

Challenge Words Write the Challenge Word that matches each definition. Use your Spelling Dictionary.

21. something at which a person is skilled
22. a star-shaped symbol used to indicate an omission of text or a reference to a footnote
23. occurring or continuing after a person's death
24. the equipment used in a particular activity
25. something that is required before something else can be done

Dictionary

Etymology The **etymology** of a word is its origin and history. In a dictionary entry, the etymology appears after the definition of a word and is enclosed in brackets. Look at the etymology below for the word *probably*. Its most modern form came from Middle English, the first language listed. Latin, the last language listed, is the word's original source.

[Middle English, from Old French, from Latin *probabilis*, provable, laudable, from *probare*, to prove, demonstrate as good, from *probus*, good.]

To find a word's etymology, you must often check the entry for its base word. In the example above, the etymology for *probably* is found under the word *probable*.

Practice Write the answer to each question below. Use your Spelling Dictionary.

1. From what Latin word did *similarly* come?
2. From what language did the word *dinghy* originate?
3. From what language did *preferable* most recently come?
4. From what word did *algebra* first come?
5. From what language did the word *sophomore* originate?
6. What was the meaning of the earliest Latin root of *liberal*?

Review: Spelling Spree

Phonetic Clues Write the Basic or Review Word that matches each phonetic respelling below.

7. prŏb´ ə blē
8. mŏn´ strəs
9. hĭn´ drəns
10. lăb´ rə tôr´ ē
11. prĕf´ ər ə bəl
12. ärk´ tĭk
13. nōō´ klē ər
14. rĕs´ tər ənt
15. mĭs´ chə vəs

16. prĭv´ ə lĭj
17. ĕn vī´ rən mənt
18. ī dĕn´ tĭ tē
19. kwŏn´ tĭ tē
20. grē´ vəs
21. gŭv´ ər nər
22. tĕm´ prə mĕn´ tl
23. dĭng´ ē
24. sĭm´ ə lər lē

Proofreading and Writing

Proofread for Spelling Find seven misspelled Basic or Review Words in this newspaper article. Write each word correctly.

Math Whiz Honored

Pilar Simpson, a sophmore at Cedarwood High School, yesterday received reconition from the National Math Association for her outstanding performance in the field of algerbra. Simpson solved a problem that had stumped university professors. "It was probably luck," said the modest mathmatics whiz. Teacher Robert Kleeman disagreed and was libral in his praise. "It's a privilege to instruct Pilar," he said. "The extent of her knowledge is comperable to that of a college student. I'm sure that in two years she will be a top canidate for a math scholarship."

Write an Introduction Speech A noted mathematician is coming to your school to speak to the Math Club. You have been chosen to present the speaker to the audience. Write the speech you will give to welcome and introduce the speaker. Try to use five spelling words.

Basic

1. algebra
2. mathematics
3. probably
4. nuclear
5. identity
6. liberal
7. recognition
8. laboratory
9. mischievous
10. temperamental
11. candidate
12. dinghy
13. hindrance
14. privilege
15. monstrous
16. grievous
17. preferable
18. arctic
19. similarly
20. sophomore

Review

21. quantity
22. comparable
23. environment
24. governor
25. restaurant

Challenge

26. prerequisite
27. asterisk
28. paraphernalia
29. forte
30. posthumous

Proofreading Marks

¶ Indent
∧ Add
⌄ Add a comma
ᵛᵛ ᵛᵛ Add quotation marks
⊙ Add a period
∽ Delete
≡ Capital letter
/ Small letter
∿ Reverse order

Expanding Vocabulary

**Spelling
Word Link**

mathematics
laboratory

Clipped Forms In Unit 34, you learned about blends and acronyms. Another way to create a new word is to shorten, or **clip**, an existing word.

LONG FORM:	mathematics	laboratory
CLIPPED FORM:	math	lab

Write the long form of each of the following clipped words. Use your Spelling Dictionary.

1. tux   3. condo   5. ad   7. vet
2. flu   4. limo   6. sax   8. disco

1. ? _____   5. ? _____
2. ? _____   6. ? _____
3. ? _____   7. ? _____
4. ? _____   8. ? _____

TEST-TAKING TACTICS

Analogies When you look at an analogy test question, pay careful attention to the order in which the stem words are stated. For example, if the first word in a stem pair is a cause and the second word is an effect, the correct answer choice will also state a cause first and an effect second—and not the reverse. If the stem pair is a whole and its part, an answer choice that presents a part and its whole is incorrect. A correct answer pair is always related in *exactly* the same way as the stem words.

Study this sample analogy test question.

ELEMENT : CALCIUM ::
(A) trolley : vehicle   (B) Venus : planet   (C) primate : gorilla
(D) e-mail : communication   (E) grocer : merchant

Now write the answers to the following questions.

9. What is the relationship between the stem words?
10. Which answer choice is related in exactly the same way as the stem words? Write its letter.

Real-World Connection

Math: Algebra All the words in the box relate to algebra. Look up these words in your Spelling Dictionary. Then write the words to complete this paragraph.

Algebra is studied worldwide because of its importance in problem solving. A math problem is often expressed as an __(1)__ , two quantities separated by an equal sign. An unknown quantity is represented by a __(2)__ such as x. Finding the value of x produces the __(3)__ to the problem. Algebra includes a variety of symbols. One familiar symbol is the minus sign, which indicates that a number is __(4)__ . Some math problems have symbols of __(5)__ , such as greater than or less than signs, in place of equal signs. In long mathematical expressions, __(6)__ are used to enclose parts of the expression that must be kept together. Other symbols include an __(7)__ , a small raised number that shows how many times a quantity is multiplied by itself, and a __(8)__ sign indicating a square root.

Spelling Word Link

algebra

equation
solution
radical
negative
variable
exponent
inequality
parentheses

TRY THIS!

True or False? Write *T* if a sentence is true and *F* if it is false.

9. A negative number is always less than zero.
10. An equation can never be solved.
11. One example of an inequality is 2 + 2 = 4.
12. An equal sign is a variable.

Fact File

The concept of "zero" was invented by the Mayans before A.D. 300 and by the Hindus a few hundred years later. The zero comes to us via Arabic books translated in the 800s.

36 Review: Units 31–35

Unit 31 Vowel Changes IV

pages 192–197

deceive	acclaim	pertain	prevail	sustain
deception	acclamation	pertinent	prevalent	sustenance

💡 **Spelling Strategy** Knowing how the vowels change in one pair of related words can help you predict changes in other pairs with the same root.

Write the word that is a synonym for each word below.

1. applicable
2. common
3. triumph
4. uphold
5. dishonesty
6. applaud

Write the word that completes each sentence.

7. Tell her only the facts that _____ directly to the case.
8. At the town meeting, the suggestion was approved by _____.
9. Strict laws make it hard for advertisers to _____ consumers.
10. I brought books for entertainment and sandwiches for _____.

Unit 32 Latin Roots IV

pages 198–203

manufacture	management	efficient	convenient	inventive
manicure	eventually	maneuver	feat	sacrifice

💡 **Spelling Strategy** Knowing the Latin roots *fac/fic/fit/fec/feat* ("to make or do"), *man* ("hand"), and *ven* ("to come") can help you spell and understand words with these roots.

Write the word that belongs in each group.

11. make, produce, _____
12. lose, forfeit, _____
13. creative, original, _____
14. supervision, direction, _____
15. ultimately, finally, _____
16. achievement, deed, _____

Write the word that matches each definition.

17. a strategic movement
18. a cosmetic treatment for the hands and fingernails
19. within easy reach
20. acting effectively with a minimum of waste, expense, or effort

Unit 33 ## Number Prefixes

pages 204–209

monarch	duel	dilemma	century	decimal
monotonous	dual	monologue	decathlon	centennial

 Spelling Strategy Remember that *mon-/mono-* ("one"), *di-* ("two"), *du-* ("two"), *dec-* ("ten"), and *cent-* ("one hundred") are number prefixes.

Write the word that can replace the underlined word or words.

21. a <u>hundred years</u> of progress
22. to face a <u>difficult choice</u>
23. a <u>contest</u> between two people
24. a <u>double</u> purpose
25. a powerful <u>king</u>
26. a <u>boring</u> routine

Write the word that completes each analogy.

27. one : annual :: one hundred : _____
28. total : sum :: fraction : _____
29. two : dialogue :: one : _____
30. running : marathon :: track and field : _____

Unit 34 ## Words New to English

pages 210–215

word processor	robotics	diskette	digital	transistor
calculator	microwave	laser	sonar	discotheque

 Spelling Strategy Knowing whether a word new to English was formed by combining word parts from other languages or by creating a **compound word**, a **blend**, or an **acronym** can help you spell the word correctly.

Write the word that matches each definition.

31. an intensified beam of light
32. a system using sound waves to locate submerged objects
33. a type of oven that can cook food very quickly
34. showing data in numbers

Write the word that fits each clue.

35. an electronic writer
36. a high-speed adder
37. a radio part
38. a round, flat information holder
39. a dance nightclub
40. the study of automated machines

Unit 35 Words Often Mispronounced pages 216–221

laboratory	mathematics	nuclear	recognition	mischievous
similarly	candidate	arctic	privilege	sophomore

💡 **Spelling Strategy** Knowing the correct pronunciation of a word will help you spell it correctly.

Write the word that completes each phrase.

41. an _____ climate
42. a _____ for mayor
43. a _____ prank
44. a chemistry _____

45. granted a special _____
46. president of the _____ class
47. a _____ power plant

Write the word that matches each definition.

48. the study of numbers and their forms or arrangements
49. the act of knowing or identifying from past experience
50. in nearly the same way

Challenge Words   Units 31–35   pages 192–221

denounce	deficit	centipede	simulation	forte
denunciation	manifest	diphthong	synthesizer	asterisk

Write the word that is either a synonym or an antonym for each word below.

51. surplus
52. recommendation
53. obvious
54. condemn
55. specialty

Write the word that fits each clue.

56. This may signal you to look for a footnote.
57. This is often used to produce electronic music.
58. An example of this is the |ou| sound in *shout*.
59. This is not the real thing.
60. This has many legs.

Spelling-Meaning Strategy

The Latin Root *tain/ten*

Everyone knows that a container is used to hold things. Not everyone is aware, however, that the meaning of the word *container* comes from the Latin root *tain* or *ten*, meaning "to hold." You have learned many words with this root, all of which have something to do with holding. The word *maintain*, for example, originally meant "to hold in the hand" and later came to mean "to support" and, finally, "to keep up." *Sustain* means "to hold up," and *pertain* means "to relate"— in other words, to hold to a topic.

The words below also contain the root *tain/ten*.

ob**tain**	**ten**ement	**ten**ure
tenet	enter**tain**	**ten**acious

con**tain**er
main**tain**
sus**tain**
per**tain**

Think

- How does the root *tain/ten* contribute to the meaning of each word? Look up the words in your Spelling Dictionary.

- In Unit 31, you learned that the spelling of a root can change in predictable ways. How is the root spelled in each word above?

Apply and Extend

Complete these activities on a separate piece of paper.

1. Write six sentences. Use one word from the word box above in each sentence.
2. Can you think of other words that belong to the same family as *container*, *maintain*, *sustain*, and *pertain*? With a partner, make a list of related words. Then look up the Latin root *tain/ten* in your Spelling-Meaning Index. Add to your list any other related words that you find.

Summing Up

The Latin root *tain* or *ten* means "to hold." Words that contain the same root are often related in spelling and meaning. Knowing some of the words in a family can help you to use and spell the others correctly.

*Urban archae-
ology is a new,
but rapidly
growing, branch
of archaeology.
Instead of pre-
historic or classical
civilizations, urban
archaeologists
study past cultures
of our own cities.
What do they find
there?*

from

"Urban Archaeology"

A rtifacts, or human-made objects of historical interest, are among the most important finds at archaeological sites. They include various items, ranging from buttons and coins to pottery and glassware. Some of the most unusual artifacts found by an urban archaeologist were metal cars from an early toy train set, which were discovered at a subway construction site in Atlanta, Georgia.

Artifacts serve many important scientific roles. Urban archaeologists study them to help date sites; to learn of trade routes by determining the country of origin; and to help figure out the site's function. A site's function is the primary kind of activity that occurred there, such as a household or domestic activity, commerce or trade, or the duties of government.

Sometimes natural objects, such as seeds or animal bones, are found with artifacts. These are called ecofacts. A recent excavation in Manhattan turned up a rich lode of ecofacts that included turkey bones, oyster shells, and even watermelon seeds.

What is valuable about a three-hundred-year-old watermelon seed? It tells us that the people who lived in seventeenth-century New York raised and ate watermelons. Artifacts help indicate how the earliest American settlers lived, worked, and played; ecofacts give information about what they ate.

Think and Discuss

1. This excerpt is part of a longer report. What do you think is the **topic** of the entire report?
2. What is the **main idea** of each paragraph in the excerpt? What is the **topic sentence** in each one?

The Writing Process

Research Report

Writing a research report allows you to learn more about something that interests you. Choose a topic to research and write a brief report. Use the guidelines, and follow the Writing Process.

Guidelines for Writing a Research Report

✓ State each main idea in a topic sentence, and support main ideas with subtopics and details.

✓ Arrange paragraphs and details in a logical order.

✓ Include an introduction, a conclusion, and a bibliography.

1 ▶ Prewriting
- List some questions about your topic. As you research, take notes to answer your questions. Make bibliography cards for your sources.
- Organize your notes into an outline. Make each question a main topic, and arrange the notes into subtopics and details.

2 ▶ Draft
- Write, following your outline.
- Write a paragraph for each main topic. Support each main topic with subtopics and details.
- Add an introduction and a conclusion.
- Write a bibliography, alphabetizing your sources.

3 ▶ Revise
- If necessary, reword your introduction to make it more interesting.
- Add details or delete those that don't belong.
- Revise your conclusion so that it clearly restates the main ideas.
- Have a writing conference.

4 ▶ Proofread
- Did you spell each word correctly?
- Did you use commas correctly with phrases and clauses?
- Did you use *who* and *whom* correctly?

5 ▶ Publish
- Copy your report neatly. Add a clear title.
- Share your report. Have a classmate interview you about it.

Composition Words

pertain
effect
dilemma
mathematics
prevalent
factor
century
laboratory

Student's Handbook

Extra Practice and Review

Unit 1 Consonant Changes pages 12–17

emit	submit	transmit	concede	omit
emission	submission	transmission	concession	omission

💡 **Spelling Strategy** Knowing how consonants change in one pair of words can help you predict changes in words with similar spelling patterns.

Write the word that completes each sentence.
1. We barely heard the radio message because of the poor _____.
2. From the list, _____ the names of people who have moved.
3. Some rulers demand the complete _____ of their subjects.

Write the word that matches each definition.
4. the act of leaving something out
5. the act of giving off
6. the act of admitting as true
7. to send out, as by radio
8. to give off
9. to yield to authority
10. to admit as true

Unit 2 Greek Word Parts I pages 18–23

pathology	symptom	synthetic	oxygen	homogenized
pathetic	empathy	syndicate	apathy	photogenic

💡 **Spelling Strategy** Knowing the Greek word parts *path* ("disease; feeling"), *syn/sym* ("together; same"), *gen* ("born; produced"), and *prot* ("first") can help you spell and understand words with these parts.

Write the word that fits each clue.
11. Most fashion models are this.
12. This kind of thing is unnatural.
13. You need this to breathe.
14. Milk is this.
15. This is an organization.
16. This kind of thing is pitiful.

Write the word that completes each analogy.
17. caring : concern :: understanding : _____
18. mind : psychology :: disease : _____
19. kindness : cruelty :: concern : _____
20. clue : hint :: sign : _____

Unit 3 Latin Prefixes I   pages 24–29

transportation	subway	transplant	submarine	transform
transparent	subside	subdivide	subtotal	subtitle

Spelling Strategy   Remember the meanings of the Latin prefixes *trans-* ("across; over; through") and *sub-* ("under; near; beneath").

Write a word by changing each underlined prefix below.

21. preside   23. entitle   25. deportation
22. byway   24. implant

Write the word that matches each definition.

26. capable of being seen through   29. a ship that operates underwater
27. to split a part into smaller parts   30. a part of a sum
28. to change the appearance or
    shape of

Unit 4 Words from Names   pages 30–35

atlas	mercury	museum	hypnosis	pasteurize
fate	jovial	fury	tantalize	galvanized

Spelling Strategy   Knowing the origin of words that come from names can help you spell and understand the meanings of the words.

Write the words that complete the paragraph.

Today I went to a science **(31)** . One exhibit showed how dairies **(32)** milk. An exhibit of metals showed the uses of **(33)** , a liquid metal, and showed how steel is **(34)** to prevent rust. An **(35)** showed the sources of the world's metal supplies. An exhibit called "The Mind" explained how **(36)** is used to affect thought.

Write the word that is a synonym for each word below.

37. destiny   38. tempt   39. jolly   40. rage

Cycle 1

Unit 5   Homophones

pages 36–41

chord	choral	site	canvas	phase
cord	coral	cite	canvass	faze

💡 **Spelling Strategy**   Remember to think about meaning when using a **homophone**, a word that sounds like another but has a different spelling and meaning.

Write the word that completes each phrase.
41. a _____ for a building
43. a G major _____
45. to _____ an example
42. a _____ of development
44. to knot a _____
46. to _____ for votes

Write the word that completes each analogy.
47. orchestra : instrumental :: choir : _____
48. hull : wood :: sail : _____
49. green : jade :: reddish-orange : _____
50. delight : please : upset : _____

Challenge Words   Units 1–5

pages 12–41

provoke	synthesis	protocol	caret	pathos
provocation	thespian	epicure	carat	nemesis
subconscious	subsequent	subculture		

Write the word that is a synonym or an antonym for each word.
51. combination
53. preceding
55. humor
52. arouse
54. actor

Write the word that completes each sentence.
56. During the ceremony, applause was not considered proper _____.
57. Some people believe that dreams express our _____ thoughts.
58. A gentle dog would never bite or snap without _____.
59. Proofreaders use a _____ to show where a missing word belongs.
60. Joan was Nat's _____ because she won every game they played.
61. Even the most refined _____ will find this meal delicious.
62. Immigrant groups within a country may have their own _____.
63. The diamond in the ring weighed one _____.

Unit 7 Absorbed Prefixes   pages 48–53

announcer	commentary	accent	allude	illusion
collision	collaborate	collapse	accumulate	aggravate

💡 **Spelling Strategy** Remember that *ad-* ("to; toward"), *in-* ("in; not"), and *con-* ("with; together") can be **absorbed prefixes** when their last letter changes to match the beginning consonant of the base word to which they are added.

Write the word that belongs in each group.

1. fall, tumble, _____
2. stress, emphasis, _____
3. gather, collect, _____
4. explanation, interpretation, _____
5. crash, impact, _____
6. cooperate, conspire, _____

Write the word that best matches each definition.

7. an appearance or impression that has no real basis
8. to refer to indirectly
9. to make worse
10. a person who brings something to public notice

Unit 8 Greek Word Parts II   pages 54–59

terminology	geology	zoology	biology	apology
mythology	theology	anthology	analogy	ecology

💡 **Spelling Strategy** Knowing the Greek word parts *log* and *logy* ("an oral or written expression; the science, theory, or study of") can help you spell and understand words with these parts.

Write the word that completes each sentence.

11. The scientist in the _____ lab was examining plant cells.
12. My love of animals had led me to study _____.
13. Those concerned with _____ work to clean up the environment.
14. Students of _____ learn about the history of religion.

Write the word that fits each clue.

15. The Greeks are famous for this.
16. This could be a book of poems.
17. This is often technical.
18. This makes a comparison.
19. This expresses regret.
20. This involves rocks.

Cycle 2

Unit 9   Latin Prefixes II

interstate	interference	intermediate	counteract
superlative	intervention	intersection	supermarket
counterclockwise	intravenous		

💡 **Spelling Strategy**   Remember the meanings of the Latin prefixes *inter-* ("between"), *intra-* ("within"), *super-* ("over; greater") and *counter-* ("opposing").

Write a word by changing each underlined prefix.

21. relative
22. interact

23. conference
24. prevention

Write the word that completes each phrase.

25. to travel on an _____ highway
26. groceries from a _____
27. to advance from beginner to _____ level

28. a stop sign at an _____
29. to wind the hands _____
30. an _____ medication

Unit 10   Words from Spanish

pages 66–71

savanna	lariat	pueblo	stampede	tornado
alfalfa	sierra	jaguar	bronco	armada

💡 **Spelling Strategy**   Knowing how to pronounce a word from Spanish will often help you spell it.

Write the word that completes each analogy.

31. toss : ball :: twirl : _____
32. boat : fleet :: ship : _____
33. crowd : rush :: herd : _____
34. trees : forest :: grass : _____
35. snow : blizzard :: wind : _____
36. kitten : wildcat :: colt : _____

Write the word that fits each definition.

37. a rugged mountain range
38. a large feline animal

39. a flat-roofed dwelling
40. a plant used to feed cattle

Unit 11 Words Often Confused

pages 72–77

persecute	accede	vocation	vial	regimen
prosecute	exceed	avocation	vile	regiment

 Spelling Strategy To avoid confusing words with similar spellings and pronunciations, think of the meanings of the words.

Write the word that fits each definition below.

41. to give one's assent
42. a hobby
43. to be greater than
44. a military unit of ground troops

45. an occupation
46. disgusting
47. to oppress or harass

Write the word that completes each sentence.

48. For better health, follow this _____ of diet and exercise.
49. The tiny _____ contained a few drops of the costly perfume.
50. A sign says that the owner will _____ trespassers.

Challenge Words   Units 7–11

pages 48–77

counterproductive	eminent	etymology	prologue
interscholastic	imminent	logistics	bravado
incommunicado	renegade	corroborate	
commemorate	intersperse	irrelevant	

Write the word that fits each definition.

51. between schools
52. introduction
53. outstanding

54. word origin
55. traitor
56. confirm

57. honor
58. scatter

Write the word that can replace the underlined word or words.

59. The prisoner was held without means of communicating.
60. The planned details of the military operation are top secret.
61. No one was fooled by the bully's show of false courage.
62. A negative attitude is harmful to any effort.
63. The thunder warned us that a downpour was about to occur.
64. Some of these facts are not applicable to your research topic.

Cycle 3

Unit 13 Vowel Changes I

pages 84–89

vegetable	stability	infinite	indicative	deprivation
vegetation	stable	finite	indicate	deprive

Spelling Strategy To remember the spelling of the schwa sound in some words, think of a related word in which the pronunciation and spelling of the vowel are more obvious.

Write the word that is a synonym for each word below.
1. deny
2. limited
3. endless
4. plants
5. show
6. steady

Write the word that matches each definition.
7. serving to point out or show
8. part of a plant that is used as food
9. the act of taking something away from someone
10. the quality of being firm or steady

Unit 14 Latin Roots I

pages 90–95

transfer	disposal	purpose	differ	contract
preposition	distract	transpose	fertile	preference

Spelling Strategy Knowing the Latin roots *fer* ("to carry"), *pos* ("to put; place"), and *tract/trace* ("to draw; pull") can help you spell and understand words with these roots.

Write the word that completes each analogy.
11. informal : handshake :: formal : _____
12. poor : rich :: unproductive : _____
13. accept : reject :: agree : _____
14. and : conjunction :: from : _____

Write the word that fits each clue.
15. to change word order
16. a solution for litter
17. a reason for action
18. a move to a new place
19. a favorite
20. to catch someone's eye

Unit 15　Noun Suffixes I

pages 96–101

nationality	hospitality	generosity	familiarity	majority
popularity	personality	urgency	democracy	minority

Spelling Strategy   The suffixes *-cy*, *-ty*, and *-ity* form nouns when added to base words or roots. Remember the spelling patterns for these suffixes.

Write the word that completes each phrase.

21. an easygoing _____
22. to offer a guest _____
23. a donation of extreme _____
24. to win by a _____
25. a government based on _____
26. the _____ of each ambassador

Write the word that fits each clue.

27. a result of having many friends
28. a feeling that occurs in an emergency
29. an acquaintance with or knowledge of something
30. less than half of the total

Unit 16　Words from French

pages 102–107

chef	buffet	fillet	brochure	suite
mustache	memoir	opaque	rendezvous	elite

Spelling Strategy   Remember that words from French often contain silent letters, especially the final *t*. Also, French words often spell the |ē| sound with *i*, the |ā| sound with *e*, and the |sh| sound with *ch*.

Write the words that complete the paragraph.

　　The downpour made the air seem __(31)__ . Despite it, I had to leave my cozy hotel __(32)__ to __(33)__ with a friend at a nearby restaurant. My friend had read in a tourist __(34)__ that the restaurant served from an elegant __(35)__ . In honor of the rain, I chose a tasty __(36)__ of fish.

Write the word that belongs in each group.

37. autobiography, journal, _____
38. hostess, waiter, _____
39. hair, beard, _____
40. best, top, _____

Cycle 3

tragedy	metaphor	melancholy	subtle	enthusiastic
adjourn	flourish	minuscule	wretched	outrageous

💡 **Spelling Strategy** Knowing a word's origin, thinking about the meanings of its parts, and practicing the word can often help you spell the word correctly.

Write the word that is a synonym for each word below.

41. end   **43.** eager   **45.** shocking

42. sly   **44.** tiny   **46.** prosper

Write the word that matches each definition.

47. a serious play that ends with ruin for the main character

48. an atmosphere of sorrow or sadness

49. miserable

50. a figure of speech that compares two things

Challenge Words   Units 13–17   pages 84–113

mandate	superimpose	susceptible	liaison	genre
mandatory	spontaneity	anonymity	détente	prosperity
juxtapose	protractor	hypocrite	queue	

Write the word that completes each sentence.

51. Transparent paper allows you to _____ one image over another.

52. Artists may _____ pale and bright colors to create a contrast.

53. During the _____, both nations hoped that peace would last.

54. The people waiting for tickets formed a _____ four blocks long.

55. Irma measured the angle with her _____.

56. The coordinator served as a _____ between the two committees.

57. The leader had a _____ from the voters to pursue his policies.

Write the word that is a synonym or antonym for each word.

58. immune   **61.** phony   **63.** type

59. optional   **62.** impulsiveness   **64.** wealth

60. fame

237

Unit 19 Vowel Changes II
pages 120–125

restoration	punctual	tranquil	neutral	trivial
restore	punctuality	tranquility	neutrality	triviality

💡 **Spelling Strategy** To remember the spelling of the schwa sound in some words, think of a related word in which the pronunciation and spelling of the vowel are more obvious.

Write the word that is an antonym for each word below.
1. disturbance
2. importance
3. late
4. bias

Write the word that completes each sentence.
5. The beautiful music made Raul feel calm and _____.
6. The builders planned to _____ the old town hall.
7. Not wanting to take sides, Nita remained _____.
8. Avoid the _____ details and concentrate on the important facts.
9. The richness of the wood was plain to see after its _____.
10. We know Jeff will be on time because he is known for his _____.

Unit 20 Latin Roots II
pages 126–131

convert	expire	universal	reverse	perspiration
invert	versus	anniversary	introvert	vertical

💡 **Spelling Strategy** Knowing the Latin roots *ver* ("to turn") and *spir/pir* ("to breathe") can help you spell and understand words with these roots.

Write the word that completes each analogy.
11. birth : birthday :: marriage : _____
12. breathing : respiration :: sweating : _____
13. begin : start :: end : _____
14. one : all :: particular : _____

Write the word that completes each phrase.
15. to _____ to a new faith
16. to shift the car into _____
17. the Cubs _____ the Cardinals
18. to _____ a saltshaker
19. a shy, quiet _____
20. a _____ pole to support a tent

Cycle 4

Unit 21	Noun Suffixes II		pages 132–137

historian	librarian	novelist	custodian	idealism
guitarist	conformist	civilian	soloist	realism

💡 **Spelling Strategy**   Remember the meanings of the noun suffixes *-ian* and *-ist* ("one who does or studies") and of the noun suffix *-ism* ("the act, profession, or theory of").

Write the word that fits each clue.

21. studies past events
22. writes fiction
23. is not in the army
24. strums a stringed instrument
25. has keys to every door of a building
26. lends books of all kinds

Write the word that completes each sentence.

27. The _____ stepped forward to sing, and the choir fell silent.
28. Rafael prefers _____ to other styles of painting.
29. A _____ likes to blend in with the crowd.
30. Courage and _____ kept her from lowering her high standards.

Unit 22	Words from Other Languages		pages 138–143

villa	pizza	gondola	opera	macaroni
violin	confetti	pretzel	influenza	umbrella

💡 **Spelling Strategy**   Remember that English has borrowed words from many languages.

Write the word that fits each clue.

31. Toss this to celebrate.
32. This is played with a bow.
33. Spend your vacation in this.
34. Stay dry with this.
35. A "bug" spreads this.

Write the word that completes each analogy.

36. frosting : cake :: cheese : _____
37. instrument : orchestra :: singer : _____
38. car : taxi :: boat : _____
39. flat : cracker :: twisted : _____
40. pillow : ravioli :: elbow : _____

Unit 23 Words Often Misspelled II   pages 144–149

acreage	vacancy	pamphlet	acquaintance	exquisite
forfeit	anxious	abundant	catastrophe	inevitable

 Spelling Strategy   Knowing a word's origin, thinking about the meanings of its parts, and practicing the word can often help you spell the word correctly.

Write the word that is a synonym for each word below.

41. uneasy   **43.** certain   **45.** plentiful
42. lose   **44.** beautiful   **46.** disaster

Write the word that fits each clue.

47. This person may be friendly without being your friend.
48. You can stay in a hotel if it has this.
49. You need a lot of this for a farm.
50. This usually contains written information.

Challenge Words   Units 19–23   pages 120–149

economy	revert	pessimism	tempera	bouillon
economics	vice versa	wanderlust	aesthetic	linguist
optimism	pistachio	inverse	bureaucrat	

Write the words that complete the paragraph.

   Amy seemed content working as a government __(51)__ , but she secretly longed to travel the world. This __(52)__ made her dream of drinking __(53)__ in France, eating a __(54)__ nut in Turkey, and treating her __(55)__ sense to art in Italy. Why, she might even buy some __(56)__ paints and become an artist herself, or learn ten languages and become a __(57)__ . Her dreams were farfetched, but __(58)__ kept her hopeful.

Write the word that matches each definition.

59. thrifty management   **62.** return
60. related to finances   **63.** a gloomy outlook
61. opposite   **64.** other way around

Cycle 5

Unit 25 Vowel Changes III

produce	retain	introduce	resume	abstain
production	retention	introduction	resumption	abstention

💡 **Spelling Strategy**   Knowing how the vowels change in one pair of related words can help you predict changes in other pairs with the same root.

Write the word that is a synonym for each word below.

1. beginning
2. refrain
3. creation
4. continue
5. keep
6. make

Write the word that completes each sentence.

7. An _____ from voting may mean that the voter is undecided.
8. Improve your _____ of dates and facts by saying them aloud.
9. The director will _____ the play with a few opening words.
10. At the _____ of this meeting, we will finish our discussion.

Unit 26 Latin Roots III
pages 162–167

complexity	imply	sentry	reconstruct	sensation
destruction	resent	sensor	applicable	multiplication

💡 **Spelling Strategy**   Knowing the Latin roots *plic/plex/ply/pli* ("to fold"), *sens/sent* ("to feel"), and *struct* ("to build") can help you spell and understand words with these roots.

Write the word that belongs in each group.

11. addition, division, _____
12. suggest, hint, _____
13. ruin, wreckage, _____
14. gatekeeper, guard, _____
15. appropriate, pertinent, _____
16. rebuild, restore, _____

Write the word that completes each analogy.

17. siren : alarm :: radar : _____
18. thought : idea :: feeling : _____
19. compliment : appreciate :: insult : _____
20. easy : simplicity :: hard : _____

Unit 27 Adjective Suffixes

pages 168–173

mountainous	gradual	cautious	mobile	tremendous
artificial	fragile	precious	social	hysterical

 Spelling Strategy The suffixes *-al*, *-ile*, and *-ous* ("of; relating to; capable of; characterized by; full of") form adjectives when added to base words or roots. Remember the spelling patterns for these suffixes.

Write the word that is an antonym for each word below.

21. flat **22.** stationary **23.** worthless **24.** sudden **25.** sturdy

Write the word that completes each sentence.

26. She prefers natural flavorings in food to _____ ones.

27. The falling rocks made a _____ noise.

28. Always be _____ when crossing a busy street.

29. The _____ committee plans parties, dances, and picnics.

30. The father quieted the frightened child's _____ sobbing.

Unit 28 Words from Places

pages 174–179

denim	jersey	satin	gauze	dungarees
tuxedo	muslin	damask	spa	Rugby

Spelling Strategy Knowing the origin of words that come from the names of places can help you spell and understand the meanings of the words.

Write the words that complete the paragraph.

My brother wore a formal black __(31)__ to his wedding. That was quite a change from his usual outfit, which consists of ragged __(32)__ and a faded __(33)__ jacket over a football __(34)__. Those clothes suit him better, but they would have looked out of place next to the bride's shiny, white __(35)__ gown.

Write the word that fits each clue.

36. This cloth is very plain cotton.

37. This cloth has patterns on it.

38. You can see through this cloth.

39. This is a ball game.

40. This is a vacation spot.

Cycle 5

Unit 29 Single or Double Consonants pages 180–185

applicant	referral	occupation	committee	essential
tariff	paraffin	possession	harass	shrubbery

Spelling Strategy Remember that double consonants can occur when a prefix is absorbed or before a suffix beginning with a vowel. Double consonants in other words must be remembered.

Write the word that matches each definition.

41. the act of owning
42. career
43. necessary
44. to bother
45. a tax
46. a group of bushes
47. the act of directing to a person or place

Write the word that completes each analogy.

48. prize : contestant :: job : _____
49. lightbulb : glass :: candle : _____
50. teacher : class :: chairperson : _____

Challenge Words Units 25–29 pages 156–185

ferocious	replica	reconnaissance	ambiguous	succinct
ferocity	pliable	intellectual	notorious	sardonic
implicit	frieze	laconic	collateral	

Write the word that matches each definition.

51. brief and clear
52. fierce
53. vague
54. sarcastic
55. very intelligent
56. known unfavorably
57. easily bent
58. security for a loan
59. a decoration across a wall

Write the word that fits each clue.

60. A person who is this does not say much.
61. This might be a military exploration.
62. This painting may look like an original work of art.
63. A statement that is this is not direct.
64. Some wild animals display this.

Unit 31 Vowel Changes IV

pages 192–197

proclaim	maintain	exclaim	perceive	conceive
proclamation	maintenance	exclamation	perception	conception

 Spelling Strategy Knowing how the vowels change in one pair of related words can help you predict changes in other pairs with the same root.

Write the word that matches each definition.
1. to form or develop in the mind
2. to announce officially and publicly
3. to become aware of
4. to keep up
5. to cry out suddenly
6. a plan, thought, or idea

Write the word that completes each analogy.
7. "Why?" : question :: "Oh!" : _____
8. knowledge : learning :: understanding : _____
9. whisper : secret :: shout : _____
10. neglect : decay :: upkeep : _____

Unit 32 Latin Roots IV

pages 198–203

factory	manual	profit	benefit	defect
effect	manipulate	factor	convention	preventive

 Spelling Strategy Knowing the Latin roots *fac/fic/fit/fec/feat* ("to make or do"), *man* ("hand"), and *ven* ("to come") can help you spell and understand words with these roots.

Write the word that belongs in each group.
11. fault, flaw, _____
12. handbook, instructions, _____
13. help, advantage, _____
14. handle, operate, _____
15. result, outcome, _____
16. gain, winnings, _____

Write the word that matches each definition.
17. designed to hinder
18. a consideration
19. a formal assembly or meeting
20. a building in which goods are manufactured

Cycle 6

Unit 33 Number Prefixes   pages 204–209

monk	decade	monopoly	monotone	duet
diploma	centigrade	monogram	monorail	duplex

💡 **Spelling Strategy**   Remember that *mon-/mono-* ("one"), *di-* ("two"), *du-* ("two"), *dec-* ("ten"), and *cent-* ("one hundred") are number prefixes.

Write the word that completes each phrase.

21. to receive a high school _____
22. to sing a _____ with a friend
23. a _____ with the initials C.F.T.
24. to speak in a dull _____
25. one hundred degrees _____
26. to last for a _____

Write the word that fits each clue.

27. This may carry passengers through a city.
28. This person spends much time in prayer.
29. Two families may live in this building.
30. This business faces no competition.

Unit 34 Words New to English   pages 210–215

software	android	photocopy	smog	antibiotic
space shuttle	amplifier	brunch	scuba	supersonic

💡 **Spelling Strategy**   Knowing whether a word new to English was formed by combining word parts from other languages or by creating a **compound word**, a **blend**, or an **acronym** can help you spell the word correctly.

Write the words that complete the paragraph.

   Near Mars, the __(31)__ swerved off course. There seemed to be an error in the computer __(32)__. Radio signals from Earth became weak, even with the __(33)__ at maximum volume. Being an __(34)__, however, Imo did not panic.

Write the word that matches each definition.

35. a type of medicine
36. a reproduction
37. faster than the speed of sound
38. fog mixed with smoke
39. a late-morning meal
40. an air tank used by a diver

Unit 35 Words Often Mispronounced   pages 216–221

algebra	probably	identity	liberal	temperamental
dinghy	hindrance	monstrous	grievous	preferable

💡 **Spelling Strategy**   Knowing the correct pronunciation of a word will help you spell it correctly.

Write the word that belongs in each group.

41. block, obstacle, _____
42. sailboat, canoe, _____
43. moody, changeable, _____

44. huge, enormous, _____
45. likely, presumably, _____
46. generous, ample, _____

Write the word that completes each analogy.

47. good: desirable :: better : _____
48. angle : geometry :: number : _____
49. happy : sad :: joyous : _____
50. address : location :: name : _____

Challenge Words   Units 31–35   pages 192–221

pronounce	prerequisite	posthumous	aerospace	decibel
pronunciation	semiconductor	circumvent	hologram	digraph
paraphernalia	monochrome	facsimile	artifact	

Write the word that matches each definition.

51. required
52. copy
53. after death

54. go around
55. utter properly
56. unit of sound

57. how a word is spoken
58. an object made by humans

Write the word that completes each sentence.

59. The _____ looked just like a three-dimensional object.
60. Mike refused to go on the hike until he had the proper _____.
61. Silicon, a _____, acts as an efficient path for electricity.
62. The *th* in *bath* is a _____ because it stands for one sound.
63. Her best painting is a _____ in various shades of blue.
64. The _____ engineers were designing a new spacecraft.

Writer's Resources

Capitalization and Punctuation Guide

Abbreviations

Abbreviations are shortened forms of words. Most abbreviations begin with a capital letter and end with a period.

Titles	Mr. *(Mister)*	Ms. *(any woman)*	Sr. *(Senior)*
	Mrs. *(married woman)*	Dr. *(Doctor)*	Jr. *(Junior)*
	Note: *Miss* is not an abbreviation and does not end with a period.		

Initials	John F. Kennedy *(John Fitzgerald Kennedy)*
	P. D. James *(Phyllis Dorothy James)*

Days of the week	Sat. *(Saturday)*
	Tues. *(Tuesday)*

Months of the year	Feb. *(February)*
	Sept. *(September)*
	Note: Do not abbreviate *May, June,* and *July.*

Time	A.M. (midnight to noon)
	P.M. (noon to midnight)

Words used in addresses	St. *(Street)*	Rte. *(Route)*	Pkwy. *(Parkway)*
	Rd. *(Road)*	Apt. *(Apartment)*	Mt. *(Mount or Mountain)*
	Ave. *(Avenue)*	Blvd. *(Boulevard)*	Expy. *(Expressway)*
	Dr. *(Drive)*		

Words used in business	Co. *(Company)*	Corp. *(Corporation)*
	Inc. *(Incorporated)*	Ltd. *(Limited)*

Other abbreviations

Some abbreviations are written in all capital letters, with a letter standing for each important word.

P.D. *(Police Department)*	P.O. *(Post Office)*
R.N. *(Registered Nurse)*	M.A. *(Master of Arts)*

Abbreviations for units of measure use neither capital letters nor periods. The only exception is the abbreviation for *inch*.

mph *(miles per hour)*   in. *(inch)*   l *(liter)*

(continued)

Other abbreviations (continued)	**Abbreviations of government agencies or national organizations do not usually have periods.** PBS *(Public Broadcasting Service)* NATO *(North Atlantic Treaty Organization)*

States	**The United States Postal Service uses two capital letters and no period in each of its state abbreviations.**

AL *(Alabama)*   LA *(Louisiana)*   OH *(Ohio)*
AK *(Alaska)*   ME *(Maine)*   OK *(Oklahoma)*
AZ *(Arizona)*   MD *(Maryland)*   OR *(Oregon)*
AR *(Arkansas)*   MA *(Massachusetts)*   PA *(Pennsylvania)*
CA *(California)*   MI *(Michigan)*   RI *(Rhode Island)*
CO *(Colorado)*   MN *(Minnesota)*   SC *(South Carolina)*
CT *(Connecticut)*   MS *(Mississippi)*   SD *(South Dakota)*
DE *(Delaware)*   MO *(Missouri)*   TN *(Tennessee)*
FL *(Florida)*   MT *(Montana)*   TX *(Texas)*
GA *(Georgia)*   NE *(Nebraska)*   UT *(Utah)*
HI *(Hawaii)*   NV *(Nevada)*   VT *(Vermont)*
ID *(Idaho)*   NH *(New Hampshire)*   VA *(Virginia)*
IL *(Illinois)*   NJ *(New Jersey)*   WA *(Washington)*
IN *(Indiana)*   NM *(New Mexico)*   WV *(West Virginia)*
IA *(Iowa)*   NY *(New York)*   WI *(Wisconsin)*
KS *(Kansas)*   NC *(North Carolina)*   WY *(Wyoming)*
KY *(Kentucky)*   ND *(North Dakota)*

Numbers	**Spell out numbers under one hundred and numbers at the beginning of a sentence. Use numerals for numbers over one hundred.** My team has *twenty-five* players. *Two hundred sixty* people were in the audience. There are *147* apartments in my building.

Titles

Underlining	**Titles of books, magazines, newspapers, long musical works, plays, works of art, movies, and TV series are underlined. The important words and the first and last words are capitalized.** Dogsong *(book)* As You Like It *(play)* Miami Herald *(newspaper)* Mona Lisa *(painting)* Requiem *(musical work)* Nature *(TV series)*

Quotations

Quotation marks

Titles of short stories, articles, songs, poems, and book chapters are enclosed in quotation marks.

"The Party" *(short story)*   "If" *(poem)*
"Crewelwork" *(article)*   "Saxon Art" *(chapter)*
"America" *(song)*

Quotation marks with commas and periods

Quotation marks are used to set a speaker's exact words apart from the rest of a sentence. The first word of a direct quotation begins with a capital letter. Question marks and exclamation points that belong to the quotation are placed inside the quotation marks. Question marks and exclamation points that do not belong to the quotation are placed outside the quotation marks. Commas separate a quotation from the rest of the sentence. Always place periods and commas inside quotation marks.

"Where," Duane asked, "did I leave my keys?"
Did Jamal say, "I am going to Miami on my vacation"?
Megan replied, "I don't know what time it is."

Bibliography

The basic organization of a bibliography is alphabetical. If the author's name is not given, list the title first, and alphabetize it by the first important word of the title.

Books

List the author's name (last name first), the book title, the city where the publisher is located, the publisher's name, and the year of publication. Note the punctuation.

Schmitt, Lois. Smart Spending: A Consumer's Guide. New York: Simon & Schuster, 1989.

Encyclopedia article

List the author's name (last name first), then the title of the article (in quotation marks). Next, give the title of the encyclopedia (underlined), and the year of publication of the edition you are using. Note the punctuation.

Mann, Alan E. "Prehistoric People." The World Book Encyclopedia. 1997 ed.

(continued)

Encyclopedia article *(continued)*	**If the author of the article is not given, begin your listing with the title of the article.** "Charles River." <u>Collier's Encyclopedia</u>. 1997 ed.
Magazine or newspaper article	**Study these examples carefully. Note the order and the punctuation.** MAGAZINE: Kirschner, Suzanne. "From School to Space." <u>Popular Science</u>, June 1998, pp. 56–57. NEWSPAPER: Martin, Douglas. "Macy's Balloons Are Heavy Subject." <u>The New York Times</u>, November 3, 1998, Sec. A, p. 27. NEWSPAPER: (no author) "Turner Considers Run for Presidency." <u>Boston Globe</u>, November 16, 1998, Sec. A, p. 12. **Here is another way that you can write these entries:** MAGAZINE: Kirschner, Suzanne. "From School to Space." <u>Popular Science</u> June 1998: 56–57. NEWSPAPER: Martin, Douglas. "Macy's Balloons Are Heavy Subject." <u>The New York Times</u> 3 Nov. 1998, sec. A: 27.

Capitalization

Rules for capitalization	**Capitalize geographical names such as cities, states, countries, continents, bodies of water, geographical features, and geographical areas. Do not capitalize small words like *the* and *of*.** <u>P</u>aris <u>A</u>sia <u>R</u>ock of <u>G</u>ibraltar <u>V</u>ermont <u>Y</u>angtze <u>R</u>iver <u>E</u>astern <u>E</u>urope <u>B</u>razil <u>R</u>io <u>G</u>rande the <u>N</u>ortheast **Do not capitalize directions.** We live ten miles east of Philadelphia. **Capitalize titles or their abbreviations when used with a person's name.** <u>G</u>overnor Bradford <u>S</u>enator Smith <u>D</u>r. Lin **Capitalize proper adjectives.** We ate at a <u>M</u>exican restaurant. She is <u>F</u>rench. **Capitalize the names of months and days.** My birthday is on the last <u>M</u>onday in <u>M</u>arch.

Rules for capitalization	**Capitalize the names of organizations, businesses, institutions, and agencies.**

(continued)

Capitalize the names of organizations, businesses, institutions, and agencies.

National Hockey League   The Status Company
Franklin Mint   Federal Aviation Administration

Capitalize names of holidays and other special events, streets, highways, buildings, bridges, monuments, historical events, periods of time, and documents.

Veterans Day	Golden Gate Bridge	Jazz Age
Route 9	Lincoln Memorial	Bill of Rights
World Trade Center	French Revolution	

Capitalize the first and last words and all important words in the titles of books, newspapers, stories, songs, poems, reports, and outlines. (Articles, short conjunctions, and short prepositions are not capitalized unless they are the first or last word.)

A Wizard of Earthsea	"The Road Not Taken"
The New York Times	"Canadian National Parks"
"The Necklace"	"The Exports of Italy"
"Over the Rainbow"	

Capitalize the first word of each main topic and subtopic in an outline.

I. Types of libraries
   A. Large public library
   B. Bookmobile

Capitalize the first word in the greeting and closing of a letter.

Dear Marcia,   Dear Mr. Olsen: Your friend,   Yours truly,

Capitalize nationalities, languages, religions, religious terms, and specific school subjects followed by a number.

Canadian	Old English	Menorah	Geography 101
Spanish	Buddhism	Koran	History I

Punctuation

End marks	**A period (.) ends a declarative or imperative sentence. A question mark (?) follows an interrogative sentence. An exclamation point (!)**

(continued)

End marks
(continued)

is used after an exclamatory sentence and after an interjection that expresses strong feeling.

The stapler is on my desk. *(declarative)*

Look up the spelling of that word. *(imperative)*

How is the word spelled? *(interrogative)*

This is your best poem so far! *(exclamatory)*

Wow! We've just won the essay prize. *(interjection)*

Apostrophe

To form the possessive of a singular noun, add an apostrophe and *s*.

sister's   family's   Tess's   Jim Dodge's

To form the possessive of a plural noun that ends in *s*, add an apostrophe only.

sisters'   families'   Smiths'   Evanses'

For a plural noun that does not end in *s*, add an apostrophe and *s*.

women's   alumni's   mice's   brothers-in-law's

Use an apostrophe and *s* to form the plural of letters, numerals, symbols, and words that are used as words.

s's   i's   2's   *'s   yes's and no's

Use an apostrophe in contractions in place of dropped letters. Do not use contractions in formal writing.

isn't *(is not)*   they've *(they have)*   it's *(it is)*

Colon

Use a colon to separate the hour from the minute.

7:30 P.M.   8:15 A.M.

Use a colon after the greeting in a business letter.

Dear Mrs. Trimby: Dear Realty Homes:

Use a colon before a list introduced by words like *the following* or *these*. Do not use a colon after a verb or a preposition.

Call the following: Tara, Rebecca, Shawn, and Felipe.

Next year I am taking English, history, and math.

He arrived with a suitcase, a coat, and an umbrella.

Comma

Use commas to separate words in a series.

Nick asked if we had any apples, pears, or grapes.

Comma
(continued)

Use commas between two or more adjectives that come before a noun. Do not use a comma if the adjectives are used together to express a single idea.
Her shrill, urgent cry was alarming.
The tired British tourists decided to rest.

Use a comma to separate the simple sentences in a compound sentence.
Some students were at lunch, but others were studying.

Use commas after words, phrases, and clauses that come at the beginning of sentences.
No, you cannot avoid the deadline.
Following the applause, the speaker continued.
When you are in doubt, ask for advice.

Use commas to separate interrupters such as *of course*, *however*, and *by the way* from the rest of the sentence.
Tamika, of course, was late for the bus again.
The driver, however, had forgotten the directions.

Use commas to set off an appositive from the rest of the sentence when the appositive is not necessary to the meaning of the sentence.
The writer Charles Dickens created complex plots.
(The appositive is necessary to the meaning.)
Texas, the Lone Star State, borders Mexico.
(The appositive is extra, not needed for meaning.)

Use a comma to separate a noun in direct address.
Kevin, help me fix this.   How was your trip, Pa?

Use a comma to separate the month and day from the year. Use a comma to separate the year from the rest of the sentence. Do not use commas if a specific day is not included.
January 12, 1999, is the date of the banquet.
Halley's comet appeared last during April 1986.

Use a comma after an interjection that expresses mild emotion.
Gee, I hope the bus comes soon.

(continued)

Comma
(continued)

Use a comma between the names of a city and a state in an address. If the address is within a sentence, also use a comma after the name of the state. Do not use a comma before the ZIP code.
Does Chicago, Illinois, have the world's tallest building?
Denise lives at 10 Palm Court, Lima, OH 45807.

Use a comma after the greeting in a friendly letter and after the closing in all letters.
Dear Joann,   Sincerely yours,

Use commas to set off a nonessential phrase or clause, which adds optional information not necessary to the meaning of the sentence. If a phrase or clause is essential, do not use commas.
Emily Dickinson, who was born in 1830, was a poet.
(The clause is not necessary to the meaning.)
The man who read the poem is my father.
(The clause is necessary to the meaning.)

Semicolon

Use a semicolon to connect independent clauses that are closely related in thought or that have commas within them.
There were five movie tickets left; Billy needed six.
He bought nuts, dates, and figs; we ate them all.

Use a semicolon to join two independent clauses when the second clause begins with an adverb such as *however*, *therefore*, or *consequently*.
It was growing dark; however, there were no clouds.

Hyphens, dashes, parentheses

Use a hyphen to join the parts of compound numbers, to join two or more words that work together as one adjective before a noun, or to divide a word at the end of a line.
thirty-two   long-range plans
Raphael is known as one of Italy's many magnificent painters.

Use dashes to show a sudden change of thought.
The sky grew dark—it could mean snow.

Use parentheses to enclose unnecessary information.
Natasha was reelected (once more) as treasurer.

Letter Models

Friendly Letter

Use correct letter format, capitalization, and punctuation in a friendly letter. A friendly letter has **five** parts.

1 The **heading** contains your complete address and the date.

2 The **greeting**, or salutation, usually includes the word *Dear* and the name of the person to whom you are writing.

3 The **body** of the letter is your message. Indent each paragraph.

4 The **closing** appears under the last paragraph and lines up with the heading. Some common closings are *Your friend*, *Love*, and *Take care*.

5 The **signature** is your first name. Sign it under the closing.

Study this model.

Heading ┄┄→

> 208 Highland Avenue
> Akron, OH 44305
> July 12, 1999

Greeting ┄┄→ Dear Sondra,

Body ┄┄→
> It wasn't very smart of me to break my arm in the hottest part of summer. Do you know how badly I'd like to go swimming? At least I broke my left arm and not the right one. Otherwise I couldn't even write this letter!
>
> I hope you're enjoying summer vacation a lot. I'll look forward to seeing you at the picnic. Meanwhile, do an extra dive in the pool for me!

Closing ┄┄→ Your friend,

Signature ┄┄→ Tammy

Writer's Resources

Letter Models

Business Letter

Use correct letter format, capitalization, and punctuation in a business letter. A business letter has **six** parts.

1. The **heading** is the same as in a friendly letter.
2. The **inside address** includes the name and address of the person or business that will receive the letter.
3. The **greeting** follows the inside address. If you do not know whom to address, use *Dear Sir or Madam* or the company's name. Use a colon (:) after the greeting.
4. The **body** is your message. Be direct and polite.
5. The **closing** is formal. Use such closings as *Yours truly* or *Sincerely yours*.
6. The **signature** is your full name. Write it under the closing. Print or type your name under your signature.

Study this model.

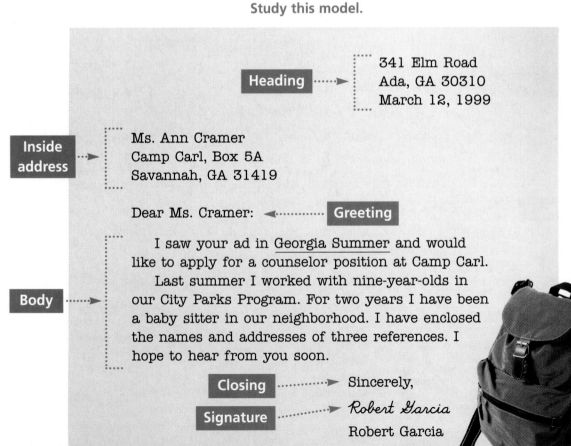

Heading

341 Elm Road
Ada, GA 30310
March 12, 1999

Inside address

Ms. Ann Cramer
Camp Carl, Box 5A
Savannah, GA 31419

Dear Ms. Cramer: ◄········· Greeting

Body

I saw your ad in Georgia Summer and would like to apply for a counselor position at Camp Carl.
Last summer I worked with nine-year-olds in our City Parks Program. For two years I have been a baby sitter in our neighborhood. I have enclosed the names and addresses of three references. I hope to hear from you soon.

Closing ···········► Sincerely,

Signature ···········► *Robert Garcia*
Robert Garcia

Using the Thesaurus

Why Use a Thesaurus?

A **thesaurus** is a reference that can help you make your writing clearer and more interesting. Use it to find a word to replace an overused word or to find an exact word to say what you mean.

How to Use This Thesaurus

This thesaurus includes main entries for words you often use. The **main entry words** appear in blue and are in alphabetical order. The main entry for *interesting* is shown below. Each main entry includes

- the **part of speech**, a **definition**, and a **sample sentence** for the main entry word;
- several **subentry words** that could be used in place of the main entry word, with a definition and a sample sentence for each one;
- **antonyms**, or opposites, for the main entry word.

For example   **How would you decide which subentry to use to replace *interesting* in this sentence?**

> *The movie was so **interesting** that we did not hear the doorbell.*

1. Find each subentry word given for *interesting*. They are *creative*, *engrossing*, and *individualistic*.
2. Read the definition and the sample sentence for each subentry. Decide which subentry fits the meaning of the sentence most closely.

> *The movie was so **engrossing** that we did not hear the doorbell.*

Part of speech   hygienic

Main entry word

adj. clean and free of germs. *al foods are best prepared in **hygienic*** *gs.*

interesting *adj.* arousing or holding interest or attention. *Our trip to Peru was interesting and informative.* ◄··· Definition

creative original and expressive. *This poetry is very **creative** but not very useful.* ···► Sample sentence

free of microorg Subentries *ptic instruments.*

engrossing occupying the complete attention of. *The story was so **engrossing** that it kept me awake.*

ate perfectly clean. *They kept their mmaculate condition.*

individualistic different from others; distinctive. *I always recognize Van Gogh's individualistic style of painting.*

remaining in a pure state; *d. From the mountaintop we looked he **pristine** wilderness of the national*

Antonyms

antonyms: boring, commonplace, monotonous, tedious

257

Using the Thesaurus

Using the Thesaurus Index

The Thesaurus Index will help you find a word in this Thesaurus. The Thesaurus Index lists **all** of the main entry words, the subentries, and any antonyms included in the Thesaurus. The words in the Thesaurus Index are in alphabetical order.

When you look in the Thesaurus Index, you will see that words are shown in three ways.

Main entry words are shown in blue. For example, the word *interesting* is a main entry.

Antonyms are shown in regular print. For example, *irrelevant* is an antonym.

Subentries are shown in dark print. For example, *irritant* is a subentry.

I

identical **adverse** *adj.*
identical **different** *adj.*
immaculate hygienic *adj.*
insignificant **important** *adj.*
insufficient **plentiful** *adj.*
interesting *adj.*
intervene obstruct *v.*
intrude go *v.*
invade go *v.*
irrelevant **important** *adj.*
irritant nuisance *n.*

Practice Look up each word below in the Thesaurus Index. Write the main entry word for each word.

1. sad   2. emigrate   3. abhor   4. delirious   5. empathetic

Use the Thesaurus to choose a more exact word to replace each underlined word. Rewrite each sentence, using the new word.

6. My sister and I sometimes have <u>juvenile</u> disagreements.
7. Last summer we tried to <u>make</u> a doghouse together.
8. However, we could not agree on a <u>site</u> for the doghouse.
9. The <u>consequence</u> was that my sister quit the whole project.
10. Nonetheless, she did <u>like</u> the completed doghouse.

Thesaurus Index

Thesaurus Index

message **communication** *n.*

migrate **go** *v.*

minuscule **colossal** *adj.*

miscellaneous **different** *adj.*

miserable **sad** *adj.*

mobile **stationary** *adj.*

moderate **gradual** *adj.*

mold **make** *v.*

monotonous **interesting** *adj.*

monstrous **colossal** *adj.*

motive **consequence** *n.*

N

negotiation **transaction** *n.*

neutrality **fight** *n.*

noiseless **quiet** *adj.*

nuisance *n.*

O

obstruct *v.*

obtain **win** *v.*

occasional **plentiful** *adj.*

opposite **adverse** *adj.*

optimistic **adverse** *adj.*

origin **consequence** *n.*

origin **end** *n.*

originate **make** *v.*

outcome **consequence** *n.*

outset **end** *n.*

P

pact **transaction** *n.*

particular **universal** *adj.*

pathetic **sad** *adj.*

pathological **hygienic** *adj.*

peace **fight** *n.*

period **phase** *n.*

perpendicular **upright** *adj.*

phase *n.*

photocopy **make** *v.*

place **site** *n.*

pleasure **nuisance** *n.*

plentiful *adj.*

polluted **hygienic** *adj.*

position **site** *n.*

possessed **wild** *adj.*

precipitous **gradual** *adj.*

predominate **succumb** *v.*

prefer **like** *v.*

prevail **succumb** *v.*

prevalent **plentiful** *adj.*

prevent **obstruct** *v.*

primitive **wild** *adj.*

pristine **hygienic** *adj.*

produce **make** *v.*

progressive **gradual** *adj.*

prohibit **obstruct** *v.*

prominent **important** *adj.*

prone **upright** *adj.*

protest **succumb** *v.*

puny **colossal** *adj.*

pure **hygienic** *adj.*

Q

quiet *adj.*

R

ramble **go** *v.*

range **go** *v.*

rare **plentiful** *adj.*

rational **wild** *adj.*

rationale **consequence** *n.*

raving **wild** *adj.*

raze **make** *v.*

rebellious **wild** *adj.*

reckless **wild** *adj.*

recommend **like** *v.*

reconciliation **fight** *n.*

refined **wild** *adj.*

refractory **wild** *adj.*

relocate **go** *v.*

remain **go** *v.*

report **communication** *n.*

representation **sign** *n.*

resent **like** *v.*

reserved **quiet** *adj.*

reside **go** *v.*

restless **stationary** *adj.*

result **consequence** *n.*

retain **win** *v.*

retard **obstruct** *v.*

retreat **go** *v.*

revel **like** *v.*

rhythm **beat** *n.*

right *adj.*

ripe **juvenile** *adj.*

roam **go** *v.*

rove **go** *v.*

S

sacrifice **win** *v.*

sad *adj.*

sane **wild** *adj.*

satin **fabric** *n.*

savage **wild** *adj.*

scarce **plentiful** *adj.*

season **phase** *n.*

secure **win** *v.*

seemly **right** *adj.*

sensible **right** *adj.*

serene **wild** *adj.*

settle **go** *v.*

shape **make** *v.*

sign *n.*

significant **important** *adj.*

similar **different** *adj.*

site *n.*

solution **consequence** *n.*

sophomoric **juvenile** *adj.*

source **end** *n.*

spat **fight** *n.*

special **universal** *adj.*

spotless **hygienic** *adj.*

stable **stationary** *adj.*

Thesaurus Index

Thesaurus

A

adverse *adj.* not favorable; hostile. *The new tax caused an **adverse** reaction.*
averse opposed; reluctant. *Duane was not **averse** to singing, as long as someone sang with him.*
contrary completely different; opposed. *The two reviewers had **contrary** opinions about the film.*
inauspicious boding ill; unfavorable. *Despite an **inauspicious** beginning, the trip actually went smoothly.*
opposite contrary in nature or tendency. *My mom and dad hold **opposite** views in politics.*
antonyms: auspicious, beneficial, concurring, favorable, identical, optimistic

---

assent *n.* agreement, especially in a formal or impersonal manner. *The students could not leave the room without the teacher's **assent**.*
acceptance favorable reception or approval. *Kim was so sure of his **acceptance** on the team that he bought a team shirt.*
agreement an arrangement or understanding between two parties. *We worked out a final **agreement** that satisfied both sides.*
approbation the act of approving, especially officially. *To be passed, the law required the **approbation** of the governor.*
compliance action or obedience in accordance with a rule, request, or command. *Every member paid dues in **compliance** with the rules.*
consent agreement and acceptance; permission. *Leah was not allowed up in the balloon without her parents' **consent**.*
antonyms: conflict, difference, disagreement, dissent, divergence

B

beat *n.* a periodic pulsation or throb. *Dr. Diaz listened to the **beat** of my heart.*
accent a stress or special emphasis. *When Sid was first learning Spanish, he often placed the **accent** on the wrong syllables of words.*
cadence the general rise and fall of the voice in speaking. *The **cadence** of the actor's voice matched the music.*
measure the notes and rests between two successive bars in a musical staff. *The pianist paused briefly after the fourth **measure**.*
rhythm a musical pattern formed by a series of notes or beats that are of different lengths and have different stresses. *Lee tapped her foot in time with the **rhythm** of the song.*
tempo the speed at which a musical composition is played. *We asked the band to play something with a faster **tempo**.*
undulation a regular rising and falling. *The mother and child rocked together to the gentle **undulation** of the music.*

C

catastrophe *n.* a great and sudden calamity, such as an earthquake or flood. *Cleanup efforts after the **catastrophe** were slow.*
calamity something that causes great distress and suffering. *This drought was a **calamity** that affected the entire region.*
disaster great destruction, distress, or misfortune. *Survivors of the wreck had nightmares about the **disaster**.*
hardship something that causes suffering or difficulty. *The Smiths found it difficult to endure the **hardship** of the fire.*
tragedy a disastrous event. *The death of a loved one is a personal **tragedy**.*
antonyms: advantage, benefit, blessing, boon, favor

---

colossal *adj.* very great in size, extent, or degree. *The accident was the result of a **colossal** series of errors.*

huge of great size. *The tunnel is cut through the center of a huge tree.*

monstrous enormous. *A monstrous fungus grew on the tree trunk.*

tremendous extremely large in amount or degree. *A tremendous explosion woke me from a sound sleep.*

antonyms: delicate, minuscule, puny, tiny

---

communication *n.* the exchange of thoughts, information, or messages. *The explorers waited for communication from home.*

leaflet a booklet or small pamphlet. *The library printed a small leaflet that contained its rules and hours.*

message spoken or written words or signals sent from one person or group to another. *The message was written in a code that only two people knew.*

report an oral or written account containing information, often prepared or delivered in organized form. *The report listed all of the dog officer's expenses.*

telegram a message or communication sent by telegraph. *A telegram is one of the fastest ways to send congratulations.*

---

consequence *n.* something that follows from an action or condition. *One consequence of this law will be higher taxes.*

effect something brought about by a cause or agent. *The storm had a devastating effect on the young fruit trees.*

outcome a final product. *To most people, the outcome of the election was no surprise.*

result the outgrowth of a particular action, operation, or cause. *The dam broke as a result of the heavy rains.*

solution the successful outcome of a problem. *Moving to a dry climate was the solution to his health problem.*

antonyms: cause, inducement, motive, origin, rationale

D

different *adj.* unlike. *You may be able to tell the twins apart because their hair color is slightly different.*

bizarre very strange or odd; grotesque. *Bob wore a bizarre costume covered with feathers, shells, and bottle caps.*

distinct having an identity of its own. *Each type of butterfly had distinct markings.*

diverse distinct in kind. *It was impossible to categorize such a diverse group of books.*

miscellaneous made up of a variety of different elements or ingredients. *It's not an orchard, just a miscellaneous bunch of trees.*

various of different kinds. *I had various reasons for choosing that brand of shoe.*

antonyms: analogous, homogenous, identical, similar, synonymous, uniform

E

end *n.* the finish of something. *Please hand in your papers at the end of the class.*

conclusion the close or closing part of something. *At the conclusion of the play, the audience clapped wildly.*

expiration the process of coming to a close. *I suggest you apply for a new license before the expiration of this one.*

finale the final section of something that is performed, especially the ending of a musical composition. *The finale of The 1812 Overture often includes a display of fireworks.*

termination something that has been brought to an end or has come to an end. *My brother returns to college a week after the termination of his summer job.*

antonyms: beginning, commencement, conception, origin, outset, source

F

fabric *n.* cloth or other material produced by joining fibers together. *Is that coat made of leather or fabric?*

calico a cotton cloth with a figured pattern printed on it in color. *Use calico for your kitchen curtains.*

denim a course, heavy cotton cloth used for work clothes and sports clothes. *Most blue jeans are made from denim.*

jersey a soft, elastic, knitted fabric of wool, cotton, or synthetic fibers, used for clothing. *On cold days, I wear a jersey turtleneck under a sweater.*

khaki a strong, heavy, yellowish-brown cloth, used for army uniforms. *The uniforms were made of khaki and blended in with the desert surroundings.*

satin a smooth fabric of silk, rayon, nylon, or other fibers, woven with a glossy finish on one side. *My sister wore a wedding dress of satin.*

---

fight *n.* a quarrel. *My friend and I had a fight, but later we both apologized.*

controversy an argument or debate. *The new tax law has aroused much controversy.*

duel a contest between two opponents. *The two candidates had a duel of wits.*

spat a brief, petty quarrel. *We get along, except for an occasional spat.*

antonyms: accommodation, accord, harmony, neutrality, peace, reconciliation

G

Shades of Meaning

go *v.*

1. to leave:

abscond	depart	vacate
decamp	embark	
defect	retreat	

2. to move from one place to another:

adjourn	journey	transfer
emigrate	migrate	voyage
immigrate	relocate	

3. to pass where one does not belong:

encroach	invade	trespass
intrude	transgress	

4. to move along aimlessly:

gallivant	range	stray
meander	roam	wander
ramble	rove	

antonyms: 1. approach, arrive, disembark 2. abide, endure, remain 3. lodge, reside, settle

---

gradual *adj.* occurring by small stages or degrees. *Rebuilding the school was a gradual process.*

easy not hurried; slow. *Walking to town will take ten minutes at an easy pace.*

moderate not violent, severe, or intense. *I like sailing only in a moderate breeze.*

progressive advancing steadily. *Scientists became alarmed about the progressive destruction of the ozone layer.*

step-by-step progressing by stages. *Building a house is a step-by-step process.*

subtle so slight as to be difficult to detect. *Actors can show anger through subtle facial expressions.*

antonyms: abrupt, hasty, precipitous, sudden

H

hygienic *adj.* clean and free of germs. *Commercial foods are best prepared in hygienic surroundings.*

antiseptic free of microorganisms. *Dentists use antiseptic instruments.*

immaculate perfectly clean. *They kept their home in immaculate condition.*

pristine remaining in a pure state; untouched. *From the mountaintop we looked out over the pristine wilderness of the national forest.*

pure free from foreign elements or impurities. *All our foods are made from pure, wholesome ingredients.*

spotless free from stain. *The doctor's spotless uniform increased our confidence.*

antonyms: contaminated, filthy, pathological, polluted, vile

I

important *adj.* able to determine or change the course of events or the nature of things. *This is a very important message, so write it carefully.*

critical decisive. *The last game was critical, so we played our hardest.*

crucial of the utmost importance. *I stopped because a crucial ingredient was missing.*

essential indispensable; basic. *Every writer needs a few essential reference books.*

prominent well-known; eminent. *For my report, I interviewed two prominent scientists.*

significant meaningful; notable. *July 4 is quite a significant day in American history.*

antonyms: insignificant, irrelevant, superficial, trivial, unnecessary

interesting *adj.* arousing or holding interest or attention. *Our trip to Peru was interesting and informative.*

creative original and expressive. *This poetry is very creative but not very useful.*

engrossing occupying the complete attention of. *The story was so engrossing that it kept me awake.*

individualistic different from others; distinctive. *I always recognize Van Gogh's individualistic style of painting.*

antonyms: boring, commonplace, monotonous, tedious

J

juvenile *adj.* young. *Many juvenile animals, such as fawns, have special names.*

childish thoughtless or foolish in a manner not suitable for a mature person. *Name-calling is childish, and it will solve nothing.*

childlike having a natural, spontaneous quality often associated with children. *My grandparents took a childlike pleasure in the circus.*

immature not fully grown or developed. *A tadpole is an immature frog.*

sophomoric immature and overconfident. *His report, poorly researched, was sophomoric.*

youthful having or giving the appearance or quality of youth. *Although he is ninety, Mr. Adams still has a youthful laugh.*

antonyms: adult, developed, mature, ripe

K

kind *adj.* inclined to help others and think of their welfare. *A kind person is also helpful.*

empathetic able to identify with another's situation, especially with sincere understanding and deep concern. *I could voice my fears to my empathetic uncle.*

generous willing to give or share. *Thanks to her generous help, I could afford college.*

merciful compassionate; kindhearted. *The merciful passer-by helped the injured bird.*

supportive furnishing support or assistance. *As I ran, my supportive friends cheered.*

sympathetic feeling pity or sorrow for the distress of another. *The sympathetic doctor allowed my friends to visit me.*
antonyms: aggressive, harsh, malicious

L

like *v.* to find pleasant; enjoy. *I like cats.*
appreciate to recognize the worth, quality, or importance of something. *Not all my friends appreciate modern art.*
esteem to think highly of; respect. *I esteem people who work in medicine.*
prefer to choose as more desirable; like better. *I like apples but prefer pears.*
recommend to praise or commend to another as being worthy or desirable. *I recommend the fruit salad.*
revel to take great pleasure or delight. *Liam revels in his children's laughter.*
antonyms: abhor, detest, loathe, resent

M

Word Bank

make *v.* to bring into being; to bring about or cause to exist.

assemble	fashion
build	formulate
compose	mold
construct	originate
devise	photocopy
erect	produce
fabricate	shape

antonyms: abolish, collapse *v.*, demolish, disassemble, dismantle, raze

N

nuisance *n.* a source of inconvenience or annoyance. *A dog that begs at the table can be a real nuisance in the home.*
bother an annoying thing. *Not having a sharpened pencil was a bother.*
hindrance someone or something that gets in the way; an obstacle. *Todd's small size was a hindrance in basketball.*
irritant causing irritation or annoyance. *A dripping faucet is an irritant to someone who is trying to sleep.*
antonyms: benefit, delight, gratification, pleasure

O

obstruct *v.* to hinder or halt by interference. *Parked cars obstructed the view of the street.*
impede to slow down; block. *Our progress was impeded by steep hills and valleys.*
intervene to enter a course of events so as to change it. *My parents intervened when the party got too loud.*
prevent to deprive someone of success in doing something. *The officer was able to prevent the robber's escape.*
prohibit to prevent from doing something by law or authority. *The club prohibits members from smoking on the grounds.*
retard to slow the progress of; delay. *The cold spring retarded the tree's growth.*
antonyms: encourage, expedite, facilitate, sustain

P

phase *n.* a distinct stage of development. *The first phase of our trip will be on foot.*
age a distinctive period of history or geology. *Artists drew pictures of flying machines years before the age of space travel.*

period an interval of time having a specified length. *After a period of two weeks the seed should sprout.*

season a period of the year devoted to or marked by a certain activity or by the appearance of something. *Their rainy season lasts four months.*

stage a step in development. *The fastest growth takes place in the earliest stage of life.*

term a period of time during which something lasts. *Our mayor is elected for a term of three years.*

plentiful *adj.* more than adequate. *Rice grows only in areas where water is plentiful.*

abundant existing in great supply. *The corn crop was so abundant we could not sell it all.*

copious large in quantity. *It took me hours to type my copious notes.*

generous large; ample. *I love salad, so Mother gave me a generous amount.*

prevalent widely existing or commonly occurring. *Video games are prevalent on my street, but I do not have one.*

antonyms: deficient, insufficient, occasional, rare, scarce

Q

quiet *adj.* peaceful, serene. *Alan was refreshed after his quiet vacation.*

calm not excited, composed. *Eileen has the ability to stay calm in a crisis.*

noiseless making little or no sound. *The deep carpet made our approach noiseless.*

reserved keeping one's feelings to oneself. *Pablo is too reserved to say how he feels.*

tranquil free from agitation, anxiety, etc. *The hermit chose to live a lonely but tranquil life.*

unruffled not ruffled or agitated. *Although the man was rude, Jill stayed unruffled.*

antonyms: agitated, hysterical, turbulent, upset

R

right *adj.* suitable, fitting, or proper. *We will be hiking, so wear the right clothes.*

appropriate suitable for a particular person, condition, occasion, or place. *Flowers are an appropriate gift for someone who is sick.*

conventional following accepted practice, custom, or taste. *Father always wears a conventional suit to work.*

seemly conforming to accepted standards of conduct; proper. *In Grandmother's day, it was not seemly for friends to hug.*

sensible in accordance with good judgment. *Food servers, who are on their feet all day, learn to wear sensible shoes.*

suitable appropriate to a given purpose or occasion. *A snorkel would be suitable for a guest at an underwater wedding.*

antonyms: improper, inappropriate, unsuitable, wrong

S

sad *adj.* showing, filled with, or expressing sorrow or regret. *The team members had sad faces after their loss.*

depressed gloomy; dejected. *The loss of my dog made me depressed for days.*

forlorn pitiful in appearance or condition. *The forlorn kitten cried for its mother.*

grievous causing grief, pain, or anguish. *The woman fainted after hearing the grievous news of the accident.*

melancholy sad; gloomy. *The melancholy song brought tears to our eyes.*

miserable very unhappy. *Being homesick made my little sister miserable at camp.*

pathetic arousing pity, sympathy, or sorrow. *In one pathetic scene of the movie, crowds of children are begging for food.*

wretched full of or attended by misery or woe. *The actor convincingly played the part of a wretched prisoner.*

antonyms: blithe, cheerful, enthusiastic, jovial, lighthearted

sign *n.* something that suggests a fact, quality, or condition not immediately evident. *That dark spot you see is a sign of an oil leak.*

evidence the data on which a conclusion is based. *Although no x-ray had been taken, all the evidence pointed to a broken leg.*

indicator something that serves as a sign. *A halo around the moon may be an indicator of snowy weather ahead.*

manifestation something that reveals something else. *Fever is a manifestation of the body's battle with an infection.*

representation something that represents, such as a picture, symbol, etc. *The first form of the letter a was a representation of an ox.*

symbol something that represents something else, as by association, resemblance, convention, etc. *For many people red roses are a symbol of love.*

---

site *n.* the place where something was, is, or is to be located. *This vacant lot will be the site of the new playground.*

location a place where something is found or situated. *Use the map to find the location of the campground.*

place a particular area or spot. *I need a place to store my typewriter.*

position the right or proper place for a person or thing. *The actors must be in position before the curtain rises.*

vicinity a nearby or surrounding region or place. *You'll find many places to fish in the vicinity.*

---

stationary *adj.* undergoing no change of position; not moving. *One dial moved, while the other remained stationary.*

fixed not subject to change or variation; constant. *The hands of the broken clock remained fixed at 12:19.*

immovable not able to be moved. *The cast iron stove was immovable in its current condition.*

stable resisting sudden changes of position or condition. *Make sure the shelf is stable before you use it.*

steadfast not moving; fixed in place. *The tent remained steadfast in the strong wind.*

still motionless or without commotion or disturbance. *Keep still until the song is over.*
antonyms: agitated, mobile, restless, turbulent

---

succumb *v.* to give in to something overpowering or overwhelming. *The senator did not succumb to political pressure to change his vote.*

accede to consent, agree, yield. *My parents finally acceded to my request for a dog.*

capitulate to surrender under stated conditions. *The general capitulated after assurances that no one would be taken prisoner.*

concede to give up on, often before results have been fully established. *The candidate conceded the election even before the votes were all counted.*

submit to surrender oneself to the will or authority of another. *The patient submitted himself to a battery of tests.*

yield to give in. *Lin gave me three good reasons, so I yielded to her wishes.*
antonyms: assert, endure, predominate, prevail, protest, sustain

---

T

transaction *n.* a business deal or operation. *I completed the transaction at the automatic banking machine.*

exchange trade. *Do you think that the scarf for the hat is an even exchange?*

negotiation discussion to reach an agreement. *The negotiation for the sale of the company lasted months.*

pact a formal agreement, as between nations. *The knights made solemn pacts to serve the king forever.*

understanding a reconciliation of differences; an agreement. *My sister and I have an understanding about borrowing clothes.*

U

universal *adj.* of, for, done by, or affecting all. *The country was founded upon the basis of universal rights for all citizens.*
common of the community as a whole; public. *I have a private home, but I share a common kitchen.*
comprehensive broad in scope. *We bought this car because of its comprehensive warranty.*
ubiquitous being or seeming to be everywhere at the same time. *Hungry, we looked for one of those ubiquitous fast-food restaurants.*
unanimous based on complete agreement. *This rule will take effect if the vote is unanimous.*
antonyms: exceptional, individual, local, particular, special, unique

---

upright *adj.* in a vertical position. *Make sure you store that box in an upright position.*
erect directed or pointing upward; standing upright. *Why is one goal post erect and one leaning to the left?*
perpendicular at right angles to the plane of the horizon. *When the sailboat isn't perpendicular, things roll off the deck.*
vertical directly upright. *To make this symbol, draw a vertical line with two shorter lines through it.*
antonyms: flat, horizontal, level, prone, supine

W

Shades of Meaning

wild *adj.* lacking discipline or control.

1. hard to discipline:

agitated	refractory
defiant	ungovernable
disobedient	unmanageable
rebellious	unruly

2. uncivilized:

barbaric	savage	uncultivated
primitive	uncouth	untamed

3. out of control:

delirious	hysterical	raving
frantic	insane	reckless
frenzied	mad	tumultuous
furious	possessed	violent

antonyms: 1. accommodating, compliant, easygoing, tractable 2. civilized, cultured, refined 3. rational, sane, serene

---

win *v.* to gain by means of hard work, effort, or perseverance. *Luis won the respect of everyone who worked for him.*
obtain to gain the possession of after planning or endeavor. *After much searching, Melissa finally obtained the rare stamp.*
retain to keep possession of. *During negotiations, the union retained the right to strike.*
secure to get possession of; acquire. *The studio was happy that it had been able to secure an exclusive contract.*
antonyms: concede, lose, sacrifice, submit, surrender

Spelling-Meaning Index

This Spelling-Meaning Index contains words related in spelling and meaning. The Index has four sections: Consonant Changes, Vowel Changes, Absorbed Prefixes, and Word Parts. The first two sections contain related word pairs and other words in the same word families. The last two sections contain a list of absorbed prefixes, Latin word roots and Greek word parts, and words that contain these word parts. The words in each section of this Index are in alphabetical order.

Consonant Changes

The letters in dark print show that the spelling stays the same even though the sound changes.

Consonant Changes: Silent-Sounded Consonants

To remember the spelling of a word with a silent consonant, try thinking of a related word in which the consonant is sounded.

autum**n**-autum**n**al
colum**n**-colum**n**ist
condem**n**-condem**n**ation
de**b**t-de**b**it
desi**g**n-desi**g**nate
dou**b**t-du**b**ious
hasten-**h**aste
heir-in**h**erit
mus**c**le-mus**c**ular
resi**g**n-resi**g**nation
solem**n**-solem**n**ity
ve**h**icle-ve**h**icular

Consonant Changes: Adding -ion

When you add -ion to a verb ending with t, the t often remains, though its sound changes to |sh|.

congratula**t**e-congratula**t**ions
connec**t**-connec**t**ion
coopera**t**e-coopera**t**ion
detec**t**-detec**t**ion

duplica**t**e-duplica**t**ion
evalua**t**e-evalua**t**ion
exhibi**t**-exhibi**t**ion
implica**t**e-implica**t**ion
investiga**t**e-investiga**t**ion
opera**t**e-opera**t**ion
participa**t**e-participa**t**ion
prosecu**t**e-prosecu**t**ion
punctua**t**e-punctua**t**ion
viola**t**e-viola**t**ion

Consonant Changes: t to ss, d to ss, k to c

When you add -ion to some verbs, the spelling of the base word changes. Knowing how consonants change in one pair of words may help you predict changes in other words with the same roots or similar spelling patterns.

commi**t**-commi**ss**ion
emi**t**-emi**ss**ion
omi**t**-omi**ss**ion
remi**t**-remi**ss**ion
submi**t**-submi**ss**ion
transmi**t**-transmi**ss**ion

conce**d**e-conce**ss**ion
interce**d**e-interce**ss**ion
rece**d**e-rece**ss**ion
succee**d**-succe**ss**ion

provo**k**e-provo**c**ation
revo**k**e-revo**c**ation

Spelling-Meaning Index

Vowel Changes
The letters in dark print show that the spelling stays the same even though the sound changes.

Vowel Changes:
Long to Short Vowel Sound

Words that are related in spelling and meaning may contain the same vowel but have different vowel sounds. In each word pair below, a vowel has the long vowel sound in one word and the short vowel sound in the other.

athlete-athletic
atrocious-atrocity
ferocious-ferocity
flame-flammable
grateful-gratitude
grave-gravity
humane-humanity
ignite-ignition
impede-impediment
induce-induction
introduce-introduction
meter-metric
microscope-microscopic
precise-precision
produce-production
reduce-reduction
revise-revision
suffice-sufficient

Vowel Changes:
Schwa to Long Vowel Sound

You can remember how to spell the schwa sound in some words by thinking of a related word with a long vowel sound spelled the same way.

admiration-admire
alternative-alternate
combination-combine
definition-define
deprivation-deprive
derivation-derive
disposition-dispose
genetic-gene
harmony-harmonious
immunize-immune
imposition-impose
indicative-indicate
infinite-finite
initiative-initiate
inspiration-inspire
mandatory-mandate
narrative-narrate
remedy-remedial
stability-stable
strategy-strategic
variety-various
vegetable-vegetation

Vowel Changes:
Schwa to Short Vowel Sound

You can remember how to spell the schwa sound in some words by thinking of a related word with a short vowel sound spelled the same way.

academy-academic
adapt-adaptation
economy-economics
emphasis-emphatic
excellence-excel
illustrate-illustrative
neutral-neutrality
original-origin
punctual-punctuality
restoration-restore

sequence-sequential
syllable-syllabication
symbolism-symbolic
tranquil-tranquility
triumph-triumphant
trivial-triviality

Adding Suffixes:
Long to Short Vowel Sound

When you add a suffix to a word, the vowels in the root of the word sometimes change. Knowing how the vowels change in one pair of related words can help you predict the vowel changes in other words with the same root.

abstain-abstention
detain-detention
retain-retention

maintain-maintenance
pertain-pertinent
sustain-sustenance

assume-assumption
consume-consumption
presume-presumption
resume-resumption

acclaim-acclamation
exclaim-exclamation
proclaim-proclamation

conceive-conception
deceive-deception
perceive-perception
receive-reception

denounce-denunciation
pronounce-pronunciation
renounce-renunciation

Absorbed Prefixes

Some prefixes change their spellings to match the first letter or sound of the word roots or base words to which they are attached. Knowing this can help you remember to double the consonant in some words with these prefixes. The letters in dark print highlight the prefix.

ad- "to; toward"

accede	**al**locate
accent	**al**lotted
accentuate	**al**lude
accept	**an**nouncer
acceptable	**ap**paratus
access	**ap**parel
accessory	**ap**parent
acclaim	**ap**pendage
acclamation	**ap**pendix
accommodate	**ap**petite
accompany	**ap**petizer
accomplice	**ap**pliance
accordion	**ap**plicable
account	**ap**plicant
accountant	**ap**plication
accumulate	**ap**point
accuracy	**ap**praisal
accurate	**ap**preciate
accusation	**ap**prehensive
accustomed	**ap**prentice
affectionate	**ap**propriate
affiliate	**ap**prove
aggravate	**ap**proximate
aggressive	**ar**rangement
allegiance	**ar**rest
alleviate	**ar**rival
alliance	**as**sembly
alliteration	**as**sent

Spelling-Meaning Index

assign
assignment
assimilation
assistance
assistant
assortment
assure
attach

attain
attempt
attendance
attendant
attire
attitude
attract
attribute

con- "with; together"

accommodate
collaborate
collapse
collateral
colleague
collision
commemorate
comment
commentary
commercial
commiserate
commission

commit
committee
communication
community
commute
correlation
correspond
correspondent
corroborate
corrode
corrupt

in- "in; not"

illegal
illegible
illicit
illiterate
illogical
illuminate
illusion
illustrate
illustration
illustrative
immaculate
immaterial
immature
immeasurable
immemorial
immerse

immigrant
immigrate
immobilize
immortal
immovable
irrational
irregular
irrelevant
irreparable
irreplaceable
irresistible
irresponsible
irrevocable
irrigate
irritate

ob- "to; against"

occasional
occupation
occurrence

opponent
opportunity
opposite

Word Parts

Words with the same Latin word root or Greek word part are related in spelling and meaning. Knowing the meaning of a word part can help you understand and spell the words in that family. The letters in dark print highlight the word part.

Latin Word Roots

cede or cess, "to go or yield"

abscess
access
accessible
accessory
ancestor
antecedent
cede
concede
concession
exceed
excess
excessive
intercede
intercession
necessary

necessity
predecessor
procedure
proceed
process
procession
recede
recess
recession
secede
succeed
success
succession
successor

ceive or cept, "to take"

accept
conceive
concept
conception
conceptual
deceive
deception

deceptive
except
exception
inception
intercept
perceive
perception

perceptive
receive

reception
susceptible

duc, "to lead or bring"

abduct
abduction
aqueduct
conducive
conduct
conductor
deduce
deduction
deductive
duct
educate
education
induce

induction
inductive
introduce
introduction
produce
product
production
productive
productivity
reduce
reduction
reproduce
reproduction

fac, "to make or do"

affect
affectation
affection
affectionate
artifact
benefactor
benefit
confection
confetti
counterfeit
defeat
defect
defective
deficient
deficit
effect
effective
efficient
facsimile
fact
faction

factor
factory
factual
feasible
feat
feature
forfeit
infect
infection
magnificent
manufacture
perfect
perfection
proficient
profit
sacrifice
satisfaction
satisfactory
significant
suffice
sufficient

also all words with the following suffixes:
-ification (specification, qualification);
-ify (signify, simplify)

fer, "to carry"

confer
conference
conifer
defer
differ
different
fertile
fertilizer
infer
inference

offer
prefer
preference
refer
reference
referral
suffer
transfer
transferral

fin, "to end"

affinity
confine
define
definite
definition
definitive
final
finale
finalist
finality
finalize
finance

financial
fine
finery
finesse
finish
finite
infinite
infinitesimal
infinitive
infinity
paraffin

man, "hand"

manacle
manage
management
manager
maneuver
manicotti
manicure

manifest
manipulate
manner
mannerism
manual
manufacture
manuscript

Spelling-Meaning Index

miss or **mit,** "to send, let go, or throw"

admission
admit
commissary
commission
commit
commitment
committee
compromise
demise
dismiss
emission
emit
intermission
intermittent
missile
mission

missionary
omission
omit
permission
permissive
permit
premise
promise
remiss
remission
remit
submission
submit
surmise
transmission
transmit

plic or **plex,** "to fold"

accomplice
applicable
application
apply
complex
complexity
complicate
complication
comply
duplex
duplicate
explicit
implicate
implication

implicit
imply
multiplication
multiply
perplex
pliable
pliant
pliers
plight
ply
replica
replicate
reply

pos, "to put, place"

appositive
compose
composer
composite
composition
decompose
deposit
disposal
dispose
disposition
expose
exposure
impose
imposition
imposter
indisposed
juxtapose

oppose
opposite
pose
position
positive
posture
predisposed
preposition
presuppose
proposal
propose
purpose
repository
superimpose
suppose
supposition
transpose

reg, "guide, rule, or law"

irregular
regal
regalia
regime
regimen
regiment

regimentation
region
regular
regulate
regulation
regulatory

sens or **sent,** "to feel"

assent
consensus
consent
dissent
resent
resentment
sensation
sense
sensibility
sensible

sensitive
sensitivity
sensitize
sensor
sentence
sentiment
sentimental
sentinel
sentry

sol, "alone"

desolate
desolation
sole
soliloquy

solitaire
solitary
solitude
solo

sol, "sun"

parasol
solar
solarium

solarize
solstice

sol, "whole"

consolidate
solid

solidarity
solidify

spir, "to breathe"

aspirate
aspire
conspiracy
conspire
expiration
expire
inspiration
inspire

perspiration
perspire
respiration
respirator
respire
spirit
spiritual
transpire

struct, "to build"

construct
construction
constructive
destruction
destructive
instruct
instruction

instructive
instructor
obstruct
obstruction
reconstruct
structure

sume, "to take or obtain"

assume
assumption
consume
consumer
consumption
presume

presumption
resume
resumption
subsume
sumptuous

tain or ten, "to hold"

abstain
abstention
attain
contain
container
continue
detain
detention
entertain
entertainment
lieutenant
maintain
maintenance
obtain

pertain
pertinent
retain
retention
sustain
sustenance
tenacious
tenant
tenement
tenet
tennis
tenor
tenure

tract, "to draw, pull"

abstract
attract
attraction
attractive
contract
contraction
detract
distract
distraction

extract
protractor
subtract
subtraction
trace
traceable
traction
tractor

Spelling-Meaning Index

ven, "to come"

advent
adventure
circumvent
convene
convenient
convent
convention
event
eventually
intervene

intervention
invent
invention
inventive
prevent
prevention
preventive
revenue
souvenir

ver, "to turn"

adversary
adverse
advertise
advertisement
anniversary
aversion
avert
controversy
conversation
converse
convert
culvert
diverse
diversion
divert
extrovert
introvert

inverse
invert
reverse
revert
traverse
universal
universe
versatile
verse
version
versus
vertebra
vertex
vertical
vertigo
vice versa

Greek Word Parts

ast, "star"

aster
asterisk
asteroid
astral
astrodome
astrology

astronaut
astronomer
astronomical
astronomy
disaster

gen, "born, produced"

gene
genealogy
genetic
heterogeneous
homogeneous

homogenized
hydrogen
nitrogen
oxygen
photogenic

log or logy, "speech, reason; science or study of"

analogy
anthology
anthropology
apology
archaeology
astrology
biology
cardiology
catalog
chronology
criminology
dermatology
dialogue
ecology
entomology
epilogue
etymology
eulogy
genealogy
geology
logarithm

logic
logical
logistics
logo
meteorology
mineralogy
monologue
mythology
neurology
pathology
phraseology
physiology
prologue
psychology
radiology
sociology
technology
terminology
theology
trilogy
zoology

also all words with the suffix *-logical*
(chronological, ecological)

path, "disease, feeling"

anti**path**y	**path**ology
a**path**y	**path**os
em**path**y	sym**path**y
pathetic	tele**path**y
pathological	

prot, "first"

protagonist	**prot**oplasm
protein	**prot**otype
protocol	**prot**ozoan
proton	

syn or **sym,** "together, same"

a**sym**metrical	**sym**ptom
symbol	**syn**agogue
symbolism	**syn**chronize
symbolize	**syn**dicate
symmetrical	**syn**drome
symmetry	**syn**onym
sympathetic	**syn**onymous
sympathize	**syn**tax
sympathy	**syn**thesis
symphonic	**syn**thesize
symphony	**syn**thesizer
symposium	**syn**thetic

Spelling Dictionary

Spelling Table

This Spelling Table shows many of the letter combinations that spell the same sounds in different words. Use this table for help in looking up words that you do not know how to spell.

Sounds	Spellings	Sample Words	Sounds	Spellings	Sample Words
|ă|	a, au	bat, have, laugh	|ī|	ei, i,	height, time, mind,
|ā|	a, ai,	made, later, rain,		ie, igh, uy,	pie, fight, buy,
	ay, ea, ei,	play, great, vein,		y, ye	try, dye, type
	eigh, ey	eight, they	|îr|	ear, eer,	near, deer,
|âr|	air, are,	fair, care,		eir, ere, ier	weird, here, pier
	ear, eir,	bear, their,	|j|	dge, g,	judge, germ,
	ere	where		ge, j	orange, jump
|ä|	a, al	father, calm	|k|	c, cc,	picnic, account,
|är|	ar, ear	art, heart		ch, ck, k,	school, stick, keep,
|b|	b, bb	bus, rabbit		que	antique
|ch|	c, ch, tch,	cello, chin, match,	|kw|	qu	quick
	tu	culture	|l|	l, ll	last, all
|d|	d, dd	dark, sudden	|m|	m, mb,	mop, bomb,
|ĕ|	a, ai, ay, e,	any, said, says, went,		mm, mn	summer, column
	ea, ie	head, friend	|n|	gn, kn, n,	sign, knee, nine,
|ē|	e, ea,	these, we, beast,		nn, pn	banner, pneumonia
	ee, ei, ey,	fleet, receive, honey,	|ng|	n, ng	think, ring
	i, ie,	magazine, chief,	|ŏ|	a, ho, o	was, honor, pond
	y	bumpy	|ō|	ew, o,	sew, most, hope,
|f|	f, ff, gh,	funny, off, enough,		oa, oe, ou,	float, toe, shoulder,
	ph	physical		ough, ow	though, row
|g|	g, gg, gu	get, egg, guide	|ô|	a, al, au,	walk, talk, haunt,
|h|	h, wh	hat, who		aw, o,	lawn, soft,
|hw|	wh	when		ough	brought
|ĭ|	a, e,	cottage, before,	|ôr|	oar, oor,	roar, door,
	ee, i,	been, mix, give,		or, ore,	storm, store,
	ia, u, ui,	carriage, busy, build,		our	court
	y	gym	|oi|	oi, oy	join, toy

Sounds	Spellings	Sample Words		Sounds	Spellings	Sample Words
|ou|	ou, ough, ow	loud, bough, now		|th|	th	thin, teeth
|o͝o|	oo, ou, u	good, could, put		|ŭ|	o, oe, oo, ou, u	front, come, does, flood, tough, sun
|o͞o|	eu, ew, o, oe, oo, ou, ough, u, ue, ui	neutral, flew, do, lose, shoe, spoon, you, through, truth, blue, juice		|yo͞o|	eau, ew, iew, u, ue	beauty, few, view, use, cue, fuel
|p|	p, pp	paint, happen		|ûr|	ear, er, ir, or, our, ur	learn, herd, girl, word, journey, turn
|r|	r, rh, rr, wr	rub, rhyme, borrow, write		|v|	f, v	of, very
|s|	c, ce, ps, s, sc, ss	city, fence, psychology, same, scent, lesson		|w|	o, w	one, way
				|y|	i, y	million, yes
|sh|	ce, ch, ci, s, sh, ss, ti	ocean, machine, special, sure, sheep, mission, nation		|z|	s, ss, x, z, zz	please, dessert, xylophone, zoo, blizzard
				|zh|	ge, s	garage, usual
|t|	ed, t, tt	stopped, talk, button		|ə|	a, ai, e, eo, i, ie, o, ou, u	about, captain, silent, surgeon, pencil, ancient, lemon, famous, circus
|th|	th	they, other				

Spelling Dictionary

How to Use a Dictionary

Finding an Entry Word

Guide Words
The word you want to find in a dictionary is listed in alphabetical order. To find it quickly, use the guide words at the top of each page. The two guide words name the first and last entries on the page.

Base Words
To find a word ending in **-ed** or **-ing,** you usually must look up its base word. For example, to find **emitted** or **emitting,** look up the base word **emit.**

Homographs
Homographs have separate, numbered entries. For example, **stable** meaning "resisting change" is listed as **stable¹. Stable** meaning "a shelter for horses" is listed as **stable².**

Reading an Entry

Read the dictionary entry below. Note the purpose of each part.

The **pronunciation** shows you how to say the entry word.

The **part of speech** (verb) is identified by an abbreviation *(v.).*

The **-ed** and **-ing** forms of a verb are often shown.

The **entry word** is shown, separated into syllables.

chivalry | cologne

A **sample sentence** or phrase helps to make the meaning clear.

The **definition** tells you what the word means.

chron·i·cle |krŏn´ĭ kəl| *v.* **chron·i·cled, chron·i·cling.** To record, as in a chronicle: *Almanacs chronicle the events of the year.* [Middle English, from Latin *chronica,* from Greek *khronikos,* pertaining to time, from *khronos,* time.] —**chron´i·cler** *n.*

A **run-on entry** is shown in dark type at the end of the entry.

The **etymology** tells the history and origin of the word.

chro·nol·o·gy |krə nŏl´ə jē| *n., pl.* **chro·nol·o·gies.** The arrangement of events in time; the order of events. [From Greek *khronos,* time + *logy,* speech.]

cir·cu·la·tion |sûr´kyə lā´shən| *n.*
1. The passage of something, such as

Spelling Dictionary

A

ab-. Also **a-** (before *m*, *p*, and *v*) or **au-** (before *f*) or **abs-** (before *t*). A prefix meaning "from, away, or off": **abnormal.** [Latin *ab*, away from.]

ab·duct |ăb **dukt´**| *v.* To kidnap. [Latin *abdūcere: ab-*, away + *dūcere*, to lead.]

ab·nor·mal |ăb **nôr´**məl| *adj.* Not ordinary; unusual.

a·broad |ə **brôd´**| *adv.* & *adj.* In or to foreign places: *going abroad.*

ab·stain |ăb **stān´**| *v.* To keep from doing something voluntarily; refrain: *abstain from eating candy.* [Latin *abstinēre*, to hold (oneself) back: *ab-*, away from + *tenēre*, to hold.]

ab·sten·tion |ăb **stĕn´**shən| *n.* **1.** The practice of abstaining. **2.** An act of abstaining, especially the withholding of a vote at an election.

ab·stract |**ăb´**străkt´| *or* |ăb **străkt´**| *adj.* **1.** Not concrete: *"Truth" is an abstract noun.* **2.** Having designs that do not represent recognizable people or things: *an abstract painting.* —*n.* |**ăb´**străkt´|. A brief summary of the main points of a text: *an abstract of a speech.* [From Latin *abstractus*, drawn away: *ab-*, away from + *trahere*, to pull.]

a·bun·dant |ə **bŭn´**dənt| *adj.* Existing in great supply; very plentiful: *abundant rainfall.*

a cap·pel·la |ä´kə **pĕl´**ə|. In music, without instrumental accompaniment: *sing a cappella.*

ac·cede |ăk **sēd´**| *v.* **ac·ced·ed, ac·ced·ing.** To consent; agree; yield: *I acceded to her request.*

ac·cent |**ăk´**sĕnt´| *n.* **1.** The stress placed on a particular syllable of a word. **2.** A style of speech or pronunciation that is typical of a certain region or country. [Middle English, from Latin *accentus*, "song added to (speech)."]

ac·cept·a·ble |ăk **sĕp´**tə bəl| *adj.* **1.** Fitting; suitable. **2.** Proper; correct.

ac·cep·tance |ăk **sĕp´**təns| *n.* **1.** The act of taking something offered: *the acceptance of a new job.* **2.** Favorable reception; approval: *Acceptance of seat belts among the public has greatly reduced injuries in car accidents.* **3.** Belief in something as true; agreement: *Acceptance of the theory has been slow.* [From Latin *acceptāre*, to receive: *ad-*, to + *capere*, to take.]

ac·ces·so·ry |ăk **sĕs´**ə rē| *n., pl.* **ac·ces·so·ries.** An extra that goes with and adds to the overall effect of something, as a scarf or pin worn with a dress. [Middle English *accessorie*, from Latin *accessor*, helper.]

ac·claim |ə **klām´**| *v.* To greet with loud praise: *acclaimed by the critics.* [Latin *acclāmāre*, to shout at: *ad-*, to + *clāmāre*, to shout.]

ac·cla·ma·tion |ăk´lə **mā´**shən| *n.* Enthusiastic praise or applause.

ac·com·mo·date |ə kŏm´ə dāt´| v.
ac·com·mo·dat·ed, ac·com·mo·dat·ing. 1.
To do (someone) a favor; oblige; help: *try to accommodate someone.* **2.** To provide with lodging or living space. **3.** To have room for; hold: *room to accommodate a large table.*

ac·com·plice |ə kŏm´plĭs| n. Someone who aids a lawbreaker in a crime. [Middle English, from Latin *ad-*, to + *con-*, together + *plex*, to fold.]

ac·cor·di·on |ə kôr´dē ən| n. A musical instrument consisting of a hand-held reed organ in which the player creates a supply of air by operating a pleated bellows contained in the instrument itself. [German *Akkordion*, from *Akkord*, agreement, "harmony."]

ac·cu·mu·late |ə kyoo´myə lāt´| v.
ac·cu·mu·lat·ed, ac·cu·mu·lat·ing. To gather together; pile up; collect: *Snow has begun to accumulate.* [Latin *accumulāre: ad-*, in addition + *cumulāre*, to pile up, from *cumulus*, a heap.]

ac·cu·ra·cy |ăk´yər ə sē| n.
1. Freedom from error; correctness: *check the results for accuracy.* **2.** Exactness; precision: *the accuracy of his aim.*

ac·quaint·ance |ə kwān´təns| n.
1. Knowledge of or familiarity with something: *acquaintance with the facts.* **2.** A person whom one knows.

a·cre·age |ā´kər ĭj| n. Land area as measured or expressed in acres.

a·cryl·ic |ə krĭl´ĭk| adj. Of any synthetic fiber or resin derived from **acrylic acid,** $C_3H_4O_2$, or some related organic chemical compound: *an acrylic blanket.*

ad |ad| n. An advertisement.

ad-. Also **ac-** (before *c*) or **af-** (before *f*) or **ag-** (before *g*) or **al-** (before *l*) or **an-** (before *n*) or **ar-** (before *r*) or **as-** (before *s*) or **at-** (before *t*). A prefix meaning "toward, to": **adhere.** [Latin, from *ad*, to, toward, or at.]

a·dapt |ə dăpt´| v. **1.** To change or adjust for a certain purpose: *adapt to a new situation.* **2.** To make or become fitted for a particular environment, condition, use, etc., as through a process of natural development: *Camels have adapted to desert conditions.* [Latin *adaptāre*, to fit to: *ad-*, to + *aptāre*, to fit.]

ad·ap·ta·tion |ăd´əp tā´shən| n.
1. The act or process of adapting; change or adjustment to meet new conditions.
2. Something that is produced by being adapted.

ad·journ |ə jûrn´| v. To bring (a meeting or session) to an official end, putting off further business until later: *adjourn the meeting.*

ad-lib |ăd lĭb´| Informal. v. **ad-libbed, ad-lib·bing.** To make up (lines, music, movements, etc.) while performing: *ad-lib a joke.*

a·do·be |ə dō´bē| n. Brick made of clay and straw that is dried in the sun. [Spanish *adobe*, from Arabic *attōba*, *al-tōba*, "the brick."]

ad·ver·sar·y |ăd´vər sĕr´ē| n., pl. **ad·ver·sar·ies.** An opponent or enemy. [Latin *adversārius*, opponent, from *adversus*, adverse.]

ad·verse |ăd vûrs´| or |ăd´vûrs´| adj. Not favorable; hostile: *adverse criticism.*

ad·ver·tise·ment |ăd´vər tīz´mənt| or |ăd vûr´tĭs mənt| or |-tĭz-| n. A public notice, as in a newspaper or on the radio, to call attention to a product, a meeting, etc. [Middle English *a(d)vertisen*, from Old French *a(d)vertir* (present participle *advertissant*), advert.]

aer·i·al |âr´ē əl| *or* |ā îr´ē əl| *adj.*
1. Of, in, or caused by the air. **2.** Of, for, or
by aircraft.

aer·o·bics |â rō´bĭks| *n.* (*used with a
sing. or pl. verb*). A system of physical
conditioning that involves vigorous exercise,
as calisthenics, combined with dance routines.
[From Greek *aero-*, air + *bios*, life.]

aer·o·space |âr´ə spās´| *adj.* Of or related
to the science and technology of flight both in
the earth's atmosphere and in outer space.
[From Greek *aer*, air + Latin *spatium*, space.]

aes·thet·ic |ĕs thĕt´ĭk| *adj.* A form of
the word **esthetic.** Of or sensitive to what is
beautiful; artistic.

af·fec·tion·ate |ə fĕk´shə nĭt| *adj.*
Having or showing affection; tender; loving.

a·fi·ci·o·na·do |ə fĭsh´ē ə nä´dō| *n., pl.*
a·fi·ci·o·na·dos. An admirer; devotee.
[Spanish *aficionar*, to incite affection.]

a·gen·cy |ā´jən sē| *n., pl.* **a·gen·cies.**
A business or service authorized to act for
others: *a detective agency.*

ag·gra·vate |ăg´rə vāt´| *v.*
ag·gra·va·ted, ag·gra·vat·ing. 1. To make
worse: *aggravate an injury.* **2.** To irritate;
provoke. [Latin *aggravāre*, to make heavier:
ad-, in addition to + *gravāre*, to burden, from
gravis, heavy.]

ag·gres·sive |ə grĕs´ĭv| *adj.* Bold;
forceful: *an aggressive salesperson.* [Latin
aggredī (past participle *aggressus*), to approach
(with hostility), attack: *ad-*, toward + *gradī*, to
step, go.]

ag·ile |ăj´əl| *or* |ăj´īl| *adj.* Able to move
quickly and easily; graceful.

ag·ri·cul·ture |ăg´rĭ kŭl´chər| *n.* The
science, art, and business of cultivating the
soil in order to produce useful crops and
livestock; farming.

aisle |īl| *n.* **1.** A passageway between rows
of seats, as in a church or theater.
2. Any passageway, as between counters or
shelves in a supermarket.

Pronunciation Key

ă	pat	ŏ	pot	û	fur
ā	pay	ō	go	*th*	**the**
â	care	ô	paw, **for**	th	**thin**
ä	father	oi	**oil**	hw	**wh**ich
ĕ	pet	ŏŏ	book	zh	usual
ē	be	ōō	boot	ə	**a**go, item
ĭ	pit	yōō	cute		pencil, at**o**m
ī	ice	ou	**out**		circus
î	near	ŭ	cut	ər	butter

al·fal·fa |ăl făl´fə| *n.* A plant with
cloverlike leaves and purple flowers, grown as
feed for cattle and other livestock. [Spanish,
from Arabic *al-fasfasah*.]

al·ge·bra |ăl´jə brə| *n.* A branch of
mathematics dealing with problems involving
known and unknown numbers and their
relations. The unknown numbers are often
represented by letters or other symbols.
[Medieval Latin, from Arabic *al-jebr*.]

a·li·en |ā´lē ən| *or* |āl´yən| *n., pl.*
a·li·ens. A person living in one country
though a citizen of another; a foreigner:
registration of aliens.

al·le·giance |ə lē´jəns| *n.* Loyalty or
devotion to one's country, to a king, or to a
cause: *pledge allegiance.* [Middle English
allegeaunce, from *liege*: *ad-*, to + *liege*, lord.]

al·li·ance |ə lī´əns| *n.* **1.** A formal
agreement or union between nations,
organizations, or individuals. **2.** Any union
or relationship by family ties, marriage,
friendship, etc.

al·lit·er·a·tion |ə lĭt´ə rā´shən| *n.* The
repetition of consonants for poetic or
rhetorical effect. [From *ad-*, to + Latin *littera*,
letter.]

al·lude |ə lōōd´| *v.* **al·lud·ed, al·lud·ing.**
To refer to indirectly; mention casually or in
passing. [Latin *allūdere*, to play with, jest at:
ad-, to + *lūdere*, to play, from *lūdus*, game.]

al·pha·bet·i·cal |ăl´fə **bĕt´**ĭ kəl| or
al·pha·bet·ic |ăl´fə **bĕt´**ĭk| *adj.*
Arranged in the order of the alphabet.
al·ter·nate |**ôl´**tər nāt´| or |ăl-| *v.*
al·ter·nat·ed, al·ter·nat·ing. To do,
perform, use, or occur in turn by changing
back and forth: *alternate one's clothes.* —*n.*
|**ôl´**tər nĭt| or |ăl-|. A person acting in place
of another. [Latin *alternus,* by turns.]
al·ter·na·tive |ôl **tûr´**nə tĭv| or |ăl-| *n.*
1. One of two or more options from which
to choose: *Raising taxes may be unpopular,
but the alternatives are even worse.* **2.** A
choice between two or more options: *The
alternative is between increased taxes or a
budget deficit.*
am·a·teur |**ăm´**ə chŏŏr´| or |-chər| or
|-tyŏŏr´| *n.* **1.** A person who engages in an
art, science, or sport for enjoyment rather
than for money. **2.** A person who does
something without professional skill.
[French, from Latin *amātōr,* lover, from
amāre, to love.]
am·bi·ance |**ăm´**bē əns| *n.* The special
atmosphere surrounding a person, place, or
thing.
am·big·u·ous |ăm **bĭg´**yŏŏ əs| *adj.*
Having two or more possible meanings or
interpretations; unclear: *an ambiguous
statement.*
am·bro·sia |ăm **brō´**zhə| *n.* In Greek
mythology, the food of the gods.
am·pli·fi·er |**ăm´**plə fī´ər| *n.* A device,
especially an electronic device, that increases
the volume of sounds. [Latin *amplificāre:
amplus,* ample + *facere,* to make.]
a·nal·o·gy |ə **năl´**ə jē| *n., pl.*
a·nal·o·gies. An inference that if two
unrelated things are alike in some ways they
are probably alike in others: *a large collection
of cases from which judges could draw analogies.*
[Greek *analogos,* resembling: *ana-,* according
to + *logos,* word.]

an·a·lyze |**ăn´**ə līz´| *v.* **an·a·lyzed,
an·a·lyz·ing. 1.** To perform or prepare an
analysis of: *They analyzed the ore and found
iron in it.* **2.** To examine in detail.
-ance. A suffix that forms nouns from verbs:
compliance; resemblance. [Middle English
-ance, -aunce, from Old French *-ance,* from
Latin *-antia,* abstract noun suffix of *-ant,* stem
of *-āns,* present participle ending, *ant.*]
an·ces·tor |**ăn´**sĕs´tər| *n.* Any person
from whom one is descended, especially if of
a generation earlier than a grandparent.
[Middle English *ancestre,* from Latin
antecessor, "one who goes before": *ante-* +
cēdere, to go.]
an·droid |**ăn´**droid´| *n.* In science fiction,
an artificially created man. [Late Greek
androeidēs, manlike: *andr(o)* + *oid.*]
an·ec·dote |**ăn´**ĭk dōt´| *n.* A short
account of an interesting or humorous
occurrence.
an·ni·ver·sa·ry |ăn´ə **vûr´**sə rē| *n., pl.*
an·ni·ver·sa·ries. 1. The yearly returning of
the date of an event that happened in an
earlier year: *a wedding anniversary.* **2.** A
celebration on this date. [Latin *anniversārius,*
"returning yearly": *annus,* year + *vertere,* to
turn.]
an·nounc·er |ə **noun´**sər| *n.*
1. Someone who announces. **2.** A person
who announces, as on television or over a
public-address system. [Middle English
announcen, from Latin *annutiāre: ad-,* to +
nuntiāre, to announce, from *nuntius,*
messenger.]
an·o·nym·i·ty |ăn´ə **nĭm´**ĭ tē| *n.* The
condition of being unknown.
an·te·ce·dent |ăn´ti **sēd´**nt| *adj.* Going
before; preceding; prior. —*n.* Someone or
something that goes before or precedes.
[Latin *anticēdere: ante-* + *cēdere,* to go.]

an·ten·na |ăn **tĕn´**ə| *n., pl.* **an·ten·nas.**
Any of various metallic devices that are capable of projecting radio waves from a transmitter into space or intercepting radio waves and delivering them to a receiver.

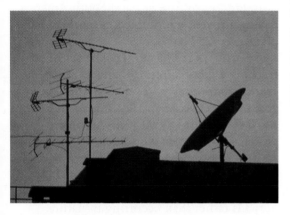

an·thol·o·gy |ăn **thŏl´**ə jē| *n., pl.*
an·thol·o·gies. A collection of writings, such as poems or short stories, by various authors. [Latin *anthologia,* from Greek "flower gathering," a collection: *antho-,* flower + *-logy,* study of.]
an·ti·bi·ot·ic |ăn´tē bī **ŏt´ĭk**| *n.* Any of a group of substances such as penicillin and streptomycin, produced by certain fungi, bacteria, and other organisms, that are capable of destroying microorganisms or stopping their growth. They are used to treat and prevent diseases. [Latin *antibioticus: anti-,* effectiveness against + *biotic,* made of life.]
an·ti·dote |ăn´tĭ dōt´| *n.* A substance that counteracts the effects of poison.
an·tique |ăn **tēk´**| *adj.* Being of ancient times. [French, from Latin *antiquus,* ancient.]
anx·i·e·ty |ăng **zī´**ĭ tē| *n., pl.*
anx·i·e·ties. A feeling of uneasiness and distress about something; worry.
anx·ious |ăngk´shəs| *or* |ăng´-| *adj.*
1. Having a feeling of uneasiness; worried: *The mother was anxious about her child.*
2. Marked by uneasiness or worry: *anxious moments.* **3.** Eagerly earnest or desirous: *anxious to begin.*

Pronunciation Key

ă	pat	ŏ	pot	û	fur
ā	pay	ō	go	*th*	**the**
â	care	ô	paw, for	th	**thin**
ä	father	oi	**oil**	hw	**which**
ĕ	pet	o͝o	book	zh	usual
ē	be	o͞o	boot	ə	ago, item
ĭ	pit	yo͞o	cute		pencil, atom
ī	ice	ou	**out**		circus
î	near	ŭ	cut	ər	butter

ap·a·thy |ăp´ə thē| *n.* Lack of feeling or interest; indifference: *the public's apathy to poverty.* [Greek *apatheia,* from *apathēs,* without feeling: *a-,* (without) + *pathos,* feeling.]
a·pol·o·gy |ə **pŏl´**ə jē| *n., pl.*
a·pol·o·gies. A statement expressing regret for an offense or fault: *make an apology for being late.* [French *apologie,* from Greek *apologiā,* speech in defense: *apo-,* defense + *logos,* speech.]
ap·par·el |ə **păr´**əl| *n.* Clothing; attire.
ap·par·ent |ə **păr´**ənt| *or* |-**pâr´**-| *adj.*
Readily understood or seen; obvious: *for no apparent reason.* [Middle English, from Old French *aparent,* present participle of *aparoir,* appear.]
ap·pli·ance |ə **plī´**əns| *n.* A machine, such as a toaster or electric stove, used to perform a household task. [Middle English *applien,* from Latin *applicāre,* to join to, apply to: *ad-,* to + *plicāre,* to fold together.]
ap·pli·ca·ble |ăp´lĭ kə bəl| *or* |ə **plĭk´**ə-| *adj.* Capable of being used; appropriate. [Middle English *applien,* from Latin *applicāre,* to join to: *ad-,* to + *plicāre,* to fold together.]
ap·pli·cant |ăp´lĭ kənt| *n.* A person who requests employment, acceptance, or admission: *an applicant for a job.*

Spelling Dictionary

ap·pli·ca·tion |ăp´lĭ kā´shən| *n.*
1. The act of putting on, upon, or to.
2. Something that is put on, such as a medicine or a cosmetic. [Latin *applicāre*, to join to: *ad-*, to + *plicāre*, to fold together.]

ap·prais·al |ə prā´zəl| *n.* **1.** The act of setting a value or price: *making appraisals of local housing markets.* **2.** The result of such an act; a valuation: *an unrealistic appraisal of his estate.*

ap·pren·tice |ə prĕn´tĭs| *n.* **1.** A person who works for another without pay in return for instruction in a craft or trade.
2. One, usually a member of a labor union, who is learning a trade: *a carpenter's apprentice.*

ap·pro·pri·ate |ə prō´prē ĭt| *adj.*
Suitable for a particular person, condition, occasion, or place; proper: *appropriate clothes.*

aq·ue·duct |ăk´wĭ dŭkt´| *n.* **1.** A large pipe or channel made to carry water from a distant source. **2.** A bridgelike structure designed to carry such a pipe or channel across low ground or a river. [Latin *aquae ductus: aquae*, genitive of *aqua*, water + *duct*, from *dūcere*, to lead.]

aq·ui·fer |ăk´wĭ fər| *or* |ä´kwĭ-| *n.* A layer of underground sand, gravel, or spongy rock in which water collects: *purify the aquifer.*

ar·chae·ol·o·gy |är´kē ŏl´ə jē| *n.* The scientific study of the remains of past human activities, such as buildings, tools, and pottery. [Late Latin *archaeologia*, "the study of antiquity," from Greek *arkhaiologia: archaeo-*, ancient + *logy*, the study or science of.]

ar·chi·tec·ture |är´kĭ tĕk´chər| *n.*
1. The art and occupation of designing and directing the construction of buildings and other large structures. **2.** A style of building: *Greek architecture.*

arc·tic |ärk´tĭk| *or* |är´tĭk| *adj.*
Extremely cold; frigid: *arctic weather.*

a·ri·a |är´ē ə| *n.* A piece written for a solo singer accompanied by instruments, as in an opera, cantata, or oratorio.

ar·ma·da |är mä´də| *or* |-mā´-| *n.* A big fleet of warships. [Spanish, from Medieval Latin *armāta*, army, fleet.]

ar·ma·dil·lo |är´mə dĭl´ō| *n., pl.*
ar·ma·dil·los. A burrowing mammal of southern North America and South America, having a covering of jointed, armorlike, bony plates.

ar·ri·val |ə rī´vəl| *n.* **1.** The act of reaching a destination: *the arrival of the general at the airport.* **2.** The attainment of a goal or objective: *arrival at a decision.*

ar·ti·fact |är´tə făkt´| *n.* An object produced by human workmanship, especially an item of primitive art. [Latin *arte*, by skill, from *ars*, art + *factum*, something made.]

ar·ti·fi·cial |är´tə fĭsh´əl| *adj.* Made by humans rather than occurring in nature.

as·cent |ə sĕnt´| *n.* **1.** The act of ascending or moving upward: *the first stages of ascent of a rocket through the atmosphere.*
2. The act of climbing up: *their ascent of Mont Blanc.*

as·pire |ə spīr´| *v.* **as·pired, as·pir·ing.**
To have a great ambition; desire strongly:
aspire to become a good player; aspire to great knowledge. [Middle English *aspiren*, from Latin *aspīrāre*, to breathe upon, favor, desire.]

as·sem·bly |ə sĕm´blē| *n., pl.*
as·sem·blies. The process of putting together a number of parts to make up a complete unit. —*modifier: assembly line.*

as·sent |ə sĕnt´| *n.* Agreement, as to a proposal, especially in a formal or impersonal manner: *desire the king's assent.*

as·sign·ment |ə sīn´mənt| *n.* **1.** The act of assigning. **2.** Something assigned, especially a task or job: *the chemistry assignment.* [Latin *assignāre: ad-*, to + *signāre*, to mark.]

as·sim·i·la·tion |ə sĭm´ə lā´shən| *n.*
The process of taking in or being taken into the cultural or social tradition of a group: *assimilation of new immigrants.*

as·sis·tant |ə sĭsˊtənt| *n.* One who assists; a helper: *a teacher's assistant.* —*adj.* Acting under the authority of another: *an assistant coach.*

as·sume |ə sōōmˊ| *v.,* **as·sumed, as·sum·ing.** To take for granted; suppose: *assume that all is well.* [Middle English *assumen,* from Latin *assūmere: ad-,* to + *sūmere,* to take.]

as·ter·isk |ăsˊtə rĭskˊ| *n.* A symbol (*) used in printed and written matter to indicate an omission or a reference to a footnote.

as·ter·oid |ăsˊtə roidˊ| *n.* Any of the numerous objects that orbit the sun, chiefly in the region between Mars and Jupiter. [Greek *asteroedēs,* like a star: *astēr,* star + *-oid,* of or resembling.]

as·trol·o·gy |ə strŏlˊə jē| *n.* The art of predicting the course of human events through the study of the positions of the stars and planets. [Middle English *astrologie,* from Greek *astrologos: astro-,* star + *logy,* study of.]

as·tro·naut |ăsˊtrə nôtˊ| *n.* A person trained to serve on the crew of a spacecraft. [From Greek *astro-,* star + *nautēs,* sailor.]

as·tro·nom·i·cal |ăsˊtrə nŏmˊĭ kəl| *adj.* Too large to be easily imagined; immense.

as·tron·o·my |ə strŏnˊə mē| *n.* The scientific study of the universe. [From Greek *astro-,* star + *-nomos,* to arrange.]

a·sy·lum |ə sīˊləm| *n.* **1.** A place of refuge. **2.** Protection offered by one country to people fleeing from persecution in another country: *The refugee requested political asylum.*

ath·let·ic |ăth lĕtˊĭk| *adj.* **1.** Of or for athletics: *athletic ability.* **2.** Of or for athletes: *a good athletic build; an athletic club.*

at·las |ătˊləs| *n.* A book or bound collection of maps. [From representations of the Greek god Atlas upholding the heavens, common in 16th-century books of maps.]

Pronunciation Key

ă	pat	ŏ	pot	û	fur
ā	pay	ō	go	*th*	the
â	care	ô	paw, for	th	thin
ä	father	oi	oil	hw	which
ĕ	pet	ōō	book	zh	usual
ē	be	ōō	boot	ə	ago, item
ĭ	pit	yōō	cute		pencil, atom
ī	ice	ou	out		circus
î	near	ŭ	cut	ər	butter

a·tri·um |āˊtrē əm| *n., pl.* **a·tri·a** |āˊtrē ə| *or* **a·tri·ums.** The open entrance court of an ancient Roman house.

a·tro·cious |ə trōˊshəs| *adj.* **1.** Extremely evil or cruel; wicked: *an atrocious crime.* **2.** Very bad; abominable: *atrocious weather.*

a·troc·i·ty |ə trŏsˊĭ tē| *n., pl.* **a·troc·i·ties.** Something atrocious, especially an extremely evil or cruel act: *wartime atrocities.*

au·to·ma·tion |ôˊtə māˊshən| *n.* The automatic operation or control of a process, machine, or system.

av·a·lanche |ăvˊə lănchˊ| *or* |-länchˊ| *n.* A large mass of material such as snow, ice, or earth that falls down the side of a mountain.

a·verse |ə vûrsˊ| *adj.* Opposed; reluctant: *Cats are usually averse to getting wet.*

av·o·ca·do |ăvˊə käˊdō| *or* |äˊvə-| *n., pl.* **av·o·ca·dos.** A tropical American fruit with leathery green or blackish skin and bland-tasting yellow-green pulp. [Spanish *aguacate,* from Nahuatl *ahuacatl* (named after the shape of the fruit).]

av·o·ca·tion |ăvˊə kāˊshən| *n.* An activity engaged in, usually for pleasure, in addition to one's regular work.

B

bac·te·ri·a |băk tîr´ē ə| *pl. n.* The less frequently used singular is **bac·te·ri·um** |băk tîr´ē əm|. Very small one-celled organisms often considered to be plants, although they usually lack green coloring.

bad·min·ton |băd´mĭn´tən| *n.* A game in which players use a light, long-handled racket to hit a shuttlecock back and forth over a high net. [After *Badminton*, in England.]

bal·co·ny |băl´kə nē| *n., pl.* **bal·co·nies.** **1.** A platform projecting from the wall of a building and surrounded by a railing. **2.** An upper section of the seats in a theater or auditorium. [Italian *balcone*, from Old Italian, scaffold, from Germanic.]

bar·be·cue |bär´bĭ kyōō´| *n.* A grill, pit, or fireplace for roasting meat, often outdoors. —*v.* **bar·be·cued, bar·be·cu·ing.** To cook (meat) over an open fire or hot coals, often with a spicy sauce. [American Spanish *barbacoa*, from Haitian Creole, framework of sticks set on posts.]

bar·i·tone |băr´ĭ tōn´| *n.* A moderately low singing voice of a man, higher than a bass and lower than a tenor.

ba·zaar |bə zär´| *n.* An Oriental market, usually consisting of a street lined with shops and stalls.

beige |bāzh| *n.* A light grayish or yellowish brown. —*adj.* Light grayish or yellowish brown.

bench |bĕnch| *v. sports.* To keep out of or remove (a player) from a team's line-up.

ben·e·fit |bĕn´ə fĭt| *n.* Something that is of help; an advantage: *The field trip was of great benefit to the students.* [Middle English *benfet*, from Norman French, from Latin *benefactum*, benefit, good deed, from *bene facere*, to do well: *bene*, well + *facere*, to do.]

be·tray·al |bĭ trā´əl| *n.* The act of betraying, especially through disloyalty and deception: *The betrayal of the prince saddened the king.*

bi-. A prefix meaning "two" or "twice": **bi·monthly; bi·sect.** [Latin *bi-, bin-,* from *bis,* twice.]

bib·li·og·ra·phy |bĭb´lē ŏg´rə fē| *n., pl.* **bib·li·og·ra·phies.** A list of the works of a specific author or publisher.

bi·o·de·grad·a·ble |bī´ō dĭ grā´də bəl| *adj.* Capable of being decomposed by natural biological processes: *biodegradable detergent.*

bi·ol·o·gy |bī ŏl´ə jē| *n.* The scientific study of living things and life processes, including growth, structure, and reproduction. Among the branches of biology are the sciences of botany, zoology, and ecology. [German *Biologie: bios-,* life + *logos,* science or study of.]

bi·op·sy |bī´ŏp´sē| *n., pl.* **bi·op·sies.** The study of tissues taken from a living person or organism, especially in an examination for the presence of disease.

bi·zarre |bĭ zär´| *adj.* Very strange or odd; grotesque: *a bizarre hat; a bizarre idea.*

bland |blănd| *adj.* **bland·er, bland·est.** Lacking distinctive taste; dull.

blank verse. A type of poetry written in unrhymed lines.

blue·print |blōō´print´| *n.* A photographic copy of architectural plans, technical drawings, etc., utilizing white lines on a blue background.

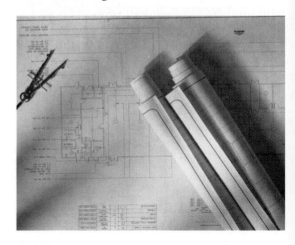

bouil·lon |bŏŏl´yŏn´| *or* |-yən´| *n.* A clear, thin soup or liquid in which meat has been boiled.

boul·e·vard |bŏŏl´ə värd´| *or* |bŏŏ´lə-| *n.* A broad city street, often lined with trees. [French, from Old French *boloart*, rampart, from Dutch *bolwerc*, from German *bulwark*.]

boy·cott |boi´kŏt´| *n.* An organized group refusal to use a product or service or to deal with a business or nation as a means of protest. —*v.* To participate in an organized group refusal: *boycott a store.* [After Charles C. *Boycott* (1832–1897), a British land agent who charged such high rents that people refused to deal with him.]

Braille, also **braille** |brāl| *n.* A system of writing and printing for the blind, in which raised dots representing letters, numbers, and punctuation are read by feeling them with the fingers. [After Louis *Braille*, French musician, educator, and inventor.]

bra·va·do |brə vä´dō| *n., pl.* **bra·va·does** or **bra·va·dos.** A show of pretended or defiant courage; false bravery. [Spanish *bravada, bravata*, from *bravo*, brave.]

brav·er·y |brā´və rē| *or* |brāv´rē| *n., pl.* **brav·er·ies.** The condition or quality of being brave; courage.

broc·co·li |brŏk´ə lē| *n.* A plant related to the cauliflower and cabbage, having green flower buds and stalks eaten as a vegetable.

bro·chure |brō shŏŏr´| *n.* A small pamphlet or booklet. [French "a stitching" (from the loose stitching of the pages) from *brocher*, to stitch.]

bron·co |brŏng´kō| *n., pl.* **bron·cos.** A small wild or half-wild horse of western North America. [Mexican Spanish, from Spanish, rough, wild, possibly from Latin *broncus.*]

brunch |brŭnch| *n.* A meal eaten late in the mornings as breakfast and lunch. [br(eakfast) + (l)unch.]

buf·fet |bə fā´| *or* |bŏŏ-| *n.* **1.** A restaurant with a counter from which food is served. **2.** A meal at which guests serve

themselves from dishes arranged on a table or sideboard. [French *buffet*.]

bul·le·tin |bŏŏl´ĭ tn| *or* |-tĭn| *n.* **1.** A statement on a matter of public interest, as in a newspaper, on television, or on radio: *a weather bulletin.* **2.** A publication, such as a periodical or pamphlet, issued by an organization.

bu·reau·crat |byŏŏr´ə krăt´| *n.* An official of a government department, or bureau.

butte |byŏŏt| *n.* A hill that rises sharply from the surrounding area and has a flat top.

but·tress |bŭt´rĭs| *n.* A structure, often of brick or stone, built against a wall for support.

by-pro·duct |bī´prŏd´əkt| *n.* **1.** Something produced in the making of something else. **2.** A secondary result; side effect: *Sawdust is a by-product of the woodworking shop.*

C

ca·fé |kă fā´| *n.* A coffeehouse or restaurant.

caf·e·te·ri·a |kăf´ĭ tîr´ē ə| *n.* A restaurant in which the customers are served at a counter and carry their meals to tables on trays. [American Spanish, coffee shop, from Spanish *cafetero*, coffee maker or seller, from *café*, coffee.]

Pronunciation Key					
ă	pat	ŏ	pot	û	fur
ā	pay	ō	go	*th*	**the**
â	care	ô	paw, for	th	**thin**
ä	father	oi	**oil**	hw	**wh**ich
ĕ	pet	ŏŏ	book	zh	usual
ē	be	ōō	boot	ə	ago, item
ĭ	pit	yŏŏ	cute		pencil, atom
ī	ice	ou	**out**		circus
î	near	ŭ	cut	ər	butter

cal·cu·la·tor |kăl´kyə lā´tər| *n.* A machine, operated by keyboard, that automatically performs the operations of arithmetic. [Latin *calculāre*, from *calculus*, small stone (used in reckoning), diminutive of *calx*, lime, limestone, from Greek *khalix*, pebble.]

cal·i·co |kăl´ĭ kō| *n., pl.* **cal·i·coes** or **cal·i·cos.** A cotton cloth with a pattern printed on it in color. [After Calicut, a city in India.]

cal·lous |kăl´əs| *adj.* Unfeeling; unsympathetic. —**cal·lous·ly** *adv.*— **cal·lous·ness** *n.*

cal·lus |kăl´əs| *n., pl.* **cal·lus·es.** A small area of the skin that has become hardened and thick through prolonged pressure or rubbing.

cam·ou·flage |kăm´ə fläzh´| *n.* The concealment or disguise of people, animals, or things through the use of colors or patterns that make them appear to be part of the natural surroundings. [French, from *camoufler*, to disguise, perhaps from *camouflet*, smoke blown into someone's nose, hence "disguise."]

cam·paign |kăm pān´| *n.* Organized activity to attain a political, social, or commercial goal.

can·cel·la·tion |kăn´sə lā´shən| *n.* **1.** The act of giving up or abandoning. **2.** A mark made on a stamp, check, etc., to indicate that it may not be used again.

can·di·date |kăn´dĭ dāt| or |-dĭt| *n.* A person who seeks or is nominated for an office, prize, honor, etc.

can·vas |kăn´vəs| *n.* Heavy cloth of cotton, hemp, or flax, used for making tents, sails, etc.

can·vass |kăn´vəs| *v.* To visit (a person or region) to get votes, hear opinions, make sales, etc.

cap·i·tal |kăp´ĭ tl| *n.* **1.** A city that is the seat of a state or national government. **2.** Wealth or property invested to produce more wealth.

cap·i·tol |kăp´ĭ tl| *n.* **1. Capitol.** The building in Washington, D.C., occupied by the Congress of the United States. **2.** The building in which a state legislature assembles.

car·at |kăr´ət| *n.* **1.** A unit of weight for precious stones, equal to 200 milligrams or about 1/140 of an ounce. **2.** A form of the word **karat.**

car·et |kăr´ĭt| *n.* A proofreading symbol used to indicate where something is to be inserted in a line of printed or written matter.

car·go |kär´gō| *n., pl.* **car·goes** or **car·gos.** The freight carried by a ship, airplane, etc. [Spanish *cargo, carga,* load.]

car·ni·val |kär´nə vəl| *n.* Any time of merrymaking; a festival.

car·rel |kăr´əl| *n.* A nook near the shelves of books in a library, used for private study.

car·tog·ra·phy |kär tŏg´rə fē| *n.* The art of making maps or charts. —**car·tog´ra·pher** *n.: The cartographer drew a map of Asia.*

car·tridge |kär´trĭj| *n.* A case holding magnetic tape and guide and feed mechanisms to be used in place of a reel in some tape players.

cash·mere |kăzh´mîr´| *or* |kăsh´-| *n.* **1.** Fine, soft wool growing beneath the outer hair of the Cashmere goat of the mountains of India and Tibet. **2.** Yarn or cloth made from this wool. [From Kashmir, a territory north of India.]

cat·a·combs |kăt´ə kōmz´| *pl. n.* A series of underground passages containing small compartments for coffins and graves.

cat·a·log or **cat·a·logue** |kăt´l ôg´| *or* |-ŏg´| *n.* A list of items, usually in alphabetical order, with a description of each. [From Greek *katalogos*, from *katalegein*, to recount: *kata*, thoroughly, + *legein*, to gather, speak.]

ca·tas·tro·phe |kə tăs´trə fē| *n.* A great calamity, such as an earthquake or flood.

ca·ter·er |kā´tər ər| *n.* A person who provides food for weddings, banquets, etc.

ca·the·dral |kə thē´drəl| *n.* Any large or important church: *married in a cathedral.*

cau·tious |kô´shəs| *adj.* Showing or having caution; careful: *a cautious driver.*

cel·lu·lose |sĕl´yə lōs| *n.* A carbohydrate that is the main component of plant tissues. It is used in making a variety of products including paper, cellophane, textiles, and explosives: *Wood contains cellulose.*

Cel·si·us |sĕl´sē əs| *or* |-shəs| *adj.* Of or concerning a temperature scale on which the freezing point of water is 0° and the boiling point of water is 100° under normal atmospheric pressure. [Originally devised by Anders *Celsius*, (1701–1744), Swedish astronomer.]

cen·ten·ni·al |sĕn tĕn´ē əl| *n.* A 100th anniversary or a celebration of it.

cent-. Indicates one hundred: **century.** [Latin *centum*, hundred.]

cen·ti·grade |sĕn´tĭ grād´| *adj.* Of or relating to a temperature scale that divides the interval between the boiling and freezing points of water into 100°; Celsius.

cen·ti·me·ter |sĕn´tə mē´tər| *n.* A unit of length; 1/100 meter.

cen·ti·pede |sĕn´tə pēd´| *n.* Any of a group of animals with a wormlike body divided into many segments, each with a pair of legs. The front pair have venom glands and are used as jaws that can give a painful bite.

Pronunciation Key

ă	pat	ŏ	pot	û	fur
ā	pay	ō	go	*th*	the
â	care	ô	paw, for	th	thin
ä	father	oi	oil	hw	which
ĕ	pet	ŏŏ	book	zh	usual
ē	be	ōō	boot	ə	ago, item
ĭ	pit	yōō	cute		pencil, atom
ī	ice	ou	out		circus
î	near	ŭ	cut	ər	butter

cen·tu·ry |sĕn´chə rē| *n., pl.* **cen·tu·ries.** A period of 100 years.

chal·lenge |chăl´ənj| *n.* An invitation or call to take part in a contest or fight to see who is better or stronger: *a challenge to a race.* —*v.* **chal·lenged, chal·leng·ing.** To call or engage in a contest or fight: *a challenge to a game.*

cham·pi·on·ship |chăm´pē ən shĭp´| *n.* A contest held to determine a champion.

char·i·ot |chăr´ē ət| *n.* A horse-drawn two-wheeled vehicle used in ancient times in battle, races, and processions: *a chariot race.*

chauf·feur |shō´fər| *or* |shō fûr´| *n.* A person who is hired to drive an automobile. [French, stoker, from *chauffer*, to warm.]

Ched·dar, also **ched·dar** |chĕd´ər| *n.* A firm, usually yellowish cheese. [From *Cheddar*, a village in England.]

chef |shĕf| *n.* A cook, especially the chief cook of a large kitchen staff, as in a restaurant. [French, from Old French *chief, chef,* chief.]

chi·ro·prac·tor |kī´rə prăk´tər| *n.* A person who practices a type of physical therapy that involves adjusting the spine or other body structures: *The chiropractor relieved the pain in the patient's back.*

chiv·al·ry |shĭv´əl rē| *n.* **1.** The medieval institution of knighthood and its customs: *the code of chivalry.* **2.** The qualities of the ideal knight, including gallantry, bravery, courtesy, honor, and devotion to the weak.

choc·o·late |chô´kə lĭt| *or* |chŏk´ə-| *or* |chôk´lĭt| *or* |chŏk´-| *n.* A sweet drink or candy made with ground roasted cacao seeds. —*adj.* Having the flavor of chocolate. [Spanish, from Aztec *xocalatl: xococ,* bitter + *atl,* water.]

cho·ral |kôr´əl| *or* |kōr´-| *adj.* Of, for, or sung by a chorus or choir.

chord |kôrd| *n.* A combination of three or more musical tones sounded at the same time.

cho·rus |kôr´əs| *or* |kōr´-| *n., pl.* **cho·rus·es.** An organized group of singers who perform together.

chron·i·cle |krŏn´ĭ kəl| *v.* **chron·i·cled, chron·i·cling.** To record, as in a chronicle: *Almanacs chronicle the events of the year.* [Middle English, from Latin *chronica,* from Greek *khronikos,* pertaining to time, from *khronos,* time.] —**chron´i·cler** *n.*

chro·nol·o·gy |krə nŏl´ə jē| *n., pl.* **chro·nol·o·gies.** The arrangement of events in time; the order of events. [From Greek *khronos,* time + *logy,* speech.]

cir·cu·la·tion |sûr´kyə lā´shən| *n.* **1.** The passage of something, such as money or news, from person to person or from place to place: *dollar bills in circulation.* **2.** The distribution of printed matter, such as newspapers and magazines: *This magazine has wide circulation.* —**modifier:** *circulation desk.*

cir·cum·vent |sûr´kəm vĕnt´| *or* |sûr´kəm vĕnt´| *v.* To avoid by or as if by passing around. [Latin *circumvenīre: circum-,* around + *venīre,* to come.]

cite |sīt| *v.* **cit·ed, cit·ing.** To quote or mention as an authority or example: *cite two cases.*

cit·i·zen·ship |sĭt´ĭ zən shĭp´| *n.* The status of a citizen with its duties, rights, and privileges: *American citizenship.*

ci·vil·ian |sĭ vĭl´yən| *n.* A person not serving in the armed forces.

civ·i·li·za·tion |sĭv´ə lĭ zā´shən| *n.* A culture and society developed by a particular nation, region, or period: *modern civilization.*

clas·si·fi·ca·tion |klăs·ə fĭ kā´shən| *n.* The act or result of arranging in categories.

clear·ance |klîr´əns| *n.* Official certification that a person is free from suspicion or guilt.

co·coa |kō´kō´| *n.* **1.** A powder made from roasted ground cacao seeds. **2.** A sweet drink made with this powder. [Spanish, from Nahuatl *cacahuatl,* cacao beans.]

col·lab·o·rate |kə lăb´ə rāt´| *v.* **col·lab·o·rat·ed, col·lab·o·rat·ing.** To work together on a project. [Latin *collabōrāre: con-,* together + *labōrāre,* to work.]

col·lapse |kə lăps´| *v.* **col·lapsed, col·laps·ing.** **1.** To fall down or inward suddenly; cave in. **2.** To break down or fall suddenly and completely: *collapse from overwork.* [Latin *collābī: con-,* together + *lābī,* slide, fall.]

col·lat·er·al |kə lăt´ər əl| *n.* Something pledged as security for a loan.

col·league |kŏl´ēg´| *n.* A fellow member of a profession, staff, or organization; an associate. [From Latin *collēga,* one chosen to serve with another: *con-,* together + *lēgāre,* to choose.]

col·li·sion |kə lĭzh´ən| *n.* The act or process of striking together; a crash. [Middle English, from Latin *collīdere,* collide: *con-,* together + *laedere,* to strike.]

co·logne |kə lōn´| *n.* A scented liquid made of alcohol and fragrant oils. [From *Cologne,* a city in western Germany.]

col·on·nade |kŏl´ə **nād**´| *n.* A series of columns placed at regular intervals.

co·los·sal |kə **lŏs**´əl| *adj.* Very great in size, extent, or degree; gigantic.

col·umn |kŏl´əm| *n.* **1.** A pillar or upright structure used in a building as a support or decoration. **2.** A feature that appears regularly in a newspaper or magazine.

col·um·nist |kŏl´əm nĭst| *or* |-ə mĭst| *n.* A person who writes a column for a newspaper or magazine.

co·me·di·an |kə **mē**´dē ən| *n.* An entertainer who makes audiences laugh.

com·mem·o·rate |kə **mĕm**´ə rāt´| *v.* **com·mem·o·rat·ed, com·mem·o·rat·ing.** To honor the memory of: *commemorate the victory.*

com·men·tar·y |kŏm´ən tĕr´ē| *n., pl.* **com·men·tar·ies.** An explanation or interpretation; a series of comments: *a news commentary.* [From Latin *comminīscī: com-,* thoroughly + *minīscī,* to think.]

com·mer·cial |kə **mûr**´shəl| *adj.* Having profit as its chief aim: *a commercial television station.* —*n.* an advertisement on radio or television.

com·mis·er·ate |kə **mĭz**´ə rāt´| *v.* To feel or express sorrow or pity for; sympathize: *One defeated candidate commiserates with another.*

com·mis·sion |kə **mĭsh**´ən| *n.* Often **Commission.** A group of people who have been given authority by law to perform certain duties: *The commission investigates false advertising.*

com·mit |kə **mĭt**´| *v.* **com·mit·ted, com·mit·ting. 1.** To do or perform: *commit a crime.* **2.** To pledge (oneself) to a position: *commit ourselves to the decision.* [Latin *committere,* to join, connect: *con-,* together + *mittere,* to send.]

com·mit·tee |kə **mĭt**´ē| *n.* A group of people chosen to do a particular job or to fulfill specified duties.

Usage: **Committee.** *Committee* takes a singular verb when it refers to the committee as a whole and a plural verb when it refers to the members of the committee as separate persons: *The committee votes every third Wednesday. The committee vote as they see fit.*

com·mu·ni·ca·tion |kə myōō´nĭ **kā**´shən| *n.* **1.** The exchange of information by speech, signals, or writing. **2.** Something communicated; a message. [Latin *commūnis,* sharing a burden, common: *con-,* together + *mūnis,* duty.]

com·mut·er |kə **myōō**´tər| *n.* A person who travels regularly between a home in one community and work in another.

com·pa·ra·ble |kŏm´pər ə bəl| *adj.* Capable of being compared; similar: *comparable in size.*

com·pe·ti·tion |kŏm´pĭ **tĭsh**´ən| *n.* Rivalry or struggle to win an advantage, success, or profit: *competition between the two teams.*

com·ple·ment |kŏm´plə mənt| *n.* Something that completes or brings to perfection.
Usage: **Complement, Compliment.** Use *complement* to mean "something that completes": *The flowers are a complement to the beautifully set table.* Use *compliment* to mean "an expression of praise": *She received many compliments on her beautifully set table.*

com·plex·i·ty |kəm´plĕk´sĭ tē| *n., pl.* **com·plex·i·ties.** The condition of being complex: *the complexity of modern civilization.* [Latin *complectere*, to entwine: *con-*, together + *plectere*, to twine, braid.]

com·pli·ca·tion |kŏm´plĭ kā´shən| *n.* **1.** Something that complicates: *Try not to add complications to an already difficult procedure.* **2.** An intricate or confused relationship of parts: *the complications of the diving equipment limit its use to experts.* [Latin *complicāre*, to fold together: *con-*, together + *plicāre*, to fold.]

com·pli·ment |kŏm´plə mənt| *n.* An expression of praise or admiration. —See Usage note at **complement.**

com·po·nent |kəm pō´nənt| *n.* Any of the parts that together make up a whole: *A large computer consists of thousands of components.*

com·pos·ite |kəm pŏz´ĭt| *adj.* Made up of distinctly different parts: *A composite face is made by putting together the eyes, mouth, nose, etc., from different pictures.* —*n.* Something made by combining different parts: *The crossbow was a composite of wood, horn, and sinew.* [Latin *con-*, together + *pōnere*, to put.]

con-. Also **col-** (before *l*) or **cor-** (before *r*) or **com-** (before *p, b,* or *m*) or **co-** (before vowels, *h,* and *gn*). A prefix meaning "together, with": **compete.** [Old Latin preposition *con.*]

con·cede |kən sēd´| *v.* **con·ced·ed, con·ced·ing.** **1.** To admit as true or real, often unwillingly or hesitantly; acknowledge: *Jenny conceded that the new house might be pleasant to live in.* **2.** To give up on (something in which one has had a strong claim or interest), often before results have been fully established: *The candidate conceded the election before all votes had been counted.* [French *concéder*, from Latin *concēdere*, to yield: *con-* + *cēdere*, withdraw.]

con·ceive |kən sēv´| *v.* To form or develop in the mind: *James Watt conceived the idea of the steam engine from watching a boiling kettle.* **2.** To grasp; understand: *conceive of an infinite space.* [Middle English *conceiven*, from Latin *concipere*, to take into the mind: *con*, comprehensively + *capere*, to take.]

con·cep·tion |kən sĕp´shən| *n.* **1.** A mental picture or understanding; idea: *the conception of the extent of the universe.* **2.** A beginning or formation of an idea: *a history of art from its earliest conception to the most complex recent works.*

con·ces·sion |kən sĕsh´ən| *n.* Something yielded or conceded: *His promise to take them fishing was a concession to their demands.* [Middle English, from Latin *concēdere*, concede.]

con·do·min·i·um |kŏn´də mĭn´ē əm| *n.* Also shortened to **condo.** An apartment building in which each apartment is owned by its tenant. [Latin *con-*, together + *dominium*, property.]

con·du·cive |kən doo´siv| *or* |-dyoo´-| *adj.* Tending to cause, promote, or help bring about: *The noisy atmosphere is not conducive to work.* [Latin *condūcere*, to lead together; *con-*, together + *dūcere*, to lead.]

con·fer |kən fûr´| *v.* **con·ferred, con·fer·ring.** To hold a conference; consult together; discuss; *confer with advisers.* [Latin *conferre*, to bring together: *con-*, together + *ferre*, to bring, bear.]

con·fet·ti |kən fĕt´ē| *n.* (used with a singular verb). Small pieces of colored paper scattered about on festive occasions. [Italian, plural of *confetto*, confection, candy, from Latin *confectus*, to put together, confect.]

con·fi·den·tial |kŏn´fĭ **dĕn**´shəl| *adj.* Told in confidence; secret: *confidential information.*

con·fine |kən **fīn**´| *v.* **con·fined, con·fin·ing. 1.** To limit in area or extent: *Nineteenth-century New York was confined to Manhattan.* **2.** To restrict in movement: *confined to bed with the flu.* **3.** To imprison: *confined in a cage.* [Latin *confīnis,* having the same border: *con-,* together + *fīnis,* border, end.]

con·form·ist |kən **fôr**´mĭst| *n.* Someone who conforms to current attitudes or practices or tries to meet other people's expectations.

con·nois·seur |kŏn´ə **sûr**´| *n.* A person with a thorough knowledge of or appreciation for a certain subject in which good taste is needed: *a connoisseur of art.* [Old French *connoisseor,* from Latin *cognōscere,* to know thoroughly: *co-,* together + *gnōscere, nōscere,* to know.]

con·quest |kŏn´kwĕst´| *or* |kŏng´-| *n.* An act of winning: *the army's conquest.*

con·science |kŏn´shəns| *n.* An inner sense in a person that distinguishes right from wrong.

con·sci·en·tious |kŏn´shē **ĕn**´shəs| *or* |kŏn´sē-| *adj.* Showing or done with care and seriousness of purpose: *a conscientious worker.*

con·scious |kŏn´shəs| *adj.* Able to perceive and understand what is happening: *He is badly injured but still conscious.*

con·sen·sus |kən **sĕn**´səs| *n.* A general agreement: *The students reached a consensus.* [From Latin *con-,* together + *sentīre,* to feel.]

con·se·quence |kŏn´sĭ kwĕns´| *or* |-kwəns| *n.* Something that follows from an action or condition.

con·ser·va·tion |kŏn´sər **vā**´shən| *n.* The act or process of conserving; a saving: *a conservation of time and human effort.*

Pronunciation Key					
ă	pat	ŏ	pot	û	fur
ā	pay	ō	go	*th*	the
â	care	ô	paw, for	th	thin
ä	father	oi	oil	hw	which
ĕ	pet	ŏŏ	book	zh	usual
ē	be	ōō	boot	ə	ago, item
ĭ	pit	yōō	cute		pencil, atom
ī	ice	ou	out		circus
î	near	ŭ	cut	ər	butter

con·serv·a·to·ry |kən **sûr**´və tôr´ē| *or* |-tōr´ē| *n., pl.* **con·ser·va·to·ries.** A school of music or dramatic art.

con·sis·ten·cy |kən **sĭs**´tən sē| *n.* Adherence or conformity to the same principles or courses of action: *His statements lack consistency.*

con·spir·a·cy |kən **spîr**´ə sē| *n., pl.* **con·spir·a·cies.** A secret plan to commit an unlawful act. [From Latin *conspīrāre,* to agree, unite, plot: *con-,* together + *spīrāre,* to breathe.]

con·sume |kən **sōōm**´| *v.* **con·sumed, con·sum·ing. 1.** To use up: *The Saturn V launch vehicle consumes 1,000 pounds of fuel per minute.* **2.** To buy and use: *Americans consume an enormous amount of cotton.* [Middle English *consumen,* from Latin *consūmere,* to take completely: *con-,* + *sūmere,* to take up.]

con·sum·er |kən **sōō**´mər| *n.* Someone who buys and uses goods and services.

con·sump·tion |kən **sŭmp**´shən| *n.* **1.** The act of eating or drinking. **2.** The act of using up. [Latin *consūmere,* to take completely: *con-,* + *sūmere,* to take up.]

con·ta·gious |kən **tā**´jəs| *adj.* **1.** Capable of being transmitted by direct or indirect contact: *a contagious disease.* **2.** Tending to spread from person to person: *contagious laughter.*

con·tam·i·nate |kən **tăm´**ə nāt| *v.*
con·tam·i·nat·ed, con·tam·i·nat·ing. To
make impure, bad, or less good by mixture or
contact; pollute; foul: *Oil contaminated the
beaches.*

con·tin·u·ous |kən **tĭn´**yo͞o əs| *adj.*
Going on without interruption; unbroken.
Usage: **Continuous, Continual.** Use
continuous to mean "without interruption":
the continuous hum of the refrigerator. Use
continual to mean "over and over again": *the
continual banging of the shutters.*

con·tin·u·um |kən **tĭn´**yo͞o əm| *n., pl.*
con·tin·u·a or **con·tin·u·ums.** Something
that can be divided into parts as small as
desired; something that extends in a smooth,
unbroken way.

con·tract |**kŏn´**trăkt´| *n.* **1.** A formal
agreement between two or more persons or
groups. **2.** A document stating the terms of
such an agreement. —*v.* |kən **trăkt´**|.
1. To make or become smaller. **2.** To
arrange by a formal agreement. **3.** To get or
acquire: *contract the mumps.* [Middle English,
from Latin *contractus*, to draw together, enter
into an agreement: *con-*, together + *trahere*, to
draw.]

con·tra·dic·tion |kŏn´trə **dĭk´**shən| *n.*
1. The act of denying or disagreeing with
something or someone or of being
inconsistent. **2.** An inconsistency;
discrepancy: *There's a contradiction in what
you're saying.*

con·tro·ver·sy |**kŏn´**trə vûr´sē| *n., pl.*
con·tro·ver·sies. 1. Argument; debate: *He
is the subject of much controversy.* **2.** A
lengthy public dispute between sides holding
opposing views: *the controversy over state aid to
private schools.* [Latin *contrōversia*, turned
against, disputed: *contrō-*, against + *versus*, to
turn.]

con·ven·ient |kən **vēn´**yənt| *adj.* **1.** Easy
to reach; within easy reach: *a convenient
location.* **2.** Suited to one's comfort, needs, or
purpose: *a convenient appliance.* [From Latin
convenīre: con-, together + *venīre*, to come.]

con·ven·tion |kən **věn´**shən| *n.* A
formal assembly or meeting: *a teacher's
convention.* [From Latin *con-*, together +
venīre, to come.]

con·vert |kən **vûrt´**| *v.* **1.** To change
into another form, substance, or condition:
convert carbon dioxide into sugar. **2.** To
change from one use to another: *convert a
home into a library.* **3.** To persuade (a
person) to adopt a particular religion or
belief: *convert to Christianity.* [Latin
convertere, to turn around, transform: *con-* +
vertere, to turn.]

cor·al |**kôr´**əl| *or* |**kŏr´-**| *n.* **1.** A hard,
stony substance formed by the skeletons of
tiny sea animals massed together in great
numbers. It is often white, pink, or reddish,
and some kinds are used for making jewelry.
2. A yellowish pink or reddish orange.
—*modifier: a coral reef.*

cord |kôrd| *n.* String or rope of twisted
strands.

cor·du·roy |**kôr´**də roi´| *or* |kôr´də **roi´**|
n. A heavy cotton cloth with a ridged surface.

cor·rob·o·rate |kə **rŏb´**ə rāt´| *v.* To
support or confirm by new evidence; attest
the truth or accuracy of: *corroborate the
statement.*

cor·rode |kə rōd´| v. **cor·rod·ed,
cor·rod·ing. 1.** To dissolve or wear away (a material, structure, etc.), especially by chemical action. **2.** To be dissolved or worn away.

counter-. A prefix meaning: **1.** Contrary; opposite: **counteract; counterclockwise. 2.** Retaliatory; in return: **counterattack. 3.** Complementary; corresponding: **countersign.** [From Latin *contrā,* opposite to, counter.]

coun·ter·act |koun´tər ăkt´| v. To lessen and oppose the effects of by contrary action; check. [From Latin *contrā,* opposing + *actus,* to do.]

coun·ter·clock·wise
|koun´tər klŏk´wīz´| adv. In a direction opposite to that of the movement of the hands of a clock.

coun·ter·feit |koun´tər fĭt| adj. Made in imitation of what is genuine in order to deceive: *a counterfeit dollar bill.* [From Latin *contrā,* opposite to + *facere,* to make.]

coun·ter·part |koun´tər pärt´| n. A person or thing exactly or very much like another, as in function, relation, etc.: *The modern counterpart of a horse and buggy is a car.* [From Latin *contrā,* opposite + *pars,* equal.]

coun·ter·pro·duc·tive
|koun´tər prə dŭk´tĭv| adj. Tending to hinder rather than serve one's purpose; harmful, not helpful.

coy·o·te |kī ō´tē| or |kī´ōt´| n. A wolflike animal common in western North America. [Mexican Spanish, from Nahuatl *coyotl.*]

cram·pon |krăm´pŏn´| n., pl. **cram·pons.** A spiked metal plate attached to the shoe to prevent slipping when climbing or walking on ice.

crev·ice |krĕv´ĭs| n. A narrow crack or opening; a fissure: *a crevice in the rock.*

crit·i·cism |krĭt´ĭ sĭz´əm| n. **1.** The act of forming and expressing judgments about the worth of something. **2.** Unfavorable

Pronunciation Key					
ă	pat	ŏ	pot	û	fur
ā	pay	ō	go	*th*	the
â	care	ô	paw, for	th	thin
ä	father	oi	oil	hw	which
ĕ	pet	o͝o	book	zh	usual
ē	be	o͞o	boot	ə	ago, item
ĭ	pit	yo͞o	cute		pencil, atom
ī	ice	ou	out		circus
î	near	ŭ	cut	ər	butter

judgment; disapproval. **3.** The art or practice of judging artistic works, such as writing or film.

cru·cial |kro͞o´shəl| adj. Of the utmost importance; decisive: *a crucial decision.*

cui·sine |kwĭ zēn´| n. A style of cooking: *French cuisine.*

cu·li·nar·y |kyo͞o´lə nĕr´ē| or |kŭl´ə-| adj. Of a kitchen or cookery: *culinary ware; culinary skill.*

cul·ti·vate |kŭl´tə vāt´| v. **cul·ti·vat·ed, cul·ti·vat·ing.** To grow and tend (plants or crops).

cul·tur·al |kŭl´chər əl| adj. Pertaining to the arts, beliefs, customs, and institutions created by people of a certain region or time.

cu·ra·tor |kyo͞o rā´tər| or |kyo͝or´ā´-| n. A person in charge of a museum or library.

cu·ri·os·i·ty |kyo͝or´ē ŏs´ĭ tē| n., pl. **cu·ri·os·i·ties.** A desire to know or learn.

cus·to·di·an |kŭ stō´dē ən| n. A person who takes care of a building; a janitor.

cus·tom·er |kŭs´tə mər| n. A person who buys goods or services.

-cy. A suffix that forms nouns: **bankruptcy; piracy.** [Middle English *-cie,* from Latin *-cia, -tia,* and Greek *-kiā, -tiā.*]

cym·bal |sĭm´bəl| n. One of a pair of musical percussion instruments consisting of a dish-shaped sheet of brass that is sounded either by being struck with a drumstick or by being struck against another identical sheet of brass.

czar |zär| *n.* A former emperor of Russia. [From Russian *tsar*, from Gothic *kaisar*, from Latin *Caesar*, emperor, from Julius Caesar.]

D

dam·ask |dăm´əsk| *n.* A rich, glossy fabric woven with patterns that show on both sides, as a silk used for draperies or a linen used for tablecloths. [Middle English *damask* (cloth), from Medieval Latin (*pannus de*) *damasco,* "(cloth of) Damascus," capital of Syria.]

da·ta·base |dā´tə bās| *or* |dăt´ə| *n.* A collection of data stored on a computer.

day·break |dā´brāk´| *n.* The time each morning when light first appears; dawn: *Farmers often get up before daybreak.*

dec-. A word part meaning "ten": **decagon; decathlon.** [Greek *deks*, from *deka*, ten.]

dec·ade |děk´ād´| *n.* A period of ten years.

de·cath·lon |dĭ kăth´lən| *or* |-lŏn´| *n.* An athletic contest in which each contestant participates in ten different track and field events.

de·ceive |dĭ sēv´| *v.* **de·ceived, de·ceiv·ing.** To make (a person) believe something that is not true; mislead. [Middle English *deceiven*, from Latin *dēcipere*, to take in, deceive: *dē* + *capere*, to take.]

de·cep·tion |dĭ sěp´shən| *n.* The act of deceiving: *practice deception.*

dec·i·bel |děs´ə bəl| *or* |-běl´| *n.* A unit used in expressing the loudness of sounds.

dec·i·mal |děs´ə məl| *n.* **1.** A numeral in the decimal system of numeration. **2.** A numeral based on 10, used with a decimal point in expressing a decimal fraction.

de·com·pose |dē´kəm pōz´| *v.* **de·com·posed, de·com·pos·ing. 1.** To separate or break down into component parts or basic elements. **2.** To decay; rot. [French *décomposer: dé-*(reversal) + *composer,* to compose.]

de·duc·tion |dĭ dŭk´shən| *n.* The act of taking away; subtraction. [Middle English *deducen*, from Latin *dēdūcere*, to lead away, infer logically: *de-*, away + *dūcere*, to lead.]

deed |dēd| *n.* A legal document showing ownership of property: *a deed to the estate.*

de·fect |dē´fěkt´| *or* |dĭ fěkt´| *n.* A lack of something necessary or desirable for completion or perfection; a deficiency: *a defect in a piece of china.* [Latin *dēfectus,* deficiency: *dē-*, away from + *facere*, to do, set.]

de·fen·sive |dĭ fěn´sĭv| *adj.* Of or for defense; protecting from attack: *defensive walls; a defensive player.* —*n.* A defensive position or attitude. ***Idiom.* on the defensive.** Expecting or being subjected to attack.

def·i·cit |děf´ ĭ sĭt| *n.* The amount by which a sum of money falls short of the required or expected amount; a shortage: *a budget deficit.* [French *déficit*, from Latin *dēficere*, to lack.]

de·fine |dĭ fīn´| *v.* **de·fined, de·fin·ing. 1.** To state the precise meaning or meanings of (a word, phrase, etc.). **2.** To describe; specify: *define one's duties.* [Middle English, *diffinen*, from Latin *dēfinīre,* to set bounds to: *dē-*, off + *finis*, boundary.]

def·i·nite |děf´ə nĭt| *adj.* **1.** Clearly defined; precise. **2.** Known beyond doubt; sure. [Middle English *diffinen*, from Latin *dēfinīre*, to set bounds to: *dē-*, off + *finis*, end, boundary.]

def·i·ni·tion |děf´ə nĭsh´ən| *n.* A statement of the precise meaning or meanings of a word, phrase, etc.

de·fin·i·tive |dĭ fĭn´ĭ tĭv| *adj.* **1.** Final; conclusive: *a definitive victory.* **2.** Being the most complete and true: *a definitive biography.*

del·i·ca·tes·sen |děl´ĭ kə těs´ən| *n.* A store that sells cooked or prepared foods, such as cheeses, salads, relishes, smoked meats, etc. [German *Delikatessen*, from French *délicatesse,* from Italian *delicato*, delicate.]

de·moc·ra·cy |dĭ **mŏk´**rə sē| *n., pl.*
de·moc·ra·cies. 1. A form of government in which power belongs to the people, who express their will through elected representatives. **2.** A country with this form of government.

den·im |**dĕn´**əm| *n.* A coarse, heavy cotton cloth used for work and sport clothes, especially blue denim, used for overalls, blue jeans, and dungarees: *a denim jacket.* [French *(serge) de Nîmes,* serge of *Nîmes,* a city in France.]

de·nounce |dĭ **nouns´**| *v.* **de·nounced, de·nounc·ing.** To express strong disapproval of: *denounce a proposed law.* [From Latin *dēnūntiāre,* make an official announcement of: *dē-,* completely + *nūntiāre,* announce.]

de·nun·ci·a·tion |dĭ nŭn´sē **ā´**shən| *or* |-shē-| *n.* The act of denouncing; open condemnation.

de·pot |**dē´**pō| *n.* **1.** A railroad or bus station. **2.** A warehouse or storehouse.

dep·ri·va·tion |dĕp´rə **vā´**shən| *n.* The condition of being deprived.

de·prive |dĭ **prīv´**| *v.* **de·prived, de·priv·ing.** To take something away from; deny: *deprived of his rights.* [Middle English *depriven,* from Latin *dēprīvāre: dē-,* completely + *prīvāre,* deprive, from *privus,* individual, private.]

de·scent |dĭ **sĕnt´**| *n.* The act or an example of going down or sloping downward: *They began the descent from the top of the mountain.*

de·sign |dĭ **zīn´**| *v.* To draw up plans for (something), especially by means of sketches or drawings. —*n.* A drawing or sketch giving the details of how something is to be made.

des·o·late |**dĕs´**ə lĭt| *adj.* **1.** Having little or no vegetation; barren. **2.** Having few or no inhabitants; deserted: *a desolate wilderness.* **3.** Lonely and sad; wretched; forlorn. —*v.* |dĕs ə **lāt´**| **des·o·lat·ed, des·o·lat·ing. 1.** To make desolate, especially to lay waste to: *A fire desolated the*

Pronunciation Key

ă	pat	ŏ	pot	û	fur
ā	pay	ō	go	*th*	the
â	care	ô	paw, for	th	thin
ä	father	oi	oil	hw	which
ĕ	pet	ŏŏ	book	zh	usual
ē	be	ōō	boot	ə	ago, item
ĭ	pit	yōō	cute		pencil, atom
ī	ice	ou	out		circus
î	near	ŭ	cut	ər	butter

forest. **2.** To make lonely, wretched, etc. [Middle English *desolat,* from Latin *dēsōlātus,* abandon: *dē-,* completely + *sōlus,* alone.]

des·o·la·tion |dĕs ə **lā´**shən| *n.* **1.** The condition of being desolate: *desolation caused by a forest fire.* **2.** The act of making desolate. **3.** A wasteland. **4.** Loneliness or misery.

de·struc·tion |dĭ **strŭk´**shən| *n.* **1.** The act of destroying. **2.** Heavy damage: *The tornado caused great destruction.* [Middle English *destruccioun,* from Latin *dēstructus,* destroy.]

de·tain |dĭ **tān´**| *v.* **1.** To delay; impede. **2.** To keep in custody; confine: *detain the suspect.* [From Latin *dētinēre,* to keep back: *dē-,* away + *tenēre,* to hold.]

de·tect |dĭ **tĕkt´**| *v.* To discover or notice the existence, presence, or fact of. —**de·tec´tion** *n.*: *detection of a false note.*

dé·tente |dā **tänt´**| *n.* An easing, as of tension, between nations. [French, a loosening.]

de·ten·tion |dĭ **tĕn´**shən| *n.* The act of delaying or keeping in custody; confinement.

de·te·ri·o·rate |dĭ **tîr´**ē ə rāt´| *v.* **de·te·ri·o·rat·ed, de·te·ri·o·rat·ing.** To make or become inferior in quality, character, or value: *The railroads deteriorated as air travel grew.*

301

di-. A word part meaning "two, twice, double": **dioxide.** [From Greek *di-*, two, twice.]

di·ag·nos·tic |dī´əg nŏs´tĭk| *adj.* Of, involving, or used in the act or process of identifying or distinguishing a disease: *The results of your diagnostic tests will not be available for several days.*

di·a·logue, also **di·a·log** |dī´ə lôg´| *or* |-lŏg´| *n.* A conversation between two or more persons. [Middle English *dialog(ue)*, from Greek *dialogos*, to converse: *dia-*, one with another + *legein*, to tell, talk.]

dic·tion·ar·y |dĭk´shə nĕr´ē| *n., pl.* **dic·tion·ar·ies. 1.** A book containing an alphabetical list of words with information given for each word. Such information includes meaning, pronunciation, etymology, usage, and synonyms. **2.** A similar book limited to one category of words: *a medical dictionary.*

dif·fer |dĭf´ər| *v.* **1.** To be unlike in form, quality, amount, or nature: *The climate often differs from one part of a state to another.* **2.** To be of a different opinion; disagree: *I beg to differ with you.* [Middle English *differen*, from Old French *differre,* be different: *dis-*, apart + *ferre*, to carry.]

dig·i·tal |dĭj´ĭ tl| *adj.* Using or representing information in the form of numbers: *a digital clock.* [From Latin *digitus*, finger.]

di·graph |dī´grăf´| *n.* A pair of letters that represents one sound, as the *ea* in *beat.*

di·lem·ma |dĭ lĕm´ə| *n.* A situation that requires a person to choose between two or more courses of action that are equally difficult or unpleasant: *I must find a solution to this dilemma.*

din·ghy |dĭng´ē| *n., pl.* **dinghies.** A small boat, especially a rowboat. [Hindi *dēngā*, boat.]

diph·thong |dĭf´thông´| *or* |-thŏng´| *or* |dĭp´-| *n.* A speech sound beginning with one vowel sound and moving to another within the same syllable. For example, *oy* in the word *boy* is a diphthong.

di·plo·ma |dĭ plō´mə| *n.* A document or certificate showing that a person has earned a degree from or completed a course of study at a school, college, or university.

di·rec·to·ry |dĭ rĕk´tə rē| *or* |dī-| *n., pl.* **di·rec·to·ries. 1.** A list of names, addresses, or other facts: *a telephone directory.* **2.** A listing of all the software contained in a computer.

dis·as·ter |dĭ zăs´tər| *or* |-zä´stər| *n.* Great destruction, distress, or misfortune. [From Italian *disastrato*, "ill-starred," from Latin *dis-*, away, without + Greek *astron,* star (because an unfavorable position of a star was thought to cause mishaps).]

dis·as·trous |dĭ zăs´trəs| *or* |-săs´-| *adj.* Causing disaster; ruinous: *disastrous floods.*

disc jockey. A radio announcer who presents and comments on recorded music.

dis·co·theque |dĭs´kə tĕk´| *or*
|dĭs´kə **tĕk**´| *n.* Also shortened to **disco.** A
nightclub that offers dancing to amplified
recorded music. [French *disco-* +
(*biblio*)*thèque*, library.]

dis·crim·i·na·tion |dĭ skrĭm´ə **nā**´shən|
n. Acts or attitudes based on prejudice;
unfairness or injustice toward a particular
group of persons: *Job discrimination is illegal.*

di·shev·eled |dĭ **shĕv**´əld| *adj.* Untidy;
not orderly; disarranged: *disheveled hair.*

disk·ette |dĭ **skĕt**´| *n.* A disk used to
store computer data; a floppy disk. [English
disk + *ette* (diminutive suffix).]

dis·miss |dĭs **mĭs**´| *v.* To direct or allow
to leave: *The teacher will dismiss the class.*
[From Latin *dis-*, away + *mittere*, to send.]

dis·miss·al |dĭs **mĭs**´əl| *n.* The act or
notice of discharging someone, as from
employment.

dis·pos·al |dĭ **spō**´zəl| *n.* The act of
throwing out or away: *the problem of waste
disposal.* [Middle English *disposen*, from Latin
dispōnere, to place here and there, arrange:
dis-, in different directions + *pōnere*, to put.]

dis·po·si·tion |dĭs´pə **zĭsh**´ən| *n.*
1. One's usual mood or attitude;
temperament: *a kind disposition.* **2.** The act
of disposing; disposal.

dis·sent |dĭ **sĕnt**´| *n.* Difference of
opinion or feeling; disagreement.

dis·tort |dĭ **stôrt**´| *v.* To give a false
account of; misrepresent: *distort the truth.*

dis·tract |dĭ **străkt**´| *v.* To draw the
attention of away from something; divert.
[Middle English *distracten*, from Latin
distrahere, to pull apart, draw away, perplex:
dis-, apart + *trahere*, to draw.]

di·va |dē´və| *n., pl.* **divas.** A leading
female singer in an opera company.

di·verse |dĭ **vûrs**´| *or* |dī-| *or*
|dī´**vûrs**´| *adj.* **1.** Distinct in kind; different:
The personalities of Bob and Jim are diverse. **2.**
Of several or many kinds: *America is a land of*

Pronunciation Key

ă	pat	ŏ	pot	û	fur
ā	pay	ō	go	*th*	**the**
â	care	ô	paw, for	th	**thin**
ä	father	oi	**oil**	hw	**wh**ich
ĕ	pet	o͝o	book	zh	usual
ē	be	o͞o	boot	ə	**a**go, item
ĭ	pit	yo͞o	cute		pencil, at**o**m
ī	ice	ou	**out**		circus
î	near	ŭ	cut	ər	butt**er**

diverse people. [Middle English *divers(e)*, from
Latin *dīversus*, contrary, from *dīvertere*, to
turn aside, divert.]

di·ver·sion |dĭ **vûr**´zhən| *or* |-shən| *or*
|dī-| *n.* **1.** Something that relaxes or
entertains; recreation: *the diversion of a royal
hunt.* **2.** The act or an example of drawing the
attention to a different course, direction, etc.

di·vulge |dĭ **vŭlj**´| *v.* **di·vulged,
di·vulg·ing.** To make known; reveal; tell:
divulge a secret.

dos·si·er |dŏs´ē ā| *or* |-ē ər| *or*
|dô´sē ā| *or* |-sē ər| *n.* A collection of
papers or documents about a particular
person or subject.

drag |drăg| *n. Slang.* Street: *the main drag.*

dram·a·tist |drăm´ə tĭst| *or* |drä´mə-|
n. A person who writes plays; a playwright.

drib·ble |drĭb´əl| *v.* To move a ball by
bouncing repeatedly, as in basketball: *He
dribbled the ball down the court.*

drought |drout| *n.* A long period with
little or no rain.

du·al |do͞o´əl| *or* |dyo͞o´-| *adj.* Composed
of two parts; double; twofold: *a dual role.*

duct |dŭkt| *n.* Any tube through which
something flows. [Latin *ductus*, a leading, a
conducting, from the past participle of *dūcere*,
to lead.]

du·el |dōō´əl| *or* |dyōō´-| *n.* **1.** A prearranged combat between two people, fought with deadly weapons to settle a point of honor. **2.** Any contest between two opponents: *a duel of wits.*

du·et |dōō ĕt´| *or* |dyōō-| *n.* **1.** A musical composition for two voices or two instruments. **2.** The two performers who present such a composition.

duf·fel |dŭf´əl| *n.* A coarse, sturdy woolen cloth with a nap on both sides. [Dutch, from *Duffel,* town near Antwerp, Belgium.]

dun·ga·ree |dŭng´gə rē´| *n.* **1.** A sturdy blue denim fabric. **2. dungarees.** Overalls or trousers made from this fabric. [Hindi *dungrī,* from *Dungrī,* a section of Bombay where it originated.]

dunk |dŭngk| *v.* In basketball, to shoot the ball through the hoop from above.

du·plex |dōō´plĕks´| *or* |dyōō´-| *n.* A house or apartment divided into two living units.

du·pli·cate |dōō´plĭ kĭt| *or* |dyōō´-| *n.* Either of two things that are exactly alike. — *v.* |dōō´plĭ kāt´| *or* |dyōō´-| To make an exact copy of: *duplicate a key.* —**du´pli·ca´tion** *n.*: *a duplication of effort.* [Latin *duplicātus,* to make twofold, from *duplex,* twofold, double.]

dye |dī| *n.* **1.** Any coloring matter used to change the color of hair, cloth, etc. **2.** A color imparted by dyeing. —*v.* **dyed, dye·ing.** To color with or become colored by a dye.

E

earth |ûrth| *n.* Often **Earth.** The planet on which humans live, the third planet of the solar system in order of increasing distance from the sun. *Idiom.* **down to earth.** Sensible, realistic.

ea·sel |ē´zəl| *n.* An upright stand or rack used to support the canvas or other material painted on by an artist or to display a picture or sign.

ec·cen·tric·i·ty |ĕk´sĕn **trĭs´ĭ tē**| *n., pl.* **ec·cen·tric·i·ties.** Odd or unusual behavior.

ec·lec·tic |ĭ klĕk´tĭk| *adj.* Choosing or consisting of what appears to be the best from various sources, systems, or styles: *eclectic architecture.*

e·col·o·gy |ĭ kŏl´ə jē| *n.* **1.** The science of the relationships between living things and their environment. **2.** The relationship between living things and their environment. [German *Ökologie*: Greek *oikos,* house + *-logy,* study or science of.]

e·co·nom·ics |ē´kə **nŏm´**ĭks| *or* |ĕk´ə-| *n. (used with singular verb).* The science that deals with the production, distribution, development, and consumption of goods and services.

e·con·o·my |ĭ kŏn´ə mē| *n., pl.* **e·con·o·mies. 1.** The careful or thrifty use or management of resources, as of income, materials, or labor: *One must practice economy in buying new clothes.* **2.** The management of the resources of a country, community, or business: *the American economy.* [Greek *oikonomos: oikos,* house + *-nomos,* managing.]

ed·u·cate |ĕj´ōō kāt´| *v.* **ed·u·cat·ed, ed·u·cat·ing.** To provide with knowledge or training, especially through formal schooling; teach. [Middle English *educaten,* from Latin *ēducāre,* to bring up, educate, from *dūcere,* to lead.]

ef·fect |ĭ fĕkt´| *n.* **1.** Something brought about by a cause or agent; a result: *The effect of advertising should be an increase in sales.* **2.** The impression produced by a specific technique: *special effects; sound effect.* [Latin *effectus,* to accomplish, work out: *ex-,* out + *facere,* to do.]

ef·fi·cient |ĭ fĭsh´ənt| *adj.* Acting or producing effectively with a minimum of waste, expense, or effort: *James Watt designed the first efficient steam engine. She is an efficient secretary.* [From Latin *efficere: ex-,* out + *facere,* to do.]

e·lec·tri·cian |ĭ lĕk **trĭsh´**ən| or
|ē ´lĕk-| *n.* A person whose work is installing,
maintaining, repairing, or operating electric
equipment.

e·lec·tron·ics |ĭ lĕk **trŏn´**ĭks| or
|ē ´lĕk-| *n. (used with a singular verb).* The
science and technology concerned with the
development and practical application of
electronic devices and systems.

el·e·vat·ed |**ĕl´**ə vā ´tĭd| *adj.* Raised or
placed above a given level: *an elevated throne.*
—*n. Informal.* A train that runs on a track
raised high enough above the ground so that
vehicles and pedestrians can pass beneath.

e·lite, also **é·lite** |ĭ **lēt´**| or |ā **lēt´**| *n.*
(*used with a plural verb*). The best or superior
members of a society or group: *the elite of the
sports world.* —*adj.* Superior. [Old French
eslite, to choose, from Latin *exlegere,* elect.]

E·liz·a·be·than |ĭ lĭz´ə **bē´**thən| or
|-**bĕth´**ən| *adj.* Of, characteristic, or
representative of the reign of Elizabeth I,
Queen of England from 1558 to 1603:
Elizabethan drama.

em·bar·rass |ĕm **băr´**əs| *v.* To feel or
cause to feel self-conscious or ill at ease.

e·mer·gen·cy |ĭ **mûr´**jən sē| *n., pl.*
e·mer·gen·cies. A serious situation or
occurrence that develops suddenly and calls
for immediate action. —*modifier: an
emergency signal.*

em·i·grate |**ĕm´**ĭ grāt| *v.* **em·i·grat·ed,
em·i·grat·ing.** To leave a native country or
region to settle in another.
Usage: **Emigrate, Immigrate.** Use the
preposition *from* after *emigrate: He emigrated
from Italy.* Use *to* after *immigrate: He
immigrated to Canada.*

em·i·nent |**ĕm´**ə nənt| *adj.* Outstanding
in performance, character, or rank;
distinguished: *an eminent scientist.*

e·mis·sion |ĭ **mĭsh´**ən| *n.* The act or
process of emitting.

Pronunciation Key					
ă	pat	ŏ	pot	û	fur
ā	pay	ō	go	*th*	**the**
â	care	ô	paw, for	th	**thin**
ä	father	oi	**oil**	hw	**which**
ĕ	pet	ŏŏ	book	zh	usual
ē	be	ōō	boot	ə	**ago,** item
ĭ	pit	yōō	cute		pencil, at**o**m
ī	ice	ou	**out**		circus
î	near	ŭ	cut	ər	butt**er**

em·it |ĭ **mĭt´**| *v.* **e·mit·ted, e·mit·ting.**
To release, give off, or send out (light, heat,
etc.). [Latin *ex-,* out + *mittere,* to send.]

em·pa·thy |**ĕm´**pə thē| *n.* Identification
with and involvement in another's situation,
especially with sincere understanding and
deep concern. [*en-,* in + *-pathy,* from Greek
empatheia, passion, feeling.]

em·pha·sis |**ĕm´**fə sĭs| *n., pl.*
em·pha·ses. 1. Special importance or
significance placed upon or imparted to
something: *a strong emphasis on foreign
languages.* **2.** Stress given to a particular
syllable, word, or phrase. [Latin, from Greek
emphainein, to exhibit, indicate: *en,* in +
phainein, to show.]

em·phat·ic |ĕm **făt´**ĭk| *adj.*
1. Expressed or performed with emphasis:
an emphatic nod. **2.** Bold and definite in
expression or action.

en·cy·clo·pe·di·a, also
en·cy·clo·pae·di·a
|ĕn sī´klə **pē´**dē ə| *n.* A book or set of books
containing articles arranged in alphabetical
order and covering one particular field or a
wide variety of subjects.

en·dan·ger |ĕn **dān´**jər| *v.* To put in
danger; imperil; jeopardize: *The oil spill
endangered thousands of birds.* —
en·dan´gered *adj.: an endangered species.*

en·deav·or |ĕn dĕv´ər| *n.* A major effort or attempt. —*v.* to attempt: *He will endeavor to break the world record.*

en·ter·tain |ĕn tər tān´| *v.* **1.** To hold the attention of; amuse. **2.** To have (a person) as a guest: *entertained her at dinner.* [Middle English *entertinen*, to maintain, from Latin *intertenēre*, to hold between: *inter-*, between + *tenēre*, to hold.]

en·thu·si·as·tic |ĕn thōō´zē ăs´tĭk| *adj.* Showing or having great interest, excitement, or admiration; eager: *The crowds gave an enthusiastic welcome to the returning heroes.*

en·trée, also **en·tree** |än´trā| *n.* The main course of a meal.

en·vi·ron·ment |ĕn vī´rən mənt| *or* |-vī´ərn-| *n.* Surroundings and conditions that affect natural processes and the growth and development of living things: *Fish and birds adapt to their environment. The children grew up in a loving environment.*

ep·ic |ĕp´ĭk| *n.* A long poem or literary work about heroic characters who perform outstanding deeds. —*adj.* Of or resembling an epic: *an epic poem.*

ep·i·cure |ĕp´ĭ kyoŏr´| *n.* A person with refined tastes in food, wine, etc.: *Many food writers are epicures.* [After *Epicurus*, Greek thinker, who advocated sensuous pleasure as the highest good.]

ep·i·logue, also **ep·i·log** |ĕp´ə lôg´| *or* |-lŏg´| *n.* A short section at the end of any literary work, often dealing with the future of its characters. [From Greek *epilegein*, to say more, to add: *epi-* in addition + *legein*, to say.]

e·qua·tion |ĭ kwā´zhən| *or* |-shən| *n.* A mathematical statement that two expressions are equal. For example, $3 + 2 = 5$, $3 \times 2 = 6$, $y = 2 + 8$, and $x + y = 18$ are all equations.

e·ques·tri·an |ĭ kwĕs´trē ən| *n.* A person who rides a horse or performs on horseback.

es·pi·o·nage |ĕs´pē ə näzh´| *or* |-nĭj| *n.* **1.** The act or practice of spying. **2.** The use of spies by a government to gain secret information about another country.

es·sen·tial |ĭ sĕn´shəl| *adj.* Of the greatest importance; indispensable; basic: *The microscope is an essential tool of science.*

et·i·quette |ĕt´ĭ kĭt| *or* |-kĕt´| *n.* Rules of correct behavior among people, in a profession, etc. [French *etiquette*, prescribed routine.]

et·y·mol·o·gy |ĕt´ə mŏl´ə jē| *n., pl.* **et·y·mol·o·gies.** The origin and development of a word as shown by its earliest use and changes in form and meaning. [Middle English *ethimologie*, from Greek *etymologiā: etymon*, earliest form of a word + *-logy*, study of.]

e·ven·tu·al |ĭ vĕn´choō əl| *adj.* Occurring at an unspecified future time; ultimate: *He never lost hope of eventual victory.* —**e·ven´tu·al·ly** *adv.*: *She will show up eventually.* [Latin *ēventus*, a coming out: *ex-*, + *venire*, to come.]

e·vict |ĭ vĭkt´| *v.* To put out (a tenant) by legal process: *They evicted the family for nonpayment of rent.*

ex-. Also **ef-** (before *f*). A prefix meaning: **1.** Removal out of or from: **expire. 2.** Former: **ex-president.** [Middle English, from Old French, from Latin *ex-,* out, out of.]

ex·ag·ger·a·tion |ĭg zăj´ə rā´shən| *n.* An overstatement: *His boast was an exaggeration.*

ex·ca·vate |ĕks´kə vāt´| *v.* **ex·ca·vat·ed, ex·ca·vat·ing.** To uncover by digging; expose to view: *They excavated ancient ruins.*

ex·ceed |ĭk sēd´| *v.* **1.** To be greater than. **2.** To go beyond the limits of: *The command exceeded his authority.*

ex·cel |ĭk sĕl´| *v.* **ex·celled, ex·cel·ling.** To be better than or superior to (others); surpass: *She excels in tennis.* [Latin *excellere,* to excel.]

ex·cel·lence |ĕk´sə ləns| *n.* The condition or quality of being superior: *artistic excellence.*

ex·cept |ĭk sĕpt´| *conj.* If it were not for the fact that; only: *I could leave early except I don't want to.* [Middle English, from Latin *exceptus,* to take out: *ex-,* out + *capere,* to take.]

ex·claim |ĭk sklām´| *v.* To cry out or speak suddenly, as from surprise. [Latin *exclāmāre,* to call out: *ex-,* out + *clāmāre,* to call.]

ex·cla·ma·tion |ĕk´sklə mā´shən| *n.* An abrupt, sudden utterance; an outcry: *an exclamation of pain.*

ex·ile |ĕg´zīl´| *or* |ĕk´sīl´| *n.* **1.** Enforced removal from one's native country; banishment: *Exile was the punishment for their political activities.* **2.** Voluntary separation from one's native country: *Many chose exile over prison.*

ex·pe·di·tion |ĕk´spĭ dĭsh´ən| *n.* A trip made by an organized group of people with a definite purpose: *an expedition to the South Pole.*

ă	pat	ŏ	pot	û	fur
ā	pay	ō	go	*th*	**the**
â	care	ô	paw, for	th	**thin**
ä	father	oi	**oil**	hw	**which**
ĕ	pet	ŏŏ	book	zh	usual
ē	be	ōō	boot	ə	**ago, item**
ĭ	pit	yōō	cute		pencil, at**o**m
ī	ice	ou	**out**		circus
î	near	ŭ	cut	ər	butt**er**

ex·per·tise |ĕk´spûr tēz´| *n.* Expert skill or knowledge: *The professional photographer shared her expertise with the camera club.*

ex·pire |ĭk spīr´| *v.* **ex·pired, ex·pir·ing.** To come to an end; terminate; cease to be effective: *His driver's license expired last month.* [Middle English *expiren,* from Latin *ex(s)pīrāre,* to breathe out: *ex-,* out + *spīrāre,* to breathe.]

ex·plic·it |ĭk splĭs´ĭt| *adj.* Clearly defined; precise: *an explicit description.* [French *explicite,* from Latin *explicitus,* past participle of *explicāre*: *ex-,* reversal + *plicāre,* to fold.]

ex·po·nent |ĭk spō´nənt| *n.* Any number or symbol, such as the 2 in $(x + y)^2$, that indicates how many times a number or other mathematical expression is multiplied by itself. The symbol is usually written above and to the right of the expression to which it applies.

ex·po·sure |ĭk spō´zhər| *n.* The act or an example of revealing or uncovering: *a newspaper's exposure of a scandal.* [From Latin *expōnere,* to put forth, expose: *ex-,* out + *pōnere,* to plan, put.]

ex·qui·site |ĕk´skwĭz ĭt| *or* |ĭk skwĭz´ĭt| *adj.* Of special beauty, charm, or elegance: *an exquisite vase.*

ex·tra·cur·ric·u·lar
|ĕk strə kə **rĭk´**yə lər| *adj.* Not part of the regular course of study: *Debating is an extracurricular activity in our school.*

ex·traor·di·nar·y |ĭk **strôr´**dn ĕr´ē| *or* |ĕk´strə **ôr´**-| *adj.* Very unusual; exceptional; remarkable.

ex·tra·ter·res·tri·al
|ĕk´strə tə **rĕs´**trē əl| *adj.* From or located outside the earth or its atmosphere.

ex·trav·a·gance |ĭk **străv´**ə gəns| *n.* Lack of restraint, especially in the spending of money.

ex·tro·vert |ĕk´strə vûrt| *n.* A person interested mainly in other people or external circumstances rather than his or her own thoughts and feelings; an outgoing person. [Latin *extro-*, variant of *extra-* + *vertere*, to turn.]

eye |ī| *n.* An organ by means of which an animal is able to see or sense light. **Idiom. see eye to eye.** To be in complete agreement.

F

fa·çade, also **fa·cade** |fə **säd´**| *n.* The main face or front of a building.

fac·sim·i·le |făk **sĭm´**ə lē| *n.* An exact copy or reproduction, as of a document, book, painting, etc. [Latin *fac simile*, make (it) similar: *fac*, imperative of *facere*, to make, do + *simile*, neuter of *similis*, similar.]

fac·tor |făk´tər| *n.* **1.** Something that helps bring about a certain result; ingredient: *Many factors contributed to his success.* **2.** A consideration: *a factor in her decision.* [From Latin *factor*, maker, doer.]

fac·to·ry |făk´tə rē| *n., pl.* **fac·to·ries.** A building or group of buildings in which goods are manufactured; a plant. [From Late Latin *factōrium*, mill, from Latin *factor*, maker, doer.]

Fahr·en·heit |făr´ən hīt´| *adj.* Of or concerning a temperature scale that indicates the freezing point of water as 32° and the boiling point of water as 212° under normal atmospheric pressure. [After Gabriel *Fahrenheit*, German physicist.]

fal·low |făl´ō| *adj.* Plowed and tilled but left unseeded during a growing season: *a fallow field.*

fa·mil·iar·i·ty |fə mĭl´**yăr´**ĭ tē| *or* |-mĭl´ē **ăr´**-| *n., pl.* **fa·mil·iar·i·ties. 1.** Acquaintance with or knowledge of something: *Familiarity with the city's streets is a necessity for a cab driver.* **2.** Friendship or informality: *the familiarity of close associates.*

fate |fāt| *n.* Something that finally happens to or befalls a person or thing; destiny: *The fate of our lost luggage is still unknown.* [After the *Fates*, Greek mythological goddesses who governed human destiny.]

faze |fāz| *v.* **fazed, faz·ing.** To upset; disconcert: *He never lets anything faze him.*

feat |fēt| *n.* An outstanding deed or accomplishment; an exploit: *The new bridge is a remarkable feat of engineering.* [Middle English *fete*, from Latin *facere*, to do.]

fe·ro·cious |fə **rō´**shəs| *adj.* Extremely cruel and fierce; savage: *a ferocious dog.*

fe·roc·i·ty |fə **rŏs´**ĭ tē| *n., pl.* **fe·roc·i·ties.** Extreme cruelty and fierceness; savageness: *the ferocity of the lions.*

fer·tile |**fûr´**tl| *adj.* Rich in material needed to support plant life; favorable to the growth of crops and plants: *fertile soil.* [Middle English, from Latin *fertilis*, from *ferre*, to bear, carry, produce.]

fic·tion |**fĭk´**shən| *n.* **1.** A product of the imagination: *fact or fiction.* **2.** Literature containing imaginary characters and events.

fil·let |fĭ lā´| *or* |fĭl´ā´| *n.* A boneless piece of meat or fish. [Middle English *filet*, from Old French, diminutive of *fil*, thread.]

fi·na·le |fĭ **năl´**ē| *or* |-**nä´**lē| *n.* The final section of something that is performed, especially the ending of a musical composition. [Italian, "final," from Latin *finālis*, final.]

fi·nal·ist |fī´nə lĭst| *n.* A contestant in the last game or games in a series of games or a tournament. [Middle English, from Latin *finālis*, from *finis*, end.]

fi·nite |fī´nīt´| *adj.* Having bounds; not infinite; limited. [Middle English *finit*, from Latin *finītus*, to limit, finish.]

flax |flăks| *n.* A plant with blue flowers, seeds that yield linseed oil, and stems that yield a light-colored fiber from which linen is made.

flo·til·la |flō tĭl´ə| *n.* A fleet of small boats. [Spanish diminutive of *flota*, fleet.]

flour·ish |flûr´ĭsh| *or* |flŭr´-| *v.* **1.** To grow well; thrive: *Flowers flourish in sunlight.* **2.** To succeed; prosper: *The lawyer's practice flourished.*

flu |flōō| *n. Informal.* Influenza.

fool·har·dy |fōōl´här´dē| *adj.* **fool·har·di·er, fool·har·di·est.** Foolishly bold; rash; reckless: *A foolhardy driver ran the stop sign.* —**fool´har´di·ness** *n.*

for·feit |fôr´fĭt| *v.* To lose or give up (something) as a penalty or fine for a failure, error, or offense: *By failing to appear and play, the opposing team forfeited the game.*

forte |fôrt| *or* |fōrt| *n.* Something in which a person excels; a strong point.

fo·rum |fôr´əm| *or* |fōr´-| *n., pl.* **fo·rums.** Often **Forum.** The public square of an ancient Roman city, especially the Forum of ancient Rome.

foy·er |foi´ər| *or* |foi´ā´| *n.* **1.** The lobby of a public building. **2.** The entrance hall of a private house or apartment. [French hearth, home, from Latin *focus*, hearth, fireplace.]

frag·ile |frăj´əl| *or* |-īl´| *adj.* Easily damaged or broken; brittle: *a fragile piece of crystal.*

frag·ment |frăg´mənt| *n.* **1.** A piece or part broken off or detached from a whole. **2.** Something incomplete or unfinished.

fran·chise |frăn´chīz´| *n.* An authorization, right, or privilege granted to a person or group, as for selling a product within a district, governing a territory, etc.: *a dry-cleaning franchise.*

fre·quen·cy |frē´kwən sē| *n.* The number of occurrences of an event within a given period: *The phone calls came with increased frequency.*

fres·co |frĕs´kō| *n., pl.* **fres·coes** or **fres·cos. 1.** The art of painting on wet plaster. **2.** A painting done in this manner: *Many frescoes were painted in Italy during the Renaissance.*

frieze |frēz| *n.* A decorative horizontal band along the upper part of a wall in a room. [French *frise*, from Medieval Latin *frisium*, *frigium*, fringe, embroidered cloth, from Latin *Phrygium*, of Phrygia, a place noted for its embroidery.]

frost·bite |frôst′bīt′| *or* |frŏst′bīt′| *n.* Injury to a part of the body as a result of exposure to freezing temperatures.

fu·ry |fyoor′ē| *n., pl.* **fu·ries.** Violent anger; rage. [From *Furies*, terrible goddesses of Greek and Roman mythology, who pursued and punished criminals.]

-fy. A suffix that forms verbs: **simplify.** [Middle English *-fien*, from Old French *-fier*, from Latin *-ficāre*, from *-ficus*.]

G

gal·va·nize |găl′və nīz′| *v.* **gal·va·nized, gal·va·niz·ing.** To put a coating of zinc on (iron or steel) as protection against rust. [French *galvanisme*, from Italian *galvanismo*, first described by Luigi Galvani.]

gar·gan·tu·an |gär găn′choo ən| *adj.* Enormous; huge. [From *Gargantua*, a giant from Rabelais' satire *Gargantua and Pantagruel*.]

gauze |gôz| *n.* A loosely woven cloth that is thin enough to see through, used especially for bandages. [Earlier *gais*, from Old French *gaze*, probably after *Gaza*, where it was supposed to be made.]

gene |jēn| *n.* A unit, located at a particular point on a chromosome, that controls or acts in the transmission of a hereditary characteristic, such as hair color or eye color in human beings, from parents to offspring. [German *Gen*, short for *Pangen*: *pan-*, all + *-gen*, from Greek *-genēs*, born.]

ge·ne·al·o·gy |jē′nē ăl′ə jē| *or* |-ŏl′-| *or* |jĕn′ē-| *n., pl.* **ge·ne·al·o·gies.** **1.** A record of the descent of a family or person from an ancestor or ancestors. **2.** Direct descent from an ancestor or ancestors; lineage. **3.** The study of ancestry and family histories. [Latin *genealogia*, from Greek: *genea*, race, generation + *-logy*, study of.]

gen·er·al·i·za·tion |jĕn′ər ə lĭ zā′shən| *n.* **1.** The act of generalizing. **2.** A general statement: *a generalization not based on fact.*

gen·er·al·ize |jĕn′ər ə līz′| *v.* **gen·er·al·ized, gen·er·al·iz·ing.** To make a general statement about a broad subject that is more or less applicable to the whole. [From Latin *generalis*, belonging to a kind or species, from *genus*, birth, race, kind, from *genēs*, born: *-gen.*]

gen·er·os·i·ty |jĕn′ə rŏs′ĭ tē| *n.* The condition or quality of being generous; willingness in giving or sharing.

ge·net·ic |jə nĕt′ĭk| *or* **ge·net·i·cal** |jə nĕt′ĭ kəl| *adj.* Of, affecting, or affected by a gene or genes. [From Latin *genesis*, birth.]

gen·re |zhän′rə| *n.* A particular type of literary, musical, or artistic composition: *The novel and the drama are different literary genres.* [French, kind, from Latin *genus*, kind.]

ge·ol·o·gy |jē ŏl′ə jē| *n.* The study of the origin, history, behavior, and structure of the earth. [Latin *geologia*: *geo-*, earth + *-logy*, study of.]

gey·ser |gī′zər| *n.* A natural hot spring that throws out a spray of steam and water from time to time. [Icelandic *Geysir*, "gusher," the name of a hot spring in Iceland.]

gon·do·la |gŏn′dl ə| *n.* A long, narrow boat with a high pointed prow and stern and often a small cabin in the middle, used for public conveyance on the canals of Venice. [Italian (Venetian dialect), *gondola*, roll, rock.]

gour·met |gŏor´mā´| *or* |gŏor mā´| *n.* A person who likes and knows fine food and drink. —*modifier: gourmet foods.* [French, from Old French *gromet*, wine merchant's servant.]

gov·er·nor |gŭv´ər nər| *n.* **1.** The person elected chief executive of a state in the United States. **2.** An official appointed to govern a colony or territory.

grad·u·al |grăj´oo əl| *adj.* Occurring in small states or degrees or by even, continuous change: *the gradual slope of a road.*

graf·fi·ti |grə fē´tē| *pl. n.* Anything drawn or written, as on a wall or door, so as to be seen by the public. [Italian, diminutive of *graffio*, a scratching, from *graffiare*, to scratch, perhaps from *grafio*, a pencil, stylus, from Greek *graphein*, to write.]

grate·ful |grāt´fəl| *adj.* **1. a.** Appreciative; thankful. **b.** Expressive of gratitude: *a grateful look.* **2.** Affording pleasure; agreeable: *grateful relief from the rays of the sun.* —**grate´ful·ly** *adv.* —**grate´ful·ness** *n.*

grat·i·tude |grăt´ĭ tood´| *or* |-tyood´| *n.* Appreciation or thankfulness, as for something received or kindness shown.

grav·i·ty |grăv´ĭ tē| *n.* **1.** The force that the earth or another celestial body exerts on any small mass close to its surface. **2.** Seriousness, importance.

griev·ance |grē´vəns| *n.* **1.** A circumstance regarded as a cause for protest: *legislation aimed at the remedy of basic grievances.* **2.** A complaint based on such a circumstance.

griev·ous |grē´vəs| *adj.* **1.** Causing grief, pain, or anguish: *a grievous wound.* **2.** Extremely serious: *a grievous error.*

gross |grōs| *adj.* Before expenses or taxes are deducted; total: *gross income.*

guar·an·tee |găr´ən tē´| *n.* **1.** Anything that makes certain a particular condition or outcome: *Money is not a guarantee of happiness.* **2.** A personal promise or assurance. —*v.* **guar·an·teed,**

Pronunciation Key						
ă	pat	ŏ	pot	û	fur	
ā	pay	ō	go	*th*	the	
â	care	ô	paw, for	th	thin	
ä	father	oi	oil	hw	which	
ĕ	pet	oo	book	zh	usual	
ē	be	oo	boot	ə	ago, item	
ĭ	pit	yoo	cute		pencil, atom	
ī	ice	ou	out		circus	
î	near	ŭ	cut	ər	butter	

guar·an·tee·ing. To promise; make certain: *to guarantee satisfaction.*

guard·i·an |gär´dē ən| *n.* **1.** Someone or something that guards, protects, or defends: *guardians of law and order.* **2.** A person who is legally responsible for the person or property of another person, such as a child, who cannot manage his or her affairs.

gui·tar·ist |gĭ tär´ĭst| *n.* A person who plays the guitar.

gulch |gŭlch| *n.* A small, shallow canyon or ravine: *Rainwater collected in the gulch.*

H

ham·mock |hăm´ək| *n.* A hanging bed or couch made of strong fabric supported by cords between two supports. [Spanish *hamaca*, from Taino.]

hang |hăng| *v.* **hung** |hŭng|, **hang·ing.** To fasten or be attached from above with no support from below; suspend. **hang out.** *Slang.* To spend one's free time in a certain place; associate with.

har·ass |hăr´əs| *or* |hə răs´| *v.* To bother or torment with repeated interruptions, attacks, etc.: *harass a speaker with whistles and shouts.*

hard·ware |härd´wâr´| *n.* **1.** Articles made of metal, as tools, nails, locks, cutlery, utensils, etc. **2.** The physical parts or equipment that make up a computer system.

har·mo·ni·ous |här **mō´**nē əs| *adj.* **1.** Marked by agreement and good will; friendly: *a harmonious meeting.* **2.** Having elements pleasingly or appropriately combined: *harmonious colors.* **3.** Pleasing to the ear; melodious: *harmonious sounds.*

har·mo·ny |**här´**mə nē| *n., pl.* **har·mo·nies. 1.** A sequence of chords used to accompany a melody. **2.** A combination of musical sounds considered to be pleasing. **3.** Agreement in feeling or opinion; good will; accord: *live in harmony.*

haz·ard·ous |**hăz´**ər dəs| *adj.* Dangerous; perilous: *a hazardous voyage.*

hi·ba·chi |hĭ **bä´**chē| *n.* A small charcoal-burning stove of Japanese origin. [Japanese: *hi*, fire + *bachi*, bowl.]

high·land |**hī´**lənd| *n.* **1.** Elevated land. **2. highlands.** A mountainous or hilly part of a country, or a region at a high elevation. *–adj.* Of or relating to a highland.

high-spir·it·ed |**hī´spĭr´**ĭ tĭd| *adj.* Having a proud or fiery disposition: *a high-spirited horse.*

hin·drance |**hĭn´**drəns| *n.* Something or someone that hinders; an obstacle: *Strong winds are a hindrance to mountain climbers.*

his·to·ri·an |hĭ **stôr´**ē ən| *or* |-**stōr´**| *n.* A person who specializes in the study of history.

hol·o·gram |**hŏl´**ə grăm´| *or* |**hō´**lə-| *n.* A three-dimensional photographic image produced with light from a laser. [Greek *holos*, whole + Latin *gramma*, something written.]

ho·mog·e·nize |hə **mŏj´**ə nīz´| *v.* **ho·mog·e·nized, ho·mog·e·niz·ing.** To spread evenly through a fluid, especially to make (milk) uniform by breaking the fat it contains into tiny particles. **—ho·mog´e·nized´** *adj.: homogenized milk.* [From Greek *homogenēs: homo-*, same + *-genēs*, born.]

hook |hŏŏk| *n.* **1.** A curved or bent object or part: *fish hook.* **2.** Something resembling such an object: *a hook of land.* **3.** In basketball, a shot made by arching the shooting hand upward while moving sideways to the basket. *—v.* To fasten or catch with a hook.

hoop |hŏŏp| *n.* **1.** In basketball, a goal consisting of an open-bottomed net fastened to a metal ring. **2.** The score, usually two points, for throwing a basketball through the hoop, or basket.

hor·i·zon·tal |hôr´ĭ **zŏn´**tl| *or* |hōr´| *adj.* Parallel to or in the plane of the horizon; intersecting a vertical line or plane at right angles.

hors d'oeuvre |ôr **dûrv´**| *n., pl.* **hors d'oeuvres** |ôr **dûrvz´**| *or* **hors d'oeuvre.** Any of various appetizers served with cocktails or before a meal. [French, outside of the ordinary meal, side dish "outside of work": *hors*, outside, from Latin *forīs* + *de*, of + *oeuvre*, work.]

hos·pi·tal·i·ty |hŏs´pi **tăl´**ĭ tē| *n., pl.* **hos·pi·tal·i·ties. 1.** Cordial and generous reception of guests. **2.** An example of being hospitable.

hos·tile |**hŏs´**təl| *or* |tīl´| *adj.* **1.** Of an enemy: *hostile troops.* **2.** Feeling or showing opposition: *hostile to the suggestion.*

hu·mane |hyŏŏ **mān´**| *adj.* Kind; compassionate; merciful.

hu·man·i·ty |hyŏŏ **măn´**ĭ tē| *n., pl.* **hu·man·i·ties. 1.** Human beings in general; humankind: *The scientist's goal was to serve humanity.* **2.** The quality or fact of being humane; kindness.

hu·mid·i·ty |hyŏŏ **mĭd´**ĭ tē| *n.* Dampness, especially of the air.

hy·brid |**hī´**brĭd| *adj.* Resulting from a combination of different types: *hybrid corn.*

hy·dro·gen |**hī´**drə jən| *n. Symbol* **H** One of the elements, a colorless, highly flammable gas. [French *hydrogène*, "water generating" (it forms water when oxidized): *hydro-*, water + *-gen*, from Greek *-genēs*, born.]

hy·giene |**hī´**jēn´| *n.* Scientific methods for the promotion of good health and the prevention of disease. [After *Hygeia*, goddess of health in Greek mythology.]

hyp·no·sis |hĭp nō´sĭs| *n., pl.* **hyp·no·ses** |hĭp nō´sēz´| **1.** A sleeplike condition into which a person passes as a result of suggestions given by another person, becoming, once in that state, very responsive to further suggestions. **2.** Hypnotism. [After *Hypnos,* Greek god of sleep: *hupnos,* sleep + *-osis,* process.]

hyp·o·crite |hĭp´ə krĭt´| *n.* A person who expresses feelings or beliefs that he or she does not actually hold; one who shows insincerity; a phony.

hy·po·ther·mi·a |hī´pō thûr´mē ə| *n.* A condition of abnormally low body temperature.

hys·ter·i·cal |hĭ stĕr´ĭ kəl| *adj.* Marked by uncontrolled emotion; violent or unrestrained.

I

-ian. A suffix that forms nouns or adjectives: **Canadian, magician.**

i·de·al·ism |ī dē´ə lĭz´əm| *n.* **1.** The practice of seeing or representing things in ideal form rather than as they usually exist in real life. **2.** The practice of pursuing one's ideals.

i·den·ti·fi·ca·tion |ī dĕn´tə fĭ kā´shən| *n.* The act of identifying or the condition of being identified.

i·den·ti·ty |ī dĕn´tĭ tē| *n., pl.* **i·den·ti·ties.** The condition of being a certain person or thing and definitely recognizable as such.

il·le·gal |ĭ lē´gəl| *adj.* Prohibited by law or by official rules, as of a game.

il·lu·mi·nate |ĭ lōō´mə nāt´| *v.* **il·lu·mi·nat·ed, il·lu·mi·nat·ing. 1.** To provide with light. **2.** To make understandable; clarify; explain: *clues that illuminate the snarled story.* [Latin *illūmināre: in-,* in + *lūmināre,* to light up, from *lūmen,* light.]

il·lu·sion |ĭ lōō´zhən| *n.* An appearance or impression that has no real basis; false

perception: *creating the illusion of depth in a painting.* [Middle English, *illusioun,* from Latin *illūdere,* to mock, jeer at: *in-,* against + *lūdere,* to play.]

il·lus·trate |ĭl´ə strāt´| *or* |ĭ lŭs´trāt´| *v.* **il·lus·trat·ed, il·lus·trat·ing.** To clarify or explain by using examples, pictures, comparisons, etc.: *illustrate the lecture with charts.* [Latin *illūstrāre: in-,* in + *lūstrāre,* to make bright.]

il·lus·tra·tive |ĭ lŭs´trə tĭv| *or* |ĭl´ə strā´tĭv| *adj.* Serving to clarify or explain through the use of examples, pictures, comparisons, etc.

im·mac·u·late |ĭ măk´yə lĭt| *adj.* Perfectly clean: *an immaculate room.* [From Latin *immaculātus: in-,* not + *maculātus,* to stain.]

im·merse |ĭ mûrs´| *v.* **im·mersed, im·mers·ing.** To cover completely in a liquid; submerge: *He immersed the pan in the stream.* [Latin *in-,* in + *mergere,* to dip.]

im·mi·grate |ĭm´ə grāt´| *v.* **im·mi·grat·ed, im·mi·grat·ing.** To move to and settle in a country or region to which one is not native. —See Usage note at **emigrate.**

im·mi·nent |ĭm´ə nənt| *adj.* About to occur; impending: *an imminent crisis.*

im·mor·tal |ĭ môr´tl| *adj.* Not subject to death; living forever: *immortal words.*

im·mune |ĭ myōōn´| *adj.* Protected; guarded; safe: *immune from attack.*

Pronunciation Key

ă	pat	ŏ	pot	û	fur
ā	pay	ō	go	*th*	**the**
â	care	ô	paw, for	th	**thin**
ä	father	oi	**oil**	hw	**which**
ĕ	pet	ŏŏ	book	zh	usual
ē	be	ōō	boot	ə	ago, item
ĭ	pit	yōō	cute		pencil, atom
ī	ice	ou	**out**		circus
î	near	ŭ	cut	ər	butt**er**

im·mu·nize |ĭm´yə nīz´| *v.*
im·mu·nized, im·mu·niz·ing. To produce
immunity in, as by vaccination or
inoculation.

im·par·tial |ĭm pär´shəl| *adj.* Not
favoring either side; fair; *an impartial witness.*

im·ple·ment |ĭm´plə mənt| *n.* A tool,
utensil, or instrument used in doing a task.

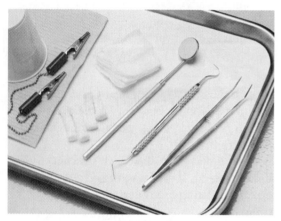

im·plic·it |ĭm plĭs´ĭt| *adj.* Implied or
understood without being directly expressed:
*Her opposition to war is implicit throughout her
book.* [Latin *implicitus*, involved, entangled,
from *implicāre*: *in-*, in + *plicāre*, to fold.]

im·ply |ĭm plī´| *v.* **im·plied, im·ply·ing,**
im·plies. To say or convey indirectly; suggest
without stating: *He turned down our request
but implied that he might change his mind
later.* [Middle English *implien*, from Latin
implicāre: *in-*, in + *plicāre*, to fold.]

im·pose |ĭm pōz´| *v.* **im·posed,**
im·pos·ing. To place (something
burdensome) on someone. [Old French
imposer, from Latin *impōnere*, to put on: *in-*,
on + *pōnere*, to put.]

in-¹. Also **il-** (before *l*) or **ir-** (before *r*) or
im- (before *b, m,* or *p*). A prefix meaning
"without, not": **inaccurate.** [Middle English,
from Old French, from Latin.]

in-². Also **il-** (before *l*) or **ir-** (before *r*) or
im- (before *b, m,* or *p*). A prefix meaning

"in, within, or into": **inbound.** [Middle
English, from Old French, from Latin.]

in·cen·tive |ĭn sĕn´tĭv| *n.* Something
that incites action or effort: *Praise is an
incentive.*

in·cog·ni·to |ĭn kŏg´nĭ tō´| *or*
|ĭn´kŏg nē´tō| *adv.* With one's identity
hidden or disguised: *The movie star traveled
incognito.*

in·come |ĭn´kŭm´| *n.* The amount of
money received during a period of time for
labor or services, from the sale of property,
etc.: *enough income to buy the house.*

in·com·mu·ni·ca·do
|ĭn´kə myōō´nĭ kä´dō| *adv.* Without the
means or right of communicating with others:
a prisoner held incommunicado. [Spanish,
from Latin *in-*, not + *comunicar*, to
communicate.]

in·dex |ĭn´dĕks´| *n., pl.* **in·dex·es** or
in·di·ces |ĭn´dĭ sēz´|. Anything that serves
to guide, point out, or aid reference; an
alphabetized listing of the names, places, and
subjects in a printed work, giving the page on
which each can be found.

in·di·cate |ĭn´dĭ kāt´| *v.* **in·di·cat·ed,**
in·di·cat·ing. To show or point out
precisely: *indicate a route.* [Latin *indicāre*, to
show, from *index*, forefinger, indicator, index.]

in·dic·a·tive |ĭn dĭk´ə tĭv| *adj.* Serving
to show or indicate: *indicative of his attitude.*

in·di·go |ĭn´dĭ gō´| *n., pl.* **in·di·gos** or
in·di·goes. 1. A plant that yields a blue dye.
2. A dye obtained from this plant. —*adj.*
Dark blue. [Spanish *indico*, from Latin
indicum, from Greek *Indikos*, Indian.]

in·di·vid·u·al·ist |ĭn´də vĭj´ōō ə lĭst| *n.*
A person independent in thought and action.

in·duce |ĭn dōōs´| *or* |-dyōōs´| *v.*
in·duced, in·duc·ing. 1. To persuade;
influence; prevail upon: *Nothing could induce
them to stay.* **2.** To reach (a conclusion or
general law) by logic. [Latin *indūcere*: *in-*, in
+ *dūcere*, to lead.]

in·duc·tion |ĭn dŭk´shən| *n.* A method of reasoning or mathematical proof in which a conclusion is reached about all members of a set by examining just a few members of the set.

in·e·qual·i·ty |ĭn´ĭ kwŏl´ĭ tē| *n., pl.* **in·e·qual·i·ties.** The condition of being unequal: *the inequality of two line segments.*

in·ev·i·ta·ble |ĭn ĕv´ĭ tə bəl| *adj.* Not capable of being avoided or prevented: *an inevitable outcome.*

in·fec·tious |ĭn fĕk´shəs| *adj.* Caused or spread by infection: *an infectious disease.*

in·fer·ence |ĭn´fər əns| *or* |-frəns| *n.* **1.** The act or process of concluding from evidence: *arrive at a conclusion by inference.* **2.** Something deduced. [Latin *inferre*, to bring in, introduce, deduce: *in-*, in + *ferre*, to bear.]

in·fi·nite |ĭn´fə nĭt| *adj.* Having no limit in space, extent, number, or time; endless: *the infinite universe.* [Latin *infinītis: in-*, not + *finītus*, finite.]

in·fin·i·tes·i·mal |ĭn´fĭn ĭ tĕs´ə məl| *adj.* Extremely small; minute. [Latin *infinītus: in-*, not + *finītus*, to limit, finish.]

in·fin·i·tive |ĭn fĭn´ĭ tĭv| *n.* A verb form that is not inflected to indicate person, number, or tense. In English, it is usually preceded by *to* or by an auxiliary verb. For example, in the phrases *wanted to leave* and *will play tomorrow*, *leave* and *play* are infinitives. [Latin *infinītus: in-*, not + *finītus*, to limit, finish.]

in·flam·ma·tion |ĭn´flə mā´shən| *n.* Redness, swelling, heat, and pain in a part of the body, resulting from injury, infection, or irritation.

in·fla·tion |ĭn flā´shən| *n.* A sharp, continuing rise in the prices of goods and services, usually attributed to an abnormal increase in available currency and credit: *The economic decline was followed by a period of inflation.*

in·flu·en·za |ĭn´floo ĕn´zə| *n.* A disease caused by viruses. Its symptoms include fever,

Pronunciation Key					
ă	pat	ŏ	pot	û	fur
ā	pay	ō	go	*th*	**the**
â	care	ô	paw, for	th	**thin**
ä	father	oi	**oil**	hw	**which**
ĕ	pet	ŏŏ	**book**	zh	usual
ē	be	ōō	**boot**	ə	**ago**, **item**
ĭ	pit	yōō	**cute**		pencil, atom
ī	ice	ou	**out**		circus
î	near	ŭ	cut	ər	butter

inflammation of the respiratory system, irritation of the intestines, and muscular pain. [Italian, *influence*, from Medieval Latin *influentia*, "a flowing in."]

in·i·ti·ate |ĭ nĭsh´ē āt´| *v.* **in·i·ti·at·ed, in·i·ti·at·ing. 1.** To begin; originate: *Saul planned to initiate the political campaign.* **2.** To admit into membership, often with a special ceremony: *Ten new members were initiated into the club.*

in·i·ti·a·tive |ĭ nĭsh´ē ə tĭv| *or* |ĭ nĭsh´ə-| *n.* **1.** The ability to begin or follow through with a plan of action or a task; ambition and determination: *She acted on her own initiative.* **2.** The first step or action; opening move: *He took the initiative and wrote a letter to the city council.*

in·spi·ra·tion |ĭn´spə rā´shən| *n.* **1.** A feeling of being inspired; stimulation of the mind or emotions. **2.** Someone or something that inspires: *Bach was an inspiration to many other composers.* [Middle English *enspiren*, from Latin *inspīrāre*, to breathe into: *in-*, into + *spīrāre*, to breathe.]

in·struc·tor |ĭn strŭk´tər| *n.* Someone who teaches; a teacher. [Middle English *instructen*, from Latin *instruere* (past participle *instructurs*), to build, instruct: *in-*, in + *struere*, to build.]

in·sur·ance |ĭn shŏŏr´əns| *n.* **1.** The business of guaranteeing to cover specified losses in the future, as in case of accident, theft, illness, or death, in return for the continuing payment of regular sums of money. **2.** A contract making such guarantees to the party insured.

in·tel·lec·tu·al |ĭn´tl ĕk´chŏŏ əl| *adj.* Of or requiring use of intelligence or the mind: *an intellectual discussion.*

in·tel·li·gence |ĭn tĕl´ə jəns| *n.* **1.** The capacity to learn, think, understand, and know; mental ability. **2.** Information; news, especially secret information about an enemy. [Latin *intelligens*, to choose between: *inter-*, between + *legere*, to gather, choose.]

inter-. A prefix meaning: "Between; among." [Middle English *inter-*, *entre-*, from Old French, from Latin *inter-*, from *inter*, between, among.]

in·ter·cede |ĭn´tər sēd´| *v.* **in·ter·ced·ed, in·ter·ced·ing.** To plead on another's behalf: *Mother interceded for her sister when grandfather was angry.* [Latin *intercēdere*, to come between: *inter*, between + *cēdere*, to go.]

in·ter·cept |ĭn´tər sĕpt´| *v.* To stop or interrupt the course or progress of: *intercept a quarterback's pass.* [Latin, to seize in transit: *inter-*, between + *capere*, to take or seize.]

in·ter·ces·sion |ĭn´tər sĕsh´ən| *n.* The act or an example of interceding.

in·ter·change·a·ble |ĭn´tər chān´jə bəl| *adj.* Capable of being switched or interchanged: *The machine has interchangeable parts.* [Old French *entrechangier: inter-*, between + *changier*, to change.]

in·ter·cit·y |ĭn´tər sĭt´ē| *adj.* Between cities: *intercity bus.*

in·ter·fer·ence |ĭn´tər fîr´əns| *n.* In various sports, an illegal obstruction of a play or player. [Old French *(s)entreferir*, to strike each other: *inter-*, between + *ferir*, to strike.]

in·ter·jec·tion |ĭn´tər jĕk´shən| *n.* **1.** The act of interrupting. **2.** A word or phrase that acts as an exclamation, such as *oh!*

in·ter·me·di·ate |ĭn´tər mē´dē ĭt| *adj.* Lying or occurring between two extremes; in between; in the middle: *of intermediate size.* [Medieval Latin *intermediātus*, from Latin *intermedius: inter-*, between + *medius*, middle.]

Interpol. An international organization of police forces from about 125 countries; International Criminal Police Organization.

in·ter·pret |ĭn tûr´prĭt| *v.* **1.** To explain or clarify the meaning or significance of: *Scientists interpret data.* **2.** To see or understand in a certain way: *He interpreted the letter to mean that the deal was off.* [Middle English *interpreten*, from Latin *interpretārī*, from *interpres*, interpreter, negotiator.]

in·ter·ro·gate |ĭn tĕr´ə gāt´| *v.* **in·ter·ro·gat·ed, in·ter·ro·gat·ing.** To question closely, as under formal conditions. [Latin *interrogāre*, to consult, question: *inter-*, between + *rogāre*, to ask.]

in·ter·rupt |ĭn´tə rŭpt´| *v.* To break in upon. —**in´ter·rup´tion** *n.: annoyed by the interruption.*

in·ter·scho·las·tic |ĭn´tər skə lăs´tĭk| *adj.* Existing or conducted between schools.

in·ter·sec·tion |ĭn´tər sĕk´shən| *n.* A corner where two or more roads intersect.

in•ter•sperse |ĭn′tər **spûrs**′| *v.*
in•ter•spersed, in•ter•spers•ing. To scatter
here and there among other things. [Latin
interspergere, to scatter among: *inter-*, among
+ *spargere*, to scatter.]

in•ter•state |ĭn′tər stāt′| *adj.* Between
or connecting two or more states: *interstate
highway.*

in•ter•ven•tion |ĭn′tər **věn**′shən| *n.* The
act or an example of intervening: *an
intervention to settle an argument.* [Latin
intervenīre, to come between: *inter-*, between
+ *venīre*, to come.]

intra-. A prefix meaning "inside of,
within": **intramural.** [From Latin *intra-*, on
the inside, within.]

in•tra•mu•ral |ĭn′trə **myo͝or**′əl| *adj.*
Carried on within a school and involving no
outsiders: *an intramural athletic program.*
[Latin, "within the walls": *intra-*, within +
mural, wall.]

in•tra•state |ĭn′trə stāt′| *adj.* Within the
boundaries of a state.

in•tra•ve•nous |ĭn′trə **vē**′nəs| *adj.*
Within or into a vein: *an intravenous
injection.* [Latin *intra-* + *vēna*, vein.]

in•trigue |ĭn′trēg′| *or* |ĭn trēg′| *n.*
1. Plotting or scheming carried on in secret.
2. A secret plot or scheme. [French, from
Italian *intrigo*, to perplex.]

in•tro•duce |ĭn′trə **do͞os**′| *or* |-**dyo͞os**′| *v.*
in•tro•duced, in•tro•duc•ing. 1. To
present (a person) by name to another or
others in order to establish an acquaintance:
introduce a young person to a grownup. **2.** To
open or begin: *She wrote a preface to introduce
her book.* **3.** To propose, create, or bring into
use or acceptance for the first time: *introduce
safer methods.*

in•tro•duc•tion |ĭn′trə **dŭk**′shən| *n.*
1. A short section at the beginning of a
book, speech, musical composition, play, etc.,
that leads into or prepares the way for what
will follow. **2. a.** The act or process of
introducing: *the introduction of the art of*

Pronunciation Key					
ă	pat	ŏ	pot	û	fur
ā	pay	ō	go	*th*	**the**
â	care	ô	paw, for	th	thin
ä	father	oi	oil	hw	which
ě	pet	o͝o	book	zh	usual
ē	be	o͞o	boot	ə	ago, item
ĭ	pit	yo͞o	cute		pencil, atom
ī	ice	ou	out		circus
î	near	ŭ	cut	ər	butter

printing in the 15th century. **b.** A particular
act of introducing: *Alice was asked to make the
introductions at the party.*

in•tro•spec•tion |ĭn′trə **spěk**′shən| *n.*
The act of looking inward to examine one's
own thoughts and feelings.

in•tro•vert |ĭn′trə vûrt′| *n.* A person
whose interest tends to center on his or her
own inner thoughts and feelings rather than
on other people and things. [New Latin
introvertere: *intro-*, inward + *vertere*, to turn.]

in•ven•tive |ĭn věn′tĭv| *adj.* Having or
showing the ability to think up new ideas,
methods, etc.; creative; original: *a highly
inventive mind.* [Middle English *inventen*, to
come upon, from Latin *invenīre*: *in-*, on +
venīre, to come.]

in•ven•to•ry |ĭn′vən tôr′ē| *or* |-tōr′ē| *n.,*
pl. **in•ven•to•ries.** The supply of goods on
hand; stock: *The store's inventory is getting low.*

in•verse |ĭn **vûrs**′| *or* |ĭn′vûrs′| *adj.*
Opposite, as in effect or character: *Addition
and subtraction are inverse operations.* [Latin
inversus, past participle of *invertere*, invert.]

in•vert |ĭn vûrt′| *v.* To turn upside down:
Invert the jar and let it stand in a pan of water.
[Latin *invertere*, to turn inside out or upside
down: *in-*, in, inward + *vertere*, to turn.]

in·ves·ti·gate |ĭn vĕs´tĭ gāt´| *v.*
in·ves·ti·gat·ed, in·ves·ti·gat·ing. 1. To look into or examine carefully in search of information. **2.** To make an investigation. [Latin *investīgāre,* to search into: *in-,* in + *vestīgāre,* to track.]

ir·i·des·cent |ĭr´ĭ dĕs´ənt| *adj.* Showing a display of rainbowlike colors: *butterflies with iridescent wings.* [From Greek *Iris,* mythical messenger of the gods who appeared as a rainbow.]

ir·reg·u·lar |ĭ rĕg´yə lər| *adj.* **1.** Not standard or uniform, as in shape, size, length, or arrangement: *an irregular coastline.* **2.** Not following a set pattern or regular schedule: *irregular rhythm.* **3.** Unusual or improper: *a highly irregular procedure.* **4.** In grammar, not following the standard pattern of inflected forms; for example, *do* is an irregular verb, with irregular principal parts. **5.** Not up to standard because of flaws or imperfections: *irregular merchandise.* [From Latin *ir-,* not + *rēgula,* ruler.]

ir·rel·e·vant |ĭ rĕl´ə vənt| *adj.* Having no relation to the subject or situation; not relevant.

ir·rev·o·ca·ble |ĭ rĕv´ə kə bəl| *adj.* Not capable of being changed or undone: *an irrevocable decision.*

-ish. A suffix that forms adjectives and means: **1.** Of the nationality of: **Finnish. 2.** Having the characteristics or qualities of: **childish. 3.** Preoccupied with: **selfish.** [Middle English *-is(c)h,* Old English *-isc,* from Germanic *-iskaz,* corresponding to Greek *-iskos,* noun suffix.]

isle |īl| *n.* An island, especially a small one.

-ism. A suffix that forms nouns and means: **1.** An act, practice, or process: **heroism. 2.** A relationship or condition: **parallelism. 3.** Characteristic behavior or quality: **individualism. 4.** A word, phrase, idiom, or usage peculiar to a language, people, etc.: **Americanism. 5.** A doctrine, theory, system, or principle: **socialism.**

i·so·la·tion |ī´sə lā´shən| *n.* The condition of being set apart from a group.

-ist. A suffix that forms nouns and means: **1.** Someone involved with a specified profession or thing: **dramatist; motorist. 2.** Someone who believes in a certain doctrine, system, etc.: **socialist. 3.** Someone characterized as having a particular trait: **romanticist.**

i·tal·ics |ĭ tăl´ĭks| *or* |ī tăl´-| *pl. n.* A style of printing type with the letters slanting to the right: *This is in italics.* [Introduced in Venice, *Italy,* in 1501.]

-ity. A suffix that forms nouns meaning "a quality or condition": **authenticity.** [Middle English *-it(i)e,* from Old French *-ite,* from Latin *-itās.*]

J

jag·uar |jăg´wär| *n.* A large, leopardlike wild cat of tropical America. [Spanish *jaguar, yaguar* and Portuguese *jaguar,* from Tupi-Guarani *jaguara, yaguara.*]

jer·sey |jûr´zē| *n., pl.* **jer·seys. 1.** A soft, elastic, knitted fabric of wool, cotton, rayon, etc., used for clothing. **2.** A garment, such as a pullover sweater or sport shirt, made of this fabric. [Originally a woolen sweater peculiar to the fishermen of *Jersey,* a British island.]

jodh·purs |jŏd´pərz| *pl. n.* Breeches worn for horseback riding that fit loosely above the knees and tightly from the knees to the ankles. [From *Jodhpur,* a city in India.]

jo·vi·al |jō´vē əl| *adj.* Full of fun and good cheer; jolly: *a jovial fellow.* [Originally "born under the influence of Jupiter" (the planet, regarded as the source of happiness), from the Latin god, Jupiter.]

jus·ti·fy |jŭs´tə fī´| *v.* **jus·ti·fied, jus·ti·fy·ing, jus·ti·fies. 1.** To show or prove to be right, just, or valid: *His fine performance justified the director's decision of casting him in the play.* **2.** To declare innocent; clear of blame: *The jury decided that the evidence justified the defendant's actions.* [Middle English *justifien* from Latin *iustificāre*, to act justly towards: *iūstus*, just + *facere*, to make.]

ju·ve·nile |jōō´və nəl| *or* |-nīl´| *adj.* **1.** Young; immature; childish: *juvenile behavior.* **2.** Of or for young people: *juvenile court.* — *n.* A young person or animal.

jux·ta·pose |jŭk´stə pōz´| *v.* **jux·ta·posed, jux·ta·pos·ing.** To place side by side: *The artist juxtaposed stripes and spots.* [Latin *juxta*, close together + French *poser*, to place.]

kin·der·gar·ten |kĭn´dər gär´tn| *n.* A class for children from four to six years of age, to prepare them for elementary school. [German *Kindergarten*, "children's garden."]

K

key·board |kē´bôrd| *or* |-bōrd| *n.* A set of keys, as on a piano, organ, typewriter, or computer: *type on a computer keyboard.*

khak·i |kăk´ē| *or* |kä´kē| *n.* A yellowish brown. —*adj.* Yellowish-brown.

ki·mo·no |kĭ mō´nə| *or* |-nō| *n., pl.* **ki·mo·nos. 1.** A long, loose robe with wide sleeves and a broad sash, worn by men and women as an outer garment. **2.** A woman's dressing gown resembling such a robe. [Japanese "thing for wearing": *ki,* to wear + *mono,* thing.]

L

lab·o·ra·to·ry |lăb´rə tôr´rē| *or* |-tōr´ē| *n., pl.* **lab·o·ra·to·ries.** A room equipped for scientific research, experiments, or testing.

lab·y·rinth |lăb´ə rĭnth´| *n.* A network of winding, connected passages through which it is difficult to find one's way without help; a maze: *a labyrinth of tunnels.*

la·con·ic |lə kŏn´ĭk| *adj.* Brief; to the point; concise. [Greek *Lakōnikos*, of or resembling the Spartans (known for their concise speech), from *Laconia*, region of Greece.]

land·scape |lănd´skāp´| *n.* **1.** A stretch of land or countryside forming a single scene or having its own special appearance or characteristics. **2.** A painting, photograph, etc., showing such a scene. [Dutch *landschap*, landscape, region: *land*, land + *schap*, condition.]

lar·i·at |lăr´ē ət| *n.* A long rope with an adjustable loop at one end, used to catch horses and cattle; a lasso. [Spanish *la reata*, lasso, rope: *la*, the + *reatar*, to tie again.]

la·ser |lā´zər| *n.* A device that emits an intense, precisely controlled beam of light. A laser may be used to cut or melt hard materials, perform delicate surgery, and transmit communication signals, among other functions. [l(ight) a(mplification by) s(timulated) e(mission of) r(adiation).]

leg·en·dar·y |lĕj´ən dĕr´ē| *adj.*
1. Based on or told of in legends: *legendary heroes.* **2.** Talked about frequently; famous: *legendary deeds.*

le·o·tard |lē´ə tärd´| *n.* Often **leotards.** A tight-fitting garment, originally worn by dancers and acrobats. [Popularized by Jules *Léotard*, 19th-century French aerialist.]

li·a·ble |lī´ə bəl| *adj.* **1.** Legally obligated or responsible: *liable for the damages.* **2.** Likely: *liable to make mistakes.*

li·ai·son |lē´ā zŏn´| *or* |lē ā´zŏn´| *n.* A channel or means of communication: *He served as the president's liaison with Congress.* [French *liaison,* "binding," from *lier,* to bind.]

li·bel |lī´bəl| *n.* **1.** A written or printed statement that unjustly damages a person's reputation or exposes him to ridicule. **2.** The act or crime of making such a statement.

lib·er·al |lĭb´ər əl| *or* |lĭb´rəl| *adj.*
1. Generous in amount; ample: *a liberal tip.*
2. Having or expressing political views that favor civil liberties, democratic reforms, and the use of governmental power to promote social progress. [Middle English, from Old French, from Latin *līberālis,* of freedom, from *līber,* free.]

li·brar·i·an |lī brâr´ē ən| *n.* A person who works in or is in charge of a library.

li·cense |lī´səns| *n.* **1.** Legal permission to do or own a specified thing. **2.** A document, card, plate, or other proof that such permission has been granted.

lieu·ten·ant |loo tĕn´ənt| *n.* An officer in the Army, Air Force, or Marine Corps ranking below a captain.

lim·ou·sine |lĭm´ə zēn´| *or*
|lĭm´ə zēn´| *n.* Also shortened to **limo.** A large, luxurious automobile. [Originally a kind of flowing mantle or coat, popularized in *Limousin,* France.]

lin·guist |lĭng´gwĭst| *n.* A person who speaks several languages fluently.

lit·er·a·ture |lĭt´ər ə chər| *n.* **1.** A body of writing in prose or verse.
2. Imaginative or creative writing, especially writing having recognized artistic value.

live·li·hood |līv´lē hood´| *n.* A person's means of support; a living.

log·ic |lŏj´ĭk| *n.* **1.** The study of the principles of reason. **2.** Rational thought; clear reasoning. [Middle English *logik,* from Old French *logique,* from Late Latin *logica,* from Greek *logikē (tekhnē),* art of reasoning.]

lo·gis·tics |lō jĭs´tĭks| *n. (used with a singular verb).* The planning and handling of details such as materials and personnel, as in a military operation. [French *logistique,* from Greek *logizein,* to calculate, from *logos,* reckoning.]

-logy. A word part meaning: **1.** An oral or written expression: **phraseology. 2.** The science, theory, or study of: **sociology.** [Middle English *-logie,* from Old French, from Latin *-logia,* from Greek, from *logos,* word, speech.]

M

mac·a·ro·ni |măk´ə rō´nē| *n.* Dried pasta, usually in the shape of hollow tubes. [Obsolete Italian *maccaroni,* plural of *maccarone.*]

ma·chin·er·y |mə shē´nə rē| *n., pl.*
ma·chin·er·ies. 1. Machines or machine parts. **2.** The working parts of a particular machine.

ma·gen·ta |mə jĕn´tə| *n.* A bright purplish red. —*adj.* Bright purplish red. [The dye was discovered in the year of the battle of *Magenta,* Italy (1859), and named for its bloodiness.]

mag·nif·i·cent |măg **nĭf´** ĭ sənt| *adj.*
1. Splendid in appearance; grand; remarkable: *a magnificent cathedral.*
2. Outstanding; excellent.

main·tain |mān **tān´**| *v.* **1.** To keep up; carry on; continue: *The train maintains a moderate speed on upgrades.* **2.** To keep in a desirable condition; keep from changing, declining, etc.: *maintain public roads.* **3.** To declare as true: *maintain one's innocence.* [Middle English *mainteine,* from Latin *manū tenēre,* "to hold in the hand": *manū,* hand + *tenēre,* to hold.]

main·te·nance |mān´tə nəns| *n.* **1.** The act of maintaining, as by supporting, preserving, etc. **2.** The work involved in care and upkeep.

ma·jor·i·ty |mə **jôr´** ĭ tē| *or* |-**jör´**-| *n.,* *pl.* **ma·jor·i·ties.** The greater number or part of something; a number more than half of a total.

mam·moth |măm´əth| *n.* An extinct elephant that had long tusks and thick hair and that lived throughout the Northern Hemisphere during the Ice Age. —*adj.* Huge; gigantic: *a mammoth wall.* [Russian *mammot',* from *Tartar mamont,* "earth" (perhaps because mammoths were thought to have burrowed).]

Pronunciation Key					
ă	pat	ŏ	pot	û	fur
ā	pay	ō	go	*th*	**the**
â	care	ô	paw, for	th	thin
ä	father	oi	oil	hw	which
ě	pet	ŏŏ	book	zh	usual
ē	be	ōō	boot	ə	ago, item
ĭ	pit	yōō	cute		pencil, atom
ī	ice	ou	out		circus
î	near	ŭ	cut	ər	butter

man·age·ment |măn´ ĭj mənt| *n.* The people who direct or supervise a business, organization, or institution. [Italian *maneggiare,* to handle, from Latin *manus,* hand.]

man·date |măn´dāt´| *n.* **1.** The results of a political election, seen as expressing the true wishes of the voters and thus used to justify the policies of the elected officials. **2.** An authoritative command or instruction. —*v.* to require.

man·da·to·ry |măn´də tôr´ē| *or* |-tōr´ē| *adj.* Required; obligatory: *A college degree is mandatory for most teaching jobs.*

ma·neu·ver |mə nōō´vər| *or* |-nyōō´-| *n.* A change in the course or position of a vehicle, as an aircraft, automobile, etc. —*v.* To make or cause to make one or more changes in course or position: *The Nautilus has to maneuver very carefully to avoid the icebergs.* [French *manoeuvre,* from Medieval Latin *man(u)opera,* manual work, from Latin *manū operārī,* to work by hand: *manus,* hand + *operārī,* to work.]

man·i·cure |măn´ ĭ kyōor´| *n.* A cosmetic treatment for the hands and fingernails. [French *manicure,* hand-care: Latin *manus,* hand + *cūra,* care.]

man·i·fest |**măn´**ə fĕst´| *adj.* Obvious; clear; apparent: *Her reasons were manifest.* —*v.* To reveal; show; display: *manifest a desire to leave.* [Middle English, from Latin *manifestus, manufestus,* palpable, grasped by hand: *manus,* hand + *-festus,* gripped.]

ma·nip·u·late |mə **nĭp´**yə lāt´| *v.* **ma·nip·u·lat·ed, ma·nip·u·lat·ing.** To operate or arrange with the hands: *manipulate the controls.* [From Latin *manipulus,* handful.]

man·ner·ism |**măn´**ə rĭz´əm| *n.* **1.** A distinctive personal trait; quirk: *an odd mannerism.* **2.** A habit or stylistic flourish that is regarded as exaggerated or affected: *He rid his speech of mannerisms.*

man·u·al |**măn´**yo͞o əl| *adj.* Requiring physical rather than mental effort: *manual labor.* —*n.* A small book of instructions; a guidebook; handbook: *a carpentry manual.* [Middle English *manuel,* from Old French, from Latin *manuālis,* of the hand, from *manus,* hand.]

man·u·fac·ture |măn´yə **făk´**chər| *v.* **man·u·fac·tured, man·u·fac·tur·ing.** To make or process (a product), especially with the use of industrial machines: *a company that manufactures cars.* [Old French *manufacture,* a making by hand, from Late Latin *manūfactus,* handmade: Latin *manū,* by hand, from *manus,* hand + *factus,* made, from *facere,* to make.]

man·u·script |**măn´**yə skrĭpt´| *n.* **1.** A handwritten or typed book, paper, article, etc., as distinguished from a printed copy. **2.** Handwriting as opposed to printing.

mas·car·a |mă **skăr´**ə| *n.* A cosmetic used to darken the eyelashes or eyebrows. [Spanish *máscara,* mask.]

math·e·mat·ics |măth´ə **măt´**ĭks| *n. (used with a singular verb).* The study of numbers, forms, arrangements, and sets, and of their relationships and properties. Arithmetic, algebra, and geometry are three branches of mathematics.

ma·tur·i·ty |mə **to͝or´**ĭ tē| *or* |**-tyo͝or´**-| *or* |**-cho͝or´**-| *n.* Adulthood; full development.

may·on·naise |mā´ə **nāz´**| *or* |**mā´**ə nāz´| *n.* A dressing made of raw egg yolk, oil, lemon juice or vinegar, and seasonings. [French, possibly named after the capture in 1756 of the city of *Mahon* by the Duke of Richelieu.]

me·di·e·val |mē´dē **ē´**vəl| *or* |mĕd ē´-| *or* |mĭd ē´-| *or* |mĭ **dē´**vəl| *adj.* Of or characteristic of the period in European history from the fall of the Roman Empire (about A.D. 500) to the rise of the Renaissance (about 1400).

mel·an·chol·y |**mĕl´**ən kŏl ē| *n.* An atmosphere of sorrow or sadness; a pervasive gloom. —*adj.* Sad; gloomy.

mem·oir |**mĕm´**wär´| *or* |-wôr´| *n.* An account of experiences that the author has lived through. [French *mémoire,* memory, from Latin *memoria,* memory.]

mem·o·ran·dum |mĕm´ə **răn´**dəm| *n., pl.* **mem·o·ran·dums** *or* **mem·o·ran·da** |mĕm´ə **răn´**də|. A written communication sent from one member or office of an organization to another or circulated generally.

men·tor |**mĕn´**tôr´| *or* |-tər| *n.* A person who gives advice and guidance; a counselor. [French, from *Mentor,* a character in Fénelon's Télémaque (1699), modeled after *Mentor,* a figure in Greek myth.]

men·u |**mĕn´**yo͞o| *n.* **1.** A list of foods and drinks available, as at a restaurant. **2. a.** A list of dishes to be served in a meal or series of meals. **b.** The dishes served. **3.** A list of options in a computer program.

mer·cu·ry |**mûr´**kyə rē| *n.* **1.** Symbol **Hg** An element, a silvery-white, poisonous metal that is a liquid at room temperature, used in thermometers and barometers: *The mercury in the barometer rose.* **2. Mercury.** The Roman god who served as messenger to the other gods and presided over commerce and travel. **3. Mercury.** The planet nearest the sun. [Middle English *Mercurie,* from Old French, from Latin *Mercurius,* Mercury, the Roman god.]

me·sa |mā´sə| *n.* A flat-topped hill or small plateau with steep sides, common in the southwestern United States. [Spanish, from Old Spanish, from Latin *mēnsa*, table.]

mes·quite |mě **skēt´**| *or* |**měs´**kēt´| *n.* A thorny shrub or tree of southwestern North America, having feathery leaves and beanlike pods.

met·a·phor |**mět´**ə fôr´| *or* |-fər| *n.* A figure of speech that compares two unlike things by stating or implying that one thing is the other. *The fog was a blanket* and *a river of light* are examples of metaphors.

me·te·or·ol·o·gy |mē´tē ə rŏl´ə jē| *n.* The scientific study of the atmosphere and its effects, especially those effects that influence weather conditions. [Greek *meteōrologia*, discussion of astronomical phenomena: *meteōron*, meteor + *-logy*, study or science of.]

me·tic·u·lous |mə tĭk´yə ləs| *adj.* **1.** Very careful and precise: *kept meticulous records.* **2.** Taking great care with details; scrupulous.

met·ro·pol·i·tan |mět´rə pŏl´ĭ tən| *adj.* Of, from, or characteristic of a major city with its suburbs: *metropolitan daily newspapers.*

mi·crobe |mī´krōb´| *n.* A living thing so small that it can be seen only through a microscope, especially one of the microorganisms that causes disease; a germ.

mi·cro·fiche |mī´krō fēsh´| *n., pl.* **mi·cro·fiche** or **-fich·es.** A sheet of microfilm capable of storing many pages of printed text, in reduced form.

mi·cro·film |mī´krə fĭlm´| *n.* A film on which written or printed material can be photographed in greatly reduced size.

mi·cro·wave |mī´krō wāv´| *n.* A high-frequency electromagnetic wave. Microwaves are used in radar and in microwave ovens. [Greek *micro*, small + *wave*.]

min·i·a·ture |mĭn´ē ə chər| *or* |mĭn´ə-| *adj.* On a greatly reduced scale from the usual.

min·i·se·ries |mĭn´ē sîr´ēz| *n.* A sequence of episodes that make up a televised dramatic production. [*mini-*, probably from both *miniature* and *minimum* + series, from Latin *seriēs*, from *serere*, to join.]

mi·nor·i·ty |mĭ nôr´ĭ tē| *or* |-nŏr´-| *or* |mī-| *n., pl.* **mi·nor·i·ties.** The smaller in number of two groups forming a whole.

min·us·cule |mĭn´ə skyōōl´| *or* |mĭ nŭs´kyōōl´| *adj.* Very small; tiny.

mis·cel·la·ne·ous |mĭs´ə lā´nē əs| *adj.*
1. Made up of a variety of different elements or ingredients: *a miscellaneous assortment of chocolates.* **2.** Not falling into a particular category: *miscellaneous items in a budget.*

mis·chie·vous |mĭs´chə vəs| *adj.* **1.** Full of mischief; naughty: *a mischievous child.* **2.** Showing a tendency to do mischief.

mis·con·cep·tion |mĭs´kən sĕp´shən| *n.* A mistaken idea; a delusion. [From Middle English *mis-*, wrong + *concepcioun*, conception, from Latin *concipere*, to conceive.]

mis·sion |mĭsh´ən| *n.* An assignment; a task: *a rescue mission; her mission in life.* [From Latin *mittere*, to let go, send.]

mo·bile |mō´bəl| *or* |-bēl´| *or* |-bīl´| *adj.* Capable of moving or being moved.

mon·arch |mŏn´ərk| *n.* A ruler or sovereign, such as a king, queen, emperor, etc.

monk |mŭngk| *n.* A member of a group of men living in a monastery and bound by vows to the rules and practices of a religious order.

mono-. A prefix meaning "one; single; alone": **monopoly.** [Middle English, from Old French, from Latin, from Greek, from *monos*, single, alone.]

mon·o·chrome |mŏn´ə krōm´| *n.* A painting done in different shades of one color.

mon·o·gram |mŏn´ə grăm´| *n.* A design made up of letters, usually the initials of a name.

mon·o·logue |mŏn´ə lôg´| *or* |-lŏg´| *n.* A long speech made by one person in a group.

mo·nop·o·ly |mə nŏp´ə lē| *n., pl.* Sole possession or control of anything.

mon·o·rail |mŏn´ə rāl´| *n.* **1.** A single rail on which a car or train of cars travels. **2.** A railway system using a track with such a rail.

mon·o·tone |mŏn´ə tōn´| *n.* A succession of sounds or words uttered in a single tone.

mo·not·o·nous |mə nŏt´n əs| *adj.* Never varied; repetitiously dull: *a monotonous diet.*

mon·strous |mŏn´strəs| *adj.* Frightful; shocking: *monstrous behavior.*

mort·gage |môr´gĭj| *n.* **1.** A legal pledge of property to a creditor as security for the payment of a loan or debt: *the mortgage of one's house to a bank.* **2.** A written agreement specifying the terms of such a pledge.

mo·sa·ic |mō zā´ĭk| *n.* A picture or design made on a surface by fitting and cementing together small pieces of colored tile, glass, stone, etc. [From Greek *mouseion*, a mosaic (after the decorations in medieval caves dedicated to the Muses).]

mos·qui·to |mə skē´tō| *n., pl.* **mos·qui·toes** or **mos·qui·tos.** Any of several winged insects of which the females bite and suck blood from animals and human beings. Some kinds transmit diseases such as malaria and yellow fever. [Spanish, from *mosca*, fly, from Latin *musca*.]

mo·tel |mō tĕl´| *n.* A hotel for motorists, usually opening directly on a parking area. [Blend of *motor* and *hotel*.]

moun·tain·ous |moun´tə nəs| *adj.* Having or characterized by many mountains.

mul·ti·pli·ca·tion |mŭl´tə plĭ kā´shən| *n.* **1.** The act or process of multiplying or increasing. **2.** A mathematical operation performed on a pair of numbers. [From Latin *multiplicāre*, from *multiplex*, having many folds.]

Muse |myooz| *n.* In Greek mythology, one of the nine sister goddesses who presided over the arts and sciences: *the Muse of dance.*

mu·se·um |myoo zē´əm| *n.* A building in which works of artistic, historical, or scientific interest are exhibited. [From Greek *mouseion*, place of the Muses.]

mus·lin |mŭz´lĭn| *n.* A cotton cloth of plain weave, either coarse or sheer, used for sheets, curtains, dresses, etc. [Italian *mussolina*, "cloth of Mosul," after *Mosul*, Iraq.]

mus·tache |mŭs´tăsh´| *or* |mə stăsh´| *n.*
The hair growing on a man's upper lip,
especially when it is not shaved off, but
shaped and groomed. [Old French
mo(u)stache, from Greek *mustax*, the upper
lip, mustache.]

my·thol·o·gy |mĭ thŏl´ə jē| *n., pl.*
my·thol·o·gies. 1. A body of myths,
especially one dealing with a specified cultural
tradition: *Greek mythology.* **2.** The study of
myths. [French *mythologie*, from Greek
muthologia: *muthos*, myth + *-logia, -logy*, the
study of.]

N

nar·cis·sus |när sĭs´əs| *n., pl.*
nar·cis·sus·es or **nar·cis·si** |när sĭs´ī´| *or*
|-sĭs´ē|. A plant related to the daffodil, with
yellow or white flowers and a trumpet-shaped
central part. [Greek *narkissos*, from *Narcissus*,
a boy in Greek myth.]

nar·rate |năr´āt´| *or* |nă rāt´| *v.*
nar·rat·ed, nar·rat·ing. 1. To give an oral
or written account of; recite. **2.** To supply
the running commentary for a motion picture
or other performance. —**nar´ra´tor** *n.*

nar·ra·tive |năr´ə tĭv| *n.* A story or
description; a narrated account. —*adj.* Telling
a story: *narrative poems.*

na·tion·al·i·ty |năsh´ə năl´ĭ tē| *n., pl.*
na·tion·al·i·ties. The status of belonging to
a particular nation by reason of origin, birth,
or naturalization: *American nationality.*

nat·u·ral·ize |năch´ər ə līz´| *or*
|năch´rə-| *v.* **nat·u·ral·ized,
nat·u·ral·iz·ing.** To give full citizenship to
(someone of foreign birth): *She was
naturalized last month.*

nec·es·sa·ry |nĕs´ĭ sĕr´ē| *adj.* Needed to
achieve a certain result or effect; essential;
requisite: *Fill out the necessary forms.*

nec·tar |nĕk´tər| *n.* **1.** In Greek
mythology, the drink of the gods: *Greek gods
ate ambrosia and drank nectar.* **2.** Any
delicious drink.

neg·a·tive |nĕg´ə tĭv| *adj.* Less than zero:
negative numbers.

ne·go·ti·ate |nĭ gō´shē āt´| *v.* To confer
or discuss (something) in order to come to
terms or an agreement: *negotiate a treaty.*

nem·e·sis |nĕm´ĭ sĭs| *n., pl.* **nem·e·ses**
|nĕm´ĭ sēz´|. An unbeatable rival: *He met his
nemesis at the tennis match.* [From *Nemesis*,
goddess in Greek mythology.]

net |nĕt| *adj.* Remaining after all necessary
additions, subtractions, or adjustments have
been made: *What was your net income?*

neu·tral |nōō′trəl| *or* |nyōō′-| *adj.* Not allied with, supporting, or favoring any side in a war, dispute, contest, or struggle for power: *a neutral nation.* [Latin, *neutrālis,* from *neuter,* neither: *ne-,* not + *uter,* either of two.]

neu·tral·i·ty |nōō trăl′ĭ tē| *or* |nyōō-| *n.* The condition, quality, or status of being neutral, especially a policy of taking no part or allying with no side in a war or dispute.

non·fic·tion |nŏn fĭk′shən| *n.* Literature that is not fiction, especially books of fact and general information, such as history books, biographies, essays, etc.

no·ti·fy |nō′tə fī′| *v.* **no·ti·fied, no·ti·fy·ing, no·ti·fies.** To let (someone) know; inform, [From Latin *nōtus,* known + *facere,* to make.]

no·to·ri·ous |nō tôr′ē əs| *or* |-tōr′-| *adj.* Known widely and regarded unfavorably; infamous: *a notorious swindler.*

nov·el·ist |nŏv′ə lĭst| *n.* A writer of novels.

nu·cle·ar |nōō′klē ər| *or* |nyōō′-| *adj.* **1.** Of, forming, or having to do with a nucleus or nuclei. **2.** Of or using energy derived from the nuclei of atoms: *a nuclear power plant.*

nui·sance |nōō′səns| *or* |nyōō′-| *n.* A source of inconvenience or annoyance; a bother.

O

ob-. Also **oc-** (before *c*) or **of-** (before *f*) or **op-** (before *p*) or **o-** (before *m*). A prefix meaning "toward, in front of, or against": **object.** [Latin *ob-,* from the preposition *ob,* to, toward, in front of, on account of, against.]

ob·struct |əb strŭkt′| *v.* **1.** To block: *obstruct the road.* **2.** To get in the way of so as to hide; cut off from view: *obstruct the view.* [From Latin: *ob-,* against + *struere,* to pile up, build.]

ob·tain |əb tān′| *v.* **1.** To gain possession of after planning or endeavor; get; acquire: *obtain an autograph.* **2.** To be established or accepted; be in use: *an ancient custom that still obtains.* [From Latin: *ob-* + *tenēre,* to hold.]

oc·ca·sion·al |ə kā′zhə nəl| *adj.* Occurring from time to time: *an occasional earthquake.*

oc·cu·pa·tion |ŏk′yə pā′shən| *n.* A means of making a living; a profession or job.

oc·cur·rence |ə kûr′əns| *n.* **1.** The act or condition of occurring, taking place, appearing, etc.: *the occurrence of an accident.* **2.** Something that happens: *a strange occurrence.*

oc·tave |ŏk′tĭv| *or* |-tāv′| *n.* The interval between one musical tone and the eighth tone above or below it: *From middle C to the C above it is an octave.*

od·ys·sey |ŏd′ĭ sē| *n.* An extended, adventurous journey. [After Odysseus, a warrior in Greek mythology.]

of·fense |ə fĕns′| *n.* **1.** A violation or crime. |ô′fĕns| *or* |ŏf′ĕns′| **2.** The act of attacking or assaulting. **3.** In sports, the team in possession of the ball or puck: *The offense took possession of the ball on the 20-yard line.*

om·e·let, also **om·e·lette** |ŏm′ə lĭt| *or* |ŏm′lĭt| *n.* A dish of beaten eggs, cooked and often folded around a filling of jelly, cheese, etc. [French *omelette,* from Old French *amelette,* "thin plate," (variant of *alumelle*) from *lemelle,* from Latin *lāmella,* thin metal plate, diminutive of *lāmina,* plate, layer.]

o·mis·sion |ō mĭsh′ən| *n.* **1.** The act or fact of omitting something or having been omitted: *the omission of several letters.* **2.** Something omitted: *omissions in the guest list.*

o·mit |ō mĭt′| *v.* **o·mit·ted, o·mit·ting.** To leave out; not include: *Omit unnecessary words.* [Latin *omittere:* *ob,* away + *mittere,* to send.]

o·paque |ō pāk´| *adj.* Not capable of letting light pass through; neither transparent nor translucent: *opaque metals.* [Partly from Middle English *opake*, partly from Old French *opaque*, both from Latin *opācus*, dark.]

op·er·a |ŏp´ər ə| *or* |ŏp´rə| *n.* A musical and dramatic work consisting of a play with stage action and the words sung to music, usually with orchestral accompaniment. [Italian, from Latin *opera*, work.]

o·pos·sum |ə pŏs´əm| *or* |pŏs´əm| *n.* A furry animal that lives mostly in trees and carries its young in a pouch. Also called *possum.*

op·por·tu·ni·ty |ŏp´ər tōō´nĭ tē| *or* |-tyōō´-| *n., pl.* **op·por·tu·ni·ties.** A time or occasion that is suitable for a particular purpose; a favorable combination of circumstances: *opportunity for advancement.*

op·po·site |ŏp´ə zĭt| *or* |-sĭt| *adj.* **1.** Placed or located directly across from something else or from each other: *the opposite sides of a house.* **2.** Contrary in nature or tendency; altogether different; contradictory: *opposite personalities.* [Middle English, from Latin *oppositus*, from *oppōnere*, oppose: *ob-*, against + *pōnere*, to put.]

op·ti·mism |ŏp´tə mĭz´əm| *n.* A tendency to take a hopeful view of a situation, or to expect the best possible outcome.

op·tom·e·trist |ŏp tŏm´ĭ trĭst| *n.* A person who examines eyes and prescribes eyeglasses and other lenses to correct visual defects: *The optometrist tested her vision.*

o·ri·en·ta·tion |ôr´ē ĕn tā´shən| *or* |-ən-| *or* |ōr´-| *n.* Introductory instruction for people in a new place or situation: *freshman orientation.* —*modifier: an orientation session.*

or·i·gin |ôr´ə jĭn| *or* |ŏr´-| *n.* The original source or cause of something: *the origin of a word.* [Middle English *origyne*, from Latin *orīgō*, from *orīrī*, to rise.]

o·rig·i·nal |ə rĭj´ə nəl| *adj.* **1.** Existing from the beginning; the first: *the original*

---

thirteen states of the Union. **2.** Being that from which a copy or translation is made: *an original painting; a book in the original German.*

-ous. A suffix that forms adjectives and means "full of or having": **joyous.** [Middle English, from Old French, from *-ous, -eus, -eux,* from Latin, *-osus,* and *-us,* adj. suffixes.]

out·ra·geous |out rā´jəs| *adj.* Exceeding all bounds of what is right or proper; shocking: *an outrageous crime; outrageous prices.*

ox·y·gen |ŏk´sĭ jən| *n. Symbol* **O** One of the elements, a colorless, odorless, tasteless gas. [French *oxygène*, "acid-former": *oxy-* (sharp, here, "acid") + *-gen,* from Greek *-genēs,* born.]

P

pac·i·fy |păs´ə fī´| *v.* **pac·i·fied, pac·i·fy·ing, pac·i·fies. 1.** To quiet; calm: *pacify a baby.* **2.** To establish peace in: *pacify the frontier.* —**pac´i·fi·ca´tion** *n.* [From Latin *pācificāre,* pax (stem *pāc-*), peace + *facere,* to make.]

pag·eant |păj´ənt| *n.* **1.** A play or dramatic spectacle usually based on an event in history. **2.** A procession or celebration.

pam·phlet |păm´flĭt| *n.* A short book or printed essay with a paper cover and no binding.

par·af·fin |pắr´ə fĭn| *n.* A waxy, white or colorless, solid mixture used to make candles, wax paper, and sealing materials.

par·a·pher·na·lia |pắr´ə fər nāl´yə| *n.* (*used with a singular or plural verb*). The equipment used in or associated with some activity; gear: *skiing paraphernalia.*

pa·ren·the·sis |pə rĕn´thĭ sĭs| *n., pl.* **pa·ren·the·ses** |pə rĕn´thĭ sēz|. Either or both of the upright curved lines, ( ), used to mark off additional remarks in printing or writing.

par·fait |pär fā´| *n.* A dessert of layers, often of ice cream with various toppings, served in a tall glass. [French, from *parfait,* perfect, from Latin *perfectus,* perfect.]

par·tic·i·pant |pär tĭs´ə pənt| *n.* Someone who participates or takes part: *participants in a card game.*

pas·ta |pä´stə| *n.* **1.** Dough made from flour and water: *Macaroni is one form of pasta.* **2.** A prepared dish of pasta.

pas·teur·ize |pắs´chə rīz´| *v.* **pas·teur·ized, pas·teur·iz·ing.** To treat a liquid with heat and then cold in order to destroy harmful microorganisms. [After Louis *Pasteur* (1822–1895), French chemist, its inventor.]

pat·ent |pắt´nt| *n.* A grant made by a government to an inventor, assuring him or her the exclusive right to manufacture, use, and sell the invention for a stated period of time.

pa·thet·ic |pə thĕt´ĭk| *adj.* Arousing pity, sympathy, or sorrow; sad; pitiful. [French *pathétique,* from Greek *pathētikos,* from *pathos,* passion, suffering.]

path·o·log·i·cal |pắth´ə lŏj´ĭ kəl| *adj.* Of, caused by, or affected with physical or mental disease: *pathological symptoms.*

pa·thol·o·gy |pə thŏl´ə jē| *n.* The scientific and medical study of disease, its causes, its processes, and its effects. [From Greek *pathologia,* study of passions: *patho-,* from Greek *pathos,* emotion, suffering + *-logy,* the study of.]

pa·thos |pā´thŏs´| *n.* A quality in something or someone that arouses feelings of pity, sympathy, tenderness, or sorrow in another. [Greek, passion, suffering.]

pe·des·tri·an |pə dĕs´trē ən| *n.* A person traveling on foot, especially on city streets.

per cap·i·ta |pər kắp´ĭ tə|. Per person; of, for, or by each individual: *per capita income.*

per·ceive |pər sēv´| *v.* **per·ceived, per·ceiv·ing. 1.** To become aware of through any of the senses, especially to see or hear. **2.** To achieve understanding of: *Try to perceive the meaning of these sentences.* [Middle English *perceiven,* from Latin *percipere,* "to seize wholly": *per-,* thoroughly + *capere,* to seize.]

per·cep·ti·ble |pər sĕp´tə bəl| *adj.* Capable of being perceived by the senses or by the mind: *a perceptible improvement in the patient's condition.* —**per·cep´ti·bil´i·ty** *n.* —**per·cep´ti·bly** *adv.* [From Latin *percipere,* to perceive.]

per·cep·tion |pər **sĕp´**shən| *n.* The act or process of perceiving.

per·fec·tion·ism |pər **fĕk´**shə nĭz´əm| *n.* A tendency to set extremely high standards and to insist on meeting them. —**per·fec´tion·ist** *n.*: *a perfectionist who tolerates no mistakes.*

pe·ri·od·i·cal |pîr´ē **ŏd´**ĭ kəl| *n.* A publication, especially a magazine, that appears at regular intervals of more than one day.

per·mit |pər **mĭt´**| *v.* **per·mit·ted, per·mit·ting.** To give permission to; allow. [Latin *per-*, through + *mittere*, to let go, send.]

per·plex |pər **plĕks´**| *v.* To confuse or puzzle; bewilder. [Latin *perplexus*, intricate: *per-*, thoroughly + *plectere*, to weave, entwine, fold.]

per·se·cute |**pûr´**sĭ kyōōt´| *v.* **per·se·cut·ed, per·se·cut·ing. 1.** To cause to suffer, especially on account of politics, religion, etc.; oppress. **2.** To annoy persistently; bother.

per·son·al·i·ty |pûr´sə **năl´**ĭ tē| *n., pl.* **per·son·al·i·ties.** The total of qualities and traits, as of character, behavior, etc., that are peculiar to each person: *a pleasing personality.*

per·son·nel |pûr´sə **nĕl´**| *n.* **1.** The staff or employees of an organization. **2.** The division of a company concerned with the selection, placement, training, etc., of employees. —***modifier:*** *a personnel manager.* ***Usage:*** **Personnel.** *Personnel* never refers to an individual; therefore it should not be used with a numeral: *All personnel* (not *five personnel*) *received raises.*

per·spec·tive |pər **spĕk´**tĭv| *n.* **1.** A view or vista: *the perspective of the city as seen from the rooftops.* **2.** A mental view of the relationships of the aspects of a subject to each other and to a whole: *a narrow perspective of the situation.*

per·spi·ra·tion |pûr´spə **rā´**shən| *n.* **1.** The salty moisture excreted through the skin by the sweat glands; sweat. **2.** The act or process of perspiring. [French *perspirer*, from Latin *perspīrāre*, breathe through: *per-*, through + *spīrāre*, to blow, breathe.]

per·sua·sive |pər **swā´**sĭv| *or* |-zĭv| *adj.* Having the power to persuade: *a persuasive speaker.*

per·tain |pər **tān´**| *v.* To have reference; relate. [Latin, to relate to: *per-*, to + *tenēre*, to hold.]

per·ti·nent |**pûr´**tn ənt| *adj.* Related to a specific matter; relevant: *pertinent topics.*

pes·si·mism |**pĕs´**ə mĭz´əm| *n.* A tendency to take the gloomiest view of a situation.

pes·ti·cide |**pĕs´**tĭ sīd´| *n.* Any chemical used to kill harmful animals or plants.

phar·ma·cist |**fär´**mə sĭst| *n.* Someone who specializes in pharmacy; a druggist.

phase |fāz| *n.* A distinct stage of development.

phe·nom·e·non |fĭ **nŏm´**ə nŏn´| *n., pl.* **phe·nom·e·na** |fĭ **nŏm´**ə nə| *or* **phe·nom·e·nons.** Any event or fact that can be perceived by the senses.

pho·to·cop·y |**fō´**tō kŏp´ē| *n., pl.* **-cop·ies.** A photographic reproduction. [*photo-*, from Greek, light + *copy*.]

pho·to·gen·ic |fō´tə **jĕn´**ĭk| *adj.* Attractive as a subject for photography. [*photo-*, from Greek, light + *-genic, -genēs*, born.]

Pronunciation Key

ă	pat	ŏ	pot	û	fur
ā	pay	ō	go	*th*	the
â	care	ô	paw, for	th	thin
ä	father	oi	oil	hw	which
ĕ	pet	ŏŏ	book	zh	usual
ē	be	ōō	boot	ə	ago, item
ĭ	pit	yōō	cute		pencil, atom
ī	ice	ou	out		circus
î	near	ŭ	cut	ər	butter

pho·tog·ra·pher |fə tŏg′rə fər| *n.* Someone who takes photographs for a living.

phy·si·cian |fĭ zĭsh′ən| *n.* A person licensed to practice medicine; a doctor.

pi·an·ist |pē ăn′ ĭst| *or* |pē′ə nĭst| *n.* Someone who plays the piano.

piece |pēs| *n.* Something considered as part of a larger quantity or group; a portion. *Idiom.* **a piece of (one's) mind.** *Informal.* Frank criticism or censure, often based on one's own attitude or opinions: *gave her a piece of his mind.*

pig·ment |pĭg′mənt| *n.* A substance or material used to give color to something.

pi·las·ter |pĭ lăs′tər| *n.* A vertical column projecting slightly from a wall.

pill |pĭl| *n.* **1.** A small lump or tablet of medicine. **2.** *Slang.* A boring or disagreeable person: *What a pill he is!*

pi·men·to |pĭ měn′tō| *n., pl.* **pi·men·tos.** A mild-flavored red pepper; a pimiento. [Spanish *pimienta*, pepper, allspice, from Late Latin *pigmenta*.]

pi·ñon |pĭn′yən| *or* |-yōn′| *n.* A pine tree of western North and South America, bearing edible seeds.

pis·ta·chi·o |pĭ stăsh′ē ō′| *n., pl.* **pis·ta·chi·os.** **1.** A tree of the Mediterranean region and western Asia, bearing small, hard-shelled nuts with a sweet green kernel. **2.** Also **pistachio nut.** The nut of such a tree. [Italian *pistacchio*, from Latin *pistācium*, from Greek *pistakion*, pistachio nut, from *pistakē*, pistachio tree, from Persian *pistah*.]

pi·ton |pē′tŏn| *n.* A metal spike fitted at one end with an eye or ring through which to pass a rope, used in mountain climbing as a hold: *Her life depended, to some extent, on the quality of her pitons.*

piz·za |pēt′sə| *n.* A baked dish, Italian in origin, consisting of a shallow, pielike crust covered with various spiced mixtures, as of tomatoes, cheese, sausage, etc. [Italian, probably from Old Italian, a point.]

plas·ter |plăs′tər| *or* |plä′stər| *n.* A mixture of sand, lime, and water, that hardens to form a smooth solid surface, used for covering walls and ceilings.

play·wright |plā′rīt′| *n.* A person who writes plays; a dramatist.

pli·a·ble |plī′ə bəl| *adj.* Easily bent or shaped without breaking; flexible. [Middle English *plyante*, from Old French *pliant*, to bend, fold, from Latin *plicāre*, to fold.]

pli·ers |plī′ərz| *n.* (*used with plural verb*). A tool with two parts attached together as in a pair of scissors, used for holding, bending, or cutting. [Middle English *plier*, from Old French *plier*, from Latin *plicāre*, to fold.]

pneu·mo·nia |nōō mōn′yə| *or* |nyōō-| *n.* Any of several usually serious diseases, caused by bacteria, viruses, chemicals, or irritation, in which the lungs become inflamed.

pol·i·ti·cian |pŏl′ ĭ tĭsh′ən| *n.* A person active in politics, especially one holding a political office.

pol·y·es·ter |pŏl′ē ĕs′tər| *n.* Any of various light, strong, weather-resistant synthetic resins used in permanent press fabrics.

pop·u·lar·i·ty |pŏp′yə lăr′ ĭ tē| *n.* The quality of being liked by many people.

por·trait |pôr´trĭt´| *or* |-trāt´| *or*
|pōr´-| *n.* A painting, photograph, or other
likeness of a person, especially one showing
the face. [French, from *portraire*, portray.]

pos·ses·sion |pə zĕsh´ən| *n.* The fact or
condition of having or possessing something:
Who has possession of the ball?

pos·si·bil·i·ty |pŏs´ə bĭl´ĭ tē| *n., pl.*
pos·si·bil·i·ties. 1. The fact or condition of
being capable of happening: *the possibility of
life on Mars.* **2.** Something that is capable of
happening: *His promotion is a possibility.*

post·hu·mous |pŏs´chə məs| *or*
|-chōō-| *adj.* Occurring or continuing after
one's death: *a posthumous award.*

pos·ture |pŏs´chər| *n.* The way in which
a person holds or carries his body; carriage: *a
person who has good posture.* [Italian *postura*,
from Latin *positūra*, from *pōnere*, to place.]

pre·cious |prĕsh´əs| *adj.* Of high price;
valuable: *precious metals.*

pre·cise |prĭ sīs´| *adj.* **1.** Definite; not
vague: *Tell me how to get there, and be precise.*
2. Particular: *on this precise spot.*

pre·ci·sion |prĭ sĭzh´ən| *n.* The
condition, property, or quality of being
precise.

pred·e·ces·sor |prĕd´ĭ sĕs´ər| *or*
|prē´dĭ-| *n.* Someone or something that
precedes another in time, especially in an
office or function: *the catapult, predecessor of
the modern rocket launcher.* [Middle English
predecessour, from Latin *praedēcessor:* Latin
prae, before + *dēcessor*, one who leaves, from
dēcēdere, to die, go away: *dē*, away + *cēdere*,
to go.]

pref·er·a·ble |prĕf´ər ə bəl| *adj.* More
desirable; preferred. [Middle English
preferren from Latin *praeferre*, to hold or set
before: *prae*, before + *ferre*, to bear.]

pref·er·ence |prĕf´ər əns| *n.* **1.** The act
of preferring; the exercise of choice: *She dressed
simply, not because she had to, but by preference.*
2. Someone or something preferred; one's
choice: *asked for a window seat, but did not
obtain his preference.* **3.** A liking for one person

or thing over another: *a preference for blue.*
[French *préférence*, from Latin *praeferēns*, present
participle of *praeferre*, to hold or set before:
prae, before + *ferre*, to bear.]

prep·o·si·tion |prĕp´ə zĭsh´ən| *n.* A
word that shows the relationship between a
noun or pronoun and another word in a
sentence. For example, the preposition *on*
in *the store on the street corner* shows the
relationship between *street corner* and *store.*
Some other common prepositions are *about,
at, by, from, in, near, of, off, out, to,* and *with.*
[Middle English *preposicioun*, from Latin
praepositiō, from *praepōnere*, to place in front:
prae, in front + *pōnere*, to place.]

pre·re·cord |prē´rĭ kôrd´| *v.* To record
(a television program, for example) at an
earlier time for later use: *a prerecorded
program.*

pre·req·ui·site |prĭ rĕk´wĭ zĭt| *adj.*
Required as a condition for something else;
necessary: *a course that is a prerequisite to
more advanced studies.* —*n.* Something that
is required.

pre·sume |prĭ zōōm´| *v.* **pre·sumed,
pre·sum·ing.** To assume to be true in the
absence of anything to the contrary; take for
granted: *I presume that she will take the job.*
[Middle English *presumen*, from Latin
praesūmere, to venture: *prae-*, before + *sūmere*,
to take.]

Pronunciation Key

ă	pat	ŏ	pot	û	fur
ā	pay	ō	go	*th*	the
â	care	ô	paw, for	th	thin
ä	father	oi	oil	hw	which
ĕ	pet	ōō	book	zh	usual
ē	be	ōō	boot	ə	ago, item
ĭ	pit	yōō	cute		pencil, atom
ī	ice	ou	out		circus
î	near	ŭ	cut	ər	butter

pre·sump·tion |prĭ **zŭmp´**shən| *n.* The act of believing or accepting as true: *a presumption of innocence.*

pret·zel |**prĕt´**səl| *n.* A thin roll of dough, often salted on the outside, baked in the form of a loose knot or stick. [German *Pretzel, Brezel,* from Old High German *brezitella,* from Latin *brachītum,* armlet, hence a ring-shaped cake.]

pre·vail |prĭ **vāl´**| *v.* **1.** To be greater in strength and influence; triumph: *"The wrong shall fail, the right prevail"* (Longfellow). **2.** To be most common or frequent: *Warm dry weather prevails in the Southwest.* **3.** To be in use; be current: *an attitude that prevailed in the 1950s.* [Middle English *prevayllen,* from Latin *praevalēre,* to be more powerful: *prae-,* beyond + *valēre,* to be strong.]

prev·a·lent |**prĕv´**ə lənt| *adj.* Widely existing or commonly occurring: *Sickness is not as prevalent in dry, cool areas as it is in hot, humid areas.*

pre·ven·tive |prĭ **vĕn´**tĭv| *adj.* Designed to prevent or hinder: *preventive steps against accidents; preventive health care.* [Middle English *preventen,* to anticipate, from Latin *praevenīre,* to come before, anticipate: *prae-,* before + *venīre,* to come.]

pri·or |**prī´**ər| *adj.* **1.** Preceding in time or order: *his prior employment.* **2.** Preceding in importance or value: *a prior consideration.*

pri·va·cy |**prī´**və sē| *n., pl.* **pri·va·cies.** The condition of being apart or secluded from others: *Her privacy is important to her.*

priv·i·lege |**prĭv´**ə lĭj| *n.* A special right, immunity, benefit, permission, etc., granted to or enjoyed by an individual, class, group, or caste.

prob·a·ble |**prŏb´**ə bəl| *adj.* **1.** Likely to happen or be true: *the probable cost of the expedition.* **2.** Relatively likely but not certain; plausible: *a probable explanation.*

prob·a·bly |**prŏb´**ə blē| Most likely; presumably. [Middle English, from Old French, from Latin *probābilis,* provable,

laudable, from *probāre,* to prove, demonstrate as good, from *probus,* good.]

pro·ceed |prə **sēd´**| *v.* **1.** To go forward or onward, especially after an interruption: *Proceed with caution.* **2.** To carry on some action or process; continue. [Middle English *proceden,* from Latin *prōcēdere: prō-,* forward + *cēdere,* to go.]

pro·claim |prō **klām´**| *or* |prə-| *v.* To announce officially and publicly; declare: *proclaim a holiday.* [Middle English *procla(y)men,* from Latin *prōclāmāre: prō-,* forward + *clāmāre,* to cry out.]

proc·la·ma·tion |prŏk´lə **mā´**shən| *n.* **1.** The act of proclaiming. **2.** Something proclaimed, especially an official public announcement: *the Emancipation Proclamation.*

pro·duce |prə **dōōs´**| *or* |-**dyōōs´**| *v.* **pro·duced, pro·duc·ing. 1.** To bring forth (something); yield: *Seeds grow up to produce plants.* **2.** To give form or shape to; make; create; manufacture: *produce parts for machines.* [Latin *prōdūcere,* to lead or bring forth: *prō-,* forward + *dūcere,* to lead.] —*n.* |**prŏd´**ōōs| *or* |-yōōs| *or* |**prō´**dōōs| *or* |-dyōōs|. Farm products, such as fruits or vegetables, raised for selling.

pro·duc·tion |prə **dŭk´**shən| *n.* **1.** The act or process of producing: *automobile production.* **2.** The output or yield of producing: *Production is down this week.*

pro·fes·sor |prə **fĕs´**ər| *n.* **1.** A teacher of the highest rank in a college or university. **2.** Any teacher or instructor.

prof·it |**prŏf´**ĭt| *n.* **1.** An advantage gained from doing something; a benefit: *decided there was little profit in complaining.* **2.** The money made in a business venture, sale, or investment after all expenses have been met: *made a profit of five cents on every paper he sold.* [From Latin *prōfectus,* advance, progress, success, profit, from the past participle of *prōficere,* to go forward, make progress, accomplish, be advantageous: *prō-,* for + *facere,* to do, make.]

prog·no·sis |prŏg **nō**´sĭs| *n., pl.*
prog·no·ses |prŏg **nō**´sēz´|. A prediction of
the likely outcome of a disease: *the doctor's
prognosis.*

pro·logue |**prō**´lôg´| *or* |-lŏg´| *n.* A
beginning section of a play, opera, or literary
work that introduces or explains what follows.
[Middle English *prolog*, from Greek *prologos*,
(speaker of) a *prologue: pro-*, before + *legein*,
to speak.]

prom·i·nent |**prŏm**´ə nənt| *adj.* **1.**
Highly noticeable; readily evident;
conspicuous: *Find the card catalog in a
prominent place.* **2.** Well-known; leading;
eminent: *a prominent politician.*

prom·ise |**prŏm**´ĭs| *n.* A vow. —*v.*
prom·ised, prom·is·ing. To give one's word;
to vow: *promise to keep the secret.* [From
Latin *pro-*, forth + *mittere*, to let go, send.]

pro·nounce |prə **nouns**´| *v.*
pro·nounced, pro·nounc·ing. **1.** To
articulate or produce (a word or speech
sound); utter in a proper or specified manner:
*used the dictionary to find out how to
pronounce unfamiliar words.* **2.** To give
utterance to; deliver formally: *pronounced a
speech.*

pro·nun·ci·a·tion |prə nŭn´sē **ā**´shən|
n. The act or manner of pronouncing words.
[Middle English *pronouncen*, from Latin
prōnūntiāre: prō-, forth + *nūntiāre*, to
declare.]

prop·a·gan·da |prŏp´ə **găn**´də| *n.*
Ideas, information, or other material
distributed for the purpose of persuading
people to follow a set of beliefs, often without
regard to truth or fairness.

pro·pos·al |prə **pō**´zəl| *n.* A suggestion;
a plan offered for consideration. [Middle
English *proposen*, from Latin *prōpōnere*, to put
or set forth, declare: *prō-*, forward + *pōnere*,
to place.]

prose |prōz| *n.* Ordinary speech or
writing as distinguished from verse or poetry.

pros·e·cute |**prŏs**´ĭ kyōōt´| *v.*
pros·e·cut·ed, pros·e·cut·ing. **1.** To
initiate or conduct a legal action against
(someone): *The victim decided not to
prosecute.* **2.** To present (a case, crime, suit,
etc.) before a court of law for punishment or
settlement.

pro·spec·tive |prə **spěk**´tĭv| *adj.* **1.**
Expected to be or occur; forthcoming; future:
a prospective bride. **2.** Possible: *prospective
customers.*

pros·per·i·ty |prŏ **spěr**´ĭ tē| *n.* The
condition of being successful; economic
success.

pro·tag·o·nist |prō **tăg**´ə nĭst| *n.* The
main character in a drama or literary work.
[Greek *prōtagōnistēs: prōt(o)-*, first + *agōnistēs*,
actor, from *agōnia*, a contest, from *agein*, to
lead.]

pro·tein |**prō**´tēn´| *n.* A main class of
food essential to the body. [French *protéine*,
"primary substance (to the body)," from
Greek *prōtos*, first.]

pro·to·col |**prō**´tə kôl´| *or* |-kōl´| *or*
|-kŏl´| *n.* The forms of ceremony and social
etiquette observed by diplomats and heads of
state. [Old French *prothocole*, from Late Greek
prōtokolon, first sheet glued to a papyrus roll,
bearing a table of contents: *prōto-* + *kollēma*,
sheets of papyrus glued together.]

pro·to·plasm |prō′tə plăz′əm| *n.* A jellylike substance that forms the living matter in all plant and animal cells. [Greek *prōtos*, first + *-plasm*, from Latin *plasma*, mold.]

pro·to·type |prō′tə tīp′| *n.* The first full-scale model to be constucted of a new type of vehicle, machine, device, etc.: *the prototype of a new jet airplane.*

pro·trac·tor |prō trăk′tər| *n.* A semicircular instrument marked off in degrees, used for measuring and drawing angles. [Latin *prōtrahere*, to drag out, lengthen: *prō-*, out, extending + *trahere*, to drag, pull.]

prov·o·ca·tion |prŏv′ə kā′shən| *n.* The act of provoking; incitement.

pro·voke |prə vōk′| *v.* **pro·voked, pro·vok·ing.** **1.** To bring on; arouse: *The comedian provoked steady laughter.* **2.** To stir to action; incite: *Conscience provoked them to speak out.*

psy·che |sī′kē| *n.* **1.** The soul or spirit as distinguished from the body. **2.** The mind considered as the source and center of thought, feeling, and behavior. [After Psyche of Greek mythology, from *psyche, psukhē*, life, soul.]

psy·chi·a·trist |sĭ kī′ə trĭst| *or* |sī-| *n.* A physician who specializes in the treatment of mental illness. [From Psyche of Greek mythology: *psyche*, soul + *-iatry*, healing.]

psy·chol·o·gy |sī kŏl′ə jē| *n., pl.* **psy·chol·o·gies.** The scientific study of mental processes and behavior. [New Latin *psychologia: psycho-*, soul + *logy*, study of.]

pueb·lo |pwĕb′lō| *n., pl.* **pueb·los.** A flat-roofed community dwelling, up to five stories high, used by certain North American Indian tribes of the Southwest. [Spanish "people," "population," from Latin *populus*, people.]

punc·tu·al |pŭngk′chōō əl| *adj.* Acting or arriving on time; prompt. —**punc′tu·al′i·ty** *n.*

pur·pose |pûr′pəs| *n.* The intended or desired result; a goal; aim; intent: *the purpose of this exercise.* [From French *purposer*, to intend, from Latin *prōpōnere*, to put forward, propose.]

Q

qual·i·fy |kwŏl′ə fī′| *v.* **qual·i·fied, qual·i·fy·ing, qual·i·fies.** To make, be, or become eligible or qualified, as for a position, task, etc.: *Her grades qualify her for the Honor Society.* [From Latin *quālis*, of what kind + *facere*, to make.]

quan·ti·ty |kwŏn′tĭ tē| *n., pl.* **quan·ti·ties.** **1.** An amount or number of a thing or things: *a small quantity of coal.* **2.** A considerable amount or number: *Pennsylvania was the first state to produce oil in quantity.*

quar·an·tine |kwôr′ən tēn′| *or* |kwŏr′-| *n.* Any enforced confinement or isolation, especially one meant to keep a contagious disease from spreading.

queue |kyōō| *n.* A line of people awaiting their turn, as at a ticket window.

quo·ta |kwō′tə| *n.* The maximum number or proportion of persons or things that may be admitted, as to a country, group, institution, etc.: *an immigration quota; an import quota.*

R

ra·dar |rā′där′| *n.* **1.** A method of detecting distant objects and determining their position, speed, size, etc., by causing radio waves to be reflected from them and analyzing the reflected waves. **2.** The equipment used in doing this.

rad·i·cal |răd′ĭ kəl| *n.* A root, such as $\sqrt{x}$ or $\sqrt[3]{2}$, especially as indicated by a radical sign.

ra·di·ol·o·gy |rā′dē ŏl′ə jē| *n.* The use of x-rays and other radiation in medical diagnosis and treatment.

rap·pel |ră pĕl′| *n.* The act or method of descending from a mountainside or cliff by means of a double rope passed under one thigh and over the opposite shoulder. —*v.* **rap·pelled, rap·pel·ling, rap·pels.** To descend from a steep height by rappel: *Rappel down the mountain.*

ra·tion·al |răsh′ə nəl| *adj.* Consistent with or based on reason; logical: *rational behavior.*

ra·tio·nale |răsh′ə năl′| *n.* The fundamental reasons for something; a logical basis.

razz |răz| *v. Slang.* To ridicule; tease.

re·al·ism |rē′ə lĭz′əm| *n.* **1.** Concern with facts and things as they actually are rather than with ideals and dreams. **2.** The depiction of reality, as in painting, sculpture, literature, etc.

re·al·i·ty |rē ăl′ĭ tē| *n., pl.* **re·al·i·ties. 1.** The condition of occurring in fact or actuality: *Giving the speech was easier in reality than it was in my imagination.* **2.** The sum total of things that exist; the real world.

Re·al·tor |rē′əl tər| *n.* A person who buys and sells real estate for a living.

reap·er |rē′pər| *n.* A machine for harvesting: *grain harvested by a reaper.*

re·cede |rĭ sēd′| *v.* **re·ced·ed, re·ced·ing.** To move back or away from a limit, point, or mark: *The flood had receded.* [Latin *recēdere*, to go back: *re-*, back again + *cēdere*, to go.]

re·ceive |rĭ sēv′| *v.* To get or acquire (something given, offered, or transmitted): *receive payment.* [Middle English *receiven*, from Old North French *receivre*, from Latin *recipere*, to take back, regain: *re-*, back, again + *capere*, to take.]

re·cep·tive |rĭ sĕp′tĭv| *adj.* Ready or willing to receive favorably: *receptive to change.* [From Latin *recipere*, to receive.]

re·cess |rĭ sĕs′| or |rē′sĕs′| *n.* **1.** A temporary halt in or stoppage of customary activity: *a court recess ordered by the judge.* **2.** The period of time of such a halt: *played games during recess at school.* [Latin *recessus, recēdere*, to go back: *re-*, back + *cēdere*, to go.]

re·ces·sion |rĭ sĕsh′ən| *n.* The act of withdrawing or going back.

re·cip·i·ent |rĭ sĭp′ē ənt| *n.* Someone or something that gets or acquires: *recipient of an award.*

re·cip·ro·cate |rĭ sĭp′rə kāt′| *v.* **re·cip·ro·cat·ed, re·cip·ro·cat·ing.** To give or take in return: *reciprocate a favor.*

rec·og·ni·tion |rĕk′əg nĭsh′ən| *n.* The act of recognizing or the condition of being recognized.

rec·om·mend |rĕk′ə mĕnd′| *v.* To advise or counsel (a course of action).

re·con·nais·sance |rĭ kŏn′ə səns| or |-zəns| *n.* An inspection or exploration of an area, especially one made to gather information about the presence, arrangement, or activity of military forces.

re·con·struct |rē′kən strŭkt′| *v.* To construct or build again; restore. [Latin *re-*, again + *con*, together + *struere*, to build.]

rec·re·a·tion |rĕk′rē ā′shən| *n.* Refreshment of a person's mind or body after work through some activity that amuses or stimulates; play. —**rec′re·a′tion·al** *adj.*: *recreational activities.*

re·duce |rĭ do͞os′| or |-dyo͞os′| *v.* **re·duced, re·duc·ing.** To make or become less in amount, degree, size, rank, etc.; diminish; lower: *reduced their demands for wage increases.* [Middle English *reducen*, bring back, from Latin *redūcere*: *re-*, back + *dūcere*, to lead.]

re·duc·tion |rĭ dŭk′shən| *n.* The act or process of reducing: *There has been a dramatic reduction in demand for this product.*

re·fer |rĭ fûr′| *v.* **re·ferred, re·fer·ring.** To direct the attention of: *refer him to his duties.* —**re·fer′ral** *n.*: *She was given a referral to the firm from a career counselor.* [Middle English *refer(r)en*, from Latin *referre*, refer to, carry back: *re-*, back + *ferre*, to carry.]

ref·er·ence |rĕf′ər əns| or |rĕf′rəns| *n.* **1.** A note in a book or other publication that directs the reader to another part of the book or to another source of information. **2.** The source of information. —**modifier:** *a reference book.*

ref·u·gee |rĕf′yo͞o jē′| *n.* A person who flees, especially from his or her country, to find refuge from oppression, persecution, etc.: *war refugees.*

re·gal |rē′gəl| *adj.* **1.** Of a king; royal: *regal power.* **2.** Befitting a king: *regal bearing.* [From Latin *rēgālis*, royal, from *rex*, king.]

re·ga·lia |rĭ gāl′yə| *n.* **1.** The emblems and symbols of royalty, as the crown and scepter. **2.** The special symbols and costume that distinguish a certain rank, office, fraternal order, etc. **3.** Fine or fancy clothes; finery.

re·gat·ta |rĭ gä′tə| or |-găt′ə| *n.* A boat race or races, organized as a sporting event.

re·gime |rĭ zhēm′| or |rā-| *n.* **1.** A system of government: *a democratic regime.* **2.** The administration or rule of a particular leader, faction, party, etc. **3.** A form of the word *regimen.* [French *régime*, from Latin *regimen*, from *regere*, to rule.]

reg·i·men |rĕj′ə mən| or |-mĕn′| *n.* A system or method of treatment or cure.

reg·i·ment |rĕj′ə mənt| *n.* A unit of soldiers, composed of two or more battalions.

re·gion |rē′jən| *n.* **1.** An area of the earth's surface, especially a large area: *the polar regions.* **2.** A section or area of the body: *the abdominal region.* **3.** Any area, volume, realm, etc. [Latin *regiō*, direction, boundary.]

reg·u·la·tion |rĕg´yə lā´shən| *n.*
1. The act or process of controlling or
directing. **2.** The condition of being
controlled: *freedom from government
regulation.* **3.** A rule, order, or law by which
something is controlled: *traffic regulations.*
—*adj.* Conforming to a regular method,
style, rule, etc.: *a regulation uniform.* [Latin
rēgulāre, from *rēgula,* a rule.]

rel·ic |rĕl´ĭk| *n.* An object or custom
surviving from a culture or period that has
disappeared.

re·me·di·al |rĭ mē´dē əl| *adj.* Intended
to correct something, especially faulty study
habits, reading skills, etc.: *remedial reading.*

rem·e·dy |rĕm´ə dē| *n., pl.* **rem·e·dies.**
Something, such as a medicine or treatment,
used or given to relieve pain or cure disease.
[Middle English *remedie,* from Latin *remedium,*
medicine: *re-,* again + *medērī,* to heal.]

re·mis·sion |rĭ mĭsh´ən| *n.* **1.** The act
of remitting. **2.** A temporary lessening of the
intensity, seriousness, or destructive effect of a
pain, disease, or disorder.

re·mit |rĭ mĭt´| *v.* **re·mit·ted,**
re·mit·ting. 1. To send (money); transmit.
2. To cancel: *remit a fine.* [Middle English
remitten, from Latin *remittere,* to send back
release: *re-,* back + *mittere,* to send.]

ren·ais·sance |rĕn´ĭ säns´| *or* |-zäns´|
or |rĭ nā´səns| *n.* **1.** A rebirth; a revival: *an
intellectual renaissance.* **2. Renaissance.** A
period of revival of the arts and learning in
Europe, lasting from the 14th through the
16th century.

ren·dez·vous |rän´dā vōō´| *or* |-də-| *n.,
pl.* **ren·dez·vous** |rän´dā vōōz´| *or*
|-də-|. **1.** A pre-arranged meeting: *a
rendezvous of the explorers in the wilderness.*
2. A designated place for a meeting. —*v.*
ren·dez·voused |rän´dā vōōd´| *or* |-də-|,
ren·dez·vous·ing |rän´dā vōō´ĭng| *or*
|-də-|, **ren·dez·vous** |rän´dā vōōz´| *or*
|-də-|. To meet together or cause to meet
together at a certain time and place. [Old
French, from *rendez vous,* "present

yourselves": *rendez,* to render + *vous,* you,
from Latin *vos.*]

ren·e·gade |rĕn´ĭ gād´| *n.* **1.** Someone
who rejects a cause, allegiance, group, etc., in
preference for another; a deserter; a traitor. **2.**
An outlaw. [Spanish *renegado,* from Medieval
Latin *renegātus,* one who denies.]

ren·o·vate |rĕn´ə vāt´| *v.* **ren·o·vat·ed,**
ren·o·vat·ing. To renew; repair: *renovate a
cottage.*

re·pair |rĭ pâr´| *v.* To restore to proper or
useful condition, as after damage or wear.

rep·er·to·ry |rĕp´ər tôr´ē| *or* |-tōr´ē| *n.,
pl.* **rep·er·to·ries. 1.** A repertoire. **2.** A
collection, as of information.

rep·li·ca |rĕp´lĭ kə| *n.* Any copy or close
reproduction: *a replica of an early telephone.*
[Italian, *replicāre,* to repeat, from Latin
replicāre, fold back: *re-,* back + *plicāre,* to
fold.]

re·port·er |rĭ pôr´tər| *or* |-pōr´-| *n.* A
person who gathers information for news
stories that are written or broadcast.

re·sent |rĭ zĕnt´| *v.* To feel angry or bitter
about: *resent a remark.* [Old French *resentir,*
to feel strongly, from Latin *re-* + *sentir,* to
feel.]

res·er·va·tion |rĕz´ər vā´shən| *n.* An
arrangement by which space, as in a hotel or
restaurant or on an airplane, is secured in
advance.

res·pi·ra·tion |rĕs´pə rā´shən| *n.* The act or process of inhaling and exhaling; breathing. [From Latin *respīrāre: re-*, again + *spīrāre*, to breathe.]

res·tau·rant |rĕs´tər ənt| *or* |-tə ränt´| *n.* A place where meals are served to the public.

res·to·ra·tion |rĕs´tə rā´shən| *n.* **1.** The action of restoring: *The damage was too great for restoration.* **2.** A particular act of restoring: *restoration of the damaged sculptures.*

re·store |rĭ stôr´| *or* |-stōr´| *v.* **re·stored, re·stor·ing. 1.** To bring back to prior condition: *restore an old building.* **2.** To bring back into existence: *Such stories restore my faith in humanity.* [Middle English *restoren,* from Old French *restorer,* from Latin *restaurāre: re-,* back + *instaurāre,* to renew.]

re·sume |rĭ zōōm´| *v.* **re·sumed, re·sum·ing.** To begin again or continue after a break. [Latin *re-,* again + *sūmere,* to take up.]

re·sump·tion |rĭ zŭmp´shən| *n.* The act of resuming: *a resumption of diplomatic relations.*

re·tain |rĭ tān´| *v.* To keep or hold in a particular place, condition, or position. [Latin *retinēre: re-,* back + *tenēre,* to hold.]

re·ten·tion |rĭ tĕn´shən| *n.* **1.** The act or process of retaining something. **2.** The ability to retain or remember things.

re·verse |rĭ vûrs´| *n.* **1.** The opposite or contrary of something. **2.** A mechanism for moving backward, as a gear in an automobile. [Latin *reversus,* revert.]

re·vert |rĭ vûrt´| *v.* To return or go back to a former condition, belief, interest, or thought. [From Latin *reverter: re-,* back + *vertere,* to turn.]

re·vise |rĭ vīz´| *v.* **re·vised, re·vis·ing. 1.** To edit: *revise a paragraph.* **2.** To change or modify.

re·vi·sion |rĭ vĭzh´ən| *n.* **1.** The act or process of revising. **2.** A new, revised version.

re·voke |rĭ vōk´| *v.* **re·voked, re·vok·ing.** To make void; cancel. —**rev´o·ca´tion** *n.: revocation of the privilege.*

rhet·o·ric |rĕt´ə rĭk| *n.* Affected or exaggerated writing or speech.

rhine·stone |rīn´stōn´| *n.* An artificial gem, cut in imitation of a diamond. [Originally made at Strasbourg, a city near the *Rhine* river.]

ri·dic·u·lous |rĭ dĭk´yə ləs| *adj.* Deserving or inspiring laughter or mockery; absurd.

ro·bot·ics |rō bŏt´ĭks| *n. (used with a singular verb).* The study and application of the technology of robots. [Coined by Isaac Asimov in *Astounding Science Fiction,* 1941.]

Rug·by |rŭg´bē| *n.* A British form of football. [Invented at *Rugby* School, England.]

S

sac·ri·fice |săk´rə fīs´| *n.* A thing or benefit given up for the sake of serving another purpose. —*v.* **sac·ri·ficed, sac·ri·fic·ing.** To give up (something valuable) for the sake of serving another purpose, interest, or cause. [Middle English, from Latin *sacrificium: sacer,* holy, sacred + *facere,* to do, to make.]

sa·gua·ro |sə gwär´ō| *or* |-wär´ō| *n., pl.* **sa·gua·ros.** A very large cactus of the southwestern United States and Mexico, having upward-curving branches, white flowers, and red fruit.

sar·don·ic |sär dŏn´ĭk| *adj.* Mocking; cynical; sarcastic: *His sardonic laughter sent chills down my spine.* [French *sardonique*, from Latin *Sardonius (rīsus)*, bitter (laugh), from Latin *herba Sardonia*, (Italy), "Sardinian herb," a poisonous plant supposed to distort the face of the eater, from *Sardanios*, bitter, scornful.]

sat·in |săt´n| *n.* A smooth fabric of silk, rayon, nylon, and other fibers, woven with a glossy finish on one side: *a gown of beaded satin.* —*adj.* As smooth and shiny as satin; satiny. [Middle English, probably from Arabic *Zaytūn*, Arabic form of Chinese *Tseutung*, city in southern China, where it was probably first exported.]

sat·is·fac·to·ry |săt´ ĭs făk´tə rē| *adj.* Sufficient to meet a demand or requirement; adequate: *She received a satisfactory grade on the exam.*

sauer·kraut |sour´krout´| *n.* Shredded cabbage, salted and fermented in its own juice. [German *Sauerkraut: sauer*, sour, from Old High German *sūr* + *Kraut*, cabbage, from Old High German *krūt*.]

sau·té |sō tā´| *or* |sô-| *v.* To fry lightly with a little fat in an open pan. [French, "tossed (in a pan)," from *sauter*, to leap.]

sa·van·na, also **sa·van·nah** |sə văn´ə| *n.* A flat, treeless grassland of warm regions. [Earlier *zavana*, from Spanish.]

sax·o·phone |săk´sə fōn´| *n.* Also shortened to **sax.** A wind instrument having a single-reed mouthpiece, a curved conical body made of metal, and keys operated by the player's fingers. [Invented (1846) by Adolphe *Sax*.]

scaf·fold |skăf´əld| *or* |-ōld´| *n.* A temporary platform used for supporting workers in the construction, repair, or cleaning of a building.

scale |skāl| *v.* To climb up to the top of or over: *scale a mountain.*

scar·ci·ty |skăr´sĭ tē| *n., pl.* **scar·ci·ties.** Insufficient amount or supply; shortage: *Because of the drought, they experienced a scarcity of food.*

schol·ar·ship |skŏl´ər shĭp´| *n.* Money awarded to a student seeking further education, usually based on personal achievement or need.

scor·pi·on |skôr´pē ən| *n.* An animal related to the spiders, having a narrow, jointed body and a tail with a poisonous sting.

scrim·mage |skrĭm´ĭj| *n.* A practice game between members of the same team.

scu·ba |skōō´bə| *n.* A tank or tanks of compressed air worn on the back and fitted with a regulator, hose, and mouthpiece, used by divers to breathe underwater. [s(elf) c(ontained) u(nderwater) b(reathing) a(pparatus).]

scythe |sīth| *n.* A tool used for mowing or reaping, having a long, curved blade with a long, bent handle: *The farmer cut the tall weeds with a scythe.*

sec·re·ta·ry |sĕk´rĭ tĕr´ē| *n., pl.* **sec·re·tar·ies.** A person employed to do clerical work, such as typing, filing, and taking messages.

selt·zer |sĕlt´sər| *n.* **1.** A bubbly mineral water. **2.** Artificially carbonated water. [German *Selterser(wasser)*, "(water) of Nieder Selters," a district in western Germany.]

se·mes·ter |sə mĕs´tər| *n.* One of two terms, each from 15 to 18 weeks long, that make up a school year.

sem·i·con·duc·tor |sĕm´ē kən dŭk´tər| *n.* A substance, such as silicon, that conducts electricity more easily than insulators, such as rubber, do, but less easily than conductors, such as copper, do. [Latin *semi*, half + *conductor*, from Latin *conducēre*, to lead together.]

sen·sa·tion |sĕn sā´shən| *n.* **1.** Something felt keenly and briefly in the mind; a momentary strong emotion: *a sensation of having been here before.* **2.** A condition of lively public interest and excitement: *The news caused a sensation.* [Latin *sensate*, from *sēnsus*, to feel.]

sen·si·ble |sĕn´sə bəl| *adj.* Showing or in accordance with good judgment; reasonable: *a sensible decision.* [Middle English, from Latin *sēnsibilis*, from *sēnsus*, to feel.]

sen·si·tive |sĕn´sĭ tĭv| *adj.* **1.** Capable of perceiving with or as if with a sense or senses: *Bats are sensitive to sounds that we cannot hear.* **2.** Responsive to or affected by something: *Photographic film is sensitive to light. Children are sensitive to criticism.* —**sen´si·tive·ly** *adv.* —**sen´si·tiv´i·ty, sen´si·tive·ness** *n.* [Middle English, for Old French *sensitif*, from Latin *sēnsus*, to feel.]

sen·sor |sĕn´sər| *or* |-sôr´| *n.* A device that reacts to a particular type of change in its environment. [From Latin *sēnsus*, to sense, feel.]

sen·ti·ment·al |sĕn´tə mĕnt´tl| *adj.* **1.** Of the feelings; emotional: *a man with sentimental ties to the country of his birth.* **2.** Ruled or influenced by one's emotions rather than reason and practicality: *a sentimental man.* —**sen´ti·ment·al·ly** *adv.* [Middle English *sentement*, from Latin *sentīre*, to feel.]

sen·try |sĕn´trē| *n., pl.* **sen·tries.** A guard. [From Latin *sentīre*, to perceive, watch, feel.]

se·quence |sē´kwəns| *n.* The order in which things or events occur or are arranged: *the sequence of steps in the sewing manual.* [Latin *sequentia*, from *sequēns*, to follow.]

se·quen·tial |sĭ kwĕn´shəl| *adj.* Of or arranged in sequence: *sequential order.*

ser·en·dip·i·ty |sĕr´ən dĭp´ĭ tē| *n.* The accidental or unexpected discovery of something good. [Coined by Horace Walpole after the characters in the fairy tale *The Three Princes of Serendip*, who made such discoveries.]

shard |shärd| *n.* A piece of broken pottery; a potsherd: *found a buried shard.*

shoot·ing star |shōō´tĭng| *n.* A meteor.

shrub·ber·y |shrŭb´ə rē| *n.* A group or growth of bushes or shrubs; shrubs in general.

siege |sēj| *n.* The surrounding and blockading of a town or fortress by an army bent on capturing it.

si·er·ra |sē ĕr´ə| *n.* A rugged range of mountains with a jagged outline like the teeth of a saw. [Spanish, "a saw," from Latin *serra*.]

sig·nif·i·cant |sĭg nĭf´ ĭ kənt| *adj.*
1. Having a meaning. **2.** Full of meaning.
sil·hou·ette |sĭl ōō ĕt´| *n.* **1.** A drawing
consisting of the outline of something,
especially a human profile, filled in with a
solid color. **2.** An outline of something that
appears dark against a light background.
[French, short for *portrait à la silhouette*, an
incomplete object, after Étienne de *Silhouette*
(1709–1767), with reference to his fleeting
career (March–November 1759) as French
controller-general.]
sim·i·lar |sĭm´ə lər| *adj.* Related in
appearance or nature; alike though not the
same: *a wild cat similar to but smaller than a
lion.* —**sim´i·lar·ly** *adv.* [French *similaire*,
from Latin *similis*, like.]
sim·u·la·tion |sĭm´yə lā´shən| *n.* An
imitation: *a simulation of conditions on the
moon.* [Latin *simulāre*, from *similis*, similar,
like.]
si·mul·ta·ne·ous |sī´məl tā´nē əs| *or*
|sĭm´əl-| *adj.* Happening, existing, or done
at the same time.
site |sīt| *n.* **1.** The place where something
was, is, or is to be located. **2.** The place or
setting of an event.
skep·ti·cism |skĕp´tĭ sĭz´əm| *n.* A
doubting or questioning state of mind.
sketch |skĕch| *n.* **1.** A rough preliminary
drawing or painting: *a sketch of the park.* **2.**
A brief composition or outline: *a
biographical sketch.* [Dutch *schets*, from Italian
schizzo, to sketch, from Latin *schedius*, hastily
put together, from Greek *skhedios*,
impromptu.]
smog |smŏg| *or* |smôg| *n.* A fog that has
become polluted with smoke. [sm(oke) +
(f)og.]
smor·gas·bord |smôr´gəs bôrd´| *or*
|-bōrd´| *n.* A buffet meal with a variety of
dishes.
so·cial |sō´shəl| *adj.* **1. a.** Living
together in communities or similar organized
groups: *Human beings are social creatures.
Bees and ants are social insects.* **b.** Of or

typical of such a way of life or of organisms
living in this way: *the social behavior of bees;
social activities.* **2.** Fond of the company of
others; pleasant; friendly: *a social character.*
so·ci·e·ty |sə sī´ ĭ tē| *n., pl.* **so·ci·e·ties.**
1. A group of living things, usually of the
same kind, living and functioning together:
*human societies; a society of bees forming a
single hive.* **2.** A group of people sharing
mutual aims, interests, etc.: *a stamp-collecting
society.*
so·ci·ol·o·gy |sō´sē ŏl´ə jē| *or*
|sō´shē-| *n.* The scientific study of human
society and its origins, development,
organizations, and institutions. [French
sociologie: socio-, companion, partner + *logy*,
science of.]
soft·ware |sôft´wâr´| *or* |sŏft´-| *n.*
Written or printed data, such as programs,
routines, and symbolic languages, essential to
the operation of computers. [Coined after
hardware ("the machines").]
sole |sōl| *adj.* **1.** Being the only one;
single; only: *her sole purpose.* **2.** Belonging
exclusively to one person or group: *She took
sole command of the ship.* [Middle English
soul(e), sole, unmarried, alone, from Old
French, from Latin *sōlus*, alone, single.]
so·lid·i·fy |sə lĭd´ə fī´| *v.* **so·lid·i·fied,
so·lid·i·fy·ing, so·lid·i·fies.** To make or
become solid.

ă	pat	ŏ	pot	û	fur
ā	pay	ō	go	*th*	**the**
â	care	ô	paw, for	th	thin
ä	father	oi	oil	hw	which
ĕ	pet	ōō	book	zh	usual
ē	be	ōō	boot	ə	ago, item
ĭ	pit	yōō	cute		pencil, atom
ī	ice	ou	out		circus
î	near	ŭ	cut	ər	butter

so·lil·o·quy |sə lĭl′ə kwē| *n., pl.*
so·lil·o·quies. A literary or dramatic
discourse in which a character reveals his or
her thoughts without addressing them to a
listener.

sol·i·taire |sŏl′ĭ târ′| *n.* **1.** Any of a
number of card games played by one person.
2. A diamond or other gemstone set alone, as
in a ring. [Latin *sōlitārius*, solitary.]

sol·i·tar·y |sŏl′ĭ tĕr ē| *adj.* **1.** Existing
or living alone: *a solitary traveler.* **2.**
Happening, done, or passed alone: *a solitary
evening.* **3.** Remote; secluded; lonely:
solitary places. **4.** Having no or few
companions; lonely: *a solitary person.*
[Middle English, from Latin *sōlitārius*, from
sōlus, alone.]

sol·i·tude |sŏl′ĭ tōōd| *or* |-tyōōd| *n.* **1.**
The state of being alone or remote from
others; isolation. **2.** A lonely or secluded
space. [Middle English, from Old French,
from Latin *sōlitūdo*, from *sōlus*, alone.]

so·lo |sō′lō| *n., pl.* **so·los. 1.** A musical
composition or passage for a single voice or
instrument, with or without accompaniment.
2. A performance of one or more such
passages or compositions by a singer or
instrumentalist. —**so′lo·ist** *n.: a soloist
with the band.*

so·lu·tion |sə lōō′shən| *n.* **1.** An answer
to a problem. **2.** A number or function that
changes an equation into an identity when
substituted for an unknown in the equation:
What is the solution to that equation? **3.** A
number or function that makes an inequality
true when substituted for an unknown.

so·nar |sō′när′| *n.* A system, similar in
principle to radar, that uses reflected sound
waves to detect and locate underwater objects.
[so(und) na(vigation) r(anging).]

son·net |sŏn′ĭt| *n.* A 14-line poem
usually expressing a single complete thought
or idea, and having lines that rhyme
according to certain specific patterns:
Shakespearean sonnets.

soph·o·more |sŏf′ə môr′| *or* |-mōr′| *n.*
A student in his or her second year at a four-
year high school or college. —**modifier:** *the
sophomore class.* [Greek, from earlier
sophumer, arguments, from *sophum*, variant of
sophism.]

sou·ve·nir |sōō′və nîr′| *n.* Something
kept as a remembrance, as of a place or
occasion; a memento. [French "memory,"
from *souvenir*, to come to mind, recall, from
Latin *subvenīre*, come to mind: *sub-*, up to +
venīre, to come.]

sov·er·eign |sŏv′ə rĭn| *or* |sŏv′rĭn| *n.*
The chief of state in a monarchy; a king or
queen; a monarch: *the sovereign of that
country.*

spa |spä| *n.* **1.** A spring whose waters
contain dissolved mineral salts. **2.** A resort
area where such springs exist. [After *Spa*, a
resort town in Belgium.]

space shuttle. A space vehicle designed
to transport astronauts to and fro between
Earth and an orbiting space station. [From
Latin *spatium*, space + *shuttle*, move back and
forth.]

spa·ghet·ti |spə gĕt´ē| *n.* A pasta made into long, solid strings and cooked by boiling. [Italian, plural diminutive of *spago*, string.]

spec·i·fi·ca·tion |spĕs´ə fĭ kā´shən| *n.*, *pl.* **spec·i·fi·ca·tions.** A list of statements giving an exact description of a product, a structure to be constructed, an invention, etc.: The contractor followed specifications exactly.

spec·ta·tor |spĕk´tā´tər| *n.* Someone who views an event; an observer or onlooker.

spon·ta·ne·i·ty |spŏn´tə nē´ĭ tē| *or* |-nā´-| *n.* Voluntary and impulsive behavior.

spread·sheet |sprĕd´shēt| *n.* A worksheet on which financial data are laid out in rows and columns for comparative purposes.

squash¹ |skwŏsh| *or* |skwôsh| *n.* **1.** Any of several types of fleshy fruit related to the pumpkins and the gourds, eaten as a vegetable. **2.** A vine that bears such fruit. [From Algonquian *askw-*, plant + *-ash*, plural ending.]

squash² |skwŏsh| *or* |skwôsh| *v.* **1.** To beat or flatten to a pulp; crush: *squashed the peach on the pavement.* **2.** To be or become crushed or flattened: *The tomato was squashed on the floor.* [Old French *esquasser*, from Latin *exquassāre*, "to break into pieces."]

sta·bil·i·ty |stə bĭl´ĭ tē| *n.*, *pl.* **sta·bil·i·ties.** The condition or property of being stable.

sta·ble¹ |stā´bəl| *adj.* **sta·bler, sta·blest. 1. a.** Not likely to change position; firm: *a stable foundation of a house.* **b.** Not likely to change, as in condition: *a stable economy.* **2.** Not likely to be affected or overthrown: *a stable government.* [From Latin *stabilis*, standing firm.]

sta·ble² |stā´bəl| *n.* Often **stables.** A building for the shelter of horses or other domestic animals. [From Latin *stabulum*, standing place, enclosure.]

Pronunciation Key

ă	pat	ŏ	pot	û	fur
ā	pay	ō	go	*th*	the
â	care	ô	paw, for	th	thin
ä	father	oi	oil	hw	which
ĕ	pet	ŏŏ	book	zh	usual
ē	be	ōō	boot	ə	ago, item
ĭ	pit	yōō	cute		pencil, atom
ī	ice	ou	out		circus
î	near	ŭ	cut	ər	butter

stam·pede |stăm pēd´| *v.* **stam·ped·ed, stam·ped·ing.** To rush suddenly or act impulsively, as a startled herd of animals or an excited crowd does. [Mexican Spanish *estampida*, from Spanish, uproar, crash.]

stat·ic |stăt´ĭk| *n.* Random noise in a radio receiver or visible specks on a television screen, caused by atmospheric disturbances.

sta·tion·ar·y |stā´shə nĕr´ē| *adj.* Undergoing no change of position; unmoving.

sta·tion·er·y |stā´shə nĕr´ē| *n.* Writing paper and envelopes.

steth·o·scope |stĕth´ə skōp´| *n.* An instrument used to listen to sounds made with the body: *The doctor's stethoscope hung around his neck.*

stock·bro·ker |stŏk´brō´kər| *n.* A person who buys or sells stocks for a client, receiving a commission in return: *the stockbroker's recommendations.*

stra·ta |strā´tə| *or* |străt´ə| *n.* Plural of **stratum:** *in all strata of society.*

stra·te·gic |strə tē´jĭk| *adj.* **1.** Of strategy: *the strategic importance of Arctic lands.* **2.** Essential to strategy: *strategic locations.*

strat·e·gy |străt´ə jē| *n.*, *pl.* **strat·e·gies.** A plan of action. [French *stratégie*, from Greek *stratēgia*, office of a general, from *stratēgas*, general.]

Spelling Dictionary

stra·tum |strā´təm| *or* |străt´əm| *n., pl.*
stra·ta |strā´tə| *or* |străt´ə|. Any of a series
of layers or levels, especially a series of
approximately parallel layers.

stren·u·ous |strĕn´yo͞o əs| *adj.*
Requiring great effort, energy, or exertion.

struc·ture |strŭk´chər| *n.* Something
constructed, as a building, bridge, etc.
[Middle English, from Old French, from
Latin *struere*, to construct, build.]

sub-. A prefix meaning: **1.** Under or
beneath: **submarine. 2.** A subordinate or
secondary part: **subdivision. 3.** Somewhat
short of or less than: **subtropical.** [Latin
sub-, from *sub*, under, from below.]

sub·con·scious |sŭb kŏn´shəs| *adj.* Not
fully conscious but capable of becoming
conscious.

sub·cul·ture |sŭb´kŭl´chər| *n.* A
cultural subgroup distinguished from the
larger culture by race, religion, economic
status, etc.

sub·di·vide |sŭb´dĭ vīd´| *v.*
sub·di·vid·ed, sub·di·vid·ing. To divide
into smaller parts. [Middle English
subdividen, from Latin *subdīvidere*: *sub-*,
smaller + *dīvidere*, to divide.]

sub·let |sŭb lĕt´| *v.* **sub·let, sub·let·ting.**
To rent (property one holds by lease) to
another.

sub·ma·rine |sŭb´mə rēn´| *or*
|sŭb´mə rēn´| *n.* A ship that can operate
underwater.

sub·merge |səb mûrj´| *v.* **sub·merged,
sub·merg·ing.** To place or go under as if
under water or some other liquid: *submerged
the dish in soapy water.* [Latin *submergere*:
sub-, under + *mergere*, to immerse, plunge.]

sub·mis·sion |səb mĭsh´ən| *n.* **1.** The
act of submitting to the power of another.
2. The act of submitting something for
consideration.

sub·mit |səb mĭt´| *v.* **sub·mit·ted,
sub·mit·ting. 1.** To yield or surrender
(oneself) to the will or authority of another:
They submitted themselves to her judgment.

2. To commit (something) to the
consideration of another: *submit ideas to her.*
[Latin *submittere*, to place under: *sub-*, under
+ *mittere*, to send.]

sub·scribe |səb skrīb´| *v.* **sub·scribed,
sub·scrib·ing.** To contract to receive and pay
for a certain number of issues of a periodical:
subscribe to a magazine. [From Latin
subscrībere: *sub-*, under + *scrībere*, to write.]

sub·scrip·tion |səb skrĭp´shən| *n.* A
purchase made by a signed order, as for issues
of a periodical or a series of theatrical
performances: *a subscription to the opera.*

sub·se·quent |sŭb´sə kwənt| *adj.*
Following in time or order; succeeding: *heavy
rains and subsequent floods.* [Latin *subsequēns*,
to follow after: *sub-*, close to, after + *sequī*, to
follow.]

sub·side |səb sīd´| *v.* **sub·sid·ed,
sub·sid·ing.** To become less active; abate:
The child's tantrum finally subsided. [Latin
subsīdere, to sink down: *sub-*, down + *sīdere*,
to settle.]

sub·stance |sŭb´stəns| *n.* **1.** A material
of a particular kind or constitution. **2.** The
essence of what is said or written; the gist:
the substance of the report. [Middle English,
essence, from Latin *substantia*, from *substāns*,
to stand up: *sub-*, from below, up + *stāre*, to
stand.]

sub·stan·ti·ate |səb stăn´shē āt´| *v.*
sub·stan·ti·at·ed, sub·stan·ti·at·ing. To
support with proof or evidence: *substantiate
his testimony.*

sub·sume |sŭb so͞om´| *or* |-syo͞om´| *v.*
To place in a more comprehensive category or
under a general principle. [New Latin
subsumere: *sub-*, under + *sūmere*, to take up.]

sub·ter·ra·ne·an |sŭb´tə rā´nē ən| *adj.*
Situated or operating beneath the earth's
surface.

sub·ti·tle |sŭb´tīt´l| *n.* A printed
translation of the dialogue of a foreign-
language film shown at the bottom of the
screen.

sub·tle |sŭt´l| *adj.* **sub·tler, sub·tlest.**
1. So slight as to be difficult to detect or
analyze; elusive: *subtle changes.* **2.** Not
immediately obvious; abstruse: *a subtle
problem.* **3.** Characterized by slyness;
devious: *subtle actions.* —**sub´tle•ness** *n.*
—**sub´tly** *adv.*

sub·to·tal |sŭb´tōt´l| *n.* The total of a
subset chosen from a set of numbers.

sub·ur·ban |sə bûr´bən| *adj.* **1.** Of a
suburb or life in a suburb: *a suburban area.*
2. Located in a suburb: *a suburban school.*
[Latin *suburbium: sub-,* near + *urbs,* city.]

sub·way |sŭb´wā´| *n.* An underground
urban railroad.

suc·ceed |sək sēd´| *v.* To follow or come
next in time or order; to replace (another) in
an office or position: *He succeeded his mother.*
[Middle English *succeden,* from Latin
succēdere, to follow closely, go after: *sub-,*
toward, next to + *cēdere,* to go.]

suc·ces·sion |sək sĕsh´ən| *n.* The act or
process of following in order or sequence: *the
succession of events.*

suc·ces·sor |sək sĕs´ər| *n.* Someone or
something that succeeds another. [Middle
English *succeden,* from Latin *succēdere,* to
follow closely, go after: *sub-,* toward + *cēdere,*
to go.]

suc·cinct |sək sĭngkt´| *adj.* **1.** Clearly
expressed in few words; concise: *a succinct
explanation.* **2.** Characterized by brevity and
clarity.

suc·cumb |sə kŭm´| *v.* To yield or
submit to something overpowering and
overwhelming: *succumb to the pressures of
society.*

suede, also **suède** |swād| *n.* Leather
that has been rubbed to give it a soft, velvety
surface. [From French *gants de suède,* "gloves
of Sweden," from *Suède,* Sweden.]

suite |swēt| *n.* A series of connected
rooms used as a living unit. [French *sieute,*
following, retinue, from Latin *sequita.*]

---

sum·ma·ry |sŭm´ə rē| *n., pl.*
sum·ma·ries. The condensed version of
something larger: *a summary of our findings.*

sum·mit |sŭm´ĭt| *n.* The highest point or
part; the top, especially of a mountain.

sump·tu·ous |sŭmp´chŏŏ əs| *adj.* Of a
size or splendor suggesting great expense;
lavish: *a sumptuous meal.* [Middle English,
from Latin *sumptus,* expense, from *sūmere,* to
consume, spend, take.]

super-. A prefix meaning: **1.** Placement
above, over, or outside: **superimpose. 2.**
Superiority of size, quality, or degree:
superhuman. 3. A degree exceeding a
norm: **supersonic.** [From Latin *super,* above,
over.]

su·per·fi·cial |sŏŏ´pər fĭsh´əl| *adj.* Not
deeply penetrating; trivial: *a superficial
knowledge of history.* [Middle English, from
Latin *superficiēs: super-,* above, over + *faciēs,*
face.]

su·per·flu·ous |sŏŏ pûr´flŏŏ əs| *adj.*
Beyond what is required or sufficient; extra:
Many items in the budget are superfluous.

su·per·im·pose |sŏŏ´pər im pōz´| *v.*
su·per·im·posed, su·per·im·pos·ing. To
lay or place over or upon something else.

su·per·in·ten·dent
|sŏŏ´pər in tĕn´dənt| *n.* A person who
supervises or is in charge of something.
[Latin *super-,* over + *intendere,* to direct one's
attention to, intend.]

Spelling Dictionary

su·per·la·tive |sə **pûr´**lə tĭv| *or* |sŏŏ-| *adj.* Of the highest order, quality, or degree: *a superlative specimen.* [Middle English *superlatyf,* from Old French *superlative,* from Latin *superlātus,* to carry over.]

su·per·mar·ket |**sŏŏ´**pər mär kĭt| *n.* A large self-service retail store selling food and household goods.

su·per·son·ic |sŏŏ´pər **sŏn´**ĭk| *adj.* Having or caused by a speed greater than the speed of sound in a given medium. [Latin *super-,* over + *son,* sound + (adj. suffix) *ic.*]

su·per·sti·tion |sŏŏ´pər **stĭsh´**ən| *n.* **1.** A belief that some action not logically related to a course of events influences its outcome. For example, the belief that walking under a ladder is bad luck is a superstition. **2.** Any belief, practice, or rite unreasonably dependent on magic, chance, or dogma: *Some primitive midwives rely more on superstition than on medical fact.*

su·per·vise |**sŏŏ´**pər vīz´| *v.* **su·per·vised, su·per·vis·ing.** To direct and inspect the action, work, or performance of. [Medieval Latin *supervidēre* (past participle *supervīsus*), to look over: Latin *super-,* over + *vidēre,* to see.]

sur·plus |**sûr´**plŭs| *or* |-pləs| *n.* An amount or quantity in excess of what is needed or used: *Brazil produces a large surplus of coffee for export.*

sur·veil·lance |sər **vā´**ləns| *n.* The action of observing or following closely: *Those high-flying planes are used for the surveillance of enemy troop movements.*

sur·vey·or |sər **vā´**ər| *n.* A person whose work is surveying and measuring land.

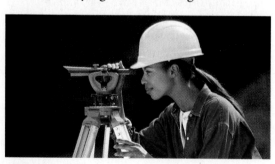

sus·cep·ti·ble |sə **sĕp´**tə bəl| *adj.* Easily influenced or impressed; sensitive to suggestions; vulnerable: *a susceptible child.* [From Latin *suscipere,* to take up, receive: *sub-,* up from under + *capere,* to take.]

sus·pense |sə **spĕns´**| *n.* **1.** The condition of being suspended. **2.** Anxious uncertainty about what will happen. [Middle English, from Latin *suspendēre,* to hang up: *sub-,* up from under + *pendēre,* to hang.]

sus·tain |sə **stān´**| *v.* **1.** To support from below; hold or prop up: *beams strong enough to sustain the weight of the roof.* **2.** To suffer and endure through; withstand: *sustain a loss.* [Middle English *suste(y)nen,* from Old French *sustenir,* from Latin *sustinēre,* to hold up: *sub-,* up from under + *tenēre,* to hold.]

sus·te·nance |**sŭs´**tə nəns| *n.* **1.** The support of life, as with food and other necessities. **2.** Something that supports life, especially food.

syl·lab·i·cate |sĭ **lăb´**ĭ kāt´| *v.* **syl·lab·i·cat·ed, syl·lab·i·cat·ing.** To form or divide into syllables. —**syl·lab´i·ca´tion** *n.: syllabication of a word.*

syl·la·ble |**sĭl´**ə bəl| *n.* A single uninterrupted sound forming part of a word or in some cases an entire word. [Middle English *sillable,* from Greek *sullabē,* "a gathering (of letters)": *sun-,* together + *lambanein,* to take, grasp.]

sym·bol |**sĭm´**bəl| *n.* Something that represents something else, as by association, resemblance, convention, etc. [Latin *symbolum,* sign, token, from Greek *sumballein,* to throw together, compare: *sun-,* together + *ballein,* to throw.]

sym·bol·ic |sĭm **bŏl´**ĭk| *adj.* **1.** Of or expressed by a symbol or symbols. **2.** Serving as a symbol.

sym·bol·ism |**sĭm´**bə lĭz´əm| *n.* **1. a.** The representation of things by means of symbols. **b.** The attachment of symbolic meaning or significance to objects, events, or relations. **3.** A system of symbols or representations.

sym·met·ri·cal |sĭ **mĕt´**rĭ kəl| *adj.* Of or showing an exact matching form and arrangement of parts on opposite sides of a boundary. [French *symmetrie*, from Latin *symmetria*, from Greek *summetros*, "of like measure": *sun-*, same + *metron*, measure.]

sym·pa·thy |**sĭm´**pə thē| *n., pl.* **sym·pa·thies.** Mutual understanding or affection between persons. [Greek *sumpathēs*, affected by like feeling: *sun-*, like + *pathos*, feelings.]

sym·pho·ny |**sĭm´**fə nē| *n., pl.* **sym·pho·nies.** A usually long and elaborate sonata for orchestra, usually consisting of four movements. [Middle English *symphonie*, harmony of sound, from Greek *sumphonos*, harmonious: *sun-*, together + *phōnē*, sound.]

symp·tom |**sĭmp´**təm| *n.* Any change in which the body departs from its normal function, feeling, or appearance, usually a sign of disease or disorder. [Greek *sumptōma*, occurrence, from *sumpiptein*, to fall together, happen: *sun-*, together + *piptein*, to fall.]

syn·a·gogue |**sĭn´**ə gŏg´| *or* |-gôg´| *n.* A building or place of meeting for Jewish worship and religious instruction. [Middle English *synagoge*, from Latin *synagōga*, from Greek *sunagōgē*, assembly, from *sunagein*, to bring together: *sun-*, together + *agein*, to lead.]

syn·chro·nize |**sĭng´**krə nīz´| *or* |**sĭn´-**| *v.* **syn·chro·nized, syn·chro·niz·ing. 1.** To operate at the same rate and together in time. **2.** To cause (two or more things) to operate in this way. [Latin *synchronos*, from Greek *sunkhronos*: *sun-*, same + *khronos*, time.]

syn·di·cate |**sĭn´**dĭ kĭt| *n.* An association of people formed to carry out any business or enterprise. [French *syndicat*, from Latin *syndicus*, from Greek *sundikos*, assistant in a court of justice: *sun-*, with + *dikē*, judgment.]

syn·drome |**sĭn´**drōm´| *n.* A set of symptoms and signs that together indicate the presence of a disease, mental disorder, or other abnormal condition. [Latin, from

Greek *sundromē*, a running together, concurrence (of symptoms): *sun-*, together + *dromos*, race.]

syn·o·nym |**sĭn´**ə nĭm| *n.* A word having a meaning similar to that of another. For example, the words *wide* and *broad* are synonyms. [Latin *synonymum*, from Greek *sunōnumos*: *sun-*, same + *onoma*, name.]

syn·the·sis |**sĭn´**thĭ sĭs| *n., pl.* **syn·the·ses** |**sĭn´**thĭ sēz´|. The combining of separate elements, parts, or substances into a single unit or whole. [Greek *suntithenai*, to put together: *sun-*, together + *tithenai*, to put.]

syn·the·siz·er |**sĭn´**thĭ sī´zər| *n.* Any of a number of electronic musical instruments that can produce a wide range of musical sounds, including sounds that imitate those of conventional instruments. [From Greek *synthesis*.]

Pronunciation Key					
ă	pat	ŏ	pot	û	fur
ā	pay	ō	go	*th*	the
â	care	ô	paw, for	th	thin
ä	father	oi	oil	hw	which
ĕ	pet	ŏŏ	book	zh	usual
ē	be	ōō	boot	ə	ago, item
ĭ	pit	yōō	cute		pencil, atom
ī	ice	ou	out		circus
î	near	ŭ	cut	ər	butter

syn·thet·ic |sĭn **thĕt´**ĭk| *adj.* Artificial; man-made: *synthetic rubber; synthetic fabrics.* [Greek *sunthetikos*, skilled in putting together, from *suntithenai*, to put together: *sun-*, together + *tithenai*, to put.]

T

tan·ta·lize |**tăn´**tə līz´| *v.* **tan·ta·lized, tan·ta·liz·ing.** To tempt or torment as if by allowing to see but keeping out of reach something desired. [After *Tantalus* of Greek mythology.]

tar·iff |**tăr´**ĭf| *n.* **1.** A list or system of duties imposed by a government on imported or exported goods. **2.** A duty imposed in such a way: *a tariff on liquor.*

tech·ni·cian |tĕk **nĭsh´**ən| *n.* A person who is skilled in a certain technical field or process.

tech·nique |tĕk **nēk´**| *n.* **1.** A systematic procedure or method by which a complicated task is accomplished, as in a science or art. **2.** The degree to which someone has mastered one or more such procedures. [French, "technical," from Greek *tekhnikos*.]

tech·nol·o·gy |tĕk **nŏl´**ə jē| *n., pl.* **tech·nol·o·gies.** The application of scientific knowledge, especially in industry and commerce. [Greek *tekhnē*, skill, art + *-logy*, science, the study of.]

tel·e·cast |**tĕl´**ĭ kăst´| *or* |-käst´| *v.* **tel·e·cast** *or* **tel·e·cast·ed, tel·e·cast·ing.** To broadcast by television. —*n. A television broadcast.* [tele(vision) + (broad)cast.]

tem·per·a |**tĕm´**pər ə| *n.* **1.** A type of paint made by mixing pigment with a sticky substance, such as egg yolk or glue, that is soluble in water. **2.** Painting done with this type of paint. [Italian, from *temperare*, to mingle, temper, from Latin *temperāre*.]

tem·per·a·ment·al |tĕm´prə **mĕn´**tl| *or* |-pər ə-| *adj.* Excessively sensitive, irritable, or changeable: *a temperamental person.*

[Middle English *temperament*, from Latin *temperāmentum*, "a mixing (of the humors)," from *temperāre*, to mingle, temper.]

te·na·cious |tə **nā´**shəs| *adj.* **1.** Holding or tending to hold firmly; persistent; stubborn. **2.** Clinging to another object or surface. [Latin *tenāx*, from *tenēre*, to hold.]

ten·ant |**tĕn´**ənt| *n.* A person who pays rent to use or occupy land, a building, or other property owned by another.

ten·e·ment |**tĕn´**ə mənt| *n.* **1.** A building to live in, especially one intended for rent. **2.** A cheap apartment house whose facilities barely meet minimum standards. [Medieval Latin *tenementum*, feudal holding, house, from Latin *tenēre*, to hold.]

ten·or |**tĕn´**ər| *n.* **1.** A voice of a male singer, higher than a baritone and lower than an alto. **2.** A person having such a voice.

ten·ure |**tĕn´**yər| *or* |-yŏŏr´| *n.* **1.** The holding of something, as an office; occupation. **2. a.** The period of holding something. **b.** Permanence of position, granted an employee after a specified number of years: *The professor received tenure.* [Old French, earlier *tenéure*, from *tenir*, to hold.]

ter·mi·nol·o·gy |tûr´mə **nŏl´**ə jē| *n., pl.* **ter·mi·nol·o·gies.** The technical terms of a particular trade, science, or art; nomenclature. [Latin *terminus*, expression + *-logy*, speech.]

tes·ti·mo·ni·al |tĕs´tə **mō´**nē əl| *n.* A formal statement testifying to a particular fact.

tex·tile |**tĕk´**stəl| *or* |-stīl´| *n.* Cloth or fabric, especially when woven or knitted.

the·at·ri·cal |thē **ăt´**rĭ kəl| *adj.* Of or suitable for the theater: *theatrical performance.*

the·ol·o·gy |thē **ŏl´**ə jē| *n.* The systematic study of religion. [Greek *theos*, god + *-logy*, study of.]

ther·mal |**thûr´**məl| *adj.* Of, using, producing, or caused by heat: *thermal clothing.*

thes·pi·an |**thĕs´**pē ən| *n.* An actor or actress: *The thespian received a standing ovation.* [From *Thespis*, Greek poet of the sixth century B.C.]

thresh·er |**thrĕsh´**ər| *n.* A machine used for separating kernels of grain from straw in cereal plants.

to·ken |**tō´**kən| *n.* **1.** A symbol: *The ring is a token of friendship.* **2.** A piece of stamped metal used as a substitute for currency: *a bus token.* **Idiom. by the same token.** In the same manner; likewise.

toll |tōl| *n.* A fixed tax for a privilege, as passage across a bridge.

tomb |tōōm| *n.* **1.** A vault or chamber for the burial of the dead. **2.** Any place of burial.

tongue |tŭng| *n.* A fleshy, muscular organ, attached in most vertebrates to the bottom of the mouth, that is the main organ of taste, moves to aid in chewing and swallowing, and, in human beings, acts in speech. **Idiom. hold (one's) tongue.** To be or keep silent.

tor·na·do |tôr **nā´**dō| *n., pl.* **tor•na•does** or **tor•na•dos.** A violent atmospheric disturbance in the form of a column of air several hundred yards wide spinning at speeds of 300 miles per hour and faster, usually accompanied by a funnel-shaped downward extension of a thundercloud. [Spanish *tronada*, thunderstorm.]

tour·na·ment |**tōōr´**nə mənt| *or* |**tûr´**-| *n.* A contest composed of a series of elimination·games or trials: *a tennis tournament.*

tox·in |**tŏk´**sĭn| *n., pl.* **tox•ins.** A poison produced by a plant, animal, or microorganism, having protein structure and capable of causing poisoning when introduced into the body but capable also of stimulating production of an antitoxin: *toxins caused by bacteria.*

trace |trās| *v.* **traced, trac•ing.** To follow something back to its source: *trace a lost letter; tracing the origins of his family back to the American Revolution.* —**trace´a•ble** *adj.*: *a vase traceable to the Ming Dynasty.* [Middle English, a path, a course, from French *tracier*, to make one's way, from Latin *tractus*, a dragging.]

trac·tion |**trăk´**shən| *n.* The friction that prevents a wheel from slipping or skidding over the surface on which it runs. [Medieval Latin *tractiō*, from Latin *trahere*, to draw, pull.]

trag·e·dy |**trăj´**ĭ dē| *n., pl.* **trag•e•dies. 1.** A serious play that ends with great misfortune or ruin for the main character or characters. **2.** The branch of drama that includes such plays.

tran·quil |**trăng´**kwĭl| *or* |**trăn´**-| *adj.* Free from agitation, anxiety, etc.: *a tranquil lake; a tranquil life.* [From Latin *tranquillus*, quiet.]

tran·quil·i·ty |trăng **kwĭl´**ĭ tē| *or* |trăn-| *n.* The quality or condition of being tranquil; calmness; peacefulness.

trans-. A prefix meaning: **1.** Across or over: **transatlantic. 2.** Beyond: **transcend.** [From Latin *trāns*, across, over, beyond, through.]

trans·ac·tion |trăn sӑk´shən| *or* |-zӑk´-| *n.* **1.** The act or process of carrying out or conducting: *the transaction of business.* **2.** Something transacted; a business deal or operation: *cash transactions only.* [Latin *trānsigere*, to carry through: *trāns-*, through + *agere*, to do.]

tran·scribe |trăn skrīb´| *v.* **tran·scribed, tran·scrib·ing. 1.** To write or type a copy of; write out fully, as from shorthand notes. **2.** To adapt or arrange (a musical composition). [Latin *trānscrībere*, to copy: *trāns-*, across + *scrībere*, to write.]

trans·fer |trăns fûr´| *or* |trăns´fər| *v.* **trans·ferred, trans·fer·ring.** To move or shift from one place, person, or thing to another: *Bees transfer pollen from one flower to another.* [Middle English *transferren*, from Old French *transferer*, from Latin *trānsferre*: *trāns-*, across + *ferre*, to carry.]

trans·form |trăns fôrm´| *v.* To change markedly in form or appearance: *A coat of paint transformed the room into a cheerful place.*

trans·fu·sion |trăns fyoo´zhen| *n.* The direct injection of whole blood, plasma, or other liquid into the bloodstream. [Middle English *transfusen*, from Latin *trānsfundere*: *trāns-*, from one place to another + *fundere*, to pour.]

tran·sient |trăn´shənt| *or* |-zhənt| *adj.* Passing with time; temporary: *transient happiness.* [Latin *trānsiēns*, present participle of *trānsīre*, to go over: *trāns-*, over, across + *īre*, to go.]

tran·sis·tor |trăn zĭs´tər| *or* |-sĭs´-| *n.* A small electronic device used to control the flow of electricity. [Originally a trademark: tran(sfer) + (re)sistor (it transfers electric signals across a resistor).]

tran·sit |trăn´sĭt| *or* |-zĭt| *n.* The act of passing over, across, or through; passage. [Latin *trānsitus*, from *trānsīre*, to go across.]

tran·si·tion |trăn zĭsh´ən| *or* |-sĭsh´-| *n.* The process of changing or passing from one form, state, subject, or place to another.

trans·late |trăns lāt´| *or* |trănz-| *or* |trăns´lāt´| *or* |trănz´-| *v.* **trans·lat·ed, trans·lat·ing.** To express or be capable of being expressed in another language: *translate a book. His novels translate well.* [Middle English *translaten*, from Latin *trānslātus*, to carry across, transfer, translate: *trāns-*, across + *lātus*, carried.]

trans·mis·sion |trăns mĭsh´ən| *or* |trănz-| *n.* **1.** The act or process of transmitting: *the transmission of news; the transmission of a disease.* **2.** Something transmitted, as by radio, television, etc., such as a voice or image.

trans·mit |trăns mĭt´| *or* |trănz-| *v.* **trans·mit·ted, trans·mit·ting. 1.** To send from one person, place, or thing to another: *transmit a message.* **2.** To send out (an electric or electronic signal), as by wire or radio. [Latin *trānsmittere*, to send across: *trāns-*, across + *mittere*, to send.]

trans·par·ent |trăns pâr´ənt| *or* |-păr´-| *adj.* Capable of transmitting light so that objects and images are clearly visible, as if there were nothing between the observer and the light source. [Middle English, from Medieval Latin *trānspārēns*: *trāns-*, through + *pārēre*, to show.]

tran·spire |trăn spīr´| *v.* **tran·spired, tran·spir·ing.** To happen; take place. [French *transpirer*, from Latin *trāns-*, out + *spīrāre*, to breathe.]

trans·plant |trăns plănt´| *or* |-plänt´| *v.* To remove (a living thing) from one place and put it in another place.

trans·por·ta·tion |trăns´pər tā´shən| *n.* A means of transport; a conveyance: *Planes are fast transportation.* [Latin *trānsportāre*: *trāns-*, from one place to another + *portāre*, to carry.]

trans·pose |trăns pōz´| *v.* **trans·posed, tran·pos·ing.** To reverse or change the order or relative positions of; put into a different order: *transpose the letters of a word.* [Latin *trāns-*, from one place to another + *poser*, to place.]

tre·men·dous |trĭ **mĕn´**dəs| *adj.*
Extremely large; enormous: *a tremendous obstacle.*

tres·pass |**trĕs´**pəs| *or* |-păs´| *v.* To invade the property or rights of another without his or her permission.

tril·o·gy |**trĭl´**ə jē| *n., pl.* **tril•o•gies.** A group of three related dramatic or literary works. [Greek *trilogia: tri-*, three + *logy*, word.]

triv·i·al |**trĭv´**ē əl| *adj.* **1.** Of little importance or significance; trifling: *trivial matters.* **2.** Ordinary; commonplace: *a trivial occurrence.* —**triv´i•al´i•ty** *n.*: *a mere triviality.* [New Latin *trivia*, "that which comes from the street," plural of *trivium*: *tri-*, three + *via*, road, way.]

trol·ley |**trŏl´**ē| *n., pl.* **trol•leys.** An electrically operated car that runs on a track; a streetcar.

tu·i·tion |tōō **ĭsh´**ən| *or* |-tyōō-| *n.* A fee for instruction, as at a college or private school.

turn·stile |**tûrn´**stīl´| *n.* A device for controlling or counting the number of persons entering a public area by admitting them one at a time between horizontal bars revolving on a central vertical post: *a subway turnstile.*

tur·quoise |**tûr´**koiz´| *or* |-kwoiz´| *n.* **1.** A bluish-green mineral containing aluminum and copper, valued in certain of its

forms as a gem. **2.** Light bluish green. —*adj.* Light bluish green. [Middle English *turkeis*, from Old French *(pierre) turqueise*, "Turkish (stone)," from *turqueis*, Turkish, Turkestan.]

tur·ret |**tûr´**ĭt| *or* |**tŭr´**-| *n.* A small tower-shaped projection on a building.

tu·to·ri·al |tōō **tôr´**ē əl| *or* |tyōō-| *adj.* Of a tutor or private instructor: *a tutorial program.*

tux·e·do, also **Tux·e·do** |tŭk **sē´**dō| *n., pl.* **tux•e•dos.** Also shortened to **tux.** A man's formal or semiformal suit, usually black, including a dinner jacket, trousers, and a black bow tie. [From the name of a country club in *Tuxedo* Park, New York, where it became popular.]

-ty¹. A suffix that forms nouns and means "a condition or quality": **loyalty.** [Middle English *-te(e), -tie*, from Latin *-tas.*]

-ty². A suffix meaning "a multiple of ten": **sixty.** [Middle English *-ty, -ti*, Old English *-tig.*]

ty·coon |tī **kōōn´**| *n.* A wealthy and powerful person in business or industry; magnate. [Japanese *taikun*, title of a shogun, from Ancient Chinese *t'ai Kiuan*, emperor: *t'ai*, great + *kiuan*, prince, sovereign.]

U

um·brel·la |ŭm **brĕl**´ə| *n.* A device for protection from the rain, consisting of a cloth cover on a collapsible frame mounted on a handle. [Italian *ombrella*, diminutive of *ombra*, shade, from Latin *umbra*.]

u·nan·i·mous |yōō **năn**´ə məs| *adj.* **1.** Sharing the same opinion: *Critics were unanimous about the play.* **2.** Based on complete agreement: *a unanimous vote.*

un·em·ploy·ment |ŭn´ĕm **ploi**´mənt| *n.* The condition of being without a job.

u·ni·form·i·ty |yōō´nə **fôr**´mĭ tē| *n.* The condition of being uniform; sameness: *uniformity of thought and action.*

u·ni·ver·sal |yōō´nə **vûr**´səl| *adj.* **1.** Extending to or affecting the whole world; worldwide: *universal peace.* **2.** Of, for, done by, or affecting all: *universal education.* [Latin *ūniversum*, the whole world, neuter of *ūniversus*, whole, entire, "turned into one": *uni-* + versus, past participle of *vertere*, to turn.]

u·ni·ver·si·ty |yōō´nə **vûr**´sĭ tē| *n., pl.* **u·ni·ver·si·ties.** A school of higher learning that offers degrees and includes programs of study in graduate school, professional schools, and regular college divisions.

ur·gen·cy |**ûr**´jən sē| *n.* Need for immediate action or attention.

u·surp |yōō **sûrp**´| *or* |-**zûrp**´| *v.* To seize and hold by force and without legal right or authority: *usurping all power; usurp a throne.*

u·til·i·ty |yōō **tĭl**´ĭ tē| *n., pl.* **u·til·i·ties.** A useful article or device. —*modifier: the utilities disk of the word-processing program.*

V

va·can·cy |**vā**´kən sē| *n., pl.* **va·can·cies.** A position, office, or accommodation that is unfilled or unoccupied.

vac·u·um |**văk**´yōō əm| *or* |-yōōm| *n.* **1. a.** The absence of matter. **b.** A space that is empty of matter. **2.** A vacuum cleaner.

val·or |**văl**´ər| *n.* Courage, bravery: *display of daring and valor.*

va·nil·la |və **nĭl**´ə| *n.* **1.** A flavoring made from the seed pods of a tropical orchid and is used in cakes, ice cream, etc. **2.** Also **vanilla bean.** The long, beanlike seed pod from which this flavoring is obtained. [Spanish, *vainila*, "little sheath," (from its elongated fruit).]

var·i·a·ble |**văr**´ē ə bəl| *n.* A variable mathematical quantity or a symbol that represents it: *Use x and y as variables in the equation.*

va·ri·e·ty |və **rī**´ĭ tē| *n., pl.* **va·ri·e·ties.** **1.** A range of difference or change resulting in lack of monotony, greater interest, etc.; diversity: *The English language allows great variety in speaking and writing.* **2.** A number of different kinds, usually within the same general grouping; an assortment: *a variety of nourishing foods.*

var·i·ous |**vâr**´ē əs| *adj.* **1.** Of different kinds: *various reasons.* **2.** Unlike; different.

var·nish |**vär**´nĭsh| *n.* **1.** An oil-based paint that dries to leave a surface with a thin, hard, glossy film that is relatively transparent and colorless. **2.** The smooth coating or finish that results from the application of varnish.

var·si·ty |**vär**´sĭ tē| *n.* The best team representing a school, college, etc. —*modifier: a varsity team; varsity players.*

veg·e·ta·ble |**vĕj**´tə bəl| *or* |**vĕj**´ĭ tə-| *n.* **1.** A plant of which the roots, leaves, stems, flowers—and in some cases the seeds, pods, or fruit—are used as food. **2.** The part of such a plant eaten as food. [Latin *vegetāre*, to enliven, from *vegēre*, to be lively.]

veg·e·ta·tion |vĕj´ĭ **tā**´shən| *n.* A growth of plants; plants or plant life in general.

ve·hi·cle |vē′ĭ kəl| *n.* **1.** A device for carrying or transporting passengers, goods, equipment, etc., especially one that moves on wheels or runners. **2.** A medium through which something is expressed or conveyed: *Oral tales were an important vehicle of culture wherever writing was unknown.*

ver·i·fi·ca·tion |vĕr′ə fĭ kā′shən| *n.* The act or process of verifying: *The instructor demanded verification of the student's facts.*

ver·i·fy |vĕr′ə fī′| *v.* **ver·i·fied, ver·i·fy·ing, ver·i·fies. 1.** To prove the truth of: *Today's astronomers have verified the findings of the ancient Greeks.* **2.** To test or check the correctness or accuracy of: *verify your addition.* [From Latin *vērus*, true + *facare*, to make.]

ver·sa·tile |vûr′sə tĭl| *or* |-tīl′| *adj.* **1.** Capable of doing many things well: *a versatile athlete.* **2.** Having varied uses or functions: *a versatile piece of machinery.* [Latin *versātilis*, from *vertere*, to turn.]

ver·sus |vûr′səs| *prep.* Against: *American team versus the German team.* [Medieval Latin, from Latin, turned toward, from the past participle of *vertere*, to turn.]

ver·te·bra |vûr′tə brə| *n., pl.* **ver·te·brae** |vûr′tə brā| *or* **ver·te·bras.** Any of the bones joined together to form the spinal column. [Latin, joint, *vertebra*, "something to turn on," from *vertere*, to turn.]

ver·ti·cal |vûr′tĭ kəl| *adj.* Perpendicular to the plane of the horizon; directly upright. [French, from Late Latin *verticālis*, from Latin *vertix.*]

vet·er·i·nar·i·an |vĕt′ər ə nâr′ē ən| *or* |vĕt′rə-| *n.* Also shortened to **vet.** A person specially trained to give medical treatment to animals.

vi·al |vī′əl| *n.* A small container for liquids.

vice ver·sa |vī′sə vûr′sə| *or* |vīs′-|. The reverse case being so; the other way around: *We learned about the exchange student's culture and vice versa.* [Latin *vice*, position + *versā*, to turn.]

vid·e·o |vĭd′ē ō′| *n.* **1.** The visual part of a television broadcast or signal as distinguished from audio. **2.** Television: *a star of stage, screen, and video.* [From Latin *vidēre*, to see.]

vile |vīl| *adj.* **vil·er, vil·est.** Hateful; disgusting.

vil·la |vĭl′ə| *n.* A country house, often a resort. [Italian, from Latin *vīlla*, country home.]

vi·o·late |vī′ə lāt′| *v.* **vi·o·lat·ed, vi·o·lat·ing.** To break; disregard: *violate a law.*

vi·o·la·tion |vī′ə lā′shən| *n.* **1.** The act of violating or the condition of being violated. **2.** An example of this: *a traffic violation.*

vi·o·lin |vī′ə lĭn′| *n.* The highest-pitched stringed instrument of the modern orchestra. [Italian *violino*, viola (instrument).]

vi·sa |vē′zə| *n.* An official authorization stamped on a passport by an official of a foreign country, permitting entry into and travel within that country.

vo·ca·tion |vō kā′shən| *n.* A profession, occupation: *making medicine his vocation.*

vol·a·tile |vŏl′ə təl| *adj.* Changeable; tending to erupt into violent action; explosive.

W

waltz |wôlts| *n.* A dance in modern triple time with a strong accent on the first beat of each measure. [German *walzan*, to roll.]

wan·der·lust |**wŏn**´dər lŭst´| *n.* A strong or irresistible impulse to travel. [German *Wanderlust: wandern*, to wander.]

word processing *n.* A system of producing typewritten documents by use of automated typewriters and electronic text-editing equipment. —**word processor** *n.*: *edit on a word processor.* [English *word* + *processor*, that which processes (1974).]

wretch·ed |**rĕch**´ĭd| *adj.* **1.** Full of or attended by misery or woe. **2.** Hateful or contemptible.

Y

yuc·ca |**yŭk**´ə| *n.* Any of several plants of dry regions of southern and western North America, having stiff, pointed leaves and a large cluster of whitish flowers.

Z

zone |zōn| *n.* An area or region distinguished or divided from a nearby one because of some special characteristic or reason: *a time zone; a postal zone.* —**zon´ing** *adj.*: *city zoning laws.*

zo·ol·o·gy |zō ŏl´ə jē| *n.* The scientific study of animals. [New Latin *zoologīa: zoo-*, animal + *-logy*, study of.]

Content Index

Numbers in **boldface** indicate pages on which a skill is introduced as well as references to the Capitalization and Punctuation Guide.

Content Index

Credits

Design and Electronic Production: Kirchoff/Wohlberg, Inc.

Handwriting Models

a b c d e f g h i
j k l m n o p q r
s t u v w x y z

A B C D E F G H I
J K L M N O P Q R
S T U V W X Y Z